Freedom Enterprise

AMERICAN BUSINESS, POLITICS, AND SOCIETY

Series editors: Andrew Wender Cohen, Shane Hamilton, Kimberly Phillips-Fein, and Elizabeth Tandy Shermer

Books in the series American Business, Politics, and Society explore the relationships over time between politics, society, and the creation and performance of markets, firms, and industries large and small. The central theme of this series is that culture, law, and public policy have been fundamental to the evolution of American business from the colonial era to the present. The series aims to explore, in particular, developments that have enduring consequences.

A complete list of books in the series is available from the publisher.

FREEDOM ENTERPRISE

Black Entrepreneurship and
Racial Capitalism in Detroit

Kendra D. Boyd

PENN

UNIVERSITY OF PENNSYLVANIA PRESS

PHILADELPHIA

Portions of chapters 4 and 5 appeared in "A 'Body of
Business Makers': The Detroit Housewives League, Black
Women Entrepreneurs, and the Rise of Detroit's African
American Business Community," *Enterprise & Society* 23,
no. 1 (March 2022): 164–205. Reproduced by permission
of Enterprise & Society/Cambridge University Press.

This book has been published with assistance
from the Claudia Clark–Rebecca Gershenson–
Megan McClintock Memorial Fund of the History
Department of Rutgers University–New Brunswick.

Published by
University of Pennsylvania Press
Philadelphia, Pennsylvania 19104-4112
www.pennpress.org

Printed in the United States of America on acid-free paper
10 9 8 7 6 5 4 3 2 1

A Cataloging-in-Publication record for this book
is available from the Library of Congress.

Hardcover ISBN 978-1-5128-2742-2
eBook ISBN 978-1-5128-2743-9

CONTENTS

List of Select Business Owners and Institutions   xi

Introduction   1

Chapter 1. Hoping: Escaping Economic Violence and
    Migrating for Business Opportunities   19

Chapter 2. Arriving: The Formation of a Black Business Community   43

Chapter 3. Hustling: Illegal Entrepreneurship and the Financing
    of Black Business   74

Chapter 4. Surviving: Black Business Organizing and Radical
    Economics During the Great Depression   102

Chapter 5. Boosting: Black Women Entrepreneurs Upbuild
    Black Business   127

Chapter 6. Booming: The Apex of Black Business in Paradise Valley   152

Chapter 7. Falling: Urban Planning and the Destruction
    of Black Business   180

Chapter 8. Fighting: The Struggle for Economic Protection
    and Inclusion   219

Epilogue   245

Notes   255

Index   325

Acknowledgments   333

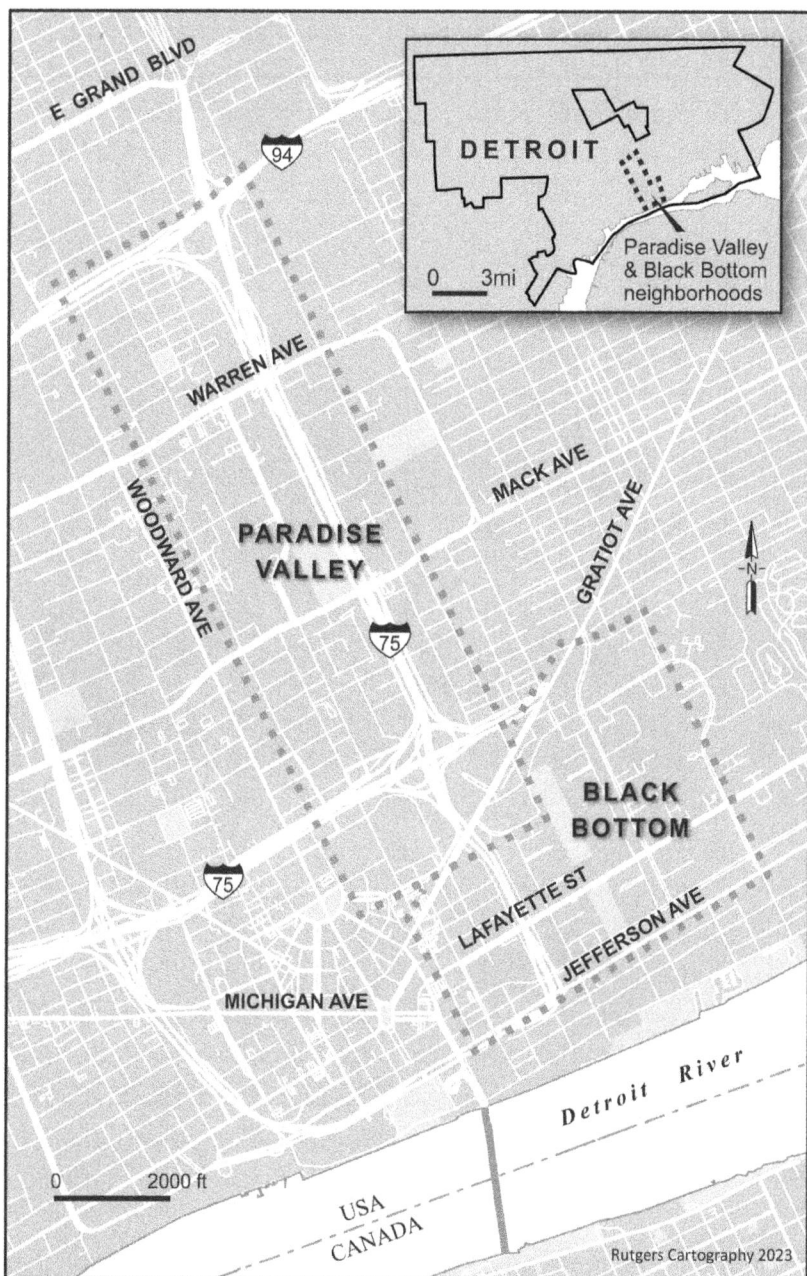

Figure 1. Detroit's African American business community was concentrated in overlapping neighborhoods known as Black Bottom and Paradise Valley. In general, Black Bottom's boundaries were considered to be: Gratiot Avenue and East Vernor Highway (north), Jefferson Avenue (south), Chene Street (east), and Brush Street (west). Paradise Valley's boundaries were considered to be: Medbury (north), Madison Street (south), Russell (east), and John R (west).

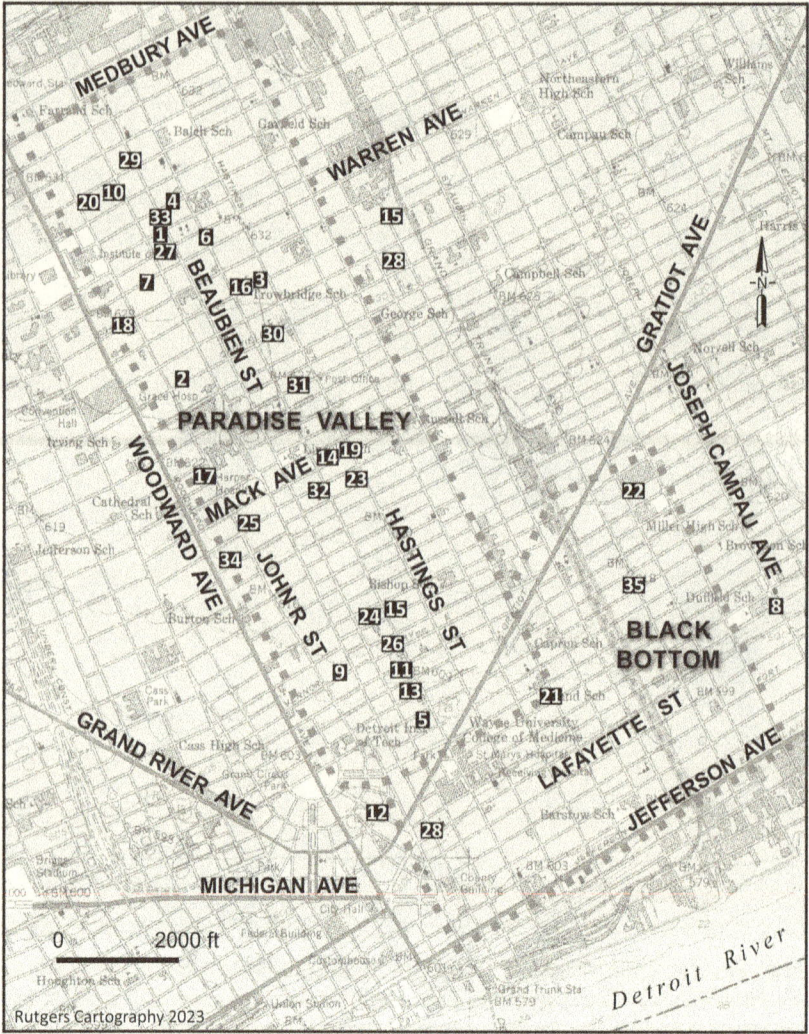

Figure 2. Select Black-owned businesses and key institutions in Black Bottom and Paradise Valley.

Select business owners and institutions mapped in Figure 2, in alphabetical order

1. A. W. Curtis Laboratories
2. Barthwell's Drug Stores
3. Bee Dew Laboratories
4. Bethel AME Church
5. Biltmore Hotel
6. Booker T. Washington Grocery
7. Booker T. Washington Trade Association and Detroit Housewives League
8. Bristol & Bristol Funeral Home
9. Davis Motors
10. Detroit Association of [Colored] Women's Clubs (DAWC)
11. *Detroit Contender* newspaper
12. Detroit Institute of Commerce
13. *Detroit Tribune* newspaper
14. Diggs Funeral Home/House of Diggs
15. Eleanora A. DeVere Hair Culturalist
16. Forest Club
17. Gotham Hotel
18. Great Lakes Mutual Insurance Company
19. Joe's Records
20. Lewis Business College (LBC)
21. Liberty Hall (UNIA)
22. Maben's Barber Shop
23. Malloy's Shoe Repair
24. Mercy Hospital
25. *Michigan Chronicle* newspaper
26. Michigan People's Finance Corporation (MPFC)
27. Paradise Valley Distributing Company (PVDC)
28. Second Baptist Church
29. Slade-Gragg Academy of Practical Arts
30. Smith Funeral Home
31. Supreme Linen and Laundry
32. Tanzy Hotel
33. Toodle's Drug Store
34. Twelve Horsemen Civic Center (IBPOEW)
35. Young's Tailoring and Dry Cleaners

LIST OF SELECT BUSINESS OWNERS AND INSTITUTIONS

1. **A. W. Curtis Laboratories**. Established by Austin W. Curtis in 1945. Born in West Virginia, Curtis was a Cornell University–trained chemist and worked with George Washington Carver at the Tuskegee Institute before migrating to Detroit in 1943. A. W. Curtis Laboratories was located at 545 Farnsworth Avenue, between Brush and Beaubien.
2. **Barthwell's Drug Stores**. Established by Sidney Barthwell in 1933. Barthwell was born in Cordele, Georgia, in 1906 and migrated to Detroit in 1920 to join his father, who worked for Ford Motor Company. After graduating with a pharmacy degree from Wayne State University, Barthwell established his first retail pharmacy and eventually expanded into manufacturing ice cream to sell at his chain of stores. By 1957 the chain had ten drugstores in the Detroit area.
3. **Bee Dew Laboratories**. Established by Vivian Nash in 1924, after she migrated to Detroit from Georgia in 1920. The company's headquarters were at 703–705 East Forest Street, between St. Antoine and Hastings. The laboratories' 47 employees manufactured cosmetic products, while over 450 agents sold the products throughout the United States and internationally.
4. **Bethel AME Church**. Originally founded in 1839 as the second Black church in Detroit, Bethel became an AME church in 1841. Shown on the map is its location at 579 Frederick Street, between Beaubien and St. Antoine, which was dedicated on June 7, 1925. The church later moved to Warren Avenue.
5. **Biltmore Hotel**. One of Detroit's early Black-owned hotels, located at 1926 St. Antoine Street, near Beacon. It was established by O. H. Banks in the mid-1910s and was later operated by Theodore Jones. Also referred to as the Hotel Biltmore, it was in operation until at least 1944.

6. **Booker T. Washington Grocery**. Established by Bertha and Berry Gordy Sr. at 5044 St. Antoine Street. The Gordys migrated to Detroit in 1921 from Sandersville, Georgia, and would become involved with the BTWTA and DHL. The Gordys were the parents of Motown Records founder Berry Gordy Jr.

7. **Booker T. Washington Trade Association and Detroit Housewives League**. Established in 1930 by William H. Peck and Fannie B. Peck (née McCampbell), the partner organizations would become the most influential Black business organizations in the city. They were headquartered at 446 East Warren Avenue, and associated with Bethel AME Church, which the Pecks led from 1928 until 1944.

8. **Bristol & Bristol Funeral Home.** Located at 1241 Joseph Campau Avenue, this funeral home was established by married couple Agnes and Vollington Bristol. Mr. Bristol immigrated from Grenada, British West Indies, and Mrs. Bristol (née Fairfax) was born in Virginia. Both received their license for embalming in 1922. Mrs. Bristol was the first Black woman in Michigan to be a licensed mortician.

9. **Davis Motors.** Established by Ed Davis in 1939. Davis was born in 1911 in Shreveport, Louisiana, and migrated to Detroit in the 1920s. Davis operated his business at 421 East Vernor Highway for over twenty years and built Davis Motor Sales into a thriving Studebaker dealership until his neighborhood was plagued by urban renewal.

10. **Detroit Association of [Colored] Women's Clubs (DAWC).** This organization was formed in 1921 from a group of eight Black women's clubs in the city. The association's home, located at 5461 Brush Street at the corner of East Ferry, was purchased in 1941. The DAWC had more than seventy affiliated clubs at its height in 1945. The organization later dropped the word "Colored" from its name.

11. *Detroit Contender* **newspaper.** Located at 2205 St. Antoine Street, the newspaper was founded by brothers Robert and Ulysses Poston. Originally from Hopkinsville, Kentucky, the Postons migrated to Detroit in 1919 to establish a newspaper. The periodical promoted Black business cooperation and Black self-determination.

12. **Detroit Institute of Commerce.** Founded by R. Louise Grooms in 1941 and located at 1308 Broadway Street, the institute offered courses in stenography, executive and finishing secretarial, junior accounting, and business administration. Besides operating the institute, Grooms worked as the chief accountant and office manager of Great Lakes Mutual Insurance Company. She was also one of the founders of Detroit's Victory Loan and Investment Company, serving as a director and secretary for twenty-five years.

13. *Detroit Tribune* **newspaper.** Located at 2146 St. Antoine Street, the newspaper was known as "the leading Negro weekly in Michigan." The *Detroit Tribune* began operating in 1933 and shortly thereafter merged with the *Detroit Independent*, becoming known as the *Tribune Independent of Michigan*. The periodical reverted to the name *Detroit Tribune* in 1935 and was known as such until 1966 when it ceased operation. The *Tribune* had several editors including Ulysses W. Boykin. Boykin also authored *A Hand Book on the Detroit Negro* in 1943 and was a key trial witness in the Mayor Reading graft scandal that exposed the inner workings of numbers gambling in Detroit.

14. **Diggs Funeral Home/House of Diggs.** Established in 1921 by Charles C. Diggs Sr., a prominent businessman (and later politician), and his wife, Mamie Diggs. The Diggs family migrated to Detroit from Mississippi and built the House of Diggs into the largest funeral business in Michigan and one of the most prominent in the nation. The business was displaced from its 689 Mack Avenue location for the Medical Center renewal project.

15. **Eleanora A. DeVere Hair Culturalist.** Founded in 1919 by Eleanora A. DeVere, this salon located at 2509 St. Antoine Street catered to Detroit's growing migrant community. DeVere trained under Madam C. J. Walker, and the salon included a retail station for Madam C. J. Walker products and also served as a distribution center for the company in order to supply agents throughout Michigan.

16. **Forest Club.** Located at 700 East Forest Street at the corner of Hastings, this club became a popular spot for nightlife entertainment in the Paradise Valley neighborhood. It was established in 1941 by Sunnie Wilson, a transplant from South Carolina. The

Forest Club spanned the entire block and had a banquet hall, a dance floor, a two-level roller-skating rink, twenty-six lanes for bowling, and a famous 107-foot-long bar.

17. **Gotham Hotel.** Located at 111 Orchestra Place (near John R Street), the Gotham boasted nine stories and more than two hundred rooms, several penthouses, an elegant lobby, a restaurant, a flower shop, and a drugstore on the first floor. Black entrepreneurs Irving Roane, John White, and Walter Norwood joined together to purchase the building in 1943. The Gotham Hotel was widely considered to be the best Black-owned hotel in the country. In 1963 the hotel was torn down to make way for the Medical Center.

18. **Great Lakes Mutual Insurance Company.** Founded in 1928, this company was touted as the largest Black-owned business in Michigan. In the 1930s and 1940s it operated from 301 East Warren Avenue and later moved its headquarters to 82 East Hancock Avenue. The company also owned and operated an apartment house called Great Lakes Manor.

19. **Joe's Records.** Joe Von Battle, a migrant from Macon, Georgia, opened this record store at 3530 Hastings Street in 1945. The popular shop was one of the few places to buy Black music in Detroit at that time. In addition to selling records, Von Battle also recorded and produced music for Black artists. The business was a vital part of Paradise Valley's vibrant music scene before it was displaced by the Chrysler Freeway.

20. **Lewis Business College (LBC).** Founded in 1939 by Violet T. Lewis, LBC was the largest and most successful of Detroit's Black business schools. Located at 5450 John R Street, the school originally educated women and became coeducational when World War II veterans wanted to take advantage of the GI Bill.

21. **Liberty Hall (UNIA).** The Detroit division of the Universal Negro Improvement Association was established in 1920 and was one of the strongest chapters, growing to over five thousand members by 1922. Detroit's UNIA purchased a building at 1516 Russell Street to house its office, which was named Liberty Hall. The UNIA's Sunshine Restaurant was located nearby at 1520 Russell.

22. **Maben's Barber Shop.** A two-chair barbershop located at 2241 Waterloo Street operated by Haywood Maben. Originally from

Augusta, Georgia (where he also operated a barbershop), Maben migrated to Detroit in the 1920s. The Marxist barber used his Detroit shop as a space to discuss radical politics during the Great Depression. The business was plowed over in 1950 to make way for the Gratiot urban renewal project.

23. **Malloy's Shoe Repair.** Located at 3409 Hastings Street, this shop was operated by husband-and-wife team Lorenzo and Helen Malloy, who were originally from Alabama. Mrs. Malloy was a longtime member of the Detroit Housewives League, serving as its president and the organization's historian. The Malloys were the foster parents of Betty Shabazz.

24. **Mercy Hospital.** Located at 668 Winder Street, this was the city's first Black-owned hospital. Mercy was established in 1917 by Drs. David and Daisy Northcross, married medical doctors from Montgomery, Alabama, who, according to their son, moved to Detroit in 1917 to escape the persecution of the Ku Klux Klan. By 1922 Mercy Hospital had moved from its original location to a new building with space for additional patients and an operating room.

25. *Michigan Chronicle* **newspaper.** Located at 268 Eliot Street, this weekly newspaper was established in 1936 by John H. Sengstacke, nephew of the *Chicago Defender*'s publisher Robert Sengstacke Abbott. The *Michigan Chronicle* was an important outlet that covered Black politics, civil rights issues, and activism in Detroit. The periodical remains in operation.

26. **Michigan People's Finance Corporation (MPFC).** Located at 606 East Vernor Highway, MPFC was chartered in 1923 and offered small loans. This financial institution was closely tied to the Detroit Urban League, which was founded in 1916 to help acclimate Black southern migrants to urban life in Detroit. John C. Dancy, longtime director of the Detroit Urban League, served as the president and treasurer of the MPFC.

27. **Paradise Valley Distributing Company (PVDC).** Located at 439 Theodore Street and founded in 1937, PVDC boasted that it was the "first and only fully owned and operated Negro beer distributing agency in the entire United States. Everything Negro from the FRONT OFFICE to the porter." By 1943, the company owned ten trucks, had forty-two employees, and sponsored scholarships for Detroit youth.

28. **Second Baptist Church.** Established in 1836, this is the oldest
    Black congregation in Michigan. Its building at 441 Monroe
    Street was erected in 1914. The Reverend Robert Bradby led
    Second Baptist Church from 1910 to 1946, and during this time
    the church was a crucial institution for facilitating the southern
    migration to Detroit and boosting Black business in the city.

29. **Slade-Gragg Academy of Practical Arts.** Located at 455 East
    Ferry Street, the academy was founded in 1947 by Rosa Slade
    Gragg as a trade school for veterans. Originally from Geor-
    gia, Gragg served as president of both the Detroit Association
    of Women's Clubs and the National Association of Colored
    Women's Clubs.

30. **Smith Funeral Home.** Located at 611 East Canfield near St.
    Antoine and Hastings Streets, this business was founded by
    Willis Eugene Smith, one of the most well-known and successful
    entrepreneurs in Detroit's Black funeral industry during the first
    half of the twentieth century. Smith was originally from Eufaula,
    Alabama, and migrated to Detroit in 1919. He opened the
    funeral home in 1929 but lost the property in the early 1960s due
    to the construction of the Chrysler Freeway.

31. **Supreme Linen and Laundry.** Located at 700 East Alexandrine
    Street, Supreme Linen was founded by Fred and Callie Allen in
    1929. The Allens were originally from Mississippi and migrated
    to Detroit in 1924. The establishment supplied tablecloths, nap-
    kins, uniforms, and aprons to Black-owned businesses in the city
    and also housed a commercial laundry. Fred Allen was deeply
    involved with the Booker T. Washington Trade Association
    and served as vice president of both the Detroit branch of the
    NAACP and the National Negro Business League.

32. **Tanzy Hotel.** Located at 2476 St. Antoine Street, this was one of
    Detroit's early Black-owned hotels, established before 1920. Pro-
    prietor B. W. Tanzy catered especially to newly arriving southern
    migrants. The Tanzy had thirty-six rooms, a dining room, and a
    dance hall, and by 1924 it regularly employed fourteen workers.

33. **Toodle's Drug Store.** Located at 5250 Beaubien Street and estab-
    lished by Dr. Aaron C. Toodle. Dr. Toodle was a pharmacist and
    successful businessman originally from Plymouth, North Caro-
    lina. Toodle had graduated from Howard University in 1917 and

migrated to Detroit in 1919. By the 1930s, Toodle's résumé in the Black business community was extensive. In addition to operating several drugstores in Detroit, Toodle was also the Michigan People's Finance Corporation's treasurer, general manager of the *Tribune-Independent* newspaper, and one of the initial entrepreneurs who mobilized to establish Detroit Memorial Park Cemetery, Detroit's first Black-owned cemetery.

34. **Twelve Horsemen Civic Center (IBPOEW).** Located at 114 Erskine Street, this facility was owned by the Improved Benevolent and Protective Order of Elks of the World. The center had a bar, an auditorium, and a ballroom as well as a large kitchen, which was equipped to serve meals for the large groups that rented the banquet hall. The Twelve Horsemen also supported Black entrepreneurship by utilizing local Black businesses as vendors.

35. **Young's Tailoring and Dry Cleaners.** Located at 1943 St. Aubin Avenue between Sherman and Maple, this shop was established by William C. Young, the father of future Detroit mayor Coleman Young. The Young family migrated to Detroit in 1923 from Alabama. The business was plowed over in 1950 to make way for the Gratiot urban renewal project. [Because Coleman Young does not mention the formal name of his father's business in his memoir, I have assigned it this moniker.]

Freedom Enterprise

Introduction

As a nine-year-old boy, Fred A. Allen made a promise to himself: "Someday I'm going to be the boss, and when I'm the boss, I'm going to see to it that our people get a few breaks." Born in 1898 near Clarksdale, Mississippi, Allen had been performing backbreaking labor in the scorching heat of a Mississippi cotton field since he was five years old. Looking back on his childhood, Allen recalled, "I was miserable and my spirit was broken. Everywhere I looked there was misery, poverty and stagnation. While the white kids my age were going to school and having fun, the Negro kids had to work 12 hours a day in the fields because our families were so poor." Allen made up his mind then and there to devote his life to raising African Americans' standard of living by starting his own business.[1]

Determined to change his lot, Fred Allen left home at age fifteen to work in Clarksdale, first as an auto mechanic and then with a cousin who drove a laundry truck. He earned fifteen dollars per week. Allen knew that in order to go into business for himself he would need to first save a significant amount of money, since white-owned banks would not provide loans to African Americans who wanted to open a business. Allen met and married his wife Callie, who worked as a tailor, and the couple moved to Houston in 1918. There, Allen could earn thirty-five dollars per week for the same work he was doing for fifteen back in Clarksdale. When the Allens learned that Fred could earn forty dollars per week working in Detroit, they migrated north in 1924. There Fred Allen would realize the goal he had been pursuing since childhood.[2]

Sharing his dream, Callie "scrimped and saved with him to help make it true."[3] The couple worked hard and saved up $6,000 before launching Supreme Linen in 1929 (Callie operated her own tailoring shop in Detroit as well). The establishment supplied tablecloths, napkins, uniforms, and aprons to Black-owned businesses, as well as some white-owned ones. The linen supply business expanded to also operate a commercial laundry in 1936 and became known as Supreme Linen and Laundry. Fred Allen had learned about this field from his cousin while living in Clarksdale, and since there were no African Americans in the industry in Detroit, the Allens decided to fill the void. While the business was most often attributed to Fred Allen, both Fred and Callie were described as the "proprietors of the Supreme Linen and Laundry" in contemporary records, and the couple described the commercial laundry as "our plant."[4] The business prospered through the couple's hard work. In just a few years, Supreme Linen serviced over three hundred businesses. By 1940, the Allens owned a large plant and a "fleet of trucks" that traversed the entire city daily, employed more than one hundred people, and had built a large family home in Detroit's North End neighborhood. By the early 1950s, Supreme Linen and Laundry was earning $200,000 annually (more than $2.2 million in 2023) and the Allens were living in Conant Gardens, the most exclusive neighborhood for African Americans in Detroit. Though he only completed the fourth grade in Mississippi, Fred Allen established one of the most profitable Black-owned businesses in Detroit in the first half of the twentieth century.[5]

The Allens' efforts not only provided them with personal wealth but also helped Fred Allen keep his childhood promise to uplift African Americans. According to Allen, one of his main objectives in becoming an entrepreneur was to create employment opportunities within his community: "As a businessman, I felt I would be able to provide good jobs for members of my race and thereby help raise their standard of living." He certainly achieved this goal with Supreme Linen, which hired African American workers. Additionally, all of the contractors, mechanics, and other workers Allen hired to prepare his 700 East Alexandrine Street laundry building were Black.[6] Allen was also deeply involved with the Booker T. Washington Trade Association, Detroit's primary organization of Black business owners and professionals, he served as vice president of both the Detroit branch of the NAACP and the National Negro Business League, and was a board member of the YMCA and Parkside Hospital, one of Detroit's first hospitals that catered to African Americans.[7] But Allen's work in strengthening Detroit's Black community did not stop there. He also became president of Wayne County Better Homes (WCBH), a construction company established by Black entrepreneurs in 1943 to build five hundred homes for African Americans through the Federal Housing Authority.[8] As well as helping to supply this necessary housing,

WCBH employed Black workers and contractors to build it. For example, the company hired Donald F. White, the first registered African American architect in the State of Michigan, to design various sites. What's more, White's firm had a reputation for appointing Black architects, engineers, and draftsmen.[9] All of these efforts had the same purpose: to provide Black Americans with greater economic autonomy.

The Allens were just one example of countless African Americans who viewed business as a route to freedom and left the South to follow their entrepreneurial dreams. Until 1910, more than 90 percent of African Americans lived in the South. During World War I, they started moving north and west in large numbers, relocating mostly to urban centers. In all, between 1910 and 1970, more than six million African Americans left the South in what became known as the Great Migration. This massive demographic shift redefined urban life throughout the country and reconfigured Black Americans' position in the U.S. economy and society. For aspiring Black entrepreneurs and those already engaged in business in the South, the Great Migration seemed like an opportunity to achieve greater economic independence, self-determination, and financial security. Faced with the ever-present obstacles that racism presented, they were able to achieve considerable gains from the 1920s through the 1940s.

In Detroit, Black migrant entrepreneurs like Fred and Callie Allen built a thriving business community, particularly in the neighborhoods known as Black Bottom and Paradise Valley (see Figure 1), which would become one of the largest and most robust in the nation.[10] Hastings Street was the most famous thoroughfare for Black business, though others, such as St. Antoine, Mack, and Forest, also bustled with commercial activities needed to sustain the migrant community. There, on Detroit's east side, Black-owned real estate firms aided African Americans in securing commercial space, in addition to housing. Migrant entrepreneurs built financial institutions and insurance companies, hotels, and a variety of professional practices. There were pharmacies, barbershops and beauty salons, taxicab companies, groceries, and restaurants, including many that specialized in southern cooking. Black Detroiters could relax at bars, clubs, billiard halls, and bowling alleys. They could shop at Black-owned clothing stores and read Black-owned newspapers (which utilized the services of Black printing shops, photography studios, and commercial art studios). Residents could choose from an array of funeral homes to provide homegoing needs when loved ones died. Funeral establishments coordinated with local Black-owned cemeteries or would ship remains back south for burial in family plots. In short, African Americans could have almost all their needs met by Detroit's Black business community.

Sadly, this success was short-lived, as postwar urban planning initiatives literally bulldozed Black Detroit's thriving business district to the ground. Funded by federal, state, and local governments, redevelopment efforts in the 1950s and 1960s cast aside Black entrepreneurs' property rights and generated glaring racial and economic injustices in the city. While ostensibly undertaken for the public good, this urban planning essentially functioned as a state-sponsored wealth redistribution program that benefited white citizens and helped maintain a system of economic white supremacy. In the process, it ravaged Detroit's Black business community and dealt a severe blow to migrant entrepreneurs who had relocated to seek economic independence and upward mobility. This book thus illuminates an understudied aspect of the ways structural racism has prevented African Americans from obtaining economic security and reveals the state's complicity in racialized economic injustices. The 1950s and 1960s witnessed several well-known victories for the Black Freedom Movement, particularly at the federal level. However, the civil rights era was also a time of devastating loss, with state initiatives rolling back the economic advancement made by the African American business community. Though an extreme example, Detroit was not the only urban center that experienced the destruction of Black-owned businesses due to urban planning; similar scenarios played out in urban Black communities across the country.

Freedom Enterprise traces the rise and fall of Detroit's Black business community and uncovers the ways migrant entrepreneurs worked to gain economic freedom within the confines of racial capitalism. In a racial capitalist system, economic and racial hierarchies intersect with and reinforce each other. As such, racism and racial oppression are linked with economic exploitation. Migrant entrepreneurs' "freedom enterprise"—their undertaking of attaining freedom through business—was curtailed by the reality of operating within U.S. racial capitalism. Many African Americans thought expanding individual and cooperative Black-owned business endeavors was imperative, since racial and economic oppression were inherently linked. And their motive in pursuing business was not necessarily to maximize their individual profit or increase their net worth but rather to make progress toward racial equality and ultimately Black freedom. Yet, in the American racial capitalist system, Black second-class economic (and political) citizenship was deeply engrained. This book aims to show how Black entrepreneurs attempted to overcome racial capitalism through their ongoing efforts at freedom enterprise.

It is important to note that racial capitalism is not a thing of the past. Racial capitalism was, and still is, an ever-present and ever-changing phenomenon that Black entrepreneurs had to contend with their entire lives, not just in the 1950s and 1960s. In many ways, the United States is still dealing with the consequences of this era. *Freedom Enterprise* joins the ongoing national conversation related to the long-term implications of racial capitalism, including the racial wealth gap. It provides valuable historical context for one aspect of contemporary concerns around generational economic regression in the Black community: urban entrepreneurs' accumulation and subsequent loss of wealth. It is well-known that there have been systemic barriers to Black economic success. Yet Black entrepreneurs in Detroit were able to accumulate wealth and build a prosperous business community. This book demonstrates that making money was not the main problem—holding onto the wealth was. Moreover, it shows that this was not due to individual business owners' deficiencies but to structural racism.

In this way, *Freedom Enterprise* intersects with current conversations about reparations and racial and economic reparative justice. Recently, the United States has seen efforts to return land taken from Black Americans and otherwise provide compensation for the past harms of municipal and state policies. These efforts are gaining traction. In October 2022, descendants of a Black California couple whose property was unjustly seized through eminent domain in the 1920s won land back from the state.[11] Discussions regarding reparations for slavery and enduring racial discrimination are increasing as more cities and states form reparations task forces. Notably, on June 29, 2023, the California Task Force to Study and Develop Reparation Proposals for African Americans recommended "a comprehensive reparations plan." In response, the city of San Francisco is considering one that could include cash payments and housing aid to African Americans. Evanston, Illinois, also approved reparations to eligible Black residents in 2021 for harm caused by "discriminatory housing policies and practices and inaction on the city's part." Evanston's reparations program may function as a model for other cities to begin to address the racial wealth gap.[12] The city of Detroit too has formed a Reparations Task Force to "develop recommendations for housing and economic development programs that address historical discrimination against the Black community in Detroit."[13] While these developments are promising, the United States has yet to sufficiently reckon with the economic consequences of postwar urban planning and take seriously the enduring injustices of racial capitalism. *Freedom Enterprise* provides useful context as the United States continues the conversation on repairing past economic harm.

Racial Capitalism and Black Entrepreneurship

I utilize the framework of "racial capitalism" for understanding southern migrants and other Black entrepreneurs' experiences in twentieth-century Detroit. Racial capitalism refers to the "development, organization, and expansion of capitalist society" wherein race is the ordering principle.[14] Black studies scholars such as Cedric Robinson, Robin D. G. Kelley, Jacquelyn Dowd Hall, Nathan Connolly, and others have outlined racial capitalism as a global economic system that requires race and class differentiation in the labor market.[15] While it does produce a system of prejudicial treatment, racial capitalism is not merely defined by racial prejudice. Rather, racial capitalism requires the exploitation of people of color to provide cheap labor for capitalist powers. Throughout history, racial capitalist regimes have taken different forms, each shaped by location, time period, and social context. As Eric Williams and Cedric Robinson demonstrate, British and American capitalism arose alongside the Atlantic slave trade and was inextricably tied to racism from the beginning.[16] In other words, capitalism in the United States is and always has been racial capitalism.[17]

This global view of racial capitalism asserts that capitalism and racism evolved together to produce what Robin D. G. Kelley has summarized as a "modern world system of 'racial capitalism' dependent on slavery, violence, imperialism, and genocide."[18] Accordingly, I write with an understanding that the inherent violence of racial capitalism continued after the end of slavery in the United States and was a key part of Black entrepreneurs' experiences throughout the twentieth century. Entrepreneurship is an understudied aspect of racial capitalism, as most scholarship on the subject in the U.S. context focuses on labor.[19] But violence was not only a tool used to extract labor from Black bodies; it was also fundamental to maintain white supremacy in the commercial sphere. Building on Jacqueline Dowd Hall's argument that lynchings "did not have to occur very often, or be witnessed directly, to be burned indelibly into the mind," I suggest that the threat of violence was an ever-present reality for African American entrepreneurs operating in the Jim Crow era, one that influenced their decisions about business and migration.[20] I also argue that, similar to extralegal violence in the Jim Crow South, the violence and economic harm of mid-century urban redevelopment projects served to keep Blacks economically subjugated and maintain a white supremacist economic system, that is, racial capitalism. Although some stories of white supremacist terror targeting Black businesses are well-known—such as the destruction of "Black Wall Street" in Tulsa, Oklahoma—I contend that we have not fully accounted for the pervasiveness of violence as a risk factor for Blacks conducting business in the United States. Black business owners were threatened constantly with capricious, irregular fits of violence, both physical and economic. In theory, capitalism is designed to cause "creative destruction," as less efficient businesses and industries are driven out by more efficient ones.[21] All businesses face risk. But *Freedom Enterprise* tells a story of entrepreneurs who had no choice but to operate in an environment of extreme peril and precarity, where the usual risks faced by all businesses intersect with the more dangerous and omnipresent threat of physical and economic anti-Black violence.

Consequently, though the title *Freedom Enterprise* plays on the term "free enterprise," this book does not endorse the idea that under the right circumstances "the market" would ultimately lead to Black liberation. I do not subscribe to the view that without racial prejudice "free enterprise" would exist and the capitalist market would be fair and neutral, although some of the business owners who appear in this book certainly did.[22] Racial capitalism does not simply impede free enterprise. Racism is foundational to the system; it is impossible to remove prejudicial structures to achieve a fair and equal economic system wherein all businesses compete freely. This book demonstrates that a capitalist political economy suffused with structural racism did allow people of color to create pockets of individual and communal entrepreneurial action. Yet the system constrained this sphere of opportunity, not only through violence but also by limiting access to capital and certain markets. In the context of business, racial capitalism produces a white supremacist economic system that limits or eliminates minority entrepreneurs' ability to engage in and profit from free enterprise. Including "racial capitalism" in the subtitle to *Freedom Enterprise* aims to capture this tension.

This is not to say that Black people were never able to turn a profit or achieve upward mobility through business. In fact, some of the book's subjects became quite affluent, defying a system that reduced many others to slavery, peonage, and imprisonment. However, just as the ideological construct of "free enterprise" disguises the way racial capitalism works, individual entrepreneurs' achievements mask the system's larger implications for African Americans on the whole. Since capitalism produces inequality—including racial inequality—being successful in business was simply not a viable route to freedom for Black America. In reality, the system failed even its most successful participants, who still faced obstacles imposed by a racist society that made it impossible for most to achieve enduring affluence or generational wealth.[23]

Freedom Enterprise examines racial capitalism from the bottom up, reconstructing migrant entrepreneurs' lived experiences, their ideas about the economy and freedom, and the community they built in Detroit. The racial capitalist system affected the lives of Black businesspeople in many ways. Segregation was key for maintaining the racial hierarchy of the political economy. The city's Black population was highly concentrated in the Black Bottom and Paradise Valley neighborhoods due to discriminatory real estate practices, and even Black entrepreneurs who lived elsewhere in the city generally established their businesses there to serve their Black clients. African American entrepreneurs had to contend with an array of obstacles linked to segregation. Just to name a few: they had limited access to commercial space (and what they did have access to was substandard), they did not have the financial support of white Detroiters who refused to shop in their neighborhoods, and they could not secure loans from white-owned banks that discriminated against them through practices such as redlining.

Unlike most Black Detroiters, Fred and Callie Allen lived in more integrated neighborhoods and Supreme Linen and Laundry did have white customers who supported the business.[24] Yet, the dynamics of racial capitalism hindered their freedom enterprise. Fred Allen described the process of starting up Supreme Linen: "Everything was going fine until I tried to buy linens. Most of the suppliers refused to sell to me and those who would wanted twice what they were charging white customers."[25] This is just one example of how racial hierarchy structured economic exploitation. Allen went to several potential customers and explained the situation to them and in solidarity they agreed to rent their linens from Allen, even though he would have to charge a higher price than white competitors. Next, white business rivals turned to anticompetitive practices. According to Allen, "The going was rough. My white competitors started cutting prices to drive me out of the business. They also threatened my customers that they wouldn't supply them once I was driven out of business. But my customers stuck with me. The situation eased when my competitors realized I was here to stay. Immediately, they quit cutting prices and supply houses charged me the same price as they charged their white customers."[26] When Allen wanted to expand the linen supply business and add a commercial laundry, he again ran into white opposition. Allen explained, "Real estate men wouldn't talk to me when I tried to buy a building to expand my business. I licked them by buying a used building at a tax sale." Fred Allen continued facing an uphill battle, since white-owned companies were the only ones producing the commercial equipment needed to outfit the laundry. According to Allen, "the nation's largest manufacturer of laundry equipment refused to deal with me. Lady luck saved the day however. A new company began manufacturing laundry equipment about this time and it agreed to sell to me."[27] The experience of combating racial capitalism at every turn was taxing for Black entrepreneurs. A 1957 *Detroit Free Press* feature on Fred Allen observed, "Allen paid a high price for his dream. The strain brought on a heart attack in 1953 and he was forced to sell out."[28]

As it was in the Jim Crow South, going up against white competitors in Detroit could be dangerous. In 1936 Supreme Linen and Laundry's night watchman was murdered while on duty. This was a major blow to Fred Allen because the slain employee, Edward McSwine, was his brother-in-law. There were several theories regarding the motive for the crime. One was that white competitors wanted to frighten Allen out of the laundry business. On the night of the murder a note was left at the scene of the crime that read "Allen, you are next."[29] Several weeks after the murder Allen received a second threatening note that warned him not to press the case any further or there would be serious consequences. Allen vowed, "No matter what has happened, or what might happen, I am staying in the laundry business."[30] About four months before the murder at Supreme Linen and Laundry, another "prosperous colored laundry" was "mysteriously burned" after the proprietor, Samuel Hood, expanded and opened a large new location at 4824 St. Antoine. Both Supreme Linen and Hood laundries were equipped with the latest laundry equipment and both plants handled a large volume of business.[31] The similarities between the laundry incidents (plus the long history of racial violence directed at Black business owners) lent credibility to the theory that white laundry operators were menacing Black entrepreneurs who were looking to expand in the industry. Events like these reminded migrant entrepreneurs that the violent hallmark of racial capitalism was ubiquitous in the United States.

Black business owners' experiences operating within racial capitalism varied, and as such they held a range of positions on capitalism and its potential for achieving freedom. Some embraced capitalist ideology, identified as part of the petite bourgeoisie, and sought to accumulate wealth. This cohort included those who solely sought personal affluence as well as those who believed that amassing wealth could lead to liberation for African Americans as a group—people like Fred Allen. Others engaged in business out of convenience or for survival without giving much thought to racial liberation. Many entrepreneurs simply wanted the economic independence of being their own boss, valuing the autonomy of not having to answer to a white employer. In fact, most of the subjects in *Freedom Enterprise* operated small businesses with few or no employees outside their families. When it came to the potential of attaining freedom through business, each entrepreneur had their own motivation and point of view.

Varied perspectives notwithstanding, Black entrepreneurs negotiated and resisted racial capitalism in a variety of ways. I am not suggesting that all of their actions constituted resistance to economic white supremacy or were attempts at freedom. However, like many African Americans who employed infrapolitics in the Jim Crow era, Black entrepreneurs engaged in daily acts of resistance while operating within the system of racial capitalism.[32] Historians have shown that Black entrepreneurs were often better positioned than laborers to be freedom leaders since economic retribution from whites was less risky for those who were self-employed.[33] In Detroit, Black business advocates worked to build the conditions for Black enterprises to succeed, cultivating research and development, opportunities for business education, and other efforts that helped the community grow in economically healthy periods and survive during ruinous ones. Engaging in a more cooperative, instructive, and community-focused variety of local capitalism was one way Detroit's Black entrepreneurs resisted racial capitalism. Still, they remained stuck in a tug-of-war between trying to pursue viable routes for freedom through business and attempting to dismantle the Jim Crow system that defined the political economy in which they operated.

Freedom Enterprise explores this tension to offer new insights into the relationship between "Black capitalism" and "racial capitalism," particularly

regarding the prospect of Black economic advancement within the system.[34] Business has long been prescribed as a means to help Black people
achieve freedom, and African American political movements focused on
building wealth through business development and ownership have cycled
throughout U.S. history. For example, racial capitalism and its dependence
on segregation inadvertently generated localized Black consumer markets
that facilitated economic success for Black nationalist groups, such as Marcus
Garvey's Universal Negro Improvement Association, as well as other "buy
Black" movements.[35] Yet efforts to advance Black entrepreneurial liberation—
whether nationalist movements in the 1920s and 1930s or Black capitalism
initiatives of the 1960s and 1970s—have not solved the problem of Black
subjugation.[36] Often, the Black community casts blame inward for their own
economic oppression, reproaching those who do not sufficiently "buy Black,"
"bank Black," or whatever slogan for economic uplift is in vogue. The problem
is not that African Americans are not adequately supportive of their communities or skilled, hardworking, creative, or innovative people. Black capitalist
efforts simply could not counteract racial capitalism enough to realize enduring Black economic advancement.[37]

Migrant Entrepreneurship and the Great Migration

Decades of scholarship on African American business history serve as a foundation for *Freedom Enterprise*.[38] Even so, my focus on the Great Migration
and its effects illuminates aspects of Black entrepreneurship that are specific
to this context and in some ways challenge predominant frameworks in Black
business history. For instance, Juliet E. K. Walker's foundational chronology
of 1900 to 1930 as the "golden age of Black business" does not apply to Detroit,
where the arrival of southern migrants created the conditions for the city's
Black business community to reach its peak in the 1940s and early 1950s. The
"Golden Age" periodization is shaped by a focus on large enterprises and corporations, as opposed to the smaller Black-owned enterprises that made up
the majority of Black business communities.[39] In addition, migrant identity
was persistent, and Black migrant entrepreneurs' experiences in Detroit were
shaped by their participation in the Great Migration in ways that resonated
long after they arrived. To better understand their distinct experiences and
deepen the complexity of this history, I propose "migrant entrepreneurship"
as a useful analytical framework.

Indeed, Detroit provides an ideal site for exploring the particularities of migrant entrepreneurship. The city's Black population increased 611 percent between 1910 and 1920—more than any other major urban center—creating unique opportunities for African Americans to pursue their entrepreneurial goals.[40] While histories of the Great Migration traditionally focus on migrants' experiences as wage laborers in northern industrial cities, Detroit's status as a mecca for Black entrepreneurship provides access to this overlooked aspect of Great Migration history.[41] This includes differences in what migration theorist Everett Lee calls "push-pull" factors—what "pushed" African Americans to leave the South (i.e., social inequality, racial and sexual violence, oppressive labor arrangements) and why certain destinations "pulled" them in (i.e., educational opportunities, political access, greater civil rights).[42] Perhaps the most widely cited pull factor of the Great Migration was the appeal of economic opportunities in the urban North.[43] However, such economic opportunities are generally discussed in terms of higher wages, occupational advancement, and the possibility of employment in sectors inaccessible to African Americans in the South.[44] But for entrepreneurially minded migrants, ideas about freedom were attached to business, not labor—a distinction that shaped the development of Detroit's Black business community.[45] In this way, the concept of migrant entrepreneurship deepens historical understandings of people's motivations and other complexities of the Great Migration story. Additionally, Detroit's premigration Black population was incredibly small, little more than 1 percent of the city's entire population. Migrants made up 85 percent of city's Black population by 1926.[46] Analyzing Detroit offers the unique opportunity to consider a Black business community comprised almost entirely of southern migrants, as compared to other cities that already had sizable African American populations prior to the Great Migration.

Finally, most studies on Detroit tend to examine the city either before or after World War II.[47] Detroit's reputation as the epitome of the postwar urban crisis, including the growth of racialized inner-city poverty, obscures the Black wealth that existed in the city in the period prior. Reperiodizing the narrative by bringing the pre- and post-1945 eras together allows me to trace the Black business community's rise *and* fall, as well as offer insight into the meaning of its destruction. While historians of urban renewal tend to emphasize housing and its effects on residents, I suggest that centering business deepens understandings of this crucial moment in U.S. history. Black business owners were in some ways more adversely affected by postwar urban redevelopment. There were several ways that urban renewal in Detroit negatively affected Black business. It dispersed their customers, created "blight by announcement," and offered woefully inadequate compensation to property owners.[48] Urban renewal policies had negative implications for many, but delayed acquisition by the city especially haunted business owners. Often, a lengthy time would pass between the announcement that an area was designated for urban redevelopment and when the city could actually take possession of the property and settle payments with owners. This could take five, ten, or more years.[49] As they watched their neighborhood customers move to other sections in the city, their sales dropped drastically, and many entrepreneurs lost all their savings and went out of business before they had a chance to obtain a payment from the city. To fully understand the meaning of business loss through postwar urban planning initiatives, we must consider that many business owners were migrant entrepreneurs and that their establishments were freedom enterprises.

Taking a longer view—from the 1910s to the 1960s—reveals that the context for understanding this Black business community's downfall is not only the political economy of Detroit, or even the urban North. The context also includes the southern experience of those who established the community. Migrant entrepreneurs had left the Jim Crow South where whites kept Blacks economically subordinate through violence and targeted business owners who became too prosperous. African Americans worried about white mobs taking away their lives, property, and wealth in their southern homes. The memories of this reality no doubt sharpened the blow to those who sought refuge in Detroit, only to then lose their livelihoods and the businesses they had spent decades building to the bulldozers of urban redevelopment. Tracing Black entrepreneurs across the Great Migration demonstrates that what happened in Detroit is a national story. Whether looking at Black business owners in the Jim Crow South or migrant entrepreneurs in the North, both suffered under the racial capitalist regime. *Freedom Enterprise* is not just about the destruction of Detroit's Black business community; it is a story about what it means to be a Black entrepreneur in America.

Locating Freedom Enterprise

Recovering the story of how Black migrants' freedom enterprise sought to overcome racial capitalism in a cohesive way has been difficult due to the challenges of the archive. The neighborhoods where Detroit's Black business community thrived—Black Bottom and Paradise Valley—were demolished by postwar highway construction and urban renewal, wiping away most evidence of the former commercial landscape. There is no reference guide as to what businesses existed in this Black community prior to urban planning initiatives, and the evidence that does exist is fragmented and scattered among various archives and within former residents' memories.[50] This archival erasure of Black businesses is another casualty of white supremacy and racial capitalism. Furthermore, there is a dearth of research material on Black-owned small businesses and everyday economic thought. Consequently, early studies of Black business focus on large enterprises like insurance companies, while this book looks in aggregate at small businesses in Detroit's Black neighborhoods.[51]

Combining business and social history methods has allowed me to tackle these archival obstacles and reconstruct Detroit's Black business community prior to urban renewal. The book's cover, depicting the bustling activity of Hastings Street in Black Bottom, symbolizes this dual emphasis on Black business and social history. The photo shows some of the area's businesses but also highlights the people who walked Hastings and lived in this community. Although *Freedom Enterprise* focuses on Black business, this book is also a social history of the people behind it. Black Detroiters are the center of the story, as they are centered in the cover photograph.[52]

Freedom Enterprise draws on an eclectic archive to locate these historical actors in time and space. In tracing entrepreneurs' journeys to Detroit, I utilized southern city directories, vital records, military draft records, and census data. Letters to northern institutions like the Urban League show that the prospect of economic advancement through business was one factor that motivated Black southerners to participate in the Great Migration. I identified the businesses of migrants who established themselves in Detroit through directories, newspaper advertisements, photographs, and Black organizational and church publications. Manuscript collections pertaining to Black entrepreneurs, business groups, and city officials allowed me to piece together the growth of Black business in the city and the obstacles that developed along the way. In addition, Black people's memories were crucial in making this study possible, particularly regarding insights into Black quotidian economic thought.[53] Memoirs and interviews from oral history collections provided valuable glimpses into the heart and soul of Detroit's Black business community. Simply put, mining a wide array of sources for anything related to Black businesses that existed before the 1950s and 1960s enabled me to construct this narrative of migrant entrepreneurs' experiences and Detroit's historic Black business community.

For this study, I employ a broad understanding of entrepreneurship and look at a range of entrepreneurial activities, including formal corporations, like insurance companies and banks; private practices, such as law firms and medical offices; and leisure establishments, like bars and pool halls. I examine contracting businesses, beauty shops, manufacturing plants, restaurants, and funeral homes as well as part-time and seasonal pursuits such as peddling goods. I also analyze illegal entrepreneurial activities as a significant part of the business landscape. This expansive framework creates a fuller picture of Detroit's Black business community and the ways migrant entrepreneurs imagined they could obtain freedom through business. In addition, focusing on smaller businesses both tells a seldom heard story and offers a distinct perspective on Black upward mobility. Most of Detroit's Black entrepreneurs were not like Madam C. J. Walker or John Merrick. The significance of small businesses with relatively low capital investment has not been adequately acknowledged in stories of twentieth-century Black urban life. *Freedom Enterprise* thus presents a novel picture of class structure and mobility—or its promise, at least—in the urban North.

Because this book draws from fragmented evidence, my strategy for capturing the story of Black business in Detroit is to combine many different entrepreneurs' experiences. This has drawbacks, however, as it can be difficult to keep track of so many individuals.[54] Figure 2 plots select business owners and institutions on a map of Black Bottom and Paradise Valley—the areas most populated by Black Detroiters—and the accompanying list provides key information. At the same time, telling a sweeping story over six decades makes it impossible to detail all the intricacies of a community. Accordingly, the narrative I present here remains incomplete, and the history of Black business development in Detroit was in reality more complex.[55] Nevertheless, I have done my best to depict a broad picture of the rise and fall of Detroit's Black business community in the early and mid-twentieth century, particularly regarding how its fate was tied up in the violence and destruction of racial capitalism.

Freedom Enterprise follows Detroit's Black entrepreneurs from the initial wave of northern migration in the 1910s and 1920s, through their efforts in building a prosperous Black business community in the 1930s and 1940s, to the destruction of that community via urban redevelopment in the 1950s and

1960s. The book's chapters are titled to represent this trajectory. The first, "Hoping," chronicles Black entrepreneurs' experiences in the U.S. South in the World War I era, prior to migrating, to explore their hopes of economic freedom in the North. Business-minded migrants left the South for many of the same reasons as nonentrepreneurial Blacks but they also had unique concerns that focused on business, such as the threat of racial violence directed specifically toward successful Black entrepreneurs. Chapter 2, "Arriving," follows these migrant entrepreneurs to Detroit, where they began to establish businesses and develop professional networks in the late 1910s into the 1920s. Despite the persistence of racial violence, illustrated by the city's large Ku Klux Klan presence and the well-known case of physician Ossian Sweet's prosecution for defending himself against a white mob, Black entrepreneurs came together to create a cohesive business community that by the late 1920s was strong enough to swiftly respond to the coming devastation of the Great Depression.

Chapter 3, "Hustling," examines illegal enterprises from the 1910s through the 1940s—a risky yet significant sector of Black Detroit's entrepreneurial activity. It demonstrates that in the context of racial capitalism, in which any business venture included the possibility of instability and violence, participating in illegal enterprise was a rational and often more profitable choice for African Americans. Moreover, the illicit marketplace was essential for financing legally operated businesses in Detroit's Black community. Chapter 4, "Surviving," considers businesses during the Great Depression, examining Black entrepreneurs' strategies to survive the crisis and advance economic recovery in their community. To promote solidarity and self-help, uplift Black business, and explore economic alternatives to capitalism, Black entrepreneurs developed critical organizations during the 1930s that would become the bedrock of the business community in the coming decades.

Chapter 5, "Boosting," highlights one of these organizations, the Detroit Housewives League (DHL), which in the 1930s and 1940s served as a vital resource for the Black business community as a whole and women entrepreneurs in particular. DHL members conducted economic research and created opportunities for business education. As businesswomen and community leaders, they significantly contributed to Black Detroit's ability to withstand the Depression and facilitated the subsequent surge in successful Black businesses as World War II revived the city's economy. Chapter 6, "Booming," discusses the apex of Detroit's migrant business community in the 1940s and 1950s. Amid another wave of wartime migration that increased the city's African American population and shifted its racial geography, Black business soared during this era, especially in the Paradise Valley area bisected by Hastings Street. Bustling with enterprise, it was in this period that Detroit's migrant entrepreneurs seemed to be making the most progress toward their freedom enterprise goals. But the impending white backlash to the city's 1943 race riot would have long-term consequences for the community.

The next decade ushered in urban planning initiatives that would demolish not only Detroit's Black business community but also migrant entrepreneurs' hopes of obtaining economic security, independence, and upward mobility through business. The seventh chapter, "Falling," explores the destructive and racist impact of postwar expressway construction and urban renewal projects, as the city targeted Black neighborhoods with fewer resources to challenge redevelopment in an attempt to push African Americans out of the area where they had built businesses. Finally, Chapter 8, "Fighting," demonstrates that Detroit's Black entrepreneurs did not simply accept the destruction of their community. They actively defended their economic interests, challenged racial discrimination, fought for inclusion in urban redevelopment processes, and asserted their own vision of urban progress. While this activism did lead to some victories, it ultimately was not enough to restore what had been lost. African Americans continued to establish businesses in Detroit after the 1960s but the era marked a sorrowful ending for the city's Black business community and the migrant entrepreneurs who had sought freedom through enterprise in the first half of the twentieth century.

*   *   *

In the United States, self-sufficiency and economic participation are central to the ideology of citizenship; being an independent economic citizen, as opposed to one deemed as dependent, has been a prerequisite for claims to political rights, state protections, and social equality. The mythical "American Dream" ideal claims that one can achieve this sort of economic citizenship—prosperity, success, and upward mobility—through hard work and is often linked to entrepreneurship. Yet this was simply not the reality for Black entrepreneurs operating in a racial capitalist system. Whether facing white vigilante mobs in the Jim Crow South or agents of the state in the urban North, Black business communities were targeted for destruction in order maintain economic white supremacy, with harmful and lasting consequences.

The following pages contain a story of economic violence and pain but also one of continual efforts to defy the restraints of racial capitalism. Black entrepreneurs' fight for freedom through enterprise—their gains and their losses—provide key insights into the relationship between Black economic development, freedom, and capitalism. It is my hope that this history can serve as a useful lesson for current discussions of economic inequalities, urban policy, and racial justice.

CHAPTER 1

Hoping: Escaping Economic Violence and Migrating for Business Opportunities

In 1920, the Black-owned *Detroit Contender* newspaper published a "special business issue" in which an article claimed that the race was not measured by its intellectual or artistic contributions but by "the number of businesses we have functioning in a community, bringing in wealth, insuring independence." Its author, most likely Robert Poston, the editor of the weekly paper, continued: "Our problem is largely one of ownership. We do not own; so consequently, we are in most cases owned.... Our salvation is in our possession. It will take business to complete the emancipation of Lincoln." When this was written, African Americans had been working to "complete the emancipation of Lincoln" for more than half a century. The article claimed that without property and the self-determination it enabled, white bosses would control African Americans' fate. It urged Blacks to become economically self-sufficient through business in order remedy this precarious situation.[1] For Poston, business was the most important measure of racial progress and would enable Blacks to accomplish what Lincoln and Reconstruction had not: true freedom.

Robert Poston was not alone in his views on the potentially liberatory role of business in Black life. During the early twentieth century, African Americans across the nation were discussing the role business could play in improving their standing in the United States. There were a variety of ideas about how to improve the economic situation of African Americans through business. Some Black intellectuals saw business advancement as the first step on the route to Black liberation, while others supposed that no real progress in economic matters could be achieved unless Blacks first attained political power and civil rights.[2] In general, most Black leaders believed that commercial advancement was fundamental for the survival of the race and that there was a need for African Americans to develop strategies not only for economic survival but also for greater independence within an economic system defined by white supremacy. One strategy was for African Americans to migrate, seeking greater opportunities outside the Jim Crow South, where the majority of the Black population resided. As Black southerners like Robert Poston chose the path of migration, many imagined businesses as a road to freedom.

This chapter traces migrant entrepreneurs' path from the South, examining the factors that influenced their decision to migrate, particularly racial violence as a "push" factor, how they obtained the knowledge that informed their destination choice, and their hopes for freedom enterprise in the North. Under racial capitalism in the Jim Crow South, anti-Black violence was an ever-present risk for entrepreneurial African Americans. The threat of lynchings caused many African Americans to fear for their lives, and entrepreneurs were no exception. With violence being a key characteristic of racial capitalism, business-minded Blacks who accrued wealth in the South often had trouble holding on to it. Racial violence directed toward Black entrepreneurs was a key tool to maintain economic white supremacy and pushed many to leave. This racial and economic violence went unchecked, given that African Americans lacked formal political power and were at the mercy of all-white southern courts and municipal governments. Thus, some Black southern migrants moved north seeking the economic independence and the security they believed business opportunities in the North could provide.

Racial Capitalism in the Jim Crow South

The dynamics of racial capitalism in the Jim Crow South greatly shaped the experiences and motivations of African Americans who would become migrant entrepreneurs. In the period following the Civil War the vast majority of Black Americans lived in southern states and were mostly agricultural laborers. Shifting from the system of race-based slavery, exploitative labor arrangements (coupled with racial violence and political disenfranchisement) were foundational to U.S. racial capitalism. Black southerners were forced into debt peonage through unfair sharecropping and tenant farming contracts and experienced perpetual poverty. Having been given no compensation or resources after emancipation, Black laborers became indebted to planters, merchants, and company stores in order to have access to land, equipment, and everyday necessities. When they could not repay their debts at the end of the season (often because they were cheated by whites), Blacks were trapped in a nonstop cycle of working without pay. This system guaranteed that most Black sharecroppers remained in peonage and had little economic independence. In addition to these labor arrangements, Blacks were also harshly penalized for minor crimes or wrongfully convicted and charged high fines and court fees. When they could not pay, they were leased out to southern businesses and industrialists that would pay their fines in exchange for their forced labor.[3] This "slavery by another name" and exploitative labor arrangements were racial capitalism at work and key features of Jim Crow, the post-Reconstruction racial caste system that would last until 1965.[4]

Some African Americans did look to entrepreneurship as an alternative to agricultural work and domestic service, and in doing so they built on a long tradition of Black business ownership and entrepreneurial activities.[5] But the hallmarks of racial capitalism curtailed African Americans' commercial efforts. Black entrepreneurs experienced discrimination in almost all areas related to operating a business. For example, they could not obtain loans from white-owned banks and were unable to enter certain sectors reserved for whites. Additionally, it was difficult for aspiring entrepreneurs to save and accumulate the needed capital to establish a business since for the most part they were confined to low-paying, unskilled occupations.[6] While there were plenty of obstacles, African Americans still managed to establish enterprises, which saw various levels of success.[7] There were notable cases of Black economic and business achievement, which included individual Black entrepreneurs and companies, as well as Black business communities, such as in Durham and Wilmington, North Carolina.[8] Still, once in business Black entrepreneurs faced subjugation in the form of threats and violence from white competitors. And any wealth gained could not protect African American business owners from the widespread anti-Blackness that existed.

Racial capitalism in the Jim Crow South depended on violence; and racial violence was key for maintaining white supremacy in both labor relations and the business world. As such, some southern Blacks sought refuge in other regions of the country. During the Civil War and Reconstruction, African Americans began migrating out of the South to the West and Midwest, and these regions would continue to be appealing destinations for Black migration in the twentieth century. African American "Exodusters" migrated west during the late nineteenth century, seeking greater freedom and a chance for economic advancement. Thus, migration and freedom enterprise were linked prior to the Great Migration of the twentieth century. Black westward migration saw the establishment of all-Black towns, such as Nicodemus, Kansas, during the late nineteenth and early twentieth centuries. In forming all-Black towns, African Americans attempted to create their own self-sufficient communities away from the racism and violence rampant in other areas. These autonomous towns offered opportunities for Blacks to own land, engage in businesses, and govern themselves. Additionally, those who migrated to western cities like Tulsa, Oklahoma, sought to build a new life that they believed would be more secure than what they could build in the South. Tulsa's "Black Wall Street" was occupied by migrant entrepreneurs who came to Oklahoma as part of the Exodusters migration, as well as part of the Tulsa oil boom.[9] But as the 1921 Tulsa Massacre demonstrated, migrant entrepreneurs could not find lasting security, no matter where they traveled to, as overt violence against Black economic self-sufficiency was crucial to the form racial capitalism took during this period.

The dynamics of racial capitalism in the Jim Crow South—particularly racial violence— "pushed" many African Americans to leave the South. While the threat of racial violence directed toward Blacks was not new, it was a major factor in the decision-making process of southern migrant entrepreneurs as they deliberated moving north and/or west as part of the Great Migration. Black entrepreneurs could experience violent backlash because of economic competition with white business owners. According to Stewart Tolnay and E. M. Beck, "There are numerous examples of lynchings that apparently had their roots in competition. Especially common were those motivated by resentment of economically successful African Americans. In some of these, no reason was given for the mob activity; in others, some alleged offense was concocted to justify the lynchings that were clearly economically motivated."[10] While plenty of African Americans engaged in business in the Jim Crow South, becoming successful and prosperous was taboo within the United States' racial capitalist system. Black entrepreneurs who achieved business success and financial independence could become targets of southern whites who had a stake in maintaining racial capitalism. In the Jim Crow South, whites were anxious to keep African Americans in their supposed "place" in the racial and economic hierarchy and would use violence in reaction to what they viewed as Black transgressions. Nearly any advancement or accomplishment by African Americans could be construed as an attack on the racial caste system.[11] This was certainly true of Black economic progress and financial achievements, and operating a successful business could be dangerous for Black southerners. Black business owners were often the targets of racial violence and intimidation, which stemmed from white competitors' anger over Black owners' success, expansion, or prosperity. The threat of violence was present not only for individual Black business owners but also entire Black business communities that were targeted during race riots. Black economic success often was not cited as the reason for a violent incident. However, an examination of cases of lynchings, race riots, and racial intimidation reveals that Black entrepreneurs frequently appear in accounts of southern anti-Black violence.

Perhaps the most well-known example of violence directed toward Black entrepreneurs due to competition is the 1892 lynching of Thomas Moss, Calvin McDowell, and William Stewart.[12] These murders thrust journalist Ida B. Wells into her decades-long antilynching campaign. McDowell and Stewart were employees of the Black-owned and operated People's Grocery Store in Memphis, and Moss led the joint stock company that owned the store. W. H. Barrett, the white owner of a rival grocery store, targeted the three men because he wanted to "reclaim his monopoly" over the area's Black trade. Barrett had been antagonistic to People's Grocery since its beginning and saw the racial unrest in Memphis in March 1892 as an opportunity to eliminate his Black competitors. Barrett harassed Moss and spread rumors of a planned mob attack on People's Grocery. When Barrett showed up at the store with nine plainclothes deputies, Blacks in the stores fired on them in self-defense, injuring three deputies. The uninjured deputies arrested several Black men, including Moss, McDowell, and Stewart, the main targets of Barrett's plan to bring down People's Grocery. Local whites then looted and destroyed the grocery store. Moss, McDowell, and Stewart were forcibly taken to an isolated field outside the city and lined up for execution. It was reported that Moss's last words before being gunned down were, "Tell my people to go West— there is no justice for them here."[13] Blacks fled Memphis after Moss's death, and his friend Ida B. Wells became an advocate for emigration.

When Thomas Moss urged Blacks to "go West," his was not a lone cry. Reverdy Ransom, an AME minister, encouraged Blacks to abandon the South in response to the violence directed at African Americans during the Atlanta Massacre of 1906. Atlanta was the leading business center of the Southeast, with an emerging Black middle class, and class was clearly at play in the white mob's actions. Walter White, a future NAACP leader, was a child during the riot and his family's home was targeted by the mob. A member of the white mob was heard saying, "That's where that nigger mail carrier lives. Let's burn it down! It's too nice for a nigger to live in."[14] Walter White's father was college educated and held a middle-class position as a postal worker, which was unusual for African Americans at the time. The fact that a Black family could afford a nice house contradicted white Atlantans' understanding of the proper racial and economic hierarchy. No doubt, Black business owners who could afford to live better than many whites were also targets during the riot. The violence in Atlanta led Ransom to urge migration out of the South to places in New England and in the Midwest. In the eyes of Ransom, "Nothing that the Negro can do, either through character, intelligence, or wealth, will change the attitude of the South toward him." He rejected the notion that Black economic advancement could be achieved in the South and reasoned that pursuing business success there was in fact counter to African Americans' freedom enterprise. Describing the violent dynamics of racial capitalism, Ransom explained that if Blacks were "too largely engaged in mercantile pursuits, having shops, stores and banks, the mob would find a ready pretext to assail in order to plot, to plunder and to steal." He asked, "Why should the Negro save money in a community where it will not pass only under certain galling limitations? Why should he own land which he cannot control, or possess property where he can neither protect nor defend it, or live where his life is less sacred than the life of a dog?"[15]

For Ransom, the answer was that Blacks had to abandon the South. In an address given at Boston's Faneuil Hall he declared, "We say to our people today, rise and emigrate from Georgia . . . depart from Mississippi . . . leave the rice swamps of the Carolinas. . . . Millions of Negroes can find liberty, prosperity and peace in the states east, west and north. They could breathe new life into the abandoned farms of New England. Michigan could easily assimilate 50,000. Ohio and Illinois have room for many more." Ransom impressed on his audience that there were more than a million Blacks who were "happy, prosperous and secure in their rights, living North of [the] Mason and Dixon line." Ransom later founded the Institutional Church and Social Settlement in Chicago, which provided assistance to Black southern migrants and offered programs to help them adjust. His settlement also hosted the National Negro Business League's three-day annual convention in 1912. Additionally, Reverdy Ransom continued to discuss the importance of Black business and economic security outside the South. For example, he was featured in a 1913 *New York Age* "A.M.E. Review" article discussing the need for African Americans to support Black-owned business in Harlem.[16]

In some cases of racial violence that involved Black business owners, it is unclear whether the violence was connected to their status as entrepreneurs. However, even ambiguous cases can provide insight into what was at stake for Black entrepreneurs who faced threats and violence in the Jim Crow South. For instance, in late 1897 and early 1898, Lonoke County, Arkansas, was bubbling with racial tension and there were several violent incidents. This included the attempted murder of Oscar Simonton, a Black merchant who owned a grocery store in Lonoke, a small town about thirty miles east of Little Rock. According to Simonton and his friends who corroborated his story, on Christmas Day 1897, a mob entered Simonton's store and threatened to kill him if he did not leave Lonoke and never return. Frightened, Oscar Simonton closed his store and remained behind barricaded doors for two days, until Monday morning when he opened up his business as usual. Simonton claimed that during the day he received another warning to leave town. As he was closing up his store on Monday night he was attacked by a white mob. Simonton was struck on the head with a blunt object, shot at several times, and struck by a single bullet.[17] He was badly injured but managed to flee from the mob and catch a train to Little Rock where he took refuge in the home of a preacher. Evidently, he did not think he would be safe back in Lonoke, and Simonton was forced to leave his affairs in the hands of friends while he hid out from those who had attacked him.[18] In early January 1898, Oscar Simonton sent friends to close up his business at Lonoke and vowed that he would not return, afraid he would be killed if he did so.[19]

It is not clear why the white mob demanded Oscar Simonton leave town forever, or why they attempted to murder him outside his store. It could very well have been because he was a business owner. Alternatively, the attack could have come about for reasons unrelated to Simonton's economic position. It is clear, however, that as soon as he became the target of racial violence, he could no longer run his business in Lonoke. This was Jim Crow racial capitalism at work. With the threat of violence an ever-present reality for African Americans, Black business owners were forced to operate in an environment of extreme risk. Entrepreneurs who were driven out of town by whites were forced to close up shop forever or start over somewhere else. The constant menace of anti-Black violence truncated Black economic development.

The racial tension in Lonoke County affected the entire Black community. At the end of January 1898, a group of whites in Lonoke attempted to drive Blacks out by leaving anonymous menacing notes around town.[20] One newspaper reported that warning notes were posted on the front gates of Black citizens' homes, threatening them with violence if they did not leave within a month. According to one Lonoke resident the notes stated: "We will give you all 30 days to leave Lonoke town, and if not gone in 30 days, you will be hung to a limb." Whites in the town attributed the notes to four or five boys who were trying to "amuse themselves." Whether or not there was an, imminent threat of lynching, Black citizens must have taken the warning seriously, as several Black families became alarmed and immediately left the town.[21] Over the next several days, Blacks began "leaving in droves" to escape the terrorism. Newspapers reported that as a result, "business is almost at a standstill."[22] According to one source, "the old peaceable negroes who have lived in Lonoke for years are taking their families and leaving town as fast as they can get away. The younger negroes are sullen and defiant."[23] This widespread intimidation of the Black community had important implications for African American entrepreneurs. Any Black business owner who received these threats had to decide whether to abandon not only their home but the business they had worked so hard to establish.

Lynchings, physical attacks, and the destruction of property were the more extreme forms of racial capitalism Black entrepreneurs experienced in the Jim Crow South. White competitors could also apply more subtle forms of pressure, then turn to threats, before resorting to violence, and it is likely that some entrepreneurs yielded to the pressure from white competitors so that they did not lose their lives. In a letter written to the *Chicago Defender* on May 16, 1917, one potential migrant from Rome, Georgia, indicated, "I am not a tramp by any means, I am a high class churchman and a business man. I am the daddy of the Transfer business in this city. And carried it on for [ten] years. Seven years ago I sold out to a white Concern."[24] The letter writer does not indicate why he sold his business to whites, but it is likely that he was pressured to sell out. If there was an impending threat of violence, this man might have sold his business to whites at whatever value they deemed fair, perhaps at a loss to the owner. A scenario like this would demonstrate just one more way that, for Black entrepreneurs, "free enterprise" was not free at all. In the system of racial capitalism, whites had an upper hand, not because of their business abilities but because of the color of their skin and the unchecked violence it allowed them to wield.

Even if they did not lose their lives to white supremacist violence, southern Black entrepreneurs like Berry Gordy Sr. could fear for their lives and decide to flee the South before it was too late. Gordy, the father of the Motown Records founder Berry Gordy Jr., migrated to Detroit in 1922 because he feared his financial success would lead to problems with local whites. Gordy was a successful businessman in Sandersville, Georgia, and in the years before his departure north, he had expanded his business activities. Gordy owned a farm from which he sold cotton, vegetables, and fruit. He also owned a beef cart and raised and sold chickens and pigs. Gordy was doing so well that he was making plans to establish a large store. Then, he sold a large number of timber stumps from his property. He received the payment in the form of a $2,600 check on a Tuesday. When several whites began pestering Gordy about cashing his check, he became suspicious. His sister warned him, "Those white people is so interested by that check. I think you should go on to Detroit and get the check cashed up there. You fool 'round here, they're liable to beat us out of it, take all our money."[25] Less than a week after receiving the check, Gordy took his sister's advice and fled Georgia. After church on Sunday, Gordy did not return to his home. He boarded a train for Detroit, where he would begin his new life as migrant entrepreneur.

Years later, Berry Gordy Sr. returned to Georgia when his father-in-law was ill and he needed to handle his financial affairs. In the process of selling his father-in-law's property, Gordy made several whites upset when he outmaneuvered attempts to cheat him. When Gordy returned to Milledgeville, Georgia, the next year a Black reverend warned him, "The white people said that you was tryin' to be smart down here. And if you were to come back down here, they was goin' to see 'bout you." The reverend went on to tell Gordy that the sheriff had "killed two or three colored people 'round there, business people," and implied that Gordy should get out of town. Gordy recalled later in life, "My sister got scared; she didn't want me to go back through Milledgeville. She wanted me to go a different route and leave there right away. But I had to go back through there to pick up a girl I was supposed to bring back to Detroit. I had promised a close friend of mine to carry the girl back to work in his store." Similar to when he initially fled Georgia, Gordy had to be stealthy. He waited until late at night to pick up the girl and then "pulled out to Detroit."[26]

Individual entrepreneurs were not the only targets of white supremacist violence. Black business communities could become the victims of white mobs and groups of business owners could experience intimidation and pressure to abandon their towns during periods of racial unrest. The 1898 massacre in Wilmington, North Carolina, is an example of how Black business owners became prime targets, even though the initial unrest was not aimed specifically at them. In this case, the city's Black community was terrorized by white mobs over two days. At the time, Wilmington was a "prosperous port town." Around two-thirds of the population was African American, and Wilmington's Black middle class was small but meaningful. Black entrepreneurs operated tailor shops and drugstores and dominated certain industries such as restaurants and barbershops.[27] Violence broke out on October 10, eventually escalating to whites gunning down Blacks on the streets.

The Wilmington Massacre (Riot) was as a political coup d'état by Southern Democrats that overthrew the legitimately elected Republican-Populist government that had support from Black and white voters. The coup installed white supremacist rule and resulted in Black disenfranchisement.[28] While the massacre was motivated by politics, witnesses' testimony indicates that whites also had economic motivations for the violence, and successful Black entrepreneurs became central targets. White businessmen were instrumental in the coup's success. A white rioter named Harry Hayden indicated that businesspeople were among those in the mob: "The Men who took down their shotguns . . . were not a mob of plug uglies. They were men of property, intelligence, culture . . . clergymen, lawyers, bankers, merchants."[29] John C. Dancy Jr., a North Carolina native who would go on to become the director of the Detroit Urban League from 1918 to 1960, was in Wilmington when the riot broke out. Dancy was ten years old at the time. He later recalled that this experience "jolted me out of my boyish dream-world and gave me a lesson in what it means to be a Negro. . . . Buildings were being burned, including the office of the Negro newspaper. Angry mobs were roaming the town in search of Negroes to kill and maim." According to Dancy, "The main targets were men like my father, whose crime was that they were successful and prosperous beyond the condition of the average white man." John Dancy also remembered that after the riot, "a number of prominent Negroes" never returned to town due to threats that had been made by riot leaders.[30] The white entrepreneurs who attacked Wilmington's Black businesspeople likely did so because they thought it was their right to be economically superior to Blacks and resented their commercial success.

Entire Black business communities could become explicit targets of violent threats and mob violence. A 1912 incident in Bluefield, West Virginia, demonstrates how whites could exploit racial unrest as an opportunity to assault Black business development and economic self-determination and drive out Black competitors. On September 11, 1912, the town of Bluefield was expecting a bloody race war to "break out at any time." Trouble had been stirring since the previous week when a Black man named Walter Johnson had been lynched. At first glance, this incident seems much like other violent clashes between whites and Blacks in the Jim Crow South. Johnson had been accused of attacking a white girl, Nita White, and it was only after the lynching that Johnson was found to be innocent. When Nita's father, George White, was arrested in connection with Johnson's murder, whites in Bluefield became enraged. As a precautionary measure, Blacks in the town began arming themselves. However, Bluefield's white citizens did not immediately turn to physically assaulting members of the Black community. Instead, "all negro businessmen on Raleigh street got letters last night [September 10] ordering them to move from Raleigh street by Saturday, or their places would be dynamited." According to Chicago's *Day Book* newspaper, the letters were signed "Lynching Committee."[31] Although the white citizens involved with the threats were not part of the business community, perhaps there was a general desire to attack Black economic power because they knew that could also lead to reduced political and social power and influence. Or maybe white competitors might have taken this as an opportunity to intimidate their competitors.

The Black business community in Bluefield had become prominent, and it is likely local whites deemed Black business owners' success a threat to the racial and economic hierarchy. The Black population of southern West Virginia had steadily grown since 1880.[32] The expansion of the coal industry and Black population created entrepreneurial opportunities for Blacks. Between 1900 and 1910, the number of African Americans in business, professional, and clerical occupations in West Virginia increased from less than 1,000 to over 1,600, a 60 percent increase in one decade. Most coal towns in southern West Virginia were segregated and African Americans operated law and medical offices, newspapers, restaurants, hotels, theaters, and undertaking establishments to cater to the growing Black population. The Black-owned *McDowell Times* newspaper spoke of the "phenom[e]nal success" of Black business and professional people in "southern tier counties of the state."[33] Some professional entrepreneurs ventured into other fields to appeal to Black coal mine workers. For instance, attorney Harry J. Capehart established a Black real estate firm that advertised to clients by asking, "Why not own a home in the coalfields where you earn your money?" Capehart sold lots in Bluefield and several other Mercer and McDowell County towns.[34]

The 1912 lynching of Walter Johnson in Bluefield was not an isolated incident. Between 1890 and 1910, there were several episodes in Mercer County where whites violently tried to drive Blacks out of the area.[35] The events in Bluefield were likely linked to heightened racial tensions brought on by an economic downturn the southern West Virginia region was beginning to experience.[36] Yet, the lynching of Walter Johnson and the subsequent threats to dynamite Black businesses demonstrate that whites were also hostile toward Black entrepreneurship and economic independence.

There were several instances of racial violence explicitly directed at Black business communities in the early twentieth century, the most notorious of which was the Tulsa Black Wall Street massacre in 1921. This was the deadliest U.S. race riot prior to the 1940s.[37] Between May 31 and June 1, 1921, armed white mobs attacked African American Tulsans, looted Black homes and businesses, and set fire to the Black section of town, particularly targeting the Black business district along Greenwood Avenue. Like Bluefield, Tulsa had also experienced a population boom driven by industry. By 1920 Oklahoma's population was two million, an increase of seven and a half times the 1890 population. Tulsa's rapid growth was spurred by oil, and the population increased from 1,390 in 1900, to 18,182 in 1910, and then to 72,075 in 1920. As Tulsa boomed, the Black community also developed and expanded. Around 1905, Blacks began living along Greenwood Avenue, which would become the center of the city's Black business district. By 1906 there was a Black-owned newspaper. A year after that there were three grocery stores and a barber, two Black doctors opened offices, and the Black business community continued to grow from there. The Black population of Tulsa doubled between 1900 and 1910, from 5 to 10 percent of the city's total population. By 1921, the year of the riot, Black Tulsa's population was 11,000. This boomtown produced opportunities for Black entrepreneurship, since African Americans were not welcome to patronize white-owned businesses. Two blocks of Greenwood Avenue north of Archer Street made up the center of Tulsa's Black business community. There were two theaters, four hotels, a dry goods store, groceries, confectionaries, restaurants, billiard halls, rooming houses, and a variety of other commercial establishments. Before the riot the area was known as the "Negro's Wall Street."[38]

On May 30, 1921, a nineteen-year-old Black man, Dick Rowland, took the elevator to use the restroom in Tulsa's Drexel building. Rowland worked as a bootblack at a nearby shoe parlor. The seventeen-year-old white girl who worked as the elevator operator accused Rowland of attacking her in the elevator (many in the Black community did not believe this to be true). The next day the police arrested Rowland and when word got around to white Tulsa, talk of lynching ensued. On the evening of May 31, a crowd of whites gathered outside the courthouse that held Rowland, eventually growing to an estimated size of 4,000. When the sheriff informed the crowd that there would be no lynching that night, the mob was not happy. There was a scuffle between a Black Tulsan and white Tulsan and shots were fired. After that, the situation escalated into an all-out race riot.[39]

As rumors of racial trouble spread, Black Tulsans started gathering on Greenwood Avenue. While some Blacks fled the city, others armed themselves with guns to defend Greenwood from white invaders. Armed whites terrorized the Greenwood district, breaking into buildings, looting, and setting fires. The first fire broke out at 1:00 a.m. (June 1) on the fringe of the Black neighborhood. White rioters who tried to cross into the Black district were met with gunfire from Black residents defending their property. However, as the night progressed, it became clear that the Black residents were outnumbered. Around 6:00 a.m. whites invaded Black Tulsa, burning and looting as they went. Members of the mob set fire to buildings along Greenwood Avenue, Tulsa's "Black Wall Street."[40]

The Black business district was completely burned out by the morning of June 1. Over one thousand homes and businesses in Black Tulsa were destroyed and smoldering, and hundreds of people were killed. The Tulsa Real Estate Exchange estimated the amount of real estate damage at $1.5 million and personal property damage at $750,000, though the true figure remains intangible. After the riot, many Black Tulsans stayed and rebuilt their lives. Some Black residents filed claims with the City of Tulsa for losses incurred during the riot. For example, Emma Gurley, a Black woman whose family owned the Gurley Hotel, filed a claim of over $150,000 in losses. However, on the night of the riot and immediately after, many Blacks moved away from Tulsa and never returned.[41] The impact of this riot was devastating for the Greenwood business district and Tulsa's "Black Wall Street." The number of business establishments decreased from 108 in 1921 to 83 in 1922. The number of professionals decreased from 33 in 1921 to 24 the following year.[42]

In general, the late 1910s and early 1920s was a violent time in the United States. The same year as the Tulsa tragedy, fifty-nine Blacks were lynched in southern or border states.[43] The Tulsa massacre followed on the heels of the Red Summer of 1919, which saw anti-Black riots across the country. Yet, even as northern and midwestern cities experienced race riots and increased Ku Klux Klan activity, the exodus to Great Migration cities continued to increase. Migrant entrepreneurs seemed to view places like Detroit as "lands of opportunity" and southern locations as more likely to erupt in the type of violence that would cost them their businesses or even their lives.

While Tulsa is the most well-known case of an attack directed at a Black business community in the early twentieth century, occurrences like this continued. A 1930 incident in Sherman, Texas, demonstrates how Black business communities could become the victims of mob violence that was originally directed at an individual and subsequently spilled over into Black neighborhoods. On the afternoon of May 9, 1930, George Hughes, a forty-one-year-old Black man, was brought into the courthouse on a charge of assaulting a white woman. A mob of several thousand stormed the courthouse, set it on fire, and killed Hughes. The mob then attached a chain to his body, tied it to an automobile, and dragged it through the streets as the crowd cheered. The next morning, the car dragging Hughes's body headed to North Sherman, a Black section of town. It was reported that leaders of the mob shouted "On to Niggertown!" This act was no doubt designed to intimidate the Black population of Sherman, estimated at 1,500 to 2,000. When the mob reached North Sherman, it turned a two-story drugstore into a "funeral pyre" for the lynching victim. This building had previously been the site of a prominent hotel, but at the time of the lynching it housed a drugstore and several other Black businesses including a beauty parlor, dance hall, and undertaking establishment. The mob set the building on fire, dumped Hughes's body, and cheered. It is clear that the mob targeted Black businesses because "adjoining [the building] were several residences occupied by white people," and the mob did not choose to burn those buildings. The mob then proceeded to destroy other Black businesses on the street. Virtually every Black store had windows broken, stock thrown on the floor, and "havoc wrought." Several members of the mob declared that they would go to the other side of town, where there was another Black section, and burn more structures.[44] This incident in Sherman demonstrates that individual Black entrepreneurs did not have to do anything to lose everything they had built to white mobs. Anti-Black violence could take place at any time, and this could subsequently lead to the destruction of Black property and dampen economic self-determination.

Southern Black business owners had experienced violence prior to the start of the Great Migration; this violence was also visible during the first wave of the migration from the 1910s through the 1930s. It is not surprising as this period was part of the nadir of American race relations. The number of lynchings decreased as the twentieth century progressed,[45] but the threat of racial violence directed at Black entrepreneurs did not disappear and incidents continued during the second wave of the migration following World War II.[46]

In the Jim Crow era, it was commonplace for whites to intimidate and threaten Black entrepreneurs, even if these threats did not always result in outward violence.[47] Racial violence was an inherent risk of operating a business for African Americans and was a key method of maintaining the white supremacist system. Violence was an effective tool to suppress Blacks' demands for political and social equality. But violence was also inherent to the form of racial capitalism in the Jim Crow South. The unfortunate reality was that even if they were successful, Black entrepreneurs always risked losing everything to racial violence. Whether as individual targets, part of a Black business community that was targeted by a mob, or as victims of violence spilling over and into the larger Black community, Black entrepreneurs operated in an economic system where one of the risks of doing business was experiencing racial violence, which could lead to property damage, the loss of wealth or financial resources, and even death.

Because mob violence could strike at any time, it was not merely the threat of death that gave lynching its power. Spontaneous racial violence reminded Blacks of their powerlessness.[48] Thus, Black entrepreneurs in the South did not need to experience racial violence firsthand to understand that it could happen to them. Even if they managed to establish an enterprise and become financially independent and prosperous, at any moment their business could be burned down or they could become a victim of lynching. This constant threat of violence influenced some Black entrepreneurs (people like Berry Gordy Sr.) to migrate north in search of freedom and prosperity—their freedom enterprise—in cities like Detroit.

Deciding to Migrate

Black entrepreneurs who participated in the Great Migration doubted that it was truly possible to have lasting business success in the southern United States and desired greater business opportunities. In explaining the circumstances that were causing Blacks to leave the South in 1918, Carter G. Woodson pointed to the lack of opportunities: "In most parts of the South the Negroes are still unable to become landowners or successful business men. Conditions and customs have reserved these spheres for the whites."[49] On April 29, 1917, one business owner and potential migrant from Temple, Texas, wrote to T. Arnold Hill, executive secretary of the Chicago Urban League, that he was "seeking to better my conditions in the business world." To do so, he had "decided to leave this state for North or West."[50] Migrant entrepreneurs went north seeking a terrain that was more equal where they could pursue economic freedom through business—their freedom enterprise.

Moving north seemed like it could provide access to "free enterprise" (or at least *freer* enterprise): southern migrant entrepreneurs hoped they might receive equal wages (and have an improved ability to save money); they anticipated gaining entry to commercial fields that were foreclosed to them in the South; and, crucially, they imagined that there would be less racial violence to curtail their commercial endeavors. In other words, migrant entrepreneurs' vision of the North as the "land of opportunity" included the expectation of greater social, political, and economic freedom that would facilitate business success. While potential migrants did not use the term "racial capitalism," their words hint at their understanding of the economic system as such and that they hoped to escape Jim Crow racial capitalism by settling in the North.

In letters potential migrants expressed the desire to move north so that they could pursue their desired trades and talents, which they felt they could not fully exploit or make a living from in the South. For example, on March 11, 1917, a fifteen-year-old boy wrote a letter to Black northerners stating, "I am talented for an artist . . . I have studied Cartooning therefore I am a Cartoonist." He intended to visit Chicago in the summer and wanted to know from the letter's recipients "can a Colored boy be an artist and make a white man's salary up there[?]"[51] On September 22, 1917, a man with a wife and mother to support wrote to R. S. Abbot, editor of the *Chicago Defender*, from Natchez, Mississippi. He expressed that his "greatest desire is to leave for a better place." He continued, "I can write short stories all of which portray negro characters but no burlesque can also write poems, have a gift for cartooning but have never learned the technicalities of comic drawing. These things will never profit me anything here in Natchez."[52] Northern Black publications might have provided a venue for this artist to profit from his talent and passion.

Some southern migrants wanted an opportunity to finally run their own business and not work at a white-owned company. A potential migrant from Memphis, Tennessee, wrote to a Black newspaper, likely the *Chicago Defender*, on June 1, 1917. The letter writer indicated that he wanted to leave the South and sought advice on how to do so. He expressed that he was seeking to secure "a good position as a first class automobeal Blacksmith or any kind pretaining to such" and also informed the letter's recipient that he had been "opporating a first class white shop here for quite a number of years one of the largest in the south and if I must say the only colored man in the city that does."[53] This potential migrant had been managing a white-owned business for years, and it is likely that this was as far as he could progress in this field if he stayed in Memphis.

There were several factors that caused Black business owners to follow the pull of economic opportunities in the North. For migrant entrepreneurs, unprecedented opportunities in Detroit developed when Black southerners moved to the city for jobs in the automobile industry. If Black business owners had previously wanted to leave the South for places like Detroit before the migration, the lack of a considerable Black consumer base had prevented this. The city's industrial boom during World War I led to an explosion in the Black population. This created a Black consumer base and made Detroit an extremely attractive place for southern migrant entrepreneurs.

Before deciding to move north to pursue their visions of freedom enterprise, potential migrants sought advice and information in order to assess the situation for Black business and their particular fields in northern cities. This allowed them to make the wisest and most profitable decisions. They requested information from knowledgeable individuals, newspapers, and institutions in the North. During the 1910s, potential migrants wrote to northern Black institutions, expressing their desire to migrate north to engage in entrepreneurship and sought advice on the best place to establish a business. For example, in April 1917 a gentleman from Decatur, Alabama, wrote a letter to the Chicago Urban League. His primary motivation in writing was to discover the possibilities for Black entrepreneurship in the North:

> Gentlemens desious of Settling in some Small Northern Town With
> a modrate Population & also Where a Colored man may open a
> business Also where one may receive fairly good wedges for a While
> ontill well enough azainted with Place to do a buiseness in other
> words Wonts to locate in Some Coming town Were agoodly no, of
> colard People is. Wonts to Work At Some occupation ontill I can
> arrange for other buiseness Just Give Me information As to the best
> placers for a young buiseness Negro to locate & make good. in. Any
> Northern State Thanking you inavance any information you may
> give in regards to Laber & buiseness.[54]

He requested a recommendation for a place where he could work making "fairly good" wages for a while, presumably so he could save up money to start his business. He also needed time to get acquainted with the new location before he felt comfortable establishing a business. The letter writer also sought demographic information in terms of up-and-coming, moderate-sized towns where there was a significant Black population. Although he was writing to the Urban League in Chicago, he made it clear that he would be willing to move to any northern state where there was opportunity for Black business development.[55] Detroit institutions also heard from potential migrants who sought information regarding the possibilities for Black business in Detroit specifically.[56] In 1917 Forrester B. Washington, the inaugural director of the Detroit Urban League, reported receiving many letters from Black entrepreneurs in the South seeking information regarding the "real situation" for Black business in Detroit.[57]

Sometimes a potential migrant might write seeking information for a community or multiple southern entrepreneurs. One person from Daphne, Alabama, wrote a letter on April 20, 1917, indicating that fifteen to twenty families in town wanted to migrate north and that "some of these people are farmers and som are cooks barbers and Black smiths but the greater part are farmers & good worker & honest people."[58] Similarly, one potential migrant from Oakdale, Louisiana, wrote to the *Chicago Defender* on April 21, 1917, indicating that "there are 3 or 4 more business men that are interested and would come. [W]rite me at once and let me know about the situation." Though the letter writer had a desire to move north to Chicago as well, they had financial matters that needed to be attended to first: "So far as me I couldn't come until I could arrange to sell out as I am in business for God knows I want to leave the South land."[59]

Some Black entrepreneurs were no doubt reluctant to leave the South and the communities where they were already established.[60] When rumors started swirling about African Americans leaving the South and going north, Black business owners likely wondered what the migration meant for them. If the available jobs in the North were for wage laborers in steel mills, packing-houses, and automobile factories, should they go? Could they make more money working as a laborer in the North than they made operating their own business in the South? Business owners probably worried that people from their communities—the folks they sold groceries to, made dresses for, and whose loved ones they buried—would be leaving. Black businesspeople had heard of and probably knew other Blacks who went north for temporary employment to make extra money in the summer but then returned to the South—people like Ossian Sweet, who went to work as a dishwasher, bellhop, and waiter in Detroit during the summers of 1910–14 and always returned to

Florida.[61] But with this widespread and unprecedented migration they could not know if their disappearing customers would ever return. As time went on and more of their clientele vanished north, southern entrepreneurs had to decide whether to stay or migrate.

Choosing to uproot was not an easy decision for southern business owners. Staying where they were already established meant not having to leave their community, build a new client base, or invest their hard-earned money in an uncertain venture up north. With these considerations, some southern entrepreneurs were probably not keen to leave, but the decision was often not solely theirs to make. In southern communities that saw dramatic decreases in population during the migration, Black entrepreneurs were compelled to leave once a significant portion of their customer base had left. In 1917 a gentleman in Memphis wrote, "At present I am employed as agent for the Interstate Life and acc'd ins. Co. but on account of the race people leaving here so very fast my present job is no longer a profitable one."[62] In some cases entire communities migrated to Detroit, and Black professionals and business owners decided to follow their clients north.[63]

Friends and family members also influenced southern entrepreneurs' decision to migrate. A woman in Greenwood, Mississippi, anonymously wrote to the *Chicago Defender* in 1917 stating:

I am very anxious to know what the chances are for business men. I am very anxious to leave the South on account of my children but my husband doesn't seem to think that he can succeed there in business, he is a merchant and also knows the barber trade what are the chances for either? Some of our folks down here have the idea that this Northern movement means nothing to any body but those who go out and labor by the day. I am willing to work myself to get a start. Tell me what we could really do. I will do most anything to get our family out of Bam. Please let this be confidential.[64]

The letter writer seems to have sought information that she could subsequently use to convince her spouse that there were in fact business opportunities for African Americans in the North. Her primary motivation was for her children to have a better future, rather than economic opportunities, but she needed to get her husband on board to make such a drastic move that could have major financial consequences.[65] For some southern entrepreneurs, the primary appeal of migrating was the social, political, and educational opportunities available in the North. Still, they had to weigh the chances of Black commercial success in the North to determine whether they could make a viable living there and leave everything behind.

The life insurance agent from Memphis, Tennessee, mentioned above wrote in his letter that "I have a number of young friends in your city who are advising me to come to Chicago and I have just about made up my mind to come." He clarified that "I am prepared to leave here at any time and must go Some place but Chicago is the place that impress me most."[66] Clearly the letter writer's friends were very influential, though he seemed to still have some reservations and stated that "before leaving here I wanted to ask some advice from you along certain lines." The advice he sought was related to business. He wanted to know if it made economic sense for him and his wife to continue paying the mortgage on their southern property and rent it out so that they could have income while they were getting established in their new northern home.[67]

Southern migrants had many skills and talents that they could use to establish a business once they arrived in the North. Hints of these talents are scattered in migrant letters, when southerners mentioned things they had done in the past or what they thought they could do in the North. For example, a thirty-one-year-old man from Dallas, Texas, wrote, "I also claims to know something about candy making."[68] While it seems this man did not operate a confectionery business in Dallas, it is conceivable that he might open such a shop after moving north. Apparently, there was a high demand for confections in the late 1910s and in the 1920s: a 1924 directory of Black businesses in Detroit listed fifty-two "Confectioneries and Confectioners."[69] Migrants like the man from Dallas could have gone north thinking they could use their skills to establish a business in their new home city.

There were more indications of the skills and experience migrants might use to establish a business in the North. One New Orleanian indicated on May 21, 1917, "I am a cook of plain meals and I have knowledge of industrial training. I recieved [sic] such training at Tuskegee Inst. some years ago and I have a letter from Mrs. Booker T. Washington bearing out such statement and letters from other responsible corporations and individuals."[70] Maybe this individual would establish a restaurant in their new northern home. A woman from Atlanta wrote on April 11, 1917, "I am a hair dresser but I will do any kind of work I can get to do I am a widow and have one child a little girl 6 years."[71] Perhaps she migrated and eventually established a hair salon. A man from Jacksonville, Florida, wrote on April 29, 1917, "i have sevrul years in laundry business as a wash man and stationery boilers fireing at this time i have charge of wash room. i am a fire man and all so a laundry wash man too."[72] He could have opened a laundry business. One man from Pensacola, Florida, had been in business for twenty years as a salesman, industrial insurance agent, collector, and business manager.[73] Similarly, a forty-year-old man from Starkville, Mississippi, was a barber with twenty years of experience.[74] From Augusta, Georgia, a man wrote to a Black newspaper: "I'm a member of the race, a normal and colloege [sic] school graduate . . . I'm a letter carrier now and am also a druggist by profession." In terms of his desired location, the man indicated, "I must say that I have nothing against Detroit, Mich."[75] This man very well might have established a drugstore in Detroit in the late 1910s or 1920s. There were others who specified they wanted to move to Detroit and that they or their family members had skills that could be used in entrepreneurial pursuits. For instance, one man from Mobile, Alabama, wrote that his wife was a seamstress and his brother-in-law a carpenter. He implored the *Chicago Defender* staff, "Please help us as we are in need of your help as we wanted to go to Detroit but if you says no we go where ever you sends us until we can get to Detroit."[76]

It is impossible to know how many southern migrants with potentially lucrative talents actually established a business once they moved north. But it is clear that in Detroit, the majority of Black-owned businesses begun in the first half of the twentieth century were established by southern migrants and/or the children of migrants. It is safe to conclude that some migrant entrepreneurs brought their skills and trades with them and established enterprises after they migrated north.

Black laborers settling in Detroit would need goods and services, and Black business owners could provide these things. This was the outlook of migrants like Dr. Ossian Sweet. Originally from Florida, Sweet received his medical degree from Howard University in Washington, D.C. He then migrated to Detroit in 1921 to establish a physician's office. His goal was to "rise in his profession and make his fortune."[77] He chose Detroit to establish his practice because he believed the city rewarded the ambitious.[78] While Sweet found it difficult to start up a practice at first, the potential rewards of migrating to Detroit outweighed the obstacles.

Migrants who wanted to pursue entrepreneurial aspirations could minimize some of the obstacles by first acquiring information about business sectors outside of the South. This information could be carried by Blacks who traveled north and then returned south. John Dancy recalled bringing news of the big city back to his friends in Wilmington, North Carolina, as a young man. After he traveled to Washington, D.C., his companions would inquire about the city. One friend in particular, Ed Jenkins, had questions that were mostly prompted by his professional interests. Jenkins was a bootblack in a barbershop in Wilmington and had ambitions to establish a barbershop outside of his hometown one day. He asked Dancy, "What kind of barber shops do they have up there? What kind of mirrors? Do the mirrors run all across the place? Do Negroes shave white people? Cut white people's hair?" These questions were designed to obtain information about the barbering field in an unknown location and the answers Dancy provided could be used to make decisions about prospects for Black business in an urban Great Migration site. Dancy was able to inform Jenkins about the "fine points of the barbering profession as practiced in the great world outside Wilmington," and Jenkins did eventually leave Wilmington and became a barber in New York City.[79]

Southerners could also gather information about potential business ventures in the North through the letters they received from acquaintances who had already migrated and settled. For example, a southern migrant living in Akron, Ohio, wrote to a friend back home, "I am making good. . . . I am wide awake on my financial plans. I have rent me a place for boarders I have 15 sleprs I began one week ago." The letter writer also indicated "I am going into some kind of business here by the first of Sept."[80] Another migrant living in Chicago wrote to her "sister": "The people are rushing here by the thousands and I know if you come and rent a big house you can get all the roomers you want. You write me exactly when you are coming. I am not keeping house yet I am living with my brother and his wife. . . . I can get a nice place for you to stop until you can look around and see what you want."[81] Presumably the recipient of the letter had inquired about the possibility of opening a boardinghouse in Chicago. The letter writer would provide assistance in the migrant's transition, and this was a useful connection for someone wanting to establish a business in an unknown land. From letters like these, southerners could learn about the kind of business opportunities that existed in the North from someone they knew and could trust to provide accurate information. Of course, the reality of establishing and operating these types of enterprises was not always conveyed in letters and there was no guarantee of success, but letters from migrants who had already settled in Great Migration cities were a crucial source of information.

As with other southern migrants, kinship networks and chain migration shaped where migrant entrepreneurs would settle. One woman (identified as "Mrs. J" in a study) left her husband and two children in Macon, Georgia, when she migrated to Detroit. The couple had decided that Mrs. J. would go to Detroit first to find employment, "look the city over," and find a home for the rest of the family to move into. The family owned a store in Georgia that was "well-stocked with groceries and a farm in the country with the crops only partially harvested." They decided that it would be best for the husband to remain in Macon until he could sell their property at the most advantageous rates. This way they were not compelled to sell their store and farm at a loss. By migrating first, Mrs. J. was able to report back about the economic conditions and do research about the chance of success Detroit.[82] Berry Gordy Sr., who migrated to Detroit and established a contracting business, chose the city because his brother had already decided to go there. Some migrant entrepreneurs moved where they knew family members had already achieved a measure of business success. Otis Sweet, the brother of Dr. Ossian Sweet, migrated to Detroit to establish his dentistry practice on the advice of his brother. Since the doctor had experienced success in operating a medical office in the Black section of the city, the dentist figured he could as well, and he was right. Within only a few months of arriving in 1923, Otis Sweet was operating his dental office near his brother's practice.[83]

*   *   *

When Black entrepreneurs left the South, they hoped for many things: to gain economic security; to be their own boss; to make a fortune; to hold onto their wealth and reap the benefits of their hard work; to build a better future for themselves and their families. They imagined that the North could be freer than the South, not just socially and politically but also economically. Participating in the Great Migration was an attempt to circumvent the suppression of Black commercial development and the anti-Black violence that were fundamental aspects of American racial capitalism. The migration to Detroit created the needed conditions for Blacks to pursue their dreams of freedom through business, their freedom enterprise: a large Black clientele, unmet need for goods and services, and an environment that was viewed as less hostile toward Black business success. Opportunities for business influenced Black migrants' decisions to leave the South, shaped their expectations of the North, and affected migration patterns. Migrant entrepreneurs did not just blindly move to the North. They sought information about demographics and locales, their particular fields, potential risks, and potential payoffs so they could make the best decisions for their personal and business futures. However, migration to Detroit offered no guarantee of wealth to the entrepreneurially minded, for racial capitalism lurked there as well. Migrant entrepreneurs would soon discover that the structural racism and violence of U.S. racial capitalism existed in every region of the United States.

CHAPTER 2

Arriving: The Formation of
a Black Business Community

In 1920, Francis H. Warren, a lawyer and expert on Black Detroit, contributed an article titled "Business Among Colored People" to the Black-owned
Detroit Contender. He wrote, "It is with great hope for future business success
that we note the recent business awakening among the Negro people in Michigan, there is large room for business enterprises and splendid profits and this
is constantly growing."[1] Warren's piece reflected the sense of optimism among
Detroit's African American entrepreneurs in the early 1920s. Due in large
part to the Great Migration, the city's population tripled between 1910 and
1930; by 1920, Detroit was already the fourth largest metropolis in the United
States with about 993,000 residents.[2] The population boom transformed possibilities for business expansion for both migrant entrepreneurs and African
Americans already living in Detroit.

These "Old Detroiters"—many of whom had also migrated from the South
years or decades before—were a tiny portion of Detroit's population prior
to the Great Migration. Initially, entrepreneurial Old Detroiters were able
to establish businesses to cater to the growing Black population; they had
long-standing connections and knowledge of the city, leaving entrepreneurs
who arrived during the migration's early years at a disadvantage.[3] At times,
the freedom enterprise of southern migrants clashed with the actions of Old
Detroiters; for example, Old Detroiter property owners seeking "splendid
profits" forced southern migrants who had limited choices as to where to
live to pay excessive rents, thus limiting their ability to save money. Many
Old Detroiters saw Black southern migrants as a nuisance who threw off the
racial balance in the city and made things worse for the long-standing Black

population. They also imagined that Black migrants would return to the South after World War I ended.[4]

Migrant entrepreneurs were determined to attain their freedom enterprises, however, and over time Detroit's Black business community would become dominated by southern migrants. These newcomers viewed the city as a desirable location for putting down permanent roots. According to a contemporaneous study, "The majority of Negroes who come to Detroit come to stay. A great many of the migrants have come directly from the South, as they have heard from friends and relatives of the better opportunities in this city than elsewhere. Detroit may be distinguished from other centers of Negro migration as a 'repository city' because the majority of Negroes who come to Detroit come to stay."[5] This unique characteristic would influence migrant entrepreneurs' work to build a strong and long-lasting business community.

But a Black business boom was not predestined or inevitable. Establishing a business in the World War I economy was an uphill battle, and the possibility that migrants would return to the South at the war's end affected Black business prospects in Detroit. An industrial depression in 1920 and 1921 also brought economic challenges to Black laborers and business owners alike. Additionally, as migrant entrepreneurs discovered, racial capitalism existed in the North too. The inner workings of racial capitalism in Detroit included features such as: discriminatory housing practices and geographic restrictions in the city and, relatedly, higher prices for property and rent; economic segregation (for the most part Black entrepreneurs could not expect to profit from conducting business with whites and catered exclusively to Black clients who earned less than whites); exclusion from certain financing opportunities (white-owned banks largely refused to provide loans to African Americans); and hostility from state actors, including police harassment, discrimination from state licensing agencies, and the targeted destruction of Black neighborhoods through the use of eminent domain (discussed in Chapter 7). Racial capitalism's manifestations in the North could look different than in the South, but there were some familiar features, such as racial violence and intimidation. Migrant entrepreneurs such as Dr. Ossian Sweet learned that, like in the Jim Crow South, African Americans in the North who became prosperous and upset the racial hierarchy could experience a violent backlash from whites. The patterns of racial discrimination in Great Migration destinations like Detroit were very much a part of the larger U.S. racial capitalist system that worked to keep Black people economically inferior to whites.[6]

African American entrepreneurs came together to combat racial capital-ism's restraints on Black business growth and develop strategies to increase Black economic development in Detroit. Many, influenced by Marcus Garvey and his Universal Negro Improvement Association (UNIA), embraced Black nationalist politics and engaged in cooperative economics in order to sur-vive, provide employment, and upbuild. An allied Black business community thus emerged in response to both the obstacles and the opportunities of the Great Migration. By the end of the 1920s, Detroit's Black business commu-nity was blossoming as migrant entrepreneurs continued pursuing freedom enterprise.

The Great Migration to Detroit

The Great Migration had a transformative demographic impact on Detroit and Black business in the city. In January 1914, Henry Ford made his famous offer of five dollars a day for unskilled laborers in his automobile factory in Highland Park, Michigan, just outside Detroit. This was a substantial amount of money at the time—more than most Black workers had ever dreamed they could earn—and Ford's offer drew workers from all around the world includ-ing many African Americans, mostly from Alabama, Georgia, Florida, and Tennessee.[7] By 1915, the increased demand in an already booming industrial sector created a labor shortage in Detroit, and many factories that had pre-viously excluded African Americans were forced to end their ban on hiring Black workers.[8] As such, emerging employment opportunities contributed to Detroit's popularity among southern migrants.

During the Great Migration years, Detroit as a whole was experiencing a boom. In 1910, the city had a total population of 465,766. This grew to 993,675 in 1920 and 1,568,662 by 1930. Detroit developed a reputation as a mecca for economic opportunity, and southerners arrived hoping they could make good in this flourishing northern city.[9] Although cities like New York and Philadelphia had long-standing and sizable Black communities before the Great Migration, Detroit had a small Black population, little more than 1 per-cent of the city's total population. However, between 1910 and 1920, Detroit's Black population increased by 611 percent; this increase was greater than that of any other major city in the United States.[10] In 1925, there were 85,000 Blacks living in Detroit; by 1930, that number had increased to 120,000. In 1940, the total had jumped to nearly 150,000. By June 1943, between 190,000 and 200,000 African Americans lived in the Motor City. In 1950, there would be more than 300,000 Blacks in Detroit.[11]

The boom in Detroit's Black population created distinct opportunities for African Americans to pursue business. It created a sizable Black consumer base and made Detroit an extremely attractive place for southern migrant entrepreneurs. High wages in the automobile industry nurtured the Black business climate by increasing the disposable income of Black industrial laborers. Prior to the Great Migration, most Black Detroiters were excluded from industrial work and were restricted to the lowest-paying and least secure jobs in the city. Most Blacks could only find work in positions such as janitors, waiters, and domestic workers—jobs that upheld economic white supremacy.[12] If Old Detroiters had entrepreneurial aspirations, these types of jobs typically did not allow them to accumulate enough capital to establish a business in Detroit before the migration. But the new wave of Black laborers settling in Detroit needed goods and services, and Black business owners could provide these things, especially in fields where whites were not willing to serve Black customers. The large increase in Detroit's Black community meant that consumers could support Black entrepreneurs operating in a wide range of business sectors.[13] Detroit's Black business community developed quickly, particularly in the Black Bottom neighborhood where many migrants settled. In the decades that followed, Detroit's Black business community, made up mostly of southern migrants, grew to become one of the largest in the country.

Most of the Black business community developed in the Black Bottom neighborhood (and would later expand to include Paradise Valley) (see Figure 1). While the area had been home to Detroit's small Black population prior to the Great Migration, the majority of Black Bottom residents were white immigrants.[14] Limited by the structures of racial capitalism, premigration Black consumers had no choice but to patronize non-Black businesses along with the few Black-owned enterprises that existed in premigration Detroit. Those who settled in Black Bottom—a neighborhood that would ultimately become synonymous with African Americans—lived and shopped within a diverse, predominately immigrant community.[15] The neighborhood was mostly residential, housing Italians, Greeks, Syrians, Germans, and Russian Jews (among others).[16] According to resident Helen Nuttall Brown, the daughter of a Black physician and businessman, Black Bottom also featured "a number of [family] businesses on corners," run by ethnic Germans and Italians.[17] Likewise, Paul B. Shirley remembered the neighborhood as a mixed area with little Black business: "When I was a kid, we would take our laundry to the Chinese laundry, and they could iron and wash your clothes."[18] According to Coleman Young, when his family moved to Black Bottom in the early 1920s, his street was "an ethnic smorgasbord. Our house was next door to an Italian family . . . there was a Syrian family down the street, a German grocery on the intersection . . . and a Jewish delicatessen around the corner."[19] African Americans frequented non-Black businesses even as many Black entrepreneurs struggled to build up their own establishments. However, opportunities for Black business began to grow once southern migrants started arriving in droves in the 1910s.

Racial segregation was a defining characteristic of the northern political economy in which migrant entrepreneurs operated. Due to racist restrictions such as discriminatory housing practices, over time Black Bottom would become overwhelmingly Black.[20] The growing concentration of African Americans in the neighborhood aided in the expansion of Black enterprises. And in turn, entrepreneurs provided essential goods and services for Detroit's growing Black community and made the city a desirable location for southern migrants. A major Black commercial hub developed around St. Antoine, Hastings, and Beaubien Streets in Black Bottom as entrepreneurs established new restaurants, retail stores, and pool halls.[21] In addition, moving services and taxicab companies that served newly arrived southerners were two of the most popular new businesses, helping migrants get settled in their new home.[22] Most of these businesses catered to Black clientele exclusively. On the one hand, the economic segregation in the North seemed to open up possibilities for Black business growth; however, the residential and economic segregation that existed was racial capitalism at work, which ultimately narrowed the possibilities for African Americans to attain freedom through business.

Uneven Entrepreneurship:
Old Detroiters and New Migrants

Old Detroiters had distinct advantages over newcomers when it came to entrepreneurship. As longtime residents, they had deeper knowledge of the area as well as political and personal connections with other Detroiters, both white and Black. They also had the benefit of not having to finance the cost of relocation from the South and were consequently more likely to have the necessary capital to start a business. Thus, during the earliest years of the migration, Blacks already living in Detroit, not newly arrived migrants, established the majority of new businesses in the city.

For African American Old Detroiters, the likelihood of gaining economic independence through business in pre–Great Migration Detroit was slight. As only 1.2 percent of Detroit's population, the small Black community did not have a strong enough client base to sustain an independent business community of its own.[23] Additionally, most white Detroiters were reluctant to patronize Black-owned establishments due to racial prejudice. This bias especially affected Black professionals like lawyers and doctors, regardless of background or qualifications. Since no white practices would hire them and it was difficult to run a profitable independent firm with only the support of Black clientele, many were left "professionals without practices."[24] In explaining Black professionals' situation in Detroit, attorney David Augustus Straker wrote in 1901 that a Black man "may sweep the lawyer's office, but cannot become his law-partner, his type writer, or his stenographer . . . he may carry the hod, but cannot contract for the building."[25] Consequently, Black doctors, architects, lawyers, and nurses often had to earn a living doing jobs far outside their education and training. This pattern of whites foreclosing Black advancement in professional fields would play a big part in the entrepreneurialization of Detroit's Black professionals—an unintended consequence of racial capitalism—once the influx of southerners arrived during the Great Migration.[26] Still, there were several doctors in pre–Great Migration Detroit among the handful of Black entrepreneurs. Dr. Levi H. Johnson, who moved to the city in 1880, was one of Detroit's best-known physicians (of any race). He had "for many years been a successful practitioner, attending to the medical wants of many of the best families of the City both white and black." Approximately 75 percent of Johnson's patients were white, and he was able to build up a "lucrative practice."[27]

Black entrepreneurs who catered to white clientele had a better chance of success. For example, African Americans dominated the barber trade, often exclusively servicing whites and refusing Blacks because they feared they would "drive away the white trade." The idea that "in order to be successful in the barber business the boss was required to draw the color line in his patronage" was widespread in pre–Great Migration Detroit.[28] Selling exclusively to whites was one strategy Old Detroiters used to navigate racial capitalism, and while this approach may have benefited individual Black entrepreneurs, it played into the segregationist practices that upheld the racial caste system. Ultimately, the status quo for Black business in the city would be upended once the Great Migration was underway.

Family ties and inheritance were crucial for Old Detroiters who wanted to establish new businesses during the early migration years. Inadequate startup capital and undercapitalization plagued Black entrepreneurs from the beginning, in large part due to features of racial capitalism operating in the North. There were not yet any Black-owned banks in Detroit and most white banks refused to lend to African Americans.[29] Unable to obtain loans from white-controlled financial institutions, Black entrepreneurs seeking to finance their enterprises had to rely on inherited assets or loans from family members. This enabled Old Detroiters to enter the marketplace quickly in the initial years of the Great Migration. Edward Watson, for example, inherited an undertaking business that his stepfather, William H. Howard, had established several years earlier. Watson's mother, Carrie, who married Howard in 1904, joined her husband as a funeral director and embalmer and it is likely that the mother-and-son team continued running the business together after Howard's death.[30] Additionally, a 1920 survey on Black Detroit reported that there was "a group who in a small degree have realized some of their ambitions. Some members of this latter group are 'old Detroiters' who have made money from real estate which their families have held on to for many years and which because of the great development of Detroit has increased a hundred fold in value."[31] In this way, family resources allowed Black entrepreneurs to take advantage of emerging business opportunities.

Black professionals who often could not maintain a business premigration now found themselves amid a sizable enough Black population to sustain their practices. Such professional enterprises proliferated in the late 1910s and 1920s—again, primarily among Old Detroiters. Physician Robert Greenidge began operating a general practice in 1915. After a few successful years, witnessing the increasing number of Black physicians in Detroit, he established an X-ray laboratory at 614 East Columbia Street to serve them. A 1924 publication noted that Greenidge's facility was "supported principally through the co-operation of [Black] physicians, and the majority of the dentists refer their patients to him for X-Ray pictures of the teeth."[32] This sort of ingenuity helped grow Detroit's Black business community.

The story of James H. Cole Jr. and Charles T. Cole—brothers who established a successful funeral home operation in the late 1910s—exemplifies Old Detroiters' entrepreneurial advantage in the early migration years. The Cole brothers benefited from long-standing community ties as well as inherited capital and business knowledge. Their father, James H. Cole Sr., was widely considered to be the wealthiest Black Detroiter in the late nineteenth century,

whose assets included a prosperous moving company and several properties. After Cole Sr.'s death, his atypically affluent family viewed the wave of
southern migration as an opportunity to further expand their business port-
folio. While his sons George and William took over Cole's Express Moving
and Cartage Company and all four siblings established a real estate enterprise with their mother, James Jr. and Charles took a different entrepreneurial
route: the mortuary business.[33]

To establish their business, the Cole brothers needed to be licensed as
embalmers by the State of Michigan Board of Mortuary Science. Licensing exam applicants were required to have apprenticed under an embalmer
licensed in Michigan for at least two years and to obtain three character references from upstanding Detroit citizens.[34] These prerequisites were significant
barriers for new migrants who wanted to enter the field but posed much less of
a problem for Old Detroiters like the Coles. James Jr. and Charles served their
apprenticeships under the Marshalls (also brothers), white morticians whose
undertaking business, started by their father, Fred, was located on Beaubien
Street across from Cole Sr.'s moving company. The Marshall and Cole brothers had probably known each other all their lives.[35] With their inheritance
and family background, James Jr. and Charles surely had enough capital and
knowledge to start their funeral homes, yet without their connection to the
Marshall brothers it would have been impossible for them to break into this
field. By 1920, James H. Cole Jr. owned two mortuary offices. A newspaper profile declared, "Mr. Cole comes from an old established family of businessmen,
which accounts for his keen and discriminating eye for business."[36] Compared
to such Old Detroiters with "established families," newly arrived migrants with
entrepreneurial aspirations were at a distinct disadvantage.

Migrants' experiences differed, but many who came to Detroit with the
goal of opening a business initially had to work for wages to accumulate the
needed startup capital. Fred and Callie Allen worked in Detroit for five years
before they had saved enough money to open a linen supply business.[37] Even
those who arrived with savings or money from selling their property in the
South generally delayed opening their businesses until they could learn the lay
of the land and make fruitful connections. For example, Willis Eugene Smith,
who left his home in Eufaula, Alabama, with six hundred dollars in savings
and would go on to establish a funeral parlor in Detroit, worked at Ford Motor
Company and sold real estate before opening his business in 1929.[38]

Moreover, while there was plenty of demand for Black entrepreneurs'
goods and services, obtaining retail space to set up a business could be

challenging and expensive. This was true for newcomers and Old Detroiters alike. The migration created a severe shortage of both residential and commercial properties, especially in the Black Bottom section of the city. The dynamics of racial capitalism in the North saw cities segregated and African Americans confined to certain neighborhoods. With limited options and increased demand, Blacks were forced to pay inflated rents for substandard accommodations. The *Detroit Free Press*, a white-owned newspaper, reported that although housing stock in the Black Bottom district had depreciated through age and lack of upkeep, rents nevertheless soared until they were disproportionately higher than those of any other neighborhood in Detroit.[39] The author of a 1917 article in the paper acknowledged that it was racial discrimination that prohibited Blacks from settling in other sections of the city and created the housing problem: "Negroes are not welcome in every neighborhood. A European, be he ever ignorant, can find localities where it is possible for him to rent, or to buy a home on easy terms. In the same district a negro would be turned away, however worthy he might be."[40] Thus, Black southerners arriving in Detroit had no choice but to settle in Black Bottom and pay whatever price landlords set.

Forrester B. Washington, the first director of the Detroit Urban League, reported in 1920 that although a lack of sufficient housing influenced Detroit's rising rents, there were also "individuals who are inflating and 'kiting' the rents higher than necessary."[41] Although whites owned much of the property in Black Bottom in the early twentieth century, African Americans did own some of the rental housing in the area. Early in the migration, some Black entrepreneurs began investing in land and/or housing and worked as real estate agents alongside their primary operations. Acknowledging that African Americans were exploited by both whites and Blacks, Washington wrote, "No less than seven Negro real estate agents have been proceeded against by the county prosecutor within the past six months for rent profiteering. This abuse is, however, not confined to the agents nor landlords but Negro business men have invested some of their capital in rent profiteering."[42] One such entrepreneur more than doubled his rents from twenty-five to sixty dollars per month.

At times the actions of Old Detroiters clashed with the freedom enterprise of southern migrants. For example, African Americans owned a group of dilapidated tenement houses near Hastings Street and Rowena known as Binga Row, named after William Binga, a Black barber and the original owner of these buildings. East-side tenements like these units often lacked hot water, toilets, and windows. But as southern migrants poured into the overcrowded neighborhood, the owners continued to rent the deteriorating units at high prices. Other landlords fashioned makeshift housing by converting sheds and stables into apartments. Due to the competition for housing in Black Bottom, African Americans were forced to pay exorbitant rents for such substandard housing.[43] Some were even swindled out of both their money and the homes for which they paid. Forrester B. Washington recounted several instances of illegal housing scams, including a Black real estate dealer who accepted deposits from five different renters with no intention of actually renting his property. Washington lamented, "There are many individuals who are taking advantage of the Negroes['] dire need for homes to absolutely rob him. . . . This situation is typical of many Negro and white real estate 'sharks' who are preying upon homeless colored people."[44] Black property owners and entrepreneurs in the real estate business thus gained wealth from exploiting other African Americans who migrated to the city in search of greater prosperity themselves. In this way and many others, Old Detroiter entrepreneurs benefited from the massive influx of southern Blacks to their city while their migrant counterparts faced new and old challenges in their chosen home.

World War I and Its Uncertain Aftermath

Although the Great War and the job opportunities it created helped propel the first wave of southern migrants to Detroit, numerous difficulties awaited them upon arrival, particularly due to the wartime economy. During World War I, the city faced shortages that made establishing and sustaining a business difficult. Fuel and food shortages and conservation efforts increased the cost of running a business and forced entrepreneurs, such as grocers, retailers, and restaurateurs, to raise prices for their goods and services. Detroit also experienced a severe coal shortage, which not only affected Black coal delivery businesses but also touched any establishment that required heat.[45] Some commercial operations passed the rising costs on to their customers. For example, in 1916, the owner of the Vaudette Theater, a "high-class vaudeville house," increased admission prices to fifteen cents, "much to his displeasure." According to him, the increase was absolutely necessary to maintain the standards to which his patrons were accustomed.[46]

Moreover, while southern migrants undoubtedly found more social liberty and opportunities in Detroit, they also soon realized that many racial and economic inequalities persisted in the North as they had in the South.

Black entrepreneurs faced discrimination in policing and the way the state enforced regulations during this period. In 1916, Detroit police temporarily shut down four Black social and entertainment clubs, all of which were legally incorporated and "serve[d] drinks, as white men's clubs do." Club representatives protested the closures, citing discrimination and arguing that since they were effectively barred from white-owned restaurants and saloons, Detroit's Black residents had no access to entertainment or public socializing. The businesses were eventually permitted to reopen, but the owners suffered lost revenue during the closure period.[47] Similarly, Berry Gordy Sr. recalled experiencing discrimination from a white inspector while operating his plastering business. According to Gordy, the white inspector would cite him for minor things, which would cost Gordy money. Yet, the same inspector let things slide for white contractors, whose work was inferior to Gordy's. This experience and others left Gordy with the impression that "it's just as bad here as it was in the South. . . . Every violation, every law or rule they make, it hits the colored man or poor man 'fore it hits anybody else."[48]

As for factory workers and other laborers lured to Detroit by wartime opportunities, some leaders in the Black community cautioned against feeling too secure in their new positions. John Dancy, the head of the Detroit Urban League as the war drew to a close, remembered, "For a while things were going along so well for the Negro community, the employment situation was so much improved that some got into the habit of congratulating ourselves. Some of the ministers were saying 'We finally made the grade,' and there was much optimism that we would roll right along. 'These factories can't get along without us,' some people were boasting." To those who were too optimistic, he warned, "For God's sake, don't say that! These people can get rid of you in a minute. They don't need you that bad."[49] Dancy was right. The feeling that Black workers were indispensable to Detroit's factories would not last long.

Armistice Day, November 11, 1918, brought uncertainty for Black workers and entrepreneurs in Detroit. It marked the end of World War I and called into question African Americans' future in the city. Dancy remembered, "The Armistice, of course, marked a change. There had been such an urgent need for labor in the war days that Negroes were grabbed as soon as they got off the train and rushed out to jobs before they had time to rent a room. It had been *too* good. I had wondered what would happen when the war was over and the soldiers came home."[50] Soon enough, an economic downturn would take a substantial toll on the city's growing Black community. The depression of 1920–21 led to mass unemployment among Black industrial workers, leaving seventeen thousand without jobs.[51] Many migrants who had come to Detroit with grand dreams of northern prosperity were disappointed and impoverished by the recession. Unable to find housing or employment, some chose to return to the South or try their luck in other northern urban centers.[52] In addition, Black entrepreneurs, who had relied on industrial workers as customers, had a difficult time selling their goods and services with so many leaving the city or living without wages.

Detroit's Black community employed various strategies to survive the 1920–21 depression. The prosperous war years had enabled many African Americans to save money. In a survey of five hundred Black families, Forrester B. Washington found that 98 percent had bank accounts, which averaged $398.[53] Black Detroiters deposited their money in accounts at white-owned local banks, national banks with branches in Detroit, and southern banks. According to Washington: "A number of depositors still maintain accounts in banks in the South. . . . They send their money regularly to these out-of-town banks. This is because many of these Negro depositors are stock holders in southern banks, owned by Negroes, and feel by keeping their accounts in these banks that they are helping themselves."[54] Those with savings were forced to dip into them during the economic downturn. According to sociologist Monroe Work, "Negro labor in the industrial centers of the North had saved a considerable amount of its earnings, and by this means was able to help tide over the period of non-employment."[55] Certainly some of Detroit's Black entrepreneurs used their savings to keep their establishments afloat, but doing so delayed plans to expand, update equipment, and otherwise continue investing in their businesses. The depression also likely shook any sense of economic security they had gained in the prior years of prosperity. And for those Detroiters who had been saving up to launch a new business, having to use those funds to survive the depression was a harsh setback.

Entrepreneurs had to devise other strategies to remain in operation, particularly in the sectors that were hit hardest. The depression greatly affected enterprises that catered to newly arrived migrants, since it caused migration to come to a standstill and even resulted in return migration. For example, the Tanzy Hotel, which claimed to be one of "the largest and finest Hostelrys in Michigan," was quite successful up until the depression. Centrally located on St. Antoine Street, the Black-owned hotel offered "reasonable rates" and "nicely furnished . . . commodious rooms." Proprietor B. W. Tanzy catered especially to migrants, advertising, "A special effort made to provide accommodations for persons coming to Detroit. Write us in advance."[56] As late as

November 1920, Mr. Tanzy did not seem to have any difficulty obtaining patrons. However, just six months later, his business was clearly suffering. A May 1921 advertisement stated, "Because of the Depression B. W. Tanzey of the Tanzey Hotel has cut the price of accommodations one-third. He has increased his space to accommodate three times as many guests as before."[57] Lowering prices was one way that entrepreneurs attempted to offset the effects of their clients' lack of employment.

While many struggled to survive the economic slump, some Black establishments actually expanded during the depression. This was the case for Mercy Hospital, Detroit's first Black hospital founded by the Northcrosses in 1917. Daisy Hill Northcross and David Northcross were both medical doctors from Montgomery, Alabama, who, according to their son, moved to Detroit in 1917 to escape the persecution of the Ku Klux Klan. By 1922 Mercy Hospital had moved from its original location to a new building with space for additional patients and an operating room.[58] However, most Black-owned businesses felt the sting of the 1920–21 depression. Black entrepreneurs who managed to stay in business realized that they needed to work together to maintain the strides they had made in the late 1910s.

The UNIA and Economic Cooperation in Detroit

The idea of cooperative business initiatives was not new to the Black community. W. E. B. Du Bois argued in his 1907 *Economic Co-Operation Among Negro Americans* that Blacks in the United Stated had long engaged in cooperative economic ventures.[59] Pooling individual resources—often insufficient on their own—and operating in tandem was a strategy to combat racial capitalism and to help African Americans gain more economic independence and political power as a group.[60] The 1920s saw an increase in cooperative attempts to advance Black Detroiters' position in business.[61]

However, banding together was no easy task for Detroit's Black business owners. The city's African American community harbored divisions related to class, religion, and approaches to racial uplift. While the various Black organizations in 1920s Detroit—including the NAACP, the Detroit Urban League, the Universal Negro Improvement Association (UNIA), and multiple church denominations—were all concerned with Black economic growth, they disagreed over how to achieve it. Groups like the Urban League and NAACP embraced an integrationist approach to economic uplift and often partnered with white philanthropists.[62] The UNIA, by contrast, called for Blacks to separate themselves from whites and unite under the banner of Africa and Black nationalism. Black professionals were often members of exclusive churches reserved for the Black elite and believed that they should act as the voice and leadership of the Black business community. Other churches were divided along class lines as well.[63] Convincing African American entrepreneurs from these different factions to cooperate in the interest of Black business was a considerable challenge.

But while they had their differences, entrepreneurs faced similar adversity from outside the Black community and had to overcome a variety of obstacles in order to run profitable, long-lasting businesses in a racial capitalist system. They experienced discrimination at almost every stage, including difficulty obtaining loans and licenses from state regulatory agencies and being charged exorbitant rents for retail space and denied access to desirable locations.[64] Black business owners also faced competition from white entrepreneurs who operated in Detroit's Black Bottom neighborhood.[65] Despite ideological disagreements, African Americans understood that the marketplace had different rules for Black and white entrepreneurs. Knowing this discriminatory climate all too well, Black business leaders recognized the necessity of putting their differences aside and embracing an ethos of cooperation. They were "allied, not united" in fighting against the restraints of racial capitalism.[66] In other words, though there were cultural, class, and social divisions, Black entrepreneurs were linked by their freedom enterprise efforts.

Marcus Garvey's Black nationalist philosophy resonated strongly with many of Detroit's entrepreneurs and aspiring business owners. Garvey founded the UNIA in Jamaica in 1914 and established the first U.S. chapter in New York City in 1917. By the mid-1920s, the UNIA had become the largest Black organization in the United States, with over seven hundred branches.[67] Garvey's ultimate goal was to universally uplift people of African descent, and economic development was fundamental to his vision of global transformation. In fact, one of the UNIA's ten founding objectives was "to conduct a world-wide commercial and industrial intercourse."[68] Black migrants in Detroit were particularly drawn to Garvey's message of self-help and uplift through business. After all, they had moved north seeking the economic autonomy they had been unable to attain in the South. As in other major cities, UNIA members in Detroit organized parades and excursions, taught African history, and rallied around the pan-African flag, which the UNIA designed.[69] All of these activities fostered feelings of dignity, self-respect, and cultural unity among Black people and pushed back against the structures of racial capitalism.[70]

Garvey traveled extensively in the late 1910s and early 1920s spreading the UNIA's message. In 1917, he wrote about the advancements of Black business owners in various parts of the United States, observing with pleasure the "commercial enterprises owned and managed by Negro people" in New York City, Boston, Philadelphia, Pittsburgh, Baltimore, Washington, and Chicago. Garvey had presumably not yet visited Detroit, or was unimpressed with the city's African American business community. Nonetheless, reflecting the sentiment and objectives of Detroit's Black entrepreneurs, Garvey proclaimed, "The acme of American Negro enterprise is not yet reached. You want more stores, more banks, and bigger enterprises."[71]

Two years later, Garvey did visit Detroit and witnessed the rising number of Black businesses. He stayed at the Biltmore Hotel, billed as "one of the best hotels, owned and operated entirely by Negroes, in this section of the country."[72] Established by O. H. Banks in the mid-1910s, the three-story brick building was located on St. Antoine Street in Black Bottom, equipped with "all the modern improvements," and offered Black travelers comfortable accommodations that would have been hard to come by in Detroit prior to the Great Migration. While local white-owned hotels generally refused to lodge Blacks, the influx of African Americans moving to and passing through Detroit offered Black entrepreneurs like Banks an opportunity to fill a niche.[73] Breaking into business sectors like the hospitality industry was exactly the sort of economic action Garvey and the UNIA promoted.

However, Garvey also imagined a future in which Blacks would make strides in all areas of business, particularly large enterprises that would allow them to be competitive on the economic and political world stage. When Garvey was in Detroit in the summer of 1919, he was in the process of raising funds for just that type of venture: the Black Star Line. This line of Black-owned steamships, intended to facilitate Black global trade, would become the most famous of the UNIA's business ventures. Garvey published a letter in the organization's national newspaper, the *Negro World*, which he penned while staying at Detroit's Biltmore Hotel. He outlined the project and a plan to raise $2 million in just five months. Asking African Americans to donate a dollar (or more), Garvey wrote, "A line of steamships owned and operated in the interest of the people, is necessary for the fuller economic and industrial development of the race."[74] The Black Star Line was to be a material manifestation of the UNIA's ideology of Black self-determination and economic independence. However, the Black Star Line not only failed as a business venture but also led to the downfall of Garvey himself.[75]

The popularity of the UNIA decreased considerably after Garvey was deported in 1927. The spectacular failure of the Black Star Line left many with the impression that Garvey was a con man who had used the organization's businesses to cheat Blacks out of their money. Rather than uplifting Black people, Garvey and the UNIA earned a reputation for harming them economically.[76] And while scholars have recognized the UNIA's positive cultural impact, the organization's financial and business dealings are widely considered disastrous.[77]

However, on a local level, the Detroit division of the UNIA had a significant economic impact on African Americans.[78] Garvey and his movement came along at a time when the Black business community needed cooperativism to survive, and the UNIA's ethos of Black nationalism was tremendously appealing. Established in 1920, the Detroit chapter of the organization was one of its strongest, growing to over five thousand members by 1922 (making it the "second largest local chapter in the world").[79] The bulk of these members were laborers, mostly employed in the automobile industry or domestic service.[80] Many of the chapter's leaders, however, were entrepreneurs, including lawyer Alonzo D. Pettiford, shoemaker F. Levi Ford, and undertaker Charles C. Diggs Sr.[81] Detroit members invested in the Black Star Line and donated to other national UNIA campaigns.[82] The chapter also purchased local real estate to house its UNIA office, located at 1516 Russell Street, which they named Liberty Hall. The chapter opened a restaurant and hired Blacks to run it, thus providing jobs to those with experience in the restaurant industry.[83] The UNIA's Sunshine Restaurant was located at 1520 Russell, close to Liberty Hall.[84] Detroit members also operated laundries, theaters, restaurants, shoeshine parlors, and drugstores under the auspices of the UNIA. As Charles Zampy, one of the Detroit UNIA's earliest members, recalled, "We did all that was possible to raise our economic standards, and we were successful until the expatriation of our leader in 1925."[85]

However, the Detroit UNIA continued after Garvey's arrest 1925. In 1926 *The Negro in Detroit* reported of the Universal Negro Improvement Association:

It is not a mere "protest" organization but tries to induce the colored people to meet injustices and denial of rights by starting all kinds of enterprises of their own with the purpose in view of finally becoming so independent of the white people financially that they can organize a government of their own in Africa. It believes that by possessing financial independence and by controlling the political power which the United States government will be forced to recognize, the Association will be able to secure for those Negroes who remain in this country and those who go to Africa a greater mead of justice and more favorable opportunities of all kinds than are otherwise possible. . . . The Detroit unit of this organization has a membership of 5,000.[86]

The Detroit chapter would continue into the 1940s.[87]

At the UNIA's height, an important channel that helped facilitate cooperation among Black entrepreneurs was the *Detroit Contender*. Established by two brothers, Robert L. Poston and Ulysses S. Poston, the paper promoted Black business cooperation and economic nationalism and was instrumental in winning support for the UNIA in Detroit.[88] Originally from Hopkinsville, Kentucky, the Poston brothers migrated to Detroit in 1919 with the intention to establish a newspaper that expressed their political views on Black self-determination. Their parents were college educated and instilled in their children (eight in all) the value of education, race pride, and Black independence. While both parents worked as teachers, the Postons' father also occasionally engaged in entrepreneurial activities, such as a running a small grocery store and a business providing custom-made suits. Although ultimately unsuccessful, these ventures likely helped inspire Robert and Ulysses to start their newspaper business.[89]

The Poston brothers established the *Hopkinsville Contender* in their Kentucky hometown with hopes of garnering economic independence and the freedom to express their political views.[90] Not atypically, the venture did not last long. Since Robert and Ulysses did not have the resources to maintain their own printing press, they needed a white-owned publishing company to print the *Hopkinsville Contender*. But after the brothers published an editorial protesting the discriminatory treatment of Black veterans forced to walk at the back of a local victory parade, their white publishers refused to print the paper any longer.[91] Outraged, the Postons decided to leave Hopkinsville and reopen their business in a city that was less hostile to Blacks, where they would have more freedom to write about race issues. After a brief and unsuccessful stint in Nashville, the brothers moved to Detroit and established the *Detroit Contender*. Within eight months, it was the most popular Black weekly in the city.[92]

Soon after they arrived in Detroit, Robert and Ulysses were introduced to the Universal Negro Improvement Association and were instantly won over by Marcus Garvey's Black nationalist ideology.[93] His message resonated with their desire to achieve independence through business—the very goal that inspired them to move to Detroit. The Postons became dedicated Garveyites and used their newspaper to publicize Garvey's philosophy on business and how it could help liberate the Black community.

The *Detroit Contender* served as a vehicle to showcase the strides being made by the city's Black entrepreneurs, foster discussions of business strategies and obstacles, and highlight the importance of economic cooperation. By creating a successful mode of Black communication, the Postons played an important role in bringing together local African American entrepreneurs. For example, the brothers invited a diverse group of Black Detroiters to contribute to a special business issue of the *Detroit Contender*. They wrote, "If your business is to uplift we are going along the same road. Let us be companionable along the way."[94] Published on November 13, 1920, the special issue profiled Black entrepreneurs from a range of backgrounds, providing each with valuable exposure. The issue also explicitly encouraged Detroit's African Americans to patronize Black-owned businesses. The Postons penned an editorial asserting, "Our people must quit begging and invest. Quit spending with others and spend with ourselves. Our purpose in running this business issue is to call your attention to some things that we are doing here in a business way with the hope of encouraging further effort among us."[95] Economic Black nationalism and cooperative economics were an important part of migrant entrepreneurs' freedom enterprise in the 1920s.

The *Contender*'s special business issue highlighted cooperative businesses in Detroit. It celebrated the Community Market Corporation, a chain of local grocery stores that was actively expanding; a third store was set to open and the proprietors were planning to enlarge their first store by taking over the entire block. They had already raised $16,000 toward this goal. The *Detroit Contender* reported that the Community Market Corporation was the result of "definite action on the part of a number of our people who believed in themselves, in their own possibility along business lines, and who had confidence in the project."[96] Likewise, the newspaper highlighted Enterprise Garage, an autobody shop located at 209 Alfred Street operated cooperatively by African Americans. The garage had investments of $8,500 and had paid employees more than $200 a week since it opened.[97] In profiling the success of cooperative Black businesses, the Postons sought to encourage further business development and joint efforts among Black entrepreneurs in Detroit.[98]

Other local organizations, such as the Detroit Urban League and Second Baptist Church, also supported economic Black nationalism and worked to increase cooperation among Black entrepreneurs. While these two groups were important in facilitating migration to Detroit, they also played significant roles in promoting Black business, especially during the early migration years. Reverend Robert Bradby of the Second Baptist Church, for instance, helped place newly arrived migrants in factory jobs and, as Beth Bates put it, "used his church effectively as a hiring hall for jobs at the FMC [Ford Motor Company]."[99] Bradby was also committed to strengthening Black business in Detroit in order to address larger economic problems facing African Americans in the city, arguing, "[The development of] business among our racial group . . . will do more for the standardization and general good of the people than any other thing that I can think of now other than the work of the church."[100] Accordingly, Bradby started the Business Boosters club through the church, which was open to Detroit Blacks regardless of religious affiliation, to encourage business ventures. This club was responsible for founding Enterprise Garage and the Community Market Corporation.

Moreover, witnessing the economic devastation of 1920–21, Bradby linked this message with the plight of laid-off workers. He implored: "If we in Detroit as a race would unify our forces and direct our attention for the next few months toward the developing of the business which you already have that is legitimate, and toward the creating of other businesses, which is badly needed, we should have done more toward the solution of your problem in this city from a civil, industrial, social, and economic standpoint than perhaps we can in any other way."[101] In this way, Reverend Bradby and the Second Baptist Church helped disseminate and apply a message of Black cooperativism in Detroit. The Detroit Urban League, led by director John C. Dancy, similarly contributed to such efforts. In 1920, for example, the organization introduced business education initiatives designed to increase African Americans' chances of success. Dancy reported, "It is our plan to inaugurate for the business[people] in the community a series of five or six lectures by some experienced man on some prescribed subject."[102]

Thus, although the 1920–21 depression hit Detroit's African American community hard, organizations and individuals worked together to ensure that the businesses they had built in the early migration years did not crumble. Many entrepreneurs embraced Marcus Garvey's philosophy of economic

Black nationalism and implemented it at a time when the city needed it most. People like Robert and Ulysses Poston, Reverend Robert Bradby, and John Dancy utilized their organizations to widely promote and advance Black business achievements. Moreover, factories in Detroit began hiring again after the depression and migration to the city increased. The summer of 1922 saw a "tremendous influx of Negroes from all parts of the country into Detroit"— around seven thousand in Dancy's estimation—and Black entrepreneurs were quick to make the most of the business opportunities generated by the new arrivals.[103]

A Thriving Business Community

After the economic blip that inaugurated the decade, Detroit's Black business community flourished in the 1920s. This growth aligned with the post–World War I prosperity experienced across the nation; Detroit was not left out of the "roaring twenties." By 1925, more than three hundred thousand workers were employed by the city's three thousand manufacturing plants.[104] Correspondingly, Detroit's Black population grew from forty thousand to eighty thousand between 1920 and 1925. By 1930, the Black population would be over one hundred twenty thousand.[105]

Businesses that experienced financial difficulties in 1920 and 1921 were able to not just recover but expand and thrive in the 1920s. The Tanzy Hotel, whose owner cut prices in order to draw in customers during the depression, seemed to be operating in full force. In 1924, the Tanzy made improvements to its subterranean dining rooms and dance hall, and Mr. Tanzy was considering installing a domed roof garden to create "a cool and delightful place to eat, as well as present a unique place from which to view a great deal of Detroit." The hotel's thirty-six rooms were well equipped with rugs, dressers, chairs, and lockers, and six rooms had running hot and cold water. The Tanzy also "constantly employed" fourteen workers in order to give patrons "maximum service at minimum cost," and so provided jobs for other African Americans in the city. Mr. Tanzy seemed optimistic about his prospects for continued success, as the hotel changed its tagline to "Watch us grow."[106]

In addition to reviving existing enterprises, a 1924 publication on Black Detroit reported, "the Negro is rapidly entering into untried fields and is gaining considerable headway."[107] These "untried fields" included businesses that Black Detroiters never imagined they could sustain before the migration so drastically increased their numbers. African Americans opened restaurants; cleaning services; hairdresser and barbershops; electrical, plumbing, and general contracting businesses; grocery and drugstores; meat and fish markets; bakeries and confectioners; autobody shops and a school for mechanics; employment agencies; jewelers; shoe repair shops; and more. The number of Black professionals also increased. In 1924, Detroit boasted fifty Black doctors (up from twenty-seven in 1920), thirty-five lawyers, twenty-five dentists (up from thirteen in 1920), and twenty-six pharmacists.[108]

Just two years later in 1926, *The Negro in Detroit*, a report prepared for the Mayor's Interracial-Committee, revealed further growth, confirming that there were now 720 business establishments in Detroit "conducted by Negroes and depending for the most part on Negro patronage. Among those, fifty-eight different types of enterprises are represented." The report highlighted some "unusual business ventures among negroes," including the Home Milling Company, established around 1922. This company manufactured cornmeal, hominy grits, and whole wheat flour in their plant at Catherine and Russell Streets. The demand for Home Milling's products was linked to the Great Migration: "there is quite a large demand of the products on the part of Southern residents in the City and the concern is doing a fair volume of business. Their cornmeal is made from specially selected white corn out of deference to the palate of Southern Negroes who do not relish meal made from yellow corn." The managers had plans to expand the business by supplying to Black-owned bakeries and by manufacturing cornmeal mush to sell to its clientele. The 1926 report also presented the findings of a survey conducted among 50 "typical" business owners. It showed that 33 of 50 were born and reared in the South, while 17 hailed from the North. Of the 50 cases, 46 percent had been in business less than five years, 68 percent less than ten years, and only 14 percent more than ten years, while the group average was six years, indicating that many of these businesses were established in the 1920s.[109]

Another of the survey's telling findings was that Detroit's Black entrepreneurs often established businesses that were unconnected to their prior occupations. An owner of a music store, for instance, was formerly employed as a shipping clerk. Perhaps those who had previously only dreamed of starting a business about which they were passionate took advantage of the new opportunity to do so. Others drew on knowledge from past jobs to launch their businesses, such as a former waiter who opened a restaurant in 1923. Another entrepreneur who had worked as a "forelady in [a] factory" established an apron manufacturing business in the 1920s.[110]

It is highly possible that this apron shop owner was Cynthia Thompson. Thompson was profiled in *Colored Detroit* in 1924 under the headline "What One Can Do *IF* One Tries." Thompson opened the Best Apron Shop on April 1, 1923, at 1535 Hastings Street after working for many years in large garment factories in Chicago—a position that gave her the experience necessary to establish a successful apron business. With only a few yards of cloth, a sewing machine, and her two industrious hands, Thompson made a few aprons and displayed them in the small window of her shop. After she made her first sale, her venture skyrocketed due to her business savvy and keen eye. Seeing an opportunity for expansion, Thompson soon began selling both women's and men's garments. By 1924, her men's department had become so popular that sales rivaled those of the women's department. Thompson also started collecting cast-off pieces of cloth to make bed quilts.[111] Her "specialty quilts" cost between four and five dollars apiece and were popular during Detroit's bitter winters. In fact, Thompson had to hire three employees in order to meet the demand.[112]

Cynthia Thompson was one of many entrepreneurs who found success in 1920s Detroit. What made her enterprise so praiseworthy was that she manufactured her own goods; many entrepreneurs viewed manufacturing as a greater benchmark of Blacks' progress in the business world and necessary to make larger economic gains. *The Negro in Detroit* acknowledged that a major reason Black entrepreneurs engaged mostly in retail and service enterprises over manufacturing was because they required a "comparatively small amount of special training and a smaller amount of initial capital."[113] The report also lamented the absence of corporations and large-scale ventures—"concerns requiring a great deal of cooperative effort and a large amount of capital goods." The surveyed establishments were mostly run by individuals and employed, on average, two workers.[114]

African Americans *were* working to launch larger enterprises. The 1920s saw efforts to establish Black-owned corporations for the first time in Detroit. By 1926, three Black insurance companies had issued approximately $5 million worth of insurance. The Great Lakes Mutual Insurance Company, which was incorporated in 1927 and began operating in 1928, would become one of the most successful Black-owned companies in Detroit.[115] Besides supplying valuable services for the growing Black population, these enterprises also provided jobs for Black Detroiters who worked as agents.

Black Detroiters knew that establishing their own financial institutions would be instrumental for the growth of Black business in the city. As such, a group of business leaders organized the Michigan People's Finance Corporation (MPFC), which was chartered on October 1, 1923.[116] By 1924 the company had two hundred individual stockholders and was providing friendly financial service to "meet both the call of opportunity and the demands of necessity." This included supporting small businesses, as the company purported to fill "a very definite need, specializing in small loans up to $500."[117] The entrepreneurs behind MPFC clearly understood that providing loans was an important step in supporting African Americans' freedom enterprise. Beyond financing new enterprises, the corporation also offered business education to the growing Black community. Managers of the MPFC edited a popular and accessible financial column in the *Detroit Independent* newspaper that featured commentary on good business practices.[118]

Such information was especially useful for Black women who had historically been pushed to the margins of the business world. They often had more incentive to engage in entrepreneurship than Black men and were hungry for this knowledge. The vast majority of Black women who migrated to Detroit during this era worked as domestics, generally enduring long hours, meager wages, constant surveillance, sexual harassment, and violence.[119] Because Detroit was, in Forrester B. Washington's words, a "metal trades town," there were simply fewer occupational options for women, who were kept out of this field. Washington explained, "It is quite reasonable to suppose that if Detroit were a great garment making center like New York or if Detroit went in for highly diversified manufacturing like Chicago that we would find colored women in a greater variety of trades as well as in factory employment in larger numbers."[120] Additionally, white companies often had policies that prohibited hiring Black women. Therefore, Black women—even those who were educated—frequently had to settle for low-paying jobs.[121] With such limited options, many saw entrepreneurship as a means of gaining the autonomy and financial benefits not possible through wage work.

Black women increasingly took the post–World War I influx of southerners as an opportunity to grow a business. Eleanora A. DeVere, who worked as a dressmaker after migrating to Detroit from South Carolina in the early 1900s, quickly became known for her skills with a needle. Some of her work—an embroidered doily and centerpiece—was featured in Michigan's 1915 Exhibit of Freedmen's Progress at the National Half Century Exposition in Chicago.[122] Like many other Black dressmakers and seamstresses, DeVere worked from home, which allowed her to enjoy considerably more independence than domestic servants or other wage workers. She set her own

Figure 3. Eleanora DeVere featured in the 1924 publication *Colored Detroit*. Courtesy of the Burton Historical Collection, Detroit Public Library.

schedule and was not under the constant, watchful eye of a white boss.[123] DeVere only had to answer to her customers and ensure they were satisfied, which apparently, judging by her success, they were.

But DeVere had greater entrepreneurial aspirations and turned to a more lucrative business once the migration got underway. In 1915, Detroit's city directory began listing Eleanora DeVere as "hairdresser" instead of "dressmaker," and she opened her own salon at 2509 St. Antoine Street in June 1919.[124] DeVere probably saved up money from her dressmaking business to finance her training as a hairdresser and start her salon. As with other Old Detroiters, the fact that she was already working in the city before the Great Migration enabled her to quickly capitalize on a new stream of Black customers. Moreover, DeVere trained under Madam C. J. Walker, the nation's

most famous Black beautician, which likely gave her a leg up in Detroit's bud-
ding beauty industry. DeVere's salon included a retail station for Madam C. J.
Walker products and also served as a distribution center for the company
that supplied agents throughout Michigan. DeVere was committed to "constant improvement," vowing to always "be courteous to her customers and
to do her work absolutely satisfactorily." While she started out with just one
employee, by 1924 DeVere employed six "industrious young women" to help
handle the increasing volume of customers. Her business was one of the most
popular Black beauty salons in Detroit into the 1920s.[125]

When asked in an interview for the *Detroit Contender* if she had any regrets
about her decision to open her salon, DeVere replied, "My only regret is that
I did not enter into business for myself years before I did."[126] For her, other
Old Detroiters, and the many migrant entrepreneurs who came north seeking economic security, self-determination, and prosperity, Detroit did in fact
seem to be a land of opportunity. However, as some Black entrepreneurs discovered, their business successes and personal wealth could also lead to a
violent backlash from northern whites.

White Backlash to Black Success

In the 1920s, as Black entrepreneurs sought to grow their businesses and
build a business community, the Ku Klux Klan (KKK) was experiencing a
rebirth. Midwestern cities like Detroit saw increasing numbers of Klan membership among whites. Some founders of this new iteration of the KKK were
business owners who stood for "One Hundred Percent Americanism."[127]
They opposed foreign-born competition and despised African Americans'
mounting presence in northern cities. In the early 1920s, white proprietors
increasingly refused to deal with Black customers.[128] Although such segregation facilitated Black business growth, it also created a hostile environment.
Racial capitalism was dynamic, and its manifestations shifted over time. In
the 1920s overt violence and intimidation in Detroit let migrant entrepreneurs know that anti-Black violence was not only a feature of the Jim Crow
system in the South. Racial violence and intimidation were key to maintaining racial capitalism in the North as well.

In 1921, C. H. Norton, the KKK's organizer for the Midwest, moved to
Detroit to expand membership in Michigan. Three years later in 1924, Detroit's
Klan had swelled to thirty-five thousand members.[129] The Indiana edition of

the *Fiery Cross*, "the leading Klan paper of America," reported in 1923 that KKK membership and enthusiasm in Michigan had increased so dramatically that "it has been found necessary to publish a Michigan edition."[130] Klan newspapers included business directories and advertisements to promote enterprises owned by KKK members. Their advertisements were not always subtle; one cleaning business, for instance, claimed to "keep klothes klean."[131] The twelve-page Michigan edition of the *Fiery Cross* began circulating in late August 1923.[132] And it is probable that it also contained advertisements for businesses owned by members of the Detroit Klan. Additionally, Detroit Klansmen created the Symwa Club (Spend Your Money with Americans).[133]

Heightened racism in the 1920s directly impacted Black business owners and professionals. A notable example is that of Ossian Sweet, a Detroit doctor originally from Florida who purchased a home in a white neighborhood in 1925. Sweet migrated to Detroit in 1921, and after several years in the city, he seemed to have fulfilled his goal to "rise in his profession and make his fortune."[134] His practice was successful and by May 1925 he had saved $3,500 as a down payment to purchase a three-bedroom bungalow at 2905 Garland Street for $18,500.[135] Using the profits from his business to purchase a home in a wealthier neighborhood should have been a sound investment. However, since that home was in a white area, Sweet was breaching Detroit's barrier of de facto residential segregation. This type of segregation was commonplace in northern cities. Blacks habitually earned less than whites and paid higher prices for rent, making it more difficult for African Americans to save money and become homeowners in the first place. Moreover, whites in Detroit and elsewhere employed discriminatory real estate practices such as restrictive covenants to keep Blacks out of their neighborhoods.[136] If they were interested in purchasing homes in white neighborhoods, would-be Black homeowners found that white real estate agents would not work with them, bankers would not give them mortgages, and they could not obtain insurance coverage.[137] All of these elements were northern racial capitalism at work. However, some African Americans, particularly entrepreneurs, were occasionally able to defy the white supremacist economic hierarchy and purchase property in all-white neighborhoods.

Ossian Sweet and his wife, Gladys, moved into their new home on September 8, 1925. They knew that their decision to live in an all-white neighborhood was risky; when a white mob descended upon their house the next evening, it was not their first encounter with mob violence. Dr. Sweet had witnessed a brutal lynching as a child, the smell of scorched flesh forever burned into his mind.[138] Later, while in medical school at Howard University in Washington, D.C., he watched a gang of white soldiers and sailors drag a Black man from a streetcar during the 1919 race riot. Gladys Sweet's family knew well the tragic outcomes of racial violence in the North. Her cousin, a police officer, was one of several Blacks killed during the 1919 Chicago race riot.[139] Thus, on the night of September 9 when hundreds of angry whites crowded around 2905 Garland Street and began throwing rocks and bricks though the window of their new home, the Sweets and their friends inside knew they could very well lose their lives. To defend themselves and the Sweets' newly acquired property, the occupants armed themselves with guns. As the situation escalated, one of them fired a shot out the window, which struck and killed a white member of the mob.[140]

The Sweets and nine associates were charged with murder, and the famous trials that ensued would set a precedent for Black self-defense in Detroit. Many scholars have analyzed the Sweet trials for their influence on residential segregation in northern cities and for defense attorney Clarence Darrow's success in convincing an all-white jury to acquit the Black defendants.[141] However, in the context of the Great Migration and the growth of Black entrepreneurship, the case also reveals an important aspect of Blacks' long struggle for economic freedom.

Reminiscent of migrant entrepreneurs' experiences in the Jim Crow South, there were consequences for becoming prosperous in the North too. As discussed in Chapter 1, Black entrepreneurs who became "too successful" risked a violent reaction from southern whites. Pushing up against the boundaries of the racial capitalist order in their new homes could also lead to dangerous encounters. African Americans had long believed that acquiring property was crucial to economic freedom. While many attempted to buy land in the South, in northern cities like Detroit Blacks mostly sought property in the form of housing. In 1925, most Black Detroiters were not in a position to do this, especially outside the city's designated Black section. As the first with the means to afford homes in all-white neighborhoods, entrepreneurs like Dr. Sweet experienced violent reactions.

In fact, two other prominent Black entrepreneurs also confronted racist violence after they moved into majority-white neighborhoods earlier that year. In June 1925, a white mob of two hundred—which would grow to over one thousand—surrounded the home of Dr. Alexander Turner mere hours after he took possession of the property. The crowd threw stones and broke windows, and the throng stormed into the house to steal Turner's belongings.

When the mob's ringleader, a member of the Tireman Avenue Improvement Association, demanded that Turner sign the deed to his house over to the organization, they all received a police escort to Turner's office so he could transfer the property.[142]

The other incident involved Agnes and Vollington Bristol, a married couple who operated the Bristol & Bristol Funeral Home and owned multiple residential properties. In 1925, the Bristols rented a house that they owned (but did not live in) to several Black families, who subsequently received threatening notes. In early July, the Bristols decided to move into the home themselves. The day after the move, a white mob formed outside their house and began throwing stones and shooting at the Bristols' home. Police were able to disperse the crowd, but tensions in the area remained high for several days, and the Bristols continued to face death threats and hostile encounters with whites until they moved out of the neighborhood.[143] The cases of Ossian Sweet, Alexander Turner, and Agnes and Vollington Bristol exemplify the physical violence and threats that Black entrepreneurs experienced as a result of buying property in segregated neighborhoods. For migrant entrepreneurs, incidents like these demonstrated that racial violence and intimidation were inherent characteristics of racial capitalism nationwide.

These violent encounters demonstrate that white Detroiters not only opposed the idea of Blacks moving into all-white neighborhoods but were enraged by African Americans' audacity in "buying the best goddamned house on the block"[144]—that they were successful and affluent enough to purchase a home in such neighborhoods. Likewise, Black entrepreneurs like Ossian Sweet saw whites' violent response as an attack on a long-term investment, on the wealth they had worked hard to accumulate. When the police came to his door after shots were fired on that September night and asked, "What in the hell are you fellows shooting about?" Ossian Sweet gave this answer: "They are ruining my property."[145]

In his defense of the Sweets, attorney Clarence Darrow successfully argued that people, regardless of their race, had the right to protect their family and property. Darrow's closing arguments on May 18, 1926, asked the all-white jury to reflect on why there were so many African Americans in Detroit: "Gentlemen, why are they here? They came here as you came here, under the laws of trade and business, under the instincts to live. . . . Your factories were open to them. Mr. Ford hired them. The automobile companies hired them. Everybody hired them. . . . You and I are willing to give them work, too. We are willing to have them in our homes to take care of the children and do the rough work that we shun ourselves. . . . The colored people must live some-where."[146] While Darrow's statement was true for most southern Blacks who migrated to Detroit, his argument ironically did not fit the Sweets' case. This idea contributes to the erasure of Black entrepreneurs in the narrative of the Great Migration. Dr. Sweet had not come to Detroit to work in an automobile factory or do "rough work" for whites. As a member of the Black middle class, Gladys Sweet did not work in a white home taking care of white children. Migrant entrepreneurs traveled north to work hard, make smart business decisions, enjoy the profits of their labor, and have enduring success. They perhaps underestimated how difficult that would be, with racial violence being an ever-present risk of doing business while Black in America.

An Allied Black Business Community

In 1929, the Michigan People's Finance Corporation (MPFC) began con-struction on a new building at the corner of St. Antoine Street and Vernor Highway. Hailed as the "first co-operative step in the matter of building that has been attempted in Detroit," Black entrepreneurs celebrated the structure as one of the major "forward steps the Negroes in this Community are mak-ing towards bettering their economic status." The space was to have six offices and five stores, and Black entrepreneurs rented out all of them before the building was even completed.[147] The entire venture—establishing the MPFC itself (in 1923), constructing a new building, Black entrepreneurs' support and personal gains in renting the space—is a prime example of how business cooperation in Detroit enabled individual success and benefited the Black community's freedom enterprise as a whole. The obstacles African Amer-icans faced in their attempts to establish and expand profitable businesses required that they work together. Relying on cooperative endeavors like the MPFC and on one another, Blacks in Detroit built an allied and flourishing business community in the 1920s.

Significantly, many of these cooperative enterprises provided essential ser-vices that Black Detroiters often had difficulty accessing. For example, prior to 1925, attempting to patronize white-operated cemeteries resulted in humili-ating and frustrating restrictions, segregated entrances, and inequitably high prices. This discriminatory treatment motivated a group of Black entrepre-neurs to jointly purchase land and set up a cemetery of their own: Detroit Memorial Park Cemetery (the first Black-owned cemetery in Michigan). Their goal was to charge reasonable prices while allowing people to bury their loved ones with dignity.[148] Founding Detroit Memorial Park Cemetery was one way Black entrepreneurs worked toward strengthening the Black business community and uplifting the race.

Charles C. Diggs Sr., a successful funeral director who arrived in Detroit on the eve of the Great Migration in 1913, spearheaded the project. Like many Black entrepreneurs and professionals, Diggs originally worked in a different industry entirely—shoe repair—but eventually saved enough money to study embalming and begin a more lucrative career. Diggs established his own funeral home in 1921, and just four years later he endeavored to organize a cemetery that would benefit Detroit's growing Black community.[149] Diggs had been heavily involved in the UNIA—he managed the Detroit UNIA's property and was the head of the Board of Trustees—and although he ultimately left the organization, he remained committed to cooperative economic uplift and Black self-determination.[150]

Establishing Detroit Memorial Park Cemetery was a massive undertaking that required the cooperation of Black physicians, hospitals, embalmers, and funeral directors. In 1925, Diggs approached twenty associates with the idea of establishing a Black-owned cemetery. The group included Dr. Robert Greenidge, Reverend Bradby of the Second Baptist Church, fellow funeral directors, and other local entrepreneurs and professionals. Diggs asked them to each invest in five shares of stock to launch the venture. This initial group of investors were experienced businesspeople, which allowed them to pool their resources and skills. They used their $25,000 collective investment to purchase sixty acres of land just outside of Detroit in Warren Township.[151] By 1927, Detroit Memorial Park Cemetery had conducted over three hundred burials and continued to offer "profitable investment" opportunities for African Americans. Moreover, by the 1940s, the Detroit Memorial Park Association was lucrative and financially stable enough to provide home loans to Black Detroiters who faced discrimination from white banks. Thus, the entrepreneurs who originally established the cemetery not only provided Detroit's African Americans with a vital service and ongoing financial opportunities but also built a practical mechanism to increase Black homeownership.[152] In this way, Detroit Memorial Park Cemetery exemplifies the collectivism that characterized Detroit's Black business community and enabled it to thrive in the 1920s. A commitment to the community's freedom enterprise among Black entrepreneurs was the backbone of Detroit's Black business boom in the 1920s.

*   *   *

The arrival of Black southern migrants in Detroit had a transformative impact for Black business development in the city during the 1910s and 1920s. Before the mass influx of Blacks from the South, it was not possible for African Americans to maintain an independent business community. Starting in the mid-1910s, "Old Detroiters" took advantage of the entrepreneurial opportunities that accompanied the migration and established new businesses that finally had a sizable enough Black patronage to succeed. At the same time, migrant entrepreneurs settled in Detroit and began pursuing their freedom enterprises. Though southern migrants undoubtedly found more social liberty and opportunities in Detroit, they also discovered that many racial and economic inequalities persisted. They learned that the city's political economy created an unequal playing field for African Americans and encountered violence from whites, which they had hoped to leave behind in the South. Despite the restrictions of racial capitalism in the North, the increased migration following World War I created more demand for Black entrepreneurs' goods and services and the number of Black-owned businesses increased. Crucially, the 1920–21 depression served as a catalyst for Black entrepreneurs to work together for joint economic uplift. Many were inspired by Marcus Garvey's vision of economic Black nationalism and continued to apply collectivist self-determination to their business practices long after his popularity diminished. Entrepreneurs cultivated cooperative enterprises, many of which provided essential services to African American Detroiters such as Black-owned hospitals, grocery stores, and financial institutions. Organizations like the UNIA, the Detroit Urban League, and Second Baptist Church helped foster networks that proved instrumental to Black business growth. While class and cultural schisms still existed, by the decade's end Detroiters had built an allied Black business community. However, the economic boom would not last forever. The impending stock market crash of 1929 and its aftermath would impact Detroit's Black business community in various ways. This included pushing many to turn to illegal entrepreneurial activities or deepen their existing financial ties to the illicit economy as a way to deal with the crushing disparities of racial capitalism.

CHAPTER 3

Hustling: Ilegal Entrepreneurship and the Financing of Black Business

The needs of a society determine its ethics, and in the
Black American ghettos the hero is that man who is
offered only the crumbs from his country's table but
by ingenuity and courage is able to take for himself a
Lucullan feast. . . . Stories of law violations are weighed
on a different set of scales in the Black mind than in the
white. Petty crimes embarrass the community and many
people wistfully wonder why Negroes don't rob more
banks, embezzle more funds and employ graft in unions.
"We are the victims of the world's most comprehensive
robbery. Life demands a balance. It's all right if we do a
little robbing now." This belief appeals particularly to one
who is unable to compete legally with his fellow citizens.

—Maya Angelou

The above quotation from Maya Angelou's *I Know Why the Caged Bird Sings* provides keen insight into Black quotidian thought about engaging in illegal business during the Great Migration years. This literary representation of African Americans' understanding of racial capitalism had very real connections to the lived experience of Black southern migrants in cities like San Francisco, New York, Chicago, and Detroit. In a familiar pattern, Angelou and her brother Bailey moved to California from Stamps, Arkansas, with their mother in large part due to an incident involving racial violence.[1] They settled first in Oakland and eventually in San Francisco. Angelou's mother, Vivian Baxter, was familiar with Oakland's underground economy, as she and a business partner ran a restaurant that also functioned as a casino. In San Francisco, Angelou's stepfather, Texas transplant "Daddy Clidell," was a successful businessman. He owned apartment buildings and pool halls and taught Angelou how to play various card games, including "poker, blackjack, tonk and high, low, Kick, Jack and the Game." Through her stepfather, she was introduced to "the most colorful characters in the Black underground" and listened to the stories of successful con men and entrepreneurs who engaged in illegal business. According to Angelou, "By all accounts those storytellers, born Black and male before the turn of the twentieth century, should have been ground into useless dust. Instead they used their intelligence to pry open the door of rejection and not only became wealthy but got some revenge in the bargain." Notably, she continued, "it wasn't possible for me to regard them as criminals or to be anything but proud of their achievements."[2]

Though this story is about California in the second wave of the Great Migration, it is instructive for understanding the everyday economic thought of migrant entrepreneurs in Detroit. The sentiment that African Americans were the "victims of the world's most comprehensive robbery" and "unable to compete legally with [their] fellow citizens" articulates the viewpoint of many migrant entrepreneurs who engaged in illegal business. Though historical actors did not use the term "racial capitalism," the racialized economic exploitation and hierarchy they described aligns with this framework. Knowing that they could not get a fair shake in the legal economy, entrepreneurs attempted to create a more level playing field by engaging in the illegal economy.

Illicit trade was an important sector for Detroit's Black entrepreneurs, especially during the interwar period. Many Blacks survived the depression and some profited greatly from illegal businesses and scams, or what Detroit's future mayor Coleman Young called "Black Bottom economics."[3] According to Young, "Prohibition and, in turn, the Great Depression converted Black Bottom into a haven for hustlers of every stripe."[4] Much of the Black community in Detroit recognized some forms of illegal entrepreneurship—especially "numbers" gambling, also known as "policy"—as legitimate ways of making money.[5] As Young explained, "The money was jumping from pocket to pocket in those days. If you weren't making money you either weren't trying or were inhibited by an unusual code of lawful-ness."[6] African Americans were not inherently criminal or anti-law; how-ever, the reality of U.S. racial capitalism pushed them to work the system in ways that would be most beneficial to them, which included engaging in illegal business.

Black entrepreneurs who participated in illegal economic activities under-took serious risks, such as police harassment, violence, imprisonment, and even death. Still, participating in illegal enterprise was a rational choice for Blacks in America's racial capitalist system. After all, Black business owners had always operated within an environment of extreme risk whether their ventures were legal or not. As discussed in Chapter 1, Black entrepreneurs in the Jim Crow South faced threats, violence, and death while running their businesses. Perhaps navigating the inherently violent nature of racial capital-ism lessened their aversion to the specific dangers of illicit business. Given the peril of legal and illegal enterprises alike, the opportunity to reap greater rewards through illegal entrepreneurship may have been worth the risk. Thus, despite the danger, illicit business sometimes provided the self-determination and economic freedom southern migrants sought in the North.

Additionally, illicit business was essential for financing legally operated businesses in Detroit. Since white-owned financial institutions rarely pro-vided loans to African Americans, the start-up capital for legal Black-owned establishments often originated from illegal economic activities. Some busi-ness owners also maintained illegal operations alongside their lawful enter-prises. Coleman Young recalled,

> The local hat shop was a front for the biggest numbers operation on the east side. Dave Winslow made whiskey in the rear of his sweet shop. If you were stupid enough to walk into Lonnie's shoe shine parlor and ask for a shine while the poker and blackjack games were going on—which was most of the day and night—you were liable to get your ass beaten. . . . At Ike Portlock's tailor shop . . . there was usually a crowd of men shooting craps in the backroom. Ike kept as many as eight very large fellows on his payroll as bounc-ers and stick men.[7]

This intertwining of legal and illegal business practices in Detroit's Black community reveals African Americans' strategies for navigating the limita-tions of the wider political economy of racial capitalism.

A "Wide-Open Town"

Illegal entrepreneurial activities such as prostitution, gambling, and bootleg-ging were common in Detroit throughout the first half of the twentieth cen-tury. While these pursuits particularly flourished during Prohibition and the Great Depression, Detroit had developed a reputation for vice by the 1920s. Early twentieth-century America saw vice districts increasingly encroaching on Black neighborhoods in part as a result of Progressive campaigns to clean up cities and eradicate "white slavery"—prostitution and sex trafficking. Such campaigns seem to have been more lax in Black neighborhoods, which tended to be both over- and underpoliced, and often became what Kevin Mumford has called interzones: vice districts that served both Blacks and whites. This is certainly true of Chicago and New York.[8] However, Detroit's history of vice has a somewhat different trajectory.

The Near East Side, particularly the Black Bottom neighborhood, was already regarded as the city's vice district prior to the Great Migration. As the poorest and oldest section of the city, this area housed a mix of recent immigrants, Jews, and a small Black population. Accordingly, Detroit's early vice district was not predominantly Black. But when southern Black migrants arrived in droves, discrimination in the housing market forced them to join the city's existing African American community on the Near East Side. As the Black population increased, white residents left. The area continued to house the city's vice, which became increasingly associated with African Ameri-cans, even though whites also frequented its illegal enterprises. Thus, rather than being pushed into established Black neighborhoods as in other cities, Detroit's vice district became Blacker over time.[9]

The city's illicit economy was sustained by a diverse set of circumstances, including its proximity to Canada, the closure of Chicago's "red-light" dis-trict, and the presence of industrial workers who could spend their relatively high disposable incomes on leisure activities. The Detroit-Windsor area was the busiest interchange between the United States and Canada, and illegal liquor flowed from Canada through Detroit during the Prohibition years. This illegal trade became the second most profitable industry in the region (after automobile manufacturing) and also spurred related illicit activities including prostitution and gambling.[10] Windsor hosted two race tracks that drew American customers after racetrack betting was outlawed in the United States in the early twentieth century. As head of the Detroit Urban League Forrester B. Washington noted in 1916, "The proximity of the Windsor

(Canada) races, attracted the touts, the gamblers, book-makers and all the undesirable followers of the race track from all over the country."[11] Likewise, in 1918, sociologist George E. Haynes reported, "About ten years ago, the crusade in other parts of the country against race-tracks and the popularity of a race-track in Windsor, Canada, just across the river" had brought many "undesirable" people to Detroit, including "disreputable characters of other kinds than those who follow the race track."[12] Many of these newcomers settled near St. Antoine and Hastings Streets in Black Bottom. A 1911 vice campaign in Chicago also drove illicit entrepreneurs to Detroit. Washington explained, "When the reform wave struck Chicago and cut out at least a large part of the colored Red Light district, a great many proprietors of disorderly resorts and their hangers-on came to Detroit because it had the reputation of being a wide open town."[13] Haynes likewise noted that "the freedom from police interference caused Detroit to be known as a 'wide-open town.'"[14] Moreover, the Great Migration produced a higher demand for sex workers' services in Detroit. According to some Black community leaders, "To many male newcomers the house of prostitution furnishes a social center to which he has ready access and where he receives a cordial welcome."[15]

While Black Progressive reformers took issue with these demographic and economic changes, entrepreneurially driven African Americans reaped the benefits. Forrester Washington reported in 1920 that some of the most prosperous Black Detroiters were those who had "made their money in the under-world, when Detroit was a 'wide-open town.'" Washington gave an example of an "individual in Detroit today who is worth at least $200,000. Beginning as a waiter in a Detroit hotel he has been successively a gambler, proprietor of a gambling club, buyer and owner of apartment houses which he rents to both Negroes and whites and from a business block."[16] Illegal gambling thus existed in Detroit prior to the Great Migration, and it would become vitally important to the Black business community as the city's African American population continued to grow.

The Rewards and Risks of Illegal Business

Illicit business offered Black migrants the ability to escape backbreaking labor that paid little and often involved ill treatment from white bosses. Being able to work for yourself, even if it meant breaking the law, was seen as a better option than working in an industrial job or as a domestic worker under oppressive conditions.[17] In Detroit, the Ford Motor Company (FMC) was the major industrial employer for African Americans. By the mid-1920s, the FMC was known as a "man-killing place," and Black workers were known as "Ford mules."[18] Detroit migrant Charles Denby recalled: "I never wanted to work for Ford. And I never did work there. Everyone talked about it, they said it was the house of murder. . . . Everybody knew Ford was a 'man-killing' place."[19] Henry Ford and other manufacturers encouraged dictatorial behavior among their foremen, who constantly pressed for greater production by threatening workers.[20] It was not uncommon for Black workers to make explicit comparisons to slavery and refer to the FMC as "the plantation."[21] In one former employee's opinion, "It was too goddamn hard working for Ford. That assembly line stuff is a sonofabitch, I'm telling you. That's nothing but slavery."[22] Detroiter Walter Rosser agreed that a job with Ford in the 1930s meant working in "almost slave-like conditions," while Black journalist George S. Schuyler claimed that the FMC was "run like a Georgia plantation."[23] Many migrants had come north to escape plantations and other repressive working conditions in the South. Turning to illegal business might have seemed like a logical decision for those disillusioned by the work environment in places like the Ford Motor Company.

During the Great Depression, Black workers, especially those who had relied on employment from the FMC, were in dire straits. For entrepreneurs who engaged in Black Bottom economics, laid-off workers' mistreatment likely confirmed that they had made a sound choice. As Charles Denby explained, "During the depression, everything closed down once for two or three months. The paper came out asking for men for Ford's. The next morning there was a stampede at Ford of two thousand men at five a.m. They were only hiring fifty or one hundred workers." When the crowd did not disperse after Ford agents announced that they were no longer hiring, things turned violent. "The police rode up on horses and ran at the crowd hitting us with sticks," Denby remembered. "This didn't disperse the workers. The police called the Fire Department and they hooked up their hoses and shot cold water on us. It was the middle of winter. While we waited for the streetcars our clothes froze on us as hard as bricks."[24] That was the last time Denby went to the FMC looking for work.

However, it was not the last time unemployed workers experienced violence at the hands of the FMC. On March 7, 1932, three thousand to five thousand unemployed and laid-off workers organized a hunger march to demand jobs. FMC security guards, along with the Dearborn Police Department, fired into the crowd, killing five and injuring sixty protesters.[25] Violent incidents like these taught Black migrants an important lesson about what to expect if their livelihoods depended upon industrial employment. Many African Americans who engaged in both legal and illegal entrepreneurship had greater autonomy and were not at the mercy of the caprices of the Ford Motor Company and other industrial employers.

In the 1930s, the employment situation was particularly dire for Black women, who were virtually shut out of work in the auto industry.[26] During the 1910s and 1920s, Black women mostly worked in domestic service positions, often obtained through the Detroit Urban League's Employment Office. But during the depression, domestic work became increasingly scarce. As industrial unemployment increased among white working-class men, their households necessarily reduced their reliance on weekly or monthly domestic laborers. Ernestine Wright remembered, "In the early '30s . . . Blacks didn't have any decent jobs anyway and lost what they did have, which was domestic service." Moreover, the few women who managed to secure domestic work did not make enough to live on. Domestic servants' wages dropped to as low as one dollar a day during the depression. Without viable employment options, some African American women decided to participate in illegal activities such as the numbers game or sex work.[27]

A 1926 research report noted that while "prostitution is more prevalent proportionately among the colored than among whites," it was "economic pressure which, according to authorities, drove colored women into prostitution."[28] Also writing about sex work in the early 1940s, journalist Ulysses Boykin claimed that the reason "for the large percentage of Negro women prostitutes is . . . economics. So long as sweat shop conditions exist, and low pay for women, prostitution was turned to in order to supplement their income."[29] Yet sex work did not necessarily guarantee adequate income for women. As the author of a 1933 study on prostitution in Detroit concluded, "The depression has brought no more prostitution but many more prostitutes."[30] The decline in men's wages combined with increased numbers of sex workers made prostitution more competitive and less lucrative during the 1930s. Sex workers also faced competition from "charity girls" who "exchanged sexual favors for a night out or viewed sexuality as an expression of freedom and independence."[31] Additionally, men who worked as pimps extracted a profit from women's earnings. The Detroit Urban League (DUL), for example, reported that "a certain young man who came from a good family in the South . . . had fallen in vicious company and was living in a very bad environment." The DUL found that he was "a so-called panderer living upon the earnings of immoral women, that he is one of the extreme type of 'pimps.'"[32] Conversely, some women also worked as pimps and exploited other women for profit.[33]

Black Bottom was closely monitored by the Detroit Police Department, making the risk of police harassment or violence higher for Blacks engaging in illegal business than for whites. Ulysses Boykin pointed this out with respect to prostitution, arguing that higher arrest rates among African Americans was a result of stricter law enforcement toward Blacks.[34] This was the case for other illegal activities as well. Police disproportionately arrested Black men for carrying or possessing concealed weapons between 1930 and 1945.[35] This trend would continue; in 1958, Detroit police arrested 1,793 Blacks for gambling, compared to 161 whites.[36] Police also harassed African Americans when looking for evidence of illegal activities. In 1940, Boykin complained that Detroit police would "needlessly stop vehicle operators, search their cars, and give them tickets for traffic violations when they fail to find gambling paraphernalia in such cars."[37] Such encounters with police could turn deadly. A 1926 report on crime among African Americans in Detroit outlined several incidents in which police killed sex workers and bootleggers during raids on illicit businesses.[38]

Carrying guns was common among residents of Black Bottom, in part because of the southern gun culture that migrants brought with them.[39] However, when illicit activities were prevalent during the 1930s, guns were sometimes used as a tool to conduct business. For instance, in 1935, Louis Spann, a thirty-five-year-old transplant from Alabama, established the Central Detective Agency and the National Private Police Company, which he ran out of a rented office at 1911 St. Antoine Street. In 1940, the news broke that these agencies supplied armed guards for Black-owned gambling houses. Operating under the guise of "special police"—citizens temporarily appointed as patrolmen for the city—these guards were officially licensed to carry firearms due to Spann's affiliation with three African American officers who worked on the police department's Special Investigation Squad. When four of the guards were arrested during a gambling raid, the city opened an investigation into Spann's agencies. In a statement issued through his lawyer, prominent African American attorney Harold E. Bledsoe, Spann admitted that his armed guards aided "various persons, firms and business establishments in transferring large sums of money which they had in their care and custody to banks, finance companies, and private individuals" but emphatically denied involvement in any illegal operations.[40]

This would not be Louis Spann's last encounter with the law. In 1945, he was found guilty of second-degree murder for shooting and killing twenty-one-year-old James Folks Jr. at the Royal Ark Tavern, a business Spann owned in River Rouge. According to witnesses, Spann grabbed a gun from behind the bar and fired while Folks was arguing with and slapping a woman in his establishment, after he had allegedly warned Folks against causing a disturbance.[41] Such examples illustrate that those conducting illegal (and legal) business not only had to worry about violence from police, competitors, or unhappy customers but also sometimes engaged in violence to protect their livelihoods.

Throughout the Great Depression, local Black newspapers frequently reported on illicit business activities and accompanying violent crimes. Some community leaders found this coverage of Black criminal behavior damaging to efforts to advance Blacks' social position.[42] For example, William J. Robinson, a journalist for the *Detroit Independent*, had this to say of African American gangsters: "They got out their guns and went to work, and the race in general has been made to share in their shame."[43] In the same vein, two Detroit clubwomen, Geraldine Bledsoe and Nellie Watts, wrote a letter to the editor of the Black-owned *Detroit Tribune* to complain about sensationalized coverage of Black crime. A veteran newspaperman responded to the women's letter in the subsequent issue, "I have been in the newspaper business since 1928. . . . I am in sympathy with Miss Watts and Mrs. Bledsoe's complaint." But the writer also reminded the women that a newspaper was primarily a business and "the first consideration of any business is to satisfy as many of its customers as is humanly possible." While he agreed that Black newspapers had a responsibility to their community, they also needed to be profitable. Since crime news sold more newspapers, he concluded, "Don't tell papers how to run their business."[44]

Opposition to illicit business and crime was not just a matter of respectability politics; these practices inflicted real harm on the Black community. Although some people were able to make good money this way, others suffered. As scholar Davarian Baldwin argues, "For sure, policy [gambling] was a blend of exploitation and enterprise, both capitalizing on the dire economic conditions of Black residents and circulating money back into the Black community."[45] Indeed, *Black Metropolis*, St. Clair Drake and Horace Cayton's famous 1945 study on Chicago, noted that "opponents [of illegal gambling] on religious grounds are relatively few," while a more prevalent objection related to economic harm: "There are people playing policy that should be buying something to eat or buying themselves some clothes"; "Most of the players are poor people who can't afford to gamble."[46] In Detroit, Ulysses Boykin likewise observed that "newcomers became victims of many money-baiting and 'get-rich-quick' schemes in their struggle to make a living" and that "spiritualists, cult leaders, and fortune tellers made large sums from releasing 'tips'" to gullible players of the numbers game.[47] Gambling establishments also tampered with their paraphernalia to stack the odds in the house's favor and cheat customers. For example, a policy game operating out of Detroit's Gotham Hotel utilized dice that were beveled to make it easier for the house to win. Additionally, the house marked red-backed playing cards so that workers wearing infrared contact lenses could tell what cards their patrons held.[48]

Thus, some profited from conning members of their own race and caused economic harm in the Black community. Future Detroit mayor Coleman Young inadvertently participated in a con that "exercised a conspicuous mastery of Black Bottom economics." The scheme involved selling tickets to a show with "forty French girls" that was supposed to take place in a hall on Hastings Street. After collecting the money for tickets, Young realized that the show's promoter was a fraud and made a break for it (with the money he collected) before the customers realized that there would be no performance.[49] These types of schemes were lucrative for those running them but could be devastating to those who were duped.

Still, not everyone in the Black community saw people who participated in unlawful activities as dangerous criminals or threats. Margaret Ward recalled, "St. Antoine was the street that ran the gamut of businesses, from legal to illegal. [As teenagers] my sister and I would . . . walk through St. Antoine. . . . We had never been treated in any way but with great respect. No one bothered anybody, and we were very safe and very, very secure."[50] Similarly, as a small child Lillian Duplessis would walk home from music class on Saturdays and see people engaging in illegal activity:

> The sidewalks between St. Matthews and Gratiot Avenue were just packed with men waiting to see what the policy number was gonna be, and they would write it on a little blackboard and put it up in the window. Well, my mother told me: "Those men aren't gonna bother you. You just walk straight through and act like you know where you're going, and don't look around like you're looking for anything, and they won't bother you." And sure enough, they didn't.

They would just make a path; and if someone didn't see us coming, someone would say, "Hey man, get out of the way. Don't you see that little girl coming down the street?"[51]

Reflections like these demonstrate that illicit business dealings were both common and, to an extent, accepted as a rational response to racial capitalism. Perhaps this was because many Black Detroiters themselves (or people close to them) also sometimes participated in unlawful pursuits.

The "Detroit Funnel": Prohibition and Bootlegging

The State of Michigan went dry before the nation did. In November 1916, citizens of Michigan voted in support of measures prohibiting "the manufacture, sale, giving away, bartering or furnishing of any vinous, malt, brewed, fermented, spiritous or intoxicating liquors, except for medicinal, mechanical, chemical, scientific or sacramental purposes." Prohibition went into effect in the state in early 1918.[52] The passing of prohibition legislation was largely due to the efforts of Detroit's largest firm, the Ford Motor Company, and Progressive reformers who wanted to eradicate working-class saloons.[53] Despite initial enthusiasm for a dry Detroit, the city ironically became one of the nation's major import sites for illegal alcohol during Prohibition.

Detroit's geography was ideal for trafficking illegal liquor. There was a Hiram Walker whiskey distillery across the river in Windsor, Ontario, which fostered the proliferation of smuggling operations. The Detroit River has many inlets and canals, which enabled countless bootleggers to furtively transport illegal alcohol and, if necessary, make a quick getaway. In fact, there was so much "rum-running" traffic across the river that the Detroit Tunnel was called the "Detroit Funnel." Hoping to halt the unlawful transport of liquor, the State of Michigan amended its laws at least seven times to increase Prohibition enforcement.[54]

Many ordinary people worked in the bootlegging trade. Coleman Young learned the business from his father, who routinely brokered whiskey obtained from Canada to half a dozen federal judges. According to Young, "I was not in my father's league as a hustler, but it wasn't for lack of trying. Along with several well-chosen friends, I had my own little bootleg business during prohibition." One strategy to avoid the Coast Guard that constantly patrolled the river was for bootleggers to only carry small cargoes that they

Figure 4. Bootleggers driving alcohol across the frozen Detroit River. Walter P. Reuther Library, Archives of Labor and Urban Affairs, Wayne State University.

could quickly drop into the water when law enforcement approached. Often, they would have to unload the liquor just before making it to shore. The job of young people like Coleman Young was to mark the spot where bootleggers dumped the cargo and return first thing the next morning to dive in and retrieve the goods. According to Young, once the illegal liquor made it to Detroit's shores, selling it was no problem; there were plenty of Prohibition saloons eager to buy it. But swimming in the Detroit River was no easy task; it was a highly risky aspect of the business. In fact, Young and his friends had to end their profitable operation after one of their best swimmers got caught in the undercurrent and drowned.[55]

Not everyone who smuggled liquor into Detroit used a boat. When the Detroit River froze in the winter, many simply drove alcohol exported from Canada over the ice.[56] Reginald Larrie remembered that bootleggers also built a tunnel under the Detroit River, wide enough to pull a cart through: "It was like a dumbwaiter, and they ran whiskey from Canada under the river. They had speedboats on top of the water as decoys." The police thought they were

Figure 5. A Detroit
man smuggling flasks
of alcohol. Walter P.
Reuther Library,
Archives of Labor and
Urban Affairs, Wayne
State University.

chasing the bootleggers, and the bootleggers were bringing the liquor under the water.[57] Once in Detroit, bootleggers would also use tunnels to transport alcohol between buildings.[58]

Transporters who moved through public spaces were more easily monitored by authorities and so took on the biggest risks during Prohibition. Comparatively, bootleggers who manufactured and sold liquor in their homes or businesses minimized their risk of being caught. Speakeasies were usually difficult to spot and closed off to strangers. According to Henry Biggs, "There was a speakeasy on the corner [of Woodward Avenue], a cigar store it was supposed to be, but you could go in there if you were known . . . because there was always a guard there. When they let you in, they just pushed a little button underneath the counter, and this wall would go back, and you could go in the closed back apartment."[59] While bootleggers shouldered different levels of risk depending on their approach, the business was profitable for all involved.

But the lucrative Prohibition era did not last forever. On March 22, 1933, President Franklin Roosevelt signed the Cullen-Harris Act, which authorized the sale of 3.2 percent beer.[60] This allowed legal enterprises to sell alcohol again, and many new Black-owned cafés and restaurants sprung up. By May 1933, such establishments began advertising that they were now selling beer and wine. For example, Gold's Drug Store announced that they offered "legalized 3.2 Beer," while Mack's Barbecue & Beer Palace highlighted the selection of "3.2 Beer & Wine Choice Brands" that patrons could expect at the restaurant's grand opening.[61] Similarly, the newly established Williams' Cafe advertised their selection of imported and domestic beer, "back on the scene after 15 years."[62] This boom in venues selling beer provided not only local employment but also lucrative opportunities for other Black entrepreneurs. The proprietors of the Creole Kitchen, for instance, promoted their "fine assortment of famous bottled beers" but made sure to also highlight that "Negro craftsmen" were responsible for the business's decoration and construction.[63] Likewise, entrepreneurs in the real estate sector benefited from the upsurge in businesses wanting to sell alcohol; as one W. S. Fornay advertisement suggested, "Large store, just the room and location for a Beer Garden or other Business."[64]

Restaurant and club owners likely experienced an increase in patronage and personal prosperity with the restored ability to serve "Real Beer and Wine." But despite invitations like that of the Cotton Club to "Come and Drink Prosperity Back," many of the patrons who spent their money at these new establishments were struggling financially.[65] Prohibition may have ended, but the nation's economic depression had not. Accordingly, African Americans in Detroit continued to engage in illicit business activities outside the bootlegging realm during the 1930s.

"Policy Existed as a Business": Black Detroiters and Illegal Gambling

The most profitable illicit business sector in 1930s Detroit was gambling. Known as the "numbers game," "clearinghouse," or "policy," the most popular form of gambling was essentially a lottery.[66] Though these names are often used synonymously, there were distinctions between "numbers" games. In clearinghouse, the winning three-digit number was drawn from the banks' clearinghouse reports published in daily newspapers. Players could bet as little as one cent and operators paid odds of 500 or 600 to 1; that is, a one-cent bet would pay out five or six dollars while a one-dollar bet would net the winner six hundred dollars. Since the clearinghouse numbers originated from an independent source and could not be fixed, this was viewed as a safer bet compared to policy. In policy, bets started at five cents and the numbers were drawn by spinning a wheel or shaking a container. The winning numbers were printed on long strips of paper and distributed throughout the city so players could check their numbers and collect a payout through their local numbers runner or at policy houses with names honoring migrants' southern roots, such as the "Yellow Dog" and "Alabama and Georgia."[67] Detroit businessman Sunnie Wilson described the process for playing the numbers this way: "If you wanted to play policy, you had to contact a Black numbers-man. They weren't hard to find; they operated all over town. The pickup numbers-men had their own districts and solicited business in their respective areas. They picked up your number in the morning and later that day, the numbers runners distributed a sheet listing the winning digits. You checked to see if you hit the right combination. If your numbers matched, they brought you the money the same day."[68]

The numbers game started in Detroit during the World War I wave of migration and grew as the Black population increased. Ulysses Boykin attributed the development of the numbers game to "Negroes' desire to take chances and to bet in hopes of getting enough money to help raise him from poverty."[69] It was also an accessible way for people to gamble since these games did not require a lot of money to participate—an important factor for recent migrants trying to establish themselves in a new city. By 1926, urban authorities reported:

Evidence has not been lacking that there is much gambling among the colored people of Detroit who fancy this past time. There are many establishments for games of chance. These places are usually carefully placed so as to be secure from interruption by unwelcome visitors, and in order to gain admittance to most of them a person must be vouched for by someone who is well-known to the manager of the place. These houses provide all the card games, dice, machines, put and take, and in addition many of them have departments where bets may be placed on races and such events. Although some of these places operate under the guise of social clubs and are licensed as such, many of them carry on without a license. There is very little open gambling, however, although in at least one case the "beater" for the establishment takes up his position near the place and seeks to persuade likely looking passersby to enter by quietly announcing the type of game that is going on within.[70]

Interestingly, the report included this description under the recreation section (as "commercialized vice") instead of the crime or business section. This
categorization demonstrates that locals viewed gambling's status as somewhat ambiguous—as in between the confines of the law. While gambling was
illegal, the numbers came to "have a legitimate place in the Detroit Negro
community."[71]

Some Black leaders viewed gambling as a vice and spoke out against the
numbers game. In 1928, the Colored Ministers Association organized a publicity campaign to combat the pervasiveness of the game. But by the 1930s, the
harsh economic conditions of the depression caused many such opponents to
change their position. They recognized that this illicit business provided jobs
for Blacks who would otherwise be out of work, and winnings from hitting
the right number helped families in a financial bind. Moreover, the popularity of the numbers game was simply unstoppable.[72] According to Coleman
Young, just about everyone in the community participated as business owners, employees, or players: "The only people not in the hustle were mothers
and preachers, although it was hardly unanimous in their cases, either. Even
my grandmother . . . played policy."[73]

Entrepreneur Sunnie Wilson maintained, "Policy existed as a business."[74]
Ulysses Boykin, who at one time worked in the numbers game, likewise
argued, "This racket has all the earmarks of big business and grew from a
penny game played chiefly by Negroes over twenty years ago to a ten million
dollar a year racket, giving employment to hundreds of men and women in
jobs such as clerks, writers, and pick-up men."[75] Indeed, the numbers industry grew so much during the Great Depression that by the early 1940s it was
the largest Black business sector in Detroit. And Boykin was correct: numbers operators and bankers could make huge amounts of money. Although
Wilson was not inclined to participate himself, he noted, "My friends who did
go into the numbers became millionaires."[76] Even Black Detroiters who were
college educated, well-connected, and already wealthy, such as lawyer and
businessman John Roxborough, chose to forge a path in the illicit industry.
Roxborough's success in operating some of the city's largest policy houses
and status as a "numbers racket czar" did not undermine his elite reputation.
Described in the press as "suavely college bred" and known as the richest
Black man in Detroit, Roxborough accumulated his wealth primarily from
the numbers business. Moreover, while his privilege and connections could
have landed him any job he wanted—and indeed, he was involved in an array

of local enterprises—his choice to remain a powerful force in the numbers game demonstrates just how profitable policy was and why many considered participating in it a sound business decision.[77]

Those outside Detroit's Black elite also found the numbers game to be a lucrative alternative to the jobs typically available to African Americans, especially during the depression. Often barred from the professions for which they had trained, many college graduates turned to the numbers, some becoming so successful that they chose to continue the vocation even after the economy stabilized and other positions became available.[78] In addition, for Black women, whose options were generally limited to domestic service, joining the numbers game was a welcome respite from white employers' harassment and lower wages. While it is possible that some women operated numbers businesses with their husbands, the majority worked as clerks and checkers in Detroit's gambling houses.[79] Some, such as Missouri migrant Charleszetta Waddles, also worked as pickup women. Waddles was forced to seek relief from the city after her husband was laid off, but the aid she received was not enough to provide for her children. Needing supplemental income, Waddles explained, "I learned to pick up numbers as a side thing, you know. I'd walk from house to house and pick up numbers."[80] For Waddles and many other women, this type of work was a preferable way—and sometimes the only way—to support themselves and their families.

The numbers game was so ubiquitous, even if owners of legitimate enterprises disapproved of the practice, they often felt compelled to participate in order to retain their clientele. Many barbers, beauticians, newspaper vendors, and lunch-counter workers sold numbers as an expected part of their occupational duties. Describing the bind in which Black entrepreneurs operated, a prominent dentist remarked: "What can I do when one of my patients asks me to buy a number? If I don't play with him he'll go somewhere else for his dental work."[81] It was hard enough to maintain small businesses during the depression. If customers wanted to play the numbers while ordering lunch or getting their teeth cleaned, it was in Black entrepreneurs' best interests to oblige.

Eventually, Detroit's numbers business became so extensive that workers organized and sometimes even went on strike. In 1941, for example, five hundred members of the Policy Writers Association of Metropolitan Detroit stopped work due to dissatisfaction with their overall pay and bonuses on winning slips. The strike affected seven large local policy houses including the Yellow Dog, Alabama and Georgia, and North and Westend. Rather than picket, the strikers simply refused to write any more tickets until the dispute was resolved. As the committee spokesperson reasoned, "They can't do business unless we turn in our money. All we have to do is keep a united front."[82]

Auxiliary industries arose from the numbers game as well. One Detroit man operated a business that specialized in printing slips for several large policy houses in the city, including the Big Four Policy House and North End Station. This kind of enterprise was not without risks; when caught in a raid, the owner was arrested and charged with possession of gambling equipment.[83] But the most popular numbers-adjacent businesses were those purported to aid people in the game: spiritual advisors and numerologists' services, retail goods such as lucky oils and roots or "jinx removal" candles, and dream and numerology books—products intended to translate people's dreams into predicting winning numbers.[84] Additionally, Detroit numbers banks purchased insurance from a national "Cover Bank," which underwrote local banks' bets as protection against excessive losses for numbers that were "hot" (i.e., heavily played on a particular day).[85] Numbers operators sometimes infringed upon the territory of secondary businesses. For example, eight Detroit policy house operators, including John Roxborough and Everett Watson, reprinted verbatim a 1933 dream book called *The Original Three Wise Men*. Mallory F. Banks, who published the text under the pseudonym Professor Zonie, sued the policy house owners in 1940. Although his attorney would not reveal the amount Banks was awarded, the settlement was described as "highly satisfactory."[86]

Everybody knew that the numbers business was illegal and had negative aspects, such as exploiting already vulnerable people in the community. Yet many Black Detroiters viewed the numbers business as a means of working for the common good.[87] As William Hines explained, "Of course, it was considered illegal, but that money was put to good use in the Black community, with the dollar turning over in the community five or six times. The pickup man, the lady that wrote the number, pickup man, the other pickup man, to the owner. The owner had all Blacks working for his area."[88] Numbers bankers' philanthropy also contributed to the community's positive impression. According to Sunnie Wilson, "Numbers money also helped create scholarships for young people to attend school."[89] Even Reverend William Peck, pastor of Bethel AME Church and founder of the Booker T. Washington Trade Association, acknowledged the positive role that illegal business played in the community during the depression. He affirmed, "The church which I was pastoring needed money to complete a construction contract that had begun on the church building. Mr. ____ [a numbers banker] did not wait for me to ask help of him but came and offered the full amount needed to complete the job."[90]

Significantly, in many cases the revenue from illegal sources laid the foundation for legal ventures, increasing Black economic enterprise and subsequently offering legitimate employment to youths trained in business.[91] In Detroit's Black community, the formal and informal economies were inextricably connected and as Victoria Wolcott has noted, "The depression greatly blurred the already indistinct lines between the formal and informal economy."[92] Money made from illegal entrepreneurship fed the legal economy and vice versa. As Sunnie Wilson put it, "Blacks used this money to build housing. They founded insurance companies, loan offices, newspapers, and real-estate firms. The numbers bought the Walter Norwood's Norwood Hotel and Slim Jones's Chocolate Bar."[93]

Illicit business was sometimes the only way for Blacks to establish legal enterprises. While legal financial institutions routinely refused to work with African Americans, numbers banks provided Black entrepreneurs with essential credit and loans.[94] A 1926 report on Black Detroit noted that one of the major handicaps to operating a business was securing capital from white banks. Almost half of the business owners surveyed reported "difficulty in attempting to borrow capital from the banks for the purpose of financing their concern."[95] An advertisement for the Black-owned Michigan People's Finance Corporation (MPFC) acknowledged this issue, proclaiming, "The problem of finance is a big one in both business and private life. . . . Bring us your financial problems."[96] Yet while Black-owned financial bodies were important institutions in the community, they too had limitations. For example, MPFC only offered small loans up to $500, which was inadequate startup capital for certain businesses.

Moreover, as a Black-owned enterprise, MPFC had a difficult time securing funding for its own operations. In 1929, the company was forced to repeatedly reassess its financing options for constructing a new location on the 600 block of East Vernor Highway, since the white-owned Detroit Savings Bank rejected its loan applications. After much deliberation, MPFC ultimately took out a mortgage for $24,735.95 with a 7 percent interest rate from private philanthropist Henry G. Stevens in June 1929 and added a second $10,000 mortgage in August. This loan also had an interest rate of 7 percent but, unlike the first, was to be paid back within six months. Stevens had been the first president of the Detroit Urban League when it was established in

1916. It seems the MPFC had to draw on all its connections to secure the necessary financing to construct a new office building.[97]

In addition to these difficulties, the Michigan People's Finance Corporation experienced ongoing financial struggles, even before the depression. By December 31, 1928, MPFC had outstanding loans of $28,000 and the company's 1929 semiannual review conveyed signs of financial trouble. Noting a decline in both income and interest earned compared to the previous year, the report concluded, "This is clear evidence of a frail financial structure which would, no doubt, collapse under stringent circumstances."[98] With profits continuing to decrease, the company also failed to repay Stevens's $10,000 loan within the allotted six months. In 1930, MPFC business manager Ferdinand W. Penn reported, "Up to the present time, only $500.00 has been paid on the principal, leaving a balance of $9,500."[99] MPFC continued to struggle as the depression wore on but managed to crawl along until the late 1930s.[100] Thus, despite being Detroit's primary Black financial institution throughout the 1920s and 1930s, MPFC was quite limited in what it could offer Black Detroiters interested in opening or expanding their businesses, and its fiscal fragility likely did not provide the same sense of security as a numbers bank.

Given Black-owned institutions' limitations and white-owned banks' biased practices, numbers bankers were often Black entrepreneurs' only means of securing adequate start-up capital. By the mid-1930s, there were at least thirty-five numbers banks in the city, many appropriately located in the buildings of defunct former banks.[101] According to native Detroiter Leroy Mitchell, "The backbone of the Black economics in the '30s and even maybe before that was the numbers. This is how our money was really accumulated." Referring to Sidney Barthwell, proprietor of nine drugstores and one of the city's most successful Black entrepreneurs, Mitchell continued, "Even Barthwell, the numbers guys help set him up. . . . Many Black businesses had numbers men behind them."[102] Simply put, the legal Black business community in Detroit could not have developed without capital from the numbers game.

Many entrepreneurs who enthusiastically ran numbers houses also operated legal businesses. This was prudent for those drawing their wealth from illegal endeavors, as investing in legal enterprises allowed them to spread the risk between ventures. Bill Mosley, a prominent numbers banker, owned the *Detroit Independent* newspaper, and had controlling interest in a funeral home, and the Great Lakes Mutual Insurance Company. Mosley also owned several commercial and residential properties.[103] Likewise, successful policy entrepreneur Everett Watson was in the real estate business, serving as president of Watson Realty Company and Watson Insurance Agency, among other ventures. Watson was also vice president of Wayne County Better Homes, a construction corporation launched in 1943 by a group of Detroit's Black leaders and business owners.[104] As mentioned previously, lawyer and wealthy numbers banker John Roxborough also had diverse business interests, including insurance and real estate. The "Negro financier," as Roxborough was described in the press, was the chairman of the board of directors of the Superior Life Insurance Society and vice president of the Great Lakes Land and Investment Company, though he was most famous for his role as principal manager to Joe Louis, heavyweight boxing champion of the world.[105]

When problems arose within the numbers game, Black operators banded together to manage them. One such issue was competition from whites trying to infringe upon their territory. Policy houses in Black Bottom and Paradise Valley were originally run exclusively by African Americans but in the late 1920s, whites attempted to invade the industry.[106] As a result, Detroit's Black numbers bankers organized the Associated Numbers Bankers in 1928 to protect their control of the game from white competition.[107] In 1940, a study reported on the organization and its founding:

> At present all of the principal number bankers in that city hold membership in it. Its chief purpose is to insure negro control of the racket against outside aggression. The negro group realized that if they were to maintain their control of the racket in Detroit it would be necessary for them to dissolve their minor individual differences and act as a group should an emergency arise. In fact, it was in such an emergency that the organization had its inception. In 1928 a group of Cleveland Jews attempted to break down the negro monopoly in Detroit and had almost succeeded in doing so when the negroes united their forces and drove them out. Soon after this the Associated Number Bankers was formed.

Besides providing protection, the association regulated rates of pay and winnings and divided the territory into areas to be controlled by each house.[108]

When Prohibition ended in 1933, white organized crime units looked for alternatives to the now obsolete illegal liquor trade and again tried to break into the Black gambling business. As in other cities, Black Detroit numbers bankers pushed back, determined to maintain their autonomy.[109] Sunnie Wilson recalled, "In the 1930s a group of white gangsters met with the Black numbers-men to discuss the possibility of a merger between them. . . . At this meeting the white gangsters planned a takeover of the Black numbers-men. Mr. Everett Watson attended the meeting surrounded by his bodyguards and told them all to 'go to hell.'"[110] Eventually, whites would enter the numbers game in Detroit; however, the Associated Numbers Bankers allowed African Americans to maintain control in the Black community.

African Americans' decisions and entrepreneurial strategies in operating illegal enterprises during the 1920s and 1930s were often linked to the larger goals of self-determination and economic freedom that had led them to migrate north. Illicit business provided many migrants with the lifestyle they had imagined was possible when they left the South but realized they could not achieve by working an unskilled industrial job. Coleman Young witnessed this perspective in action, as well-off numbers men sat on the street mocking Ford recruiters and laborers whom they likely viewed as fools for working harder than they did. Young remembered, "All over the streets you'd see Black guys with their pants neatly pressed and their fingernails manicured and their yellow leather shoes shined so bright it made you squint. Most of those guys came from the South, where their models for success were the highfalutin plantation owners, with their crisp clothes and smooth hands. The object was to remain unsullied by hard labor, and the young smart asses of Black Bottom seemed to have it knocked."[111] For these young men and many other Black Detroiters, numbers gambling was a profitable business that provided migrant entrepreneurs with the lifestyle they had dreamed of.

The Cost of Doing Business: Political Collusion, Payoffs, and the Detroit Numbers Game

Despite periodic efforts to clean up vice, Detroit maintained its reputation as a "wide-open town" through the 1940s, enabling illegal gambling to operate more or less consistently. Yet Black operators could not claim complete control over the business. As in other Great Migration cities, police and government cooperation was necessary for the numbers game to thrive.[112] Crackdowns on gambling establishments were often just for show, as the Detroit Police Department routinely accepted bribes and urban officials worked behind the scenes to facilitate illegal gambling in the city.[113] According to one gambler—who only spoke to journalists on the condition of anonymity—the corruption was obvious to anyone who cared to look. In a 1938 interview, he explained: "Politicians and a police department made disinterested in number gambling by political pressure are actually responsible. . . . Number operators for years have held considerable voting power. Their patrons, particularly Negroes, voted as the number bosses told them. Consequently, city officials all these years as the racket progressed, have failed to do anything about number gambling."[114] Thus, those who controlled the numbers game had significant political influence among Detroit's Black voters, and local politicians hoped to benefit from their support.[115]

Chief among these influential numbers bankers was John Roxborough, who for a time was reportedly "so strong that, did he give a party, a governor of Michigan either had to show up or give a good reason for staying away."[116] Having migrated from Louisiana in 1898 or 1899, the Roxboroughs were considered "Old Detroiters" and had long-standing political connections in the city. Both John's father, Charles Roxborough Sr., and his brother Charles Jr. had careers in politics and all three Roxborough men were trained lawyers.[117] Charles Roxborough Jr. was quite successful in the local Republican Party, even serving as Michigan's first Black state legislator from 1931 to 1932.[118]

Like his brother, John Roxborough was a staunch Republican and he employed his prominent reputation to advocate for Republican candidates. As a successful numbers operator, Roxborough was known to put his profits back into the community. Describing him as the "soft-spoken, philanthropic Negro lawyer of Detroit," one newspaper noted that "he helped numbers of young Negro men and women through college" and was "definitely a benefactor of his people." Some even referred to him the "Colored Man's Santa Claus."[119] In addition to his philanthropy, Roxborough utilized his role as manager to celebrated boxer Joe Louis to garner support from Detroit's Black voters. Of this strategy, a journalist reported, "In his method of operation, Roxborough has been politically bold particularly since he got control of Louis, who is, willy-nilly, an important political tool in Michigan." According to the journalist, "Louis, himself, did not at any time wish to be a political tool, or sledgehammer. As a matter of record, after he married, Sleepy Joe wanted to move to Chicago. But the politicians said: 'Louis stays in Michigan and helps control the vote—otherwise, no numbers racket.'"[120] Notwithstanding the reporter's familiarity with Joe Louis's wishes, Louis did join his manager's brother Charles Roxborough in touring cities across the country to promote the Republican ticket to African Americans for the 1936 and 1938 elections.[121] Other prosperous numbers bankers, such as Everett Watson, also utilized their notable affiliations to help build their gambling businesses and increase their political sway. As boxer Roscoe Toles's manager, Watson passed out free tickets to Toles's matches all around town. And like Roxborough, Watson was also accused of "exploit[ing] him cagily" for political means.[122]

The political influence of those in the numbers game would become increasingly important after 1932, when Black Detroiters began abandoning the Republican Party and voting Democrat.[123] Although in the 1937 Detroit mayoral election African Americans supported Richard Reading, a Republican, the tide was already turning.[124] In 1936 Detroit businessman Charles C. Diggs Sr. won election to the state senate, becoming the first African American to win a state office in Michigan as a Democrat. Diggs had been an active Republican in the 1920s and became a Democrat with President Franklin Roosevelt's victory in 1932. Diggs was a popular candidate; he was reelected in 1938, 1940, 1942, and in 1950, though he was blocked by state legislators from serving his 1950–52 term because he had served time in prison on graft and corruption charges.[125] According to Coleman Young, Diggs's large funeral home and insurance company were "the basis of his political machine." Young explained, "The insurance company had about a hundred agents who went door to door selling policies and carrying the partisan message. In effect, Diggs's salesmen were agents for the first Democratic organization in the Black communities of Detroit and Michigan. Until then, Blacks had always voted Republican, a tradition that went back to Abraham Lincoln. Roxborough was a Republican. But Diggs succeeded him as state senator from the Third District, and virtually all of the Black legislators from that time on—including Diggs's son, Charlie Jr. the congressman—were Democrats."[126]

When politicians were elected due in part to the support of Black numbers operators—such as Republican mayor Richard Reading, who served from 1938 to 1940—they repaid them by ordering the police department to allow those in the numbers syndicate to operate their business. Although those with strong political connections like John Roxborough made out best, this arrangement was not a direct quid pro quo, as all gambling houses also had to pay bribes to police and city officials to maintain operations and prevent harassment. This was an expensive undertaking; in 1939, the standard monthly payments for a gambling house were $5 to $15 for each patrolman, $25 to $50 for sergeants, $50 to $100 for lieutenants, and $300 for inspectors, who were also granted a monopoly on payoffs from establishments located in their precincts. Numbers operators and runners were also expected to provide gifts such as clothing, cigars, and whiskey. Any police inspector who would not go along with the bribe scheme was retired or "sent to the sticks" and replaced by one who was more cooperative.[127]

In addition to paying off members of each precinct, numbers bankers contributed to a larger "downtown pool" each month to be distributed to central figures such as the police superintendent and mayor.[128] Everett Watson, another "king of the policy racket in Detroit," collected this money from other houses, reportedly dispensing $4,000 a month (amounting to more than $85,000 in 2023) on their behalf throughout 1939.[129] Approximately half of the downtown pool went to Mayor Richard Reading; between December 1938 and August 1939, Reading pocketed $18,000 from Black numbers bankers.[130] These payments only increased over time and numbers operators "sweated and swore, and said they could hardly make expenses because of protection payments."[131]

However, there was little they could do to combat this system, as the police actively worked to close any gambling joint that did not contribute to the payoffs.[132] According to Leroy Mitchell, "They just kept busting them and busting them and busting them. A lot of times they would bust the guys in the numbers and they'd just take all of their money." Some operators attempted to avoid the police by moving their business to different neighborhoods but the loss of revenue could be devastating, and many who refused to pay for police protection went bankrupt. As Mitchell explained, "I think they just harassed them out of the situation. They just had to get out."[133]

The protections provided for numbers bankers who did participate in the payoff system could be quite elaborate. When the "heat was on"—that is, when pressured to respond to complaints from local citizens or otherwise ordered to suppress the numbers game—the police sometimes performed sham raids on gambling houses.[134] In these instances, police inspectors would tip off the establishment to give the operator time to prepare for the staged raid: "The operator would shoo away all of his regular patrons, and make a quick visit to some shelter for the needy. He hired stumble-bums at $2 a head to come and occupy seats in his book [gambling establishment], and await the arrival of the raid. The police would beat down the doors, destroy a few pieces of useless equipment left around for that purpose, and march proudly away to jail with a contingent of human scarecrows. They were quickly released by writs of habeas corpus, and never brought to trial."[135] Although numbers bankers occasionally faced genuine police raids, the most prominent operators devised their own ways to safeguard their businesses. John Roxborough and Everett Watson, for example, purportedly employed Al "Geechy" Pakeman—widely considered the "Black Mayor of Detroit"—as a "political representative." Consistently spotted in the corridors of the city's Recorder's Court, Pakeman evidently arranged for releases, bonds, and/or attorneys if the police raided Roxborough's or Watson's numbers houses and arrested patrons.[136]

Thus, despite infrequent crackdowns and the expense of bribes, police and local officials' cooperation ensured that the numbers business thrived in the 1930s. Black operators controlled the game not only in Detroit's Black community but also in nearby Dearborn, River Rouge, Inkster, Ypsilanti, Wyandotte, Ann Arbor, Mt. Clemens, and Pontiac. There, runners would pick up bets, drive them to the city, and pay out winnings directly from Detroit banks. Detroit's bankers also indirectly managed the numbers racket in Flint, Saginaw, Port Huron, and Kalamazoo, as well as in Toledo, Ohio. For these cities, Detroit-based bankers provided the backing for local operations in exchange for a percentage of the take.[137] In this way, by 1940, the Black-controlled numbers game grew into a $10 million a year industry (over $200 million in 2023 dollars).[138]

Even so, running an illegal enterprise was a precarious endeavor—a fact made obvious when a corruption scandal rocked the city. In a tragic turn of events, Detroit resident Janet McDonald took her own life and that of her eleven-year-old daughter in August 1939, with sweeping implications for Detroit's numbers business. As an act of revenge against her "two-timing" ex-boyfriend, policy manager Willie McBride, McDonald had sent letters detailing her knowledge of the city's illegal gambling to several Detroit-area newspapers, Michigan's governor, and the FBI. Exposing the "fixes" and "pay-off guys" endemic to the business, McDonald's letters triggered a state investigation into collusion between gamblers and urban officials.[139]

Specifically, the investigation examined charges of graft within Richard Reading's mayoral administration. Led by Judge Homer Ferguson, who acted as a one-man grand jury, the case hinged upon the testimony of former police inspector Raymond Boettcher. Having turned on his colleagues, Boettcher testified that he had worked as a graft paymaster and delivered money to various Detroit officials, including Mayor Reading. Reading was convicted and sentenced to four to five years in prison, alongside several other high-level bureaucrats. In all, 135 people were indicted as a result of the investigation.[140] Among them were key Black numbers bankers; John Roxborough and Everett Watson were each sentenced to two to five years in prison for "dealing in policy slips."[141]

According to Sunnie Wilson, "Black Detroiters saw the trial as a direct attack on their community."[142] And in the wake of the ordeal the new head of the police department promised to eschew the influence of gamblers and racketeers.[143] Yet Wilson continued, "Though it may have forced many numbersmen temporarily to curb their operations, the [case] never entirely stamped out gambling in the city."[144] Many Black entrepreneurs continued to brave the risks of this illegal and precarious business, intent on pursuing its substantial rewards and, they hoped, the financial freedom they sought in Detroit.

*   *   *

In his autobiography, boxing champion Joe Louis expressed what was perhaps Black Detroiters' most common response to the illegal business dealings in their midst—one of support and understanding. Louis wrote, "In those days it was hard living if you were Black, and it was harder still because the Depression was on. If you were smart enough to have your own numbers operation and you were kind and giving in the Black neighborhoods, you got as much respect as a doctor or lawyer."[145] Recognizing that Black entrepreneurs were not in a position to compete with whites and that the formal economy offered them second-class economic citizenship, many African Americans sought opportunities in the illicit economy. In some ways, bootlegging liquor or running numbers offered fairer competition and more favorable conditions. Yet engaging in illegal business required that proprietors seriously weigh the rewards against the risks, which included arrest, imprisonment, harassment from competitors and police, violence, and even death.

Even so, as Sunnie Wilson affirmed, "For Black Detroiters during this time, the most important source of economic and political power rested upon the numbers operations," and illicit entrepreneurship remained widespread on Detroit's east side throughout the 1930s.[146] Profit was not color-blind and the legal markets in which Black entrepreneurs operated were skewed by systemic racism. Illegal business was one avenue for Black Detroiters to create employment and make gains toward economic advancement, especially during the depression, and many established legal businesses with money from illicit enterprises. Engaging in illegal business constituted a critique of the existing formal economy, and as African Americans worked through unprecedented economic challenges during the depression, they imagined radical alternatives to U.S. racial capitalism.

CHAPTER 4

Surviving: Black Business Organizing and Radical Economics During the Great Depression

The Great Depression threatened to destroy all that migrant entrepreneurs had built up in the previous decades and affected both southern migrants and Old Detroiters. Old Detroiters initially had an advantage over migrant entrepreneurs when entering new markets during the first wave of the Great Migration and operated some of the longest-running Black businesses in the city. However, initial advantages were not enough to protect Old Detroiters from the grips of the depression. This was the case for James H. Cole Jr., a funeral director and the son of James H. Cole Sr., one of the most successful Black entrepreneurs in nineteenth-century Detroit. At his death in 1907, the senior Cole left behind an estate valued at approximately $200,000 and his son likely used some of this wealth to set up his undertaking business.[1] The younger Cole established his funeral home on St. Aubin Street in 1919 and experienced great success. But in the early 1930s, Cole's fortunes declined and he moved his business to St. Antoine and Livingston, perhaps to take advantage of less expensive commercial space. During the mid-1930s, he moved again, to 446 East Warren Avenue, and remained there for two to three years until he lost the building during the depression.[2]

The Great Depression was a setback for Black entrepreneurs' freedom enterprise. The dynamics of racial capitalism forced Black entrepreneurs to rely solely on African American customers and also created the conditions whereby Black workers faced disproportionate rates of unemployment. The combination of these factors made operating during the Depression years especially difficult for Detroit's Black business owners. The economic downturn caused some migrants to return south. The depression also pushed African American entrepreneurs toward a variety of survival strategies, including forming Black business organizations that promoted Black solidarity and economic self-help. Some of their organizing built on strategies Black entrepreneurs had employed during the 1920–21 depression. The Booker T. Washington Trade Association and the Detroit Housewives League utilized business boosting, similar to the Business Boosters club Reverend Bradby had formed in the 1920s. Relatedly, the Nation of Islam called for racial separation and Black economic independence, building on the work of the Universal Negro Improvement Association.

For some entrepreneurs who had believed in the potential of capitalism to lead to greater Black independence, the Great Depression caused them to doubt the viability of business as a road to freedom. The economic crisis opened both business owners' and workers' eyes to the weaknesses of capitalism. Critics of the existing economic system viewed the unprecedented depression as a moment of possibility for drastic change. U.S. racial capitalism was predicated on Black exploitation and some business owners looked to communism as an alternative that might more realistically lead to Black liberation.

Black Detroiters and the Great Depression

The depression hit the Motor City particularly hard because consumers across the country had less money to spend on luxury items, and an automobile was certainly a luxury. African Americans were affected more than any other group by the mass unemployment that industrial workers experienced during the 1930s in Detroit. The unemployment rate for Black workers was twice as high as it was for whites. While only 7.6 percent of the city's population was Black, African Americans made up 30 to 35 percent of those who received aid from relief programs.[3] Detroit Urban League director John C. Dancy explained the situation this way: "You see, first and foremost, the Negroes didn't have as much seniority as many of the whites and of course he had to go. The Negro was left out in many of these places." According to Dancy, Blacks in Detroit suffered more than whites because "there were more of them out of work and a larger percent of them out of work. And they had no office jobs, jobs like that where they could be retained."[4] The racial hierarchy of the labor market meant that Black workers were the last hired and first fired, and this would have negative implications for Black entrepreneurs who relied on Black wage laborers for patronage.

Black entrepreneurs in the city experienced unique challenges in trying to survive the Great Depression. For example, with the reduction in the Black population in Detroit, the size and purchasing power of Black businesses' consumer base shrank. Whereas new Black migrants had once poured into Detroit, between the spring of 1929 and November 1929, the influx was "almost negligible" according to the Detroit Urban League. Instead, during this period an estimated 75,000 male workers left the city.[5] Many were encouraged to leave by city leaders. Charles Denby, a Black migrant laborer, recalled, "In 1929 no one was working. . . . It got to the point where the city had to do something. . . . The city officials put in the paper that they would pay the fare of anybody who had another place to go."[6] On December 30, 1930, the *Detroit Free Press* reported that Detroit's Public Welfare Commission had "provided transportation for thousands of colored people back to their homes in the south."[7] City officials urged African Americans who were receiving aid from the city to return to their southern homeland—and many did.[8] However, most stayed on to "fight it out in their adopted homes."[9]

Competition from white-owned establishments in the Black section of town was also injurious to Black-owned business. Black proprietors in Detroit struggled to survive in the racially segregated market where they had to depend solely on the support of Black customers. According to Detroit historian Richard W. Thomas, "White competitors were well aware of the potential for profit within the Black ghetto, where racial segregation fostered a captive consumer market. But Black business and professional people were also captives, in a sense, because while white business and professional people could penetrate and exploit the ghetto market, their Black counterparts could barely get within reach of the white consumer market."[10] As they struggled to make ends meet, Black entrepreneurs often voiced strong opposition to the presence of white competitors in their community and the system of unequal economic opportunity.[11]

Black entrepreneurs developed many strategies to retain customers and combat the effects of the depression, and this included advertising. During the 1920s and 1930s, businesses across the country saw advertising as a modern way to increase efficiency, specialization, and rationalization. The idea was that with more information being provided through ads, customers would choose the best and most efficient enterprises, boosting sales and allowing companies to achieve greater economies of scale. These businesses could then lower prices and attract more customers.[12] In step with this marketing trend, Black businesses in Detroit utilized advertising to stimulate sales during the 1930s.[13] Black proprietors tried to relate to and sympathize with the economic plight of their clients in advertisements. For example, on December 28, 1930, the Ohio Barbershop placed an advertisement in the Black-owned *Detroit People's News*. In it the barbers who worked at the shop, Mr. Watkins, Mr. Lyons, and Mr. Gaines, not only advertised their services but also offered words of encouragement. The advertisement stated, "Our President Hoover said it is the moral and spiritual inspiration of a Nation more than its material progress which will determine its future." The barbers as well as the proprietor, Mrs. A. L. Turner, wished their customers and friends "A Merry Christmas and Jobs for the New Year."[14]

Black entrepreneurs also tried to attract customers by advertising their willingness to work with clients who lacked sufficient funds to pay for services up front. For instance, a little over a year into the economic crisis, Walter L. Riley, who touted himself as "the People's Funeral Director," advertised: "Customers with no money: Let us save you worry when you are in trouble with or without money—Consult Us."[15] Three years later in December 1933, A. G. Wright Funeral Home guaranteed clients "we are always at your service, with or without money."[16] Husband and wife funeral directors Vollington and Agnes Bristol assured patrons "We Consider Your Troubles Our Troubles During These Hard Times."[17]

Other strategies Black entrepreneurs used besides advertising to cope with the financial challenges of the depression were increasing, reducing, or maintaining prices of goods and services. For example, Belle's Beauty Salon placed an advertisement in the *Detroit Tribune* that stated: "In cooperation with president Roosevelt's blanket code to shorten hours, raise salaries and put more people back to work, our prices will be slightly higher beginning Sept. 1st." The shop's manager, Jeanette Coleman, hoped to have customers' support in "bringing about the good purpose and aim of the administration, that we all may experience better living conditions and better times."[18] Conversely, Mitzie-Bobette Beauty Shoppe placed an announcement (directly next to the Belle's Beauty ad in the same newspaper) informing customers that while the shop was now operating under the president's new National Recovery Administration code, "regardless of the increase in the costs of material and advance in wages," their prices would "remain the same."[19] Perhaps the proprietor, Beatrice Phillips, was trying to highlight Mitzie-Bobette

Beauty Shoppe's commitment to keeping prices low for customers, unlike its competitor Belle's Beauty Saloons.

No matter what tactics they employed, Black entrepreneurs faced the possibility of losing everything they had worked for, and some sought loans to avoid going out of business. Enterprising individuals who had available capital made loans to those hoping to hold onto their property. C. J. Cole advised potential clients "Don't Lose Your Property" and advertised that his company had "Money Available for Foreclosures and Mortgages."[20] Certainly some of those who faced the prospect of losing their property were business owners, and perhaps the services of people like C. J. Cole allowed some entrepreneurs to stay afloat. However, even an inflow of cash was not enough to save Black entrepreneurs whose customers had disappeared. Many of Detroit's Black businesses established during the 1910s and 1920s did not survive the Great Depression. Some were lost forever, others eventually reopened, and others closed shop in Detroit only to reopen in other parts of the country.

Not all business owners who faced financial difficulties or ruin stayed down forever. James H. Cole, mentioned at the opening of the chapter, was able to reopen his business at 275 East Warren and remained at that location until 1962.[21] Similarly, funeral home owner Charles C. Diggs, who had migrated to Detroit in the 1910s from Mississippi, went bankrupt in 1929 and went out of business. However, he was able to return to the funeral business in 1932, the same year he was appointed as a member of the Michigan State Parole Commission, which provided him with steady income outside of his business pursuits. Diggs managed to start again and eventually built one of the largest funeral businesses in the country, the House of Diggs.[22]

Cole and Diggs were able to bounce back from their losses. But the reality of losing everything or going bankrupt was too much for some entrepreneurs to bear. Some struggling business owners made the decision to end their lives and free themselves from the financial troubles the Great Depression brought them. In September 1933, both Dr. Leon O. Jefferson and Hewitt Watson, two prominent Black businessmen, committed suicide due to financial troubles. Jefferson had suffered from a nervous breakdown and was being treated at Dr. Ossian Sweet's hospital before he fled to his cousin's home and shot and killed himself. Jefferson had been under treatment at the hospital because he was despondent over economic conditions and had experienced "financial reverses." According to the *Detroit Tribune*, "he had lost a large sum of money in the bank failures."[23] Similarly, Hewitt Watson, an undertaker and insurance salesman, committed suicide at his mortuary at 611 East Canfield Avenue.[24] It is likely that financial troubles were too much for Watson to bear after sacrificing so much to uproot from Kentucky to start a business in Detroit.[25]

Watson and Jefferson were not the only ones who struggled with the economic damage brought on by the depression. The mental health issues that came with economic insecurity and destitution likely contributed to a rise in suicides. In 1931 the number of suicides in Detroit increased 30 percent compared to the average over the previous five-year period. Half of these suicides (with known causes) were linked to unemployment. Moreover, the economic crisis fostered other kinds of mental health problems as well. According to the Detroit Bureau of Governmental Research, from 1930 to 1932 the number of "insane" persons in Wayne County increased by roughly 70 percent.[26] Some Black migrant entrepreneurs likely experienced feelings of depression when the businesses they had invested so much in simply evaporated. For those who viewed business success as a route to freedom, they were losing not just money but their means to greater independence.

Some migrant entrepreneurs decided to go back to the South and start over when their businesses were no longer solvent. This was likely the case with William Ellis Jackson. Born on December 18, 1885, in Victoria, Texas, Jackson completed the ninth grade in the public schools of Texas before going on to study at Tuskegee Institute in Alabama and Worsham College of Embalming in Chicago.[27] On February 15, 1914, Jackson completed his course at Worsham and then returned to Texas to begin his first embalming practice in Houston. After practicing embalming there for two years, Jackson decided to migrate to Detroit and pursue his profession there.[28]

While he saved up money working as a laborer for the Detroit Shell Company, Jackson was also busy acquiring the prerequisites needed to operate as a licensed embalmer in the State of Michigan.[29] Jackson apprenticed under Charles T. Cole (brother of James H. Cole Jr.) in the field of embalming and subsequently applied to take the Michigan state examination for an embalmer's license in 1920.[30] Jackson passed his exam and opened his own funeral business. He was soon profiled in the *Detroit Contender*'s special business issue. Here, Jackson was described as "one of Detroit's popular undertakers." His establishment was located at 332 Orleans Street and carried a full line of modern funeral equipment. The profile stated: "Mr. Jackson is always ready to serve. It is this characteristic about him that has made for him legions of friends. You will find a friend to the friendless and ready to lend a helping hand."[31] Jackson also advertised in the *Detroit Contender* and highlighted his full line of equipment, refined service, and agreeable prices.[32]

While funeral homes were one of the most stable enterprises in the Black community, they were not without financial challenges.[33] As the depression continued year after year, Jackson finally decided to cut his losses and return to the South. By 1935, he was back in Texas, living in Corpus Christi. The 1940 census lists Jackson's occupation as an undertaker at his own shop, where he worked sixty hours a week.[34] Two years later Jackson was still in Corpus Christi running a funeral parlor with a partner, Joel B. Flowers. Jackson operated this enterprise until his death in late 1942.[35] For migrant entrepreneurs like William E. Jackson, the ability to return south and operate there was beneficial during the Great Depression.

For those who chose to stay in Detroit, connections to their former homes in the South were at times crucial. Having family ties and/or property in the South might be the only thing that enabled migrant entrepreneurs to ride out the depression. This was certainly the case for the Gordys. Berry Gordy Sr. had fled Sandersville, Georgia, in 1922 because he feared his financial success would lead to problems with local whites. After following his brother to Detroit, Gordy decided he would settle permanently in the city. He recalled, "I got up there in Detroit and I saw how things was. I saw a lotta people makin' money. . . . So I just know I could make big money in Detroit. I wrote for my wife, Bertha, to come up; I was gonna stay here. I told her to sell everything."[36] Many families had made property sacrifices in order to obtain the funds needed to migrate north. One man from Jacksonville, Florida, sold his horse, wagon, and cow to pay for his family's transportation north.[37] Dr. Robert R. Moton, principal of Tuskegee Institute, claimed that many southerners who left for northern cities ran off "pell-mell" without investigating and fully weighing the opportunities available to them in the North. According to Moton, "Some Negroes who own valuable property have left their homes, their cotton, their cattle and even unharvested products, and gone north."[38] However, Bertha Gordy erred on the side of caution and decided not to sell everything before she moved north to join her husband in Detroit.[39]

In Detroit, the Gordys would establish a contracting business and also purchase a grocery store.[40] Like most migrant entrepreneurs, they faced obstacles in getting established; however, the couple was able to grow their ventures into successful businesses. Regarding his contracting business Gordy remembered, "I had a good business goin' and had a lotta people workin' for me. So, when people would come to Detroit from Georgia, Mississippi, Alabama, or Tennessee, or somewhere from the Southern states, the people at the church would send 'em to me to give 'em jobs as mechanics. They made good mechanics. There was lots of 'em that I give jobs too."[41]

With the onset of the Great Depression the entrepreneurial family experienced financial troubles; it reached a point where Berry Gordy Sr. did not have enough work for his employees and could not pay them. He had no choice but to lay off his employees.[42] In order to cope with their financial troubles Berry and Bertha Gordy worked odd jobs so they could continue providing for their eight children. Bertha worked at any jobs she could find, at one point working in an office doing day work. Most of the work related to Berry Gordy Sr's trade was temporary and did not pay enough to feed a family of ten. He once worked as a carpenter for the city, but the job was only for three days. According to Gordy, "What it really came down to, I was hustlin' hard. . . . I was doing everything I could to make a livin'. I was sellin' ice, coal, wood—even collectin' junk paper to sell. I bought watermelons and sold 'em whole and by the slice."[43] As Black businesses faltered throughout the depression, proprietors and their family members often had to seek other types of work.[44]

Yet, even with all family members seeking work, many Black families still had to seek relief aid at some point during the depression, including the Gordys. Berry Gordy Sr. recalled, "I never did look to get on the Welfare . . . I held out; stood as long as I could."[45] Gordy was not the only Detroiter reluctant to seek assistance from the state. In 1930 Harry Andrews, president of the city's Public Welfare Commission, noted, "The sad part about the entire welfare problem is the fact that hundreds of men and women will go without food, clothing, or fuel, and deprive their children of these necessities, rather than appeal to charity." He added, "These people have too much pride to seek aid from the city, and they provide some of the most worthy cases."[46]

Non-business-owning people at the time did not fully recognize the struggles of Black entrepreneurs who remained in business during the depression. Berry Gordy Sr. believed his family was deserving and that he had a right to relief assistance because he "was a taxpayer," but not everyone agreed.[47] When Gordy finally went down to the relief office, some of the people in line tried to block him from getting in. According to Berry, "Some of the people saw me. They told me that I didn't need any help. Said, 'that man use to work; he's got a business; he's a big man.' Well, there was a time I was kinda big. I had people workin' for me and all. But 'cause of the Depression and bein' that there wasn't no more work, all that went down. I wasn't no big man; I was just like the rest of 'em."[48] Gordy's statement highlights the precarious nature of Black entrepreneurs' economic stability and ability to uplift themselves and their community members through business.

According to Detroit historian Roberta Hughes Wright, "During the Depression years most [Black-owned] businesses were closed, closing, or operating in the red."[49] Ulysses Boykin, who worked in the newspaper business, recognized that "those forced to seek relief aid not only included day labors but also professional workers and small businessmen of all races and nationalities."[50] Even entrepreneurs whose businesses did not fold could not always make ends meet without aid. According to Gordy, "The people down there at the welfare office said I couldn't get on. My business was the reason keepin' me off of the Welfare."[51] His connections with entrepreneurs like Charles C. Diggs and other prominent Blacks likely aided him in eventually being able to receive relief from the city.[52] Gordy was able to obtain a meeting with the mayor's secretary; he brought all of his receipts, his bank book, and other documents related to his business. After seeing the history of his business—how well he had been doing, and then the withdrawal of funds from his bank account—the secretary gave him a letter to take to the relief office. Subsequently Gordy was able to receive financial assistance. However, Gordy vowed "that soon I'd get to where I could get off, 'cause I really didn't want to be on welfare."[53]

The Gordys were not the only business owners who had to turn to the state for assistance. On January 10, 1936, John C. Dancy, director of the Detroit Urban League, wrote a letter to John J. O'Brien of the Works Progress Administration (WPA) in Detroit on behalf of Lula J. Theus, the wife of a photographer. Theus and her husband owned Theus Photo Service located at 3419 Hastings Street.[54] Dancy wrote to O'Brien, "For several years the Detroit Urban League has had on its volunteer staff of music teachers at its center at 1534 Chestnut Street a Mrs. Lula J. Theus. . . . Recently Mrs. Theus has made efforts to be taken on the W.P.A., so that she might continue this work with some pay but all of her requests have been turned down since it happens that she is married. Her husband is a photographer but earns hardly enough to pay rent. I am writing to ask if it is at all possible for Mrs. Theus to be put on W.P.A. rolls?"[55] It is not clear whether Lula Theus ever obtained a position through the WPA; however, her case demonstrates the struggles entrepreneurial families faced when they could not take advantage of New Deal programs. Theus's experience of repeatedly being turned down by the WPA was not unique. Though her marital status was one factor in her being denied,

her race very well could have been another. Black women who applied at
WPA offices were routinely told that they should "go hunt washing" and that
there were not any government jobs.[56] African Americans across the nation
experienced discrimination and could not count on New Deal agencies to
treat them as full economic citizens. In short, most New Deal programs were
not designed for the benefit of Black workers or Black business owners. Thus,
Black entrepreneurs had to rely primarily on their own efforts to weather the
Great Depression.[57]

Organizing Around Black Business

At the start of the Great Depression, African Americans compared it to the
depression Detroit had experienced in 1920–21. In the 1920s, Black entrepreneurs had used cooperative strategies to overcome financial strains and
to provide employment for Black workers who had been laid off. The work
of organizations such as the UNIA and the Boosters Club, headed by Second Baptist Church's Reverend Robert L. Bradby in the 1920s, helped create a allied Black business community in Detroit. As such, at the beginning
the Great Depression, Black entrepreneurs were able to swiftly organize in
order to work together to preserve and strengthen Black business in the city.
Throughout the 1930s, Black Detroiters made many efforts to use business
development as a solution to the economic devastation experienced in the
Black community. These included educating entrepreneurs in modern business practices, promoting individual Black businesses, forming cooperatives,
and promoting economic Black nationalism.

Reverend Bradby had advocated for Black business cooperation in the
1920s, and Reverend William H. Peck and Fannie B. Peck took up this work
in the 1930s. These church leaders built on a long-standing tradition of Black
churches serving as key sites of entrepreneurial activity and religious leaders
supporting business development in the community. As John Sibley Butler
puts it, "The fundamental institution for self-help among Afro-Americans
was the church."[58] The ties between church and business go back to the nineteenth century. For example, the North Carolina Mutual Life Insurance Company, an iconic African American–owned business, was founded in 1898.
According to historian Walter B. Weare, NC Mutual had "a profound relationship with religion." Additionally, two Black ministers founded the mutual
aid association that would develop into the Atlanta Life Insurance Company

in 1904.[59] In general, religious connections were an important feature in the life insurance industry. Weare writes: "Well into the twentieth century the business of Black insurance had not divorced itself from the traditions and practices of the early mutual benefit and burial associations, most of which were linked directly to the church."[60]

Long hubs of the Black community, churches served as sites for business planning meetings, they provided networking opportunities for entrepreneurs, and their congregations were key audiences for promoting messages of Black business development and cooperation. For example, when faced with discrimination from a white-owned trolley company in 1901, Black community leaders in Jacksonville, Florida, met at St. Paul AME church to strategize forming their own trolley company, the North Jacksonville Street Railway, Town and Improvement Company.[61] The relationship between religion and Black entrepreneurship continued in urban Great Migration destinations. In their 1945 study of Black Chicago, *Black Metropolis*, St. Clair Drake and Horace Cayton discuss the role of Black religious leaders in promoting Black-owned businesses and emphasizing the value of buying Black. The authors claim that the term "double-duty dollar" was first popularized by a Black minister and provide various examples of ministers preaching the double-duty dollar doctrine. Drake and Cayton point out that for the Black community a business was "more than a mere enterprise to make profit for the owner. From the standpoints of both the customer and the owner it becomes a symbol of racial progress. . . . And the preacher is expected to encourage his flock to trade with Negros. . . . [R]esidents of the Negro community rather generally approve of those churches and ministers who lend their support to Negro enterprises, and church members sometimes cite such actions as evidences that their pastors are 'progressive.'" However, Drake and Cayton also note that "some of the Holiness sects protest vigorously against this mixture of religion, business, and race pride, but they are definitely a minority in Bronzeville."[62] In Black Detroit, as in other Great Migration communities, churches were mainstay institutions and religious establishments promoted Black self-help and racial solidarity.[63]

Like Detroit's Second Baptist Church, Bethel AME Church embodied a self-help philosophy and worked to build Black economic institutions in the community. However, there were differences in the congregations. Whereas Second Baptist drew from the poor and Black working classes, most of Bethel AME's membership was drawn from the Black middle class.[64] In 1930 Bethel AME's pastor, Reverend William Peck, and his wife, Fannie Peck, founded the Booker T. Washington Trade Association and the Detroit Housewives League (the subjects of Chapter 5), which would become the largest and most visible Black business organizations during the Great Depression. As historian Angela Dillard notes, "Although ministers and their wives played a role in the groups' founding, the BTWTA and the Housewives' League were not religiously oriented."[65] Still, it was not a coincidence that these business-centered associations were organized in the Black church.

The Booker T. Washington Trade Association (BTWTA) and the Detroit Housewives League (DHL) were established to boost and build Black-owned business in Detroit. Members of the BTWTA and DHL organized annual trade exhibits, canvassed Black neighborhoods promoting Black businesses, produced and distributed informational publications, and sponsored education programs for entrepreneurs and consumers. These organizations grew immensely during the 1930s and remained strong throughout the 1940s. Fifty people attended the first meeting, and five years later DHL membership had increased to 10,000. At its height the organization had 12,000 members.[66] Many BTWTA members had previously been involved in 1920s business organizations, such as the Detroit Negro Business League, which was founded in 1926.[67] The previous networks that had been built among Black entrepreneurs were an important factor in the success of the Booker T. Washington Trade Association and the Detroit Housewives League.

One threat to Black economic survival that Black business organizations sought to address was competition from white-owned businesses.[68] The activism of the BTWTA and DHL centered on business education and improving business efficiency so Black entrepreneurs could become more competitive and have a better chance to compete for Black dollars in the skewed market place. One educational program these organizations created was the BTWTA Weekly Luncheons. This weekly lunch was a space where business leaders and expert guests educated entrepreneurs in modern business practices. "Visiting men and women of high standing" spoke to the attendees about specific business sectors and broadened members' business knowledge.[69] The BTWTA celebrated when a white-owned grocery and meat market, which opened on the corner of Forest and Hastings Streets, closed its doors after a few months. "We cannot believe the proprietors got rich and retired from business so soon, but rather that they could not stand the competition of so many stores operated by our group in that vicinity."[70] The group clearly attributed the Black businesses' stronger position to the efforts of the BTWTA.

The BTWTA and DHL were the most visible Black business groups during the Great Depression. However, they were not the only organizations Black entrepreneurs formed to foster business cooperation for joint economic survival. Black entrepreneurs in specific fields created their own cooperative associations. For example, sixteen Black-owned trucking, moving, and storage companies founded the Detroit Cooperative Movers Association.[71] Likewise, in April 1933, Detroit's Black manufacturers came together under the leadership of R. C. Smith, president of May Morning Manufacturing Company, to organize the National Negro Manufacturers' Association (NNMA). Its purpose was to "stimulate the sale of colored manufacturers' products among the buying public, and to create a greater demand for these products among members of the race." In order to do this, NNMA planned an advertising campaign and direct house-to-house contact with potential clients. The organization was comprised of more than half of the forty-six Black manufacturers in Detroit.[72]

Besides establishing cooperative organizations, African Americans also participated in popular movements that promoted business as a means to Black economic security. These included Father Divine's International Peace Mission movement, the Nation of Islam, and Development of Our Own. The latter two groups formed in Detroit during the 1930s and stressed Black economic independence and self-determination during the depression years. Although these groups had different philosophies on religion and interracial cooperation, they all emphasized the importance of Blacks' engagement in business ventures.[73]

Father Divine's following began in the late 1910s, but the International Peace Mission movement was most popular during the Great Depression. Father Divine, who was born George Baker, founded the new religion in Harlem, New York. According to historian Juliet E. K. Walker, Father Divine was one of the first African Americans to "introduce 'New Thought' economic principles to the Black masses. These teachings held that Blacks could use their mental capacities and positive thinking to achieve wealth."[74] Divine's message appealed to Blacks and whites across the nation, as he also espoused race neutrality. Father Divine organized his followers into units that operated businesses, including restaurants, laundries, grocery stores, and farm cooperatives. Profits from the businesses enabled Divine to provide employment, food, and shelter to struggling individuals during the Great Depression.[75] This charity helped recruit more people to join the Peace Mission movement.

However, only a small number of Black Detroiters joined Father Divine's movement. Journalist Ulysses Boykin reported in 1943, "The so-called cult movements have not grown to any great extent in Detroit as they have in large Metropolitan communities, because of the strong control of the various established religious groups over the majority of Negro religious life. There are a few followers of Father Divine, but not enough to warrant any detailed mention."[76] While there is no evidence that Father Divine had a large following in Detroit, Black entrepreneurs did sell the International Peace Mission's materials in their stores. For example, the Housewife's Lunch café sold Father Divine's publication; the proprietor was a member of the BTWTA and proudly advertised that his restaurant, located at John R and Palmer, was "dedicated to the Housewives' League of Detroit."[77] It is unclear whether DHL members read Father Divine's *New Day* publication or subscribed to his economic philosophies, but they certainly had the opportunity to learn more about his message concerning Black economic advancement. African American women made up approximately 75 to 90 percent of the Peace Mission's members.[78] As such, the economic message of Father Divine and the Peace Mission could have been popular among members of the DHL or women customers who frequented the lunch counter. If nothing else, Father Divine provided Black retailers with material to sell to those interested in Black economic development.

Around the same time Black entrepreneurs were organizing the BTWTA and DHL in 1930, Wallace Fard (later also known as Wallace Fard Muhammed), a former restaurant owner and coat salesman, formed the Black nationalist Nation of Islam (NOI). Erdmann Beynon's early study on the NOI reported that Fard made his first appearance among the Blacks of Detroit as a peddler. According to Sister Denke Majied (formerly Mrs. Lawrence Adams), "he went from house to house carrying his wares. He came first to our houses selling raincoats, and then afterwards silks. In this way he could get into the people's houses, for every woman was eager to see the nice things the peddlars had for sale."[79] With the financial constraints most Black Detroiters experienced during the depression, Fard must have been selling his goods at an attractive price. Once inside Black Detroiters' homes, Fard was able to sell silks and the Islamic religion. Denke Majied recalled, "He told us that the silks he carried were the same kind that our people used in their home country and that he had come from there. So we all asked him to tell us about our own country."[80] Fard's strategy worked. Between 1930 and 1934, 5,000 to 8,000 Black

Figure 6. Ferguson's Housewife's Lunch restaurant sold Father Divine's *New Day* publication. Courtesy of the Burton Historical Collection, Detroit Public Library.

Detroiters became members of the Nation of Islam. Most were recent migrants from the rural South, the majority having come to Detroit from small communities in Virginia, South Carolina, Georgia, Alabama, and Mississippi.[81] After 1934, the NOI expanded even more under the leadership of Elijah Muhammad (formerly Elijah Poole), a migrant from Georgia.

Black economic self-help and independence through entrepreneurship were central to the Nation of Islam's teachings. Indeed, several NOI temples and members operated various business enterprises, including grocery stores, restaurants, laundries, and farms. According to the FBI's investigative file on the NOI, "some of these institutions were organized to enable members of the [NOI] to secure freedom from the control of the 'devil' [white race] and members are urged to patronize these institutions."[82] This vision of freedom enterprise recognized that upward mobility for Blacks in the United States was curtailed by a system of economic white supremacy. According to the NOI, the solution was not integration into the system but separation from it.[83]

The NOI's Black nationalist economic philosophy was not new: the organization's message had many similarities to that of Marcus Garvey's Universal Negro Improvement Association (UNIA) and Drew Noble Ali's Moorish Science Temple.[84] In the wake of the UNIA's decline, the organization's Detroit members sought other means of community building and economic development. For example, Charles C. Diggs and J. A. Craigen left the UNIA for other economic pursuits. Diggs, in particular, became deeply involved with the BTWTA. Others who had previously been attracted to the UNIA's economic philosophy were drawn to the NOI. Elijah Muhammad, who would become the leader of the NOI in the 1930s, was a former member of the UNIA, and Malcolm X, who would join the NOI years later, was the son of Garveyites.[85] Members of the UNIA certainly saw a connection between the Detroit UNIA and the Nation of Islam. Garveyite Charles Zampy explained, "[Elijah Muhammad] was a good member of the UNIA and worked with us for many years. . . . But Elijah Poole was wise enough in arousing the Black people here in certain areas . . . to recognize that they must do something economic for their race, and since they are *Black* Muslims, then they must work as Black people. If he would have left the word 'Muslim' out, I think he would have gotten more cooperation from even those who were at one time former members of the UNIA."[86] The culture of business cooperation that had been prominent in the Detroit division of the UNIA in the 1920s was no doubt crucial for the formation and growth of the NOI in 1930s Detroit and (re)crafting members' vision of freedom enterprise.

Another prominent Detroit organization that attempted to solve the economic inequalities African Americans faced under racial capitalism was Development of Our Own. Unlike Black separatist organizations, this group stressed the importance of economic cooperation among all people of color. George Grimes started Development of Our Own in 1933, and Major Satochasi Takahashi, a reserve officer in the Japanese army, would later take over leadership of the group. According to journalist Ulysses Boykin, Takahashi "used the organization to urge Negroes to join with all other colored people, yellow, brown, and Black—against all white people."[87]

The Black-owned *Detroit Tribune* published articles relating to the activities of Development of Our Own. This included a report on Takahashi's address at a Black church and a picture of Takahashi with his African American wife. The *Detroit Tribune* was the only newspaper in the city that printed a picture of the interracial couple, and the paper received some criticism for it.[88] The *Detroit Tribune* also printed advertisements for Black businesses that were affiliated with the organization. For example, Howard Grocery advertised their "complete line of groceries and fresh meats" while also promoting its affiliation with Development of Our Own.[89] Although they had different positions on racial separatism, Development of Our Own and the Nation of Islam had similar philosophies regarding the importance of minority-owned business and Black economic development. Takahashi even capitalized on these similarities by attempting to lure some members of the Nation of Islam to join his organization. However, only a small minority of NOI members followed him into Development of Our Own.[90]

Policing and violent suppression of radical economic organizing were endemic in maintaining racial capitalism. Police officers eventually raided Development of Our Own's headquarters at 2299 East Congress Street. Takahashi and his wife were arrested, and Takahashi was deported to Japan shortly thereafter in 1934. Development of Our Own continued to operate under the leadership of Takahashi's wife and had branches in multiple cities throughout Michigan. In 1943 the organization claimed to have a membership of over twenty thousand. However, the Detroit Police Department estimated that the actual figure was less than half of that.[91] Even if Development of Our Own had slightly fewer than ten thousand members (as per the police estimate), that was a sizable following, close to that of the DHL.

The FBI and the Detroit Police Department considered the NOI a cult or "voodoo" organization; the police also regarded Development of Our Own as a threat.[92] However, many in Detroit's Black community did not see things this way.[93] Some Black Christians were uncomfortable with the NOI because of religious differences, but many agreed with the organization's message about Black economic development and self-help through business. These organizations all participated in an ongoing conversation in Detroit about the importance of maintaining and growing Black-owned businesses as a way to achieve greater freedom for the race. Still, all of these groups proposed solutions that involved operating within a capitalist system. Others would look for more radical answers to overcome the oppression of American racial capitalism.

Seeking Alternatives to Racial Capitalism

The economic breakdown in the 1930s caused some Black business owners
to doubt the viability of capitalism and they began to envision overturning
the system of racial capitalism in new ways. One such person was Haywood
Maben, a Marxist barber operating in Detroit. Maben was originally from
Augusta, Georgia, and migrated to Detroit between 1923 and 1930. Prior to
coming to Detroit, he had operated Maben & Maben Barbershop in Augusta
with his business partner Noy Maben. Once in Detroit, Haywood Maben ran
a two-chair barbershop on the city's east side at 2241 Waterloo Street.[94]

According to Coleman Young, Haywood Maben conducted civic classes
in his shop; Young remembered him as a "pontificator extraordinaire" who
"argued about economic systems" and subscribed to the theory of dialectical
materialism.[95] Maben's barbershop attracted a crowd of the "more thought-
ful men" in the neighborhood and occasionally somebody would purchase a
haircut. As Young put it, "If you weren't in the market for a political quarrel,
you didn't happen into Maben's." Most of the regulars shared the same basic
ideology, which Young described as "trade unionism with a liberal dose of
communism."[96] It is possible that Maben attended classes held by the Communist Party in Detroit. FBI informant Richard O'Hair recalled that during
his membership in the Communist Party USA he attended several evening
classes held at 10 West Warren Avenue in Detroit, where he studied dialectic
materialism.[97]

The fact that Haywood Maben was an entrepreneur and supported communism raises certain questions. For instance, why would he be interested
in a system that seemingly would not support his interest as private business
owner? And how did Black entrepreneurs with communist leanings reconcile
their existing petit bourgeois status with a potential economic revolution?
Perhaps part of the answer to these questions lies in the precarious and discriminatory nature of being a Black entrepreneur in the United States. Black
entrepreneurs did not operate in a free enterprise system because they could
not compete on equal terms with white competitors. Perhaps those who supported communism understood that white wealth was built on the exploitation of Blacks and that the racialized economic hierarchy in U.S. capitalism
would not change without drastic measures. Communism's proponents had
many visions of what a communist America could look like; perhaps Haywood Maben imagined he could still be a barber after the revolution but with
greater economic security. For Black communists, an economic revolution

seemed far more likely to lead to racial and economic equality than the existing system of racial capitalism.

One of the main reasons African Americans were drawn to communism
in the 1930s was the promise of working-class empowerment, and many
Black entrepreneurs were working-class people. Some Black entrepreneurs
had turned to business because of a lack of job opportunities, job security,
or workplace mistreatment. For African Americans who were not chasing
wealth but desired a stable income and economic security, communism
could have been an attractive option. Of the crowd who frequented Haywood
Maben's barbershop, Coleman Young noted, "There were not a lot of con-
servative . . . Booker T. Washingtonians in the barbershop crowd—with the
exception of the cobbler next door, who had attended Tuskegee Institute."[98]
In fact, Maben did not earn much more in his barbershop than an unskilled
laborer working in an auto factory.[99] While some Black entrepreneurs aspired
to amass a fortune, many others simply used the skills they had to make a
living through business. Maben probably fell in the latter group.

Black contemporaries certainly had questions regarding the relationship
of Black entrepreneurs to a workers' revolution. In a 1936 article in the *Crisis* magazine, Bettie E. Parham, former head of the Economics Department
at Shaw University and founder of Miracle Products beauty supplies, asked,
"What of the Negro Bourgeoisie?"[100] Parham argued that the small group of
Black professional and businesspeople, including lawyers, physicians, dentists, educators, and government workers, needed to choose whether to "ally
themselves with the worker, the capitalist, or remain in their neutral status."
She urged Black entrepreneurs to side with the laboring class, writing that the
Black bourgeoisie, "like the others, has suffered by the depression," and that
the "laissez faire attitude of the educated Negro toward the laborer can do
no other than lead to racial deterioration." Parham recognized the dilemma
Black entrepreneurs faced and the tensions involved in operating in a racial
capitalist system. She was all too aware that "the life blood of the Negro bourgeoisie is dependent upon the proletariat on the one hand, while they are tied
hand and foot to the capitalist on the other. . . . Extreme loyalty to either side
means death to him." Communist policies and principles might not appeal to
Black entrepreneurs because, as Parham acknowledged, "if brought to fruition [they] will doubtless tear down the hopes and accomplishments of many
years' struggle." Still, she concluded, "the white collared Negro must look
beyond his immediate circumstance into the future. He must offer himself to
be hanged upon the cross of personal sacrifice to save the suffering masses."[101]

It seems Bettie Parham did not have confidence that Black entrepreneurs would ever be able to rise above the status of second-class economic citizens under a racial capitalist system. Perhaps she reasoned that communism and supporting Black workers' struggle offered a more viable a route to freedom in the long term than enterprise.

Were other Black entrepreneurs, besides Haywood Maben and Bettie Parham, convinced that they were better-off siding with the masses over capitalists regardless of the personal financial sacrifices it entailed? Possibly. According to Richard O'Hair, an FBI informant, the Communist Party's East Side Council in Detroit consisted of different neighborhood clubs, factory branches, and professional groups, which involved doctors, lawyers, artists, and anybody with a craft. The East Side Council was chaired by Chris Alston, an African American war veteran, and had many Black members. Dr. J. Massee, a Black medical doctor whose office was located at 5205 Hastings Street, was a member of the party's Midtown Club and "paid dues, but put in few appearances at general meetings."[102] However, membership records do not exist to confirm how many other Black professionals and business owners were directly involved with the Communist Party during the 1930s.

Yet, Haywood Maben and Dr. Massee were not the only African Americans to align themselves with the communists during the depression years.[103] James Anderson was one of the primary African American communist organizers in Detroit. Anderson was codirector of the Political Action Committee of the Communist Party's Midtown Club and in 1944 helped organize the Thirteenth Congressional District Democratic Club, operated out of the Elks' building at 114 Erskine Street. According to O'Hair, Anderson had joined the party in 1932.[104] Anderson was a union man, but some Booker T. Washingtonian types also appeared sympathetic to the communist cause, or at least were willing to do business with the Communist Party in Detroit.

Richard O'Hair connected several business concerns to Communist Party activity when he testified before the House Un-American Activities Committee in 1951.[105] For example, a dentist leased a space above Mac's Drug Store for the party to hold meetings. Likewise, Iggy Barenson, who operated a newsstand near City Hall, also supplied the *Daily Worker* for all the Communist Party units in Wayne County.[106] While most of these connections seem to be with whites, O'Hair's testimony suggests a relationship between the Communist Party and Black entrepreneurs in Detroit during the Great Depression.

Dr. Aaron C. Toodle was a Black entrepreneur who might have been involved with, or at least sympathetic to, the communist cause. O'Hair remembered that Harry Glassgold, an artist involved with the party, had mentioned that Toodle "was instrumental in assisting Glassgold in his organizational work for the Communist Party in the State of Michigan." One of Glassgold's main projects was to pinpoint individuals who could be cultivated for Communist Party membership and leadership in organizations within Detroit's African American district. According to O'Hair, Toodle assisted Glassgold in creating progressive democratic organizations in the Thirteenth Congressional District.[107]

Aaron Toodle was a pharmacist and extremely successful businessman. Originally from Plymouth, North Carolina, Toodle had graduated from Howard University in 1917 and migrated to Detroit in 1919.[108] By the 1930s, Toodle's résumé in the Black business community was extensive. In addition to operating several drugstores in Detroit, Toodle was also the treasurer for Michigan People's Finance Corporation and general manager of the *Tribune-Independent* newspaper.[109] Along with Charles C. Diggs, Toodle was one of the initial entrepreneurs who mobilized and raised capital in the mid-1920s to establish Detroit Memorial Park Cemetery, Detroit's first Black-owned cemetery. Not only was Toodle one of the original twenty subscribers who purchased five shares each in 1925, he was the first president of the Board of Directors and also served as the general manager of the company during his time as board president.[110] Additionally, Dr. Toodle was a longtime trustee of Detroit's Bethel AME Church, where the Booker T. Washington Trade Association was established in 1930.[111] At the BTWTA's founding, Toodle was elected chairman of the Committee on Ways and Means. Toodle's wife, Hattie Toodle, was a founding member of the Detroit Housewives League and was elected treasurer at the group's initial meeting.[112] Throughout the 1930s and 1940s, Aaron and Hattie Toodle were deeply involved with the BTWTA and the DHL and contributed financial resources to the organizations.[113]

So why would Toodle, who seemed to epitomize the pro-capitalist "Booker T. Washingtonians," have connections to the Communist Party? There are several possible explanations. First, perhaps O'Hair misunderstood Toodle's role in helping Harry Glassgold in his organizational work for the Communist Party. Toodle was involved in local politics and might have worked with Glassgold without knowing of Glassgold's communist ties. However, it is also possible that Toodle was sympathetic to the Communist Party's cause. When campaigning for a Michigan state senate seat in 1934, Toodle highlighted that he had "helped hundreds of Negroes to secure employment, rendered much welfare service, and clothed hundreds of needy children." Toodle claimed to be "a true friend to the forgotten man and woman."[114] Perhaps Toodle chose to ally himself with the laboring class during the Great Depression. Whatever his motivation, the case of Aaron Toodle and other business owners who were communist sympathizers disrupts the common assumption that only working-class African Americans were drawn into the political movement. The emergence of entrepreneurial "fellow travelers" also provides insight into the shifting nature of entrepreneurs' freedom enterprise vision during the rocky years of the Great Depression.

Richard O'Hair also suggested a relationship between the Communist Party and two Black clubs, the Elks' Twelve Horsemen and the Detroit Association of Women's Clubs, in Detroit in the early 1940s. These clubs' membership consisted of many Black entrepreneurs. It is unlikely that they would have allowed the Communist Party to meet in their space unless they were somewhat sympathetic to their cause. According to O'Hair, from time to time the Communist Party USA rented accommodations at the Twelve Horsemen's Civic Center. On one occasion, business owner and politician Charles C. Diggs Sr. gave a speech there to the Communist Party's Midtown Club.[115] The Civic Center was located at 114 Erskine Street, and was owned by the Improved Benevolent and Protective Order of Elks of the World. The fraternal insurance business was a major industry that African Americans engaged in the early 1940s, and there were several fraternal benefit societies that operated in Detroit, including the Elks.[116] The Elks' lodge was in a prominent location, and the organization often rented out space at the Twelve Horseman as a money-making activity.

Erma Henderson, who managed the Twelve Horsemen's Civic Center, remembered the Twelve Horsemen as a luxurious facility. It had an auditorium and ballroom, as well as a huge kitchen in the basement, which was equipped to serve meals for the large groups that rented the banquet hall. The center also supported Black businesses. When the Twelve Horsemen purchased a smaller club in order to expand its property, Henderson remembered, "the renovation that took place to make this change was the first time I had seen an African American contractor granted a job."[117] The Twelve Horsemen also utilized local Black businesses for events. For special events in the ballroom, Henderson would contact Edgar Brazelton (of Brazelton's Flowers), who was an African American florist known for his elegant arrangements for weddings, banquets, and church and union events. The Twelve Horsemen was one of the major ballrooms for African Americans in the city.[118]

Various organizations used the Twelve Horsemen Civic Center as their meeting place. They included the AFL-CIO, which would hold meetings there every Wednesday, and the National Negro Labor Congress. Henderson recalled, "There was another labor group or two that would meet at the Civic Center, which caused some of the members of the Civic Center to question whether labor groups should be allowed to meet at the Civic Center."[119] Henderson did not specify which other groups used the Twelve Horsemen, but her statement gives credit to O'Hair's claim that the Communist Party used the facility. According to Henderson, some members of the Civic Center did not want the facility to be used by labor groups because "the labor organizations members were predominantly white." However, an unspoken issue could also have been that some were uneasy with the idea of communists meeting in the center. Henderson pointed out that her reason for allowing the groups to meet at Twelve Horsemen was that "labor organizations were being denied access to, and prohibited from meeting at other buildings." The Board of Directors of the Civic Center backed Henderson's decision to allow labor groups to meet at the facility.[120]

Richard O'Hair had also testified that the Midtown Club of the Communist Party held meetings at the Detroit Association of Women's Clubs (DAWC), located at 5461 Brush Street.[121] Originally called the Detroit Federation of Colored Women's Clubs, the DAWC was established in 1921, and its membership consisted of many businesswomen and women with entrepreneurial connections.[122] For example, the president of the DAWC, Rosa Slade Gragg, was the proprietor of the Slade-Gragg Academy of Practical Arts, considered to be a Tuskegee Institute of the North.[123] It is possible a woman named Elizabeth Clark convinced the DAWC leaders to allow communists to meet at their clubhouse. O'Hair remembered seeing Elizabeth Clark, an African American woman and a member of the Communist Party's Midtown Club, speak at a CPUSA general membership meeting held at the DAWC's headquarters. Clark lived at 631 East Kirby Street, just three blocks from the DAWC's clubhouse, and was actively trying to increase Black participation in the Communist Party and labor activism.[124]

Even if they disagreed with certain economic goals, perhaps Black business owners respected the Communist Party's stance on racial equality and its willingness to defend Black clients in legal cases. For many African Americans during the 1930s, the appeal of the Communist Party was the organization's promise of racial equality. As historian Timothy Tyson noted about Black activist Robert F. Williams's experience in Detroit in the early 1940s:

The Communist and socialist organizers Williams met in Detroit were "impressive to me," he recalled. "I wasn't interested in politics," he said, but "these things sounded quite good, the idea of equality, the denial of the power of one man to exploit another man, of equal justice, also the fact that men shouldn't be allowed to hog the money, or some men to hog the property, that it should be collectively owned." To Williams, this rhetoric rang more with the Sermon on the Mount and Negro spirituals than with *The Communist Manifesto* or "The Internationale." "I didn't think of them as communists from a political point of view," he said, "but saw them as what we considered friends, people who wanted to abolish racism."[125]

The Communist Party sympathized with African Americans' economic plight and recognized that the capitalist system in the United States was particularly oppressive to Black workers. This acknowledgment by a white-led organization likely appealed to Blacks who long understood that the United States' economic system was organized around their subjugation. The party's insistence that Blacks could attain full freedom only under communism was a divisive issue in the Black community. Yet, for many southern migrants who had come north to Detroit seeking freedom, the revolutionary system of communism seemed liked a viable route to economic security and equality.[126]

Certainly Black Detroiters were exposed to communist ideas and this likely swayed some to support the radical movement. According to the FBI, left-wing groups in Detroit such as the Socialist Workers Party were extremely "active in distributing pamphlets and other literature pertaining to the Negro situation" and "vie among themselves for the Negro support."[127] Robert F. Williams read the Detroit edition of the Communist Party's *Daily Worker* because "they used to have them in the bathroom, so I would read it."[128] Additionally, advertisements offering free pamphlets on the "facts on communism" appeared in Black-owned newspapers such as the *Michigan Chronicle*.[129] Most African Americans living in Detroit including Williams never joined the Communist Party, but he "read the *Daily Worker* and attended demonstrations occasionally, especially when the rallies focused on 'cases in the South' and when 'they would have Black people doing most of the speaking.'"[130]

A major factor in Black support of the Communist Party during the depression years was the International Labor Defense's (ILD) representation of African Americans in key legal battles. The ILD was the legal arm of the Communist Party USA, and this convinced Blacks that the party did not just talk about racial and economic equality but was willing to take action. The most notable case the ILD took up was that of the Scottsboro Boys. In this case, nine Black teenagers were arrested in 1931 and held for trial in Scottsboro, Alabama, falsely accused of raping two white women while riding the rails. After eight of the nine were convicted and sentenced to death, the ILD was the first to offer assistance in appealing the convictions and death penalty sentences.[131] According to Richard O'Hair, James Anderson, a prominent Black communist, joined the party in 1932 (soon after the ILD took up the Scottsboro case). It is possible that the Scottsboro case convinced Anderson and other Black Detroiters that the Communist Party was the real deal when it came to fighting anti-Black racism and racial capitalism.

Detroit had its own version of the Scottsboro case in 1934, which could have also led Black entrepreneurs to support, or be sympathetic to, the Communist Party. In this case, an African American World War I veteran named James Victory was accused of physically attacking and robbing a white woman. It was clear that Victory was innocent, since he had a rock-solid alibi.[132] The prosecution had no evidence against Victory and had to "rely solely upon the testimony of Mrs. Kay who only recognized his hair which she saw in an unlighted alley at night."[133] Maurice Sugar, a labor lawyer who worked for the ILD, successfully defended Victory.[134] Before an all-white jury, Sugar used his closing statement to passionately plead with the jury for justice, highlighting that the "Negro is doubly exploited. He is exploited as a worker and he is further exploited as a colored worker."[135] This defense of the Black proletariat, the lifeblood of Black-owned businesses, could have prompted Black entrepreneurs to support the Communist Party directly or indirectly during the 1930s.

* * *

The economic crisis of the Great Depression caused many Black businesses to go under, but it also prompted Black entrepreneurs to pursue radical economic alternatives to the (racial) capitalist system and/or organize for joint economic survival. The efforts of newly formed Black business organizations helped alleviate the economic suffering of Black entrepreneurs and were crucial to the survival of Detroit's Black business community in a time of economic crisis. The organizations formed in this period would become the bedrock of the business community as entrepreneurs continued pursuing their freedom enterprise in the coming decades.

CHAPTER 5

Boosting: Black Women Entrepreneurs Upbuild Black Business

In a 1939 letter written to Detroit Housewives League (DHL) president Christina Fuqua, local merchant Lincoln Gordon recognized "the ability of the Housewives League to boost race business." Gordon manufactured a household cleaning product called Gordon's Quality Cleanser, a mineral water softener and solvent, and he wanted the DHL's help in boosting sales. He wrote, "I shall be very pleased to have this body of business makers select or recommend to me [agents and consumers]." Gordon assured Fuqua, "As far as it is possible, I shall function for the mutual benefit of business for the race." He closed his letter by letting Fuqua know that he subscribed to the DHL's principles, asserting, "This is a written statement to display my willingness to cooperate and promote a bigger and better Racial Business."[1] As an up-and-coming entrepreneur Gordon acknowledged that the women of the Detroit Housewives League were important leaders in Detroit's Black business community and indicated that he agreed with the organization's vision of freedom enterprise.

The DHL and the Booker T. Washington Trade Association (BTWTA) were partner organizations dedicated to enriching Detroit African American business through commercial efficiency, networking, employment, and education.[2] Unlike other organizations that focused on a specific industry such as beauty culture, banking, or real estate, these organizations were established to promote Black business more broadly. DHL members were pioneers in Black women's business organizing. Founded in 1930, the DHL became a model for the National Housewives League, which was formed in 1933 in direct response to the success of the Detroit league.[3] Entrepreneurial DHL women came from a range of fields, and their knowledge and connections enabled the DHL to be a driving force behind the rise of Detroit's African American business community in the 1930s and 1940s.

Examining the Detroit Housewives League through its partnership with the Booker T. Washington Trade Association facilitates a deeper understanding of DHL women's actions and philosophy. Though "housewives" was in the organization's name, Black women were not simply involved as wives, mothers, or consumers concerned with their households but were entrepreneurs and business experts in their own right. Analyzing DHL members as businesswomen and focusing on their entrepreneurial activities reveals that they were instrumental in generating the business information and networking structures that would allow the Black business community to not only survive the Great Depression but also continue to grow into one of the most prosperous African American business communities in the 1940s.

Unlike "Don't Buy Where You Can't Work" campaigns, the Detroit Housewives League and the Booker T. Washington Trade Association did not focus their efforts on convincing white-owned businesses to hire Blacks or improving white stores' treatment of African Americans.[4] According to Helen Malloy, longtime member, onetime DHL president, and the organization's historian, "We never said don't patronize whites."[5] The DHL's actions and philosophy regarding women's purchasing power fit into the category of a "buycott." A consumer buycott is the opposite of a boycott, as boycotts often seek to punish businesses for past wrongs while buycotts aim to reward them for good deeds.[6] The Detroit Housewives League did not openly advocate boycotting white-owned businesses but rather encouraged spending in Black businesses. In their principles and bylaws, the DHL declared, "We are not engaged in any efforts of protest against business operated by other racial groups that may have a large percentage of Negro patronage. We feel that OUR BUSINESS is to support our own."[7] Both the DHL and BTWTA believed, "To throw support to Negro business in this way is a duty we owe the race. It is not a form of boycott against other groups. It is a legitimate and essential act of self-preservation."[8] They encouraged the "double-duty dollar" as part of consumers' pledge to support Black-owned businesses and reasoned that the entire Black community would benefit from this type of spending—consumers procured the goods and services they needed and their dollars would strengthen Black-owned businesses.[9] The DHL's strategy of "boosting" Black business was a fundamental aspect of the more cooperative, instructive, and community-focused variety of the local capitalism that Detroit's Black entrepreneurs engaged in to resist racial capitalism.

Launching the BTWTA and DHL

The economic downturn of the 1930s pushed African American entrepreneurs toward a variety of survival strategies, including forming organizations to promote Black self-help and boost Black business, and the Detroit Housewives League and the Booker T. Washington Trade Association were the largest and most influential of these organizations. Reverend William H. Peck was the driving force behind the BTWTA. As pastor of Bethel AME Church in Detroit, Peck felt the need to do something about the negative effects the Great Depression was having on his two-thousand-member congregation. Unemployed laborers were struggling to survive without work, and Black entrepreneurs were fighting to remain in operation. After discussing this predicament with his wife, Fannie, the pastor decided that Detroit needed a Black business organization. In April 1930, Reverend Peck called a meeting of Black business owners and professionals and formed the Booker T. Washington Trade Association.[10]

Fannie Peck was involved in the BTWTA from its inception.[11] According to an organizational history, after Reverend Peck proposed the idea of a business organization over breakfast, Fannie voiced her support and replied, "You may depend on me doing my part."[12] Two months after the BTWTA's first meeting, Fannie Peck issued her own call, and on June 10, 1930, a group of fifty Black women gathered to establish the Detroit Housewives League, an organization to foster self-help and build Black economic institutions in the community.[13] The DHL grew to have ten thousand members by 1935 and several neighborhood units within the city that belonged to the Central Committee.[14] The BTWTA and the DHL were established as partner organizations and remained intertwined throughout the 1930s and 1940s.

The two organizations made their partnership explicit, regularly referring to the BTWTA and DHL as a pair, and offered unified messages and goals. Their annual directory of Black businesses stated, "The Booker T. Washington Trade Association and the Detroit Housewives League are endeavoring to bring together in this little book the names, location[s] and telephone number[s] of those men and women who are engaged in business and the profession[s]."[15] The organizations also had a General Council composed of elected officers from both groups. Its objective was to unify the programs, operations, and plans among the BTWTA and the different units of the DHL throughout the city and "to agree upon united actions for furthering of the work."[16] Together, the BTWTA and DHL sponsored annual trade exhibits, business booster drives, educational events for entrepreneurs and consumers, and a general "program of support and improvement of Negro business."[17]

The BTWTA and DHL were not only partner organizations with a shared vision for Detroit's Black business community but also interconnected in terms of leadership, programming, and membership. The BTWTA held a "Spring Drive" in 1933—an event to help Black businesses "get a larger share of the general business in the metropolitan area of Greater Detroit." BTWTA president Reverend Peck stressed, "We can carry out this order only through the co-operation of our Business, Artisan, and Professional men and women."[18] The 1933 directory characterized the BTWTA as "an organization of Business and Professional men and women organized to stimulate and improve their business."[19] As such, the BTWTA appointed a chairperson for different industries, such as insurance, laundry products, and beauty manufacturing, with whom business owners could consult.[20] The BTWTA's weekly Luncheon Club meetings included lectures by prominent business leaders, "men and women of high standing," and the club's membership was "made up of persons who are actually engaged in business professions of some sort."[21] As one member highlighted, "Over a plate of food or cup of coffee we have been able to learn [from] the real men and women" in the business community.[22] An advertisement for the 1944 BTWTA membership drive stated: "Every woman and man interested in a business profession should carry a membership."[23] Both business men and women came together to address the problems Black business owners faced under racial capitalism.

Even though many of the women in the DHL were leaders in the Black business community, the league's founders' decision to use the term "housewives" in the title of the organization helped obscure Black women's business leadership and activism. The name "Housewives League" is a misnomer, as most DHL members worked outside the home. Certainly, some members of the DHL identified as housewives, but the gendered culture of the time also influenced the naming of the league. Historian Victoria Wolcott notes that "the feminine nature of the league's work, the emphasis on women's roles as consumers, marked the movement as 'respectable' in spite of its militant tactics."[24] In the early twentieth century, middle-class Black women often espoused a politics of respectability as a strategy to navigate the racism and sexism in their lives.[25] To combat negative stereotypes of Black women, middle-class leaders "endorsed the popular belief that women were more nurturing, moral, and altruistic" than men and that men's nature was selfish and aggressive.[26] Women who embodied characteristics like assertiveness, ambition, or shrewdness in business did not fit into this model. Respectability politics also shaped the way Black women could enter into public space and lead on public platforms, limiting how they could lay claim to public business leadership roles.[27]

Many were concerned about how Black businesswomen would be viewed or treated by men in their community in the 1930s and 1940s. DHL member and entrepreneur Violet T. Lewis experienced firsthand the issues that accompanied being a successful entrepreneur and prominent female business leader. Lewis's business success and stature were direct factors in the breakup of her marriage. According to her daughters, "Daddy was married to a woman with a strong personality. Not having a comparable or complementing personality, Daddy's ego could not endure his perceived subservient role in the marriage. The more Mother grew in stature in the community, the more successful her business became, the more she became empowered, the less Daddy felt like a partner in her success. Mother tried to be inclusive and Daddy tried to support her, but he was always playing the second role and people rarely asked or knew about Mr. Lewis."[28] DHL women likely obscured their entrepreneurial prowess, perhaps to help their spouses save face or because it was necessary to placate businessmen in the community. Calling themselves "housewives" even when they were entrepreneurs could have protected business-minded DHL members from inter- and intraracial social backlash and provided them with political, social, and economic benefits. Nevertheless, by choosing the name "Housewives League" for their organization, entrepreneurial DHL women facilitated the erasure of their business backgrounds and expertise from historical narratives.

On the other hand, DHL women's use of the term "housewife" was a savy decision. Choosing this gendered, cross-class, economic term allowed the Detroit Housewives League to include women who were engaging in the economy as workers, business owners or wives of business owners, and consumers. Through their actions, we can see that Black women were utilizing and transforming existing economic language to fashion a new kind of identity and professional role for themselves. In the 1930s and 1940s, DHL women considered the word "housewife" to be very much about business, and their actions offer a new view on the position of "housewife" in the early to mid-twentieth century.

Entrepreneurial "Housewives": DHL
Women's Business Expertise

The Detroit Housewives League was not the first local organization to bring Black businesswomen together to advocate for their own entrepreneurial interests. In September 1928, two years before Fannie Peck launched the DHL, Black women who worked in Detroit's Black business and professional offices established the Elliotorian Business Women's Club (EBWC). Its leader, Elizabeth Nelson Elliot, was a secretary who realized that Black women secretaries, bookkeepers, and clerks needed more support in order to fulfill their potential of becoming a "viable community force." She also wanted to encourage young women to pursue business careers.[29] The EBWC's goals were to "stimulate interest in Detroit's businesses, build an educational program, study the needs of businesswomen, develop leadership qualities," and facilitate professional women's entry into "public and private white-collar occupations."[30] By 1931, EBWC had 33 members (all women, some of whom were also DHL members) and 118 "patrons," prominent leaders who supported the organization but were not official members. These patrons included several people who were involved in the newly established DHL and BTWTA. In 1936, William and Fannie Peck became Elliotorian patrons while simultaneously leading the BTWTA and DHL.[31]

These links between the DHL and the Elliotorian Business Women's Club are important. First, the EBWC demonstrates that Black businesswomen had their own ideas about how to improve Black Detroit's economic life prior to 1930. They would bring this background and knowledge to their work with the DHL and BTWTA. Second, that the Elliotorian Business Women's Club was founded in 1928 shows that Black women were organizing to build up the Black business community before the Great Depression hit and that they were organizing for their own interests as entrepreneurs. Neither the Elliotorian Business Women's Club nor the Detroit Housewives League was comprised solely of businessmen's "housewives."

In the 1930s, most of the DHL's ten thousand members were working-class women. However, the leadership—those who shaped the organization's philosophy and strategies and who collaborated with the BTWTA—consisted largely of businesswomen. A review of early DHL member lists as well as minutes from organizational meetings reveals that many of the women in leadership roles were entrepreneurs or had experience working in family businesses. Helen Malloy's oral history confirms that women were often recruited to be involved with the DHL because of their business experience. Malloy indicated that she spent a lot of time working in the shoe business with her husband before beginning her work with the Detroit Housewives League. According to Malloy, the DHL "came and got me" because of her affiliation with the family business.[32] She also indicated that most of the early DHL members either were in business for themselves or had husbands who owned businesses.[33] For example, DHL founder Fannie Peck established the Fannie Peck Credit Union, the first Black credit union to receive a state charter in Michigan. Peck's credit union provided vital loans to Black community members until at least 1985.[34] A 1943 publication on Black Detroit reported that the Fannie Peck Credit Union was among the four largest and best-known Black credit unions in Detroit.[35] Peck's credit union was critical because of white financial institutions' long-standing practice of discriminating against Black borrowers. In addition, in her capacity as DHL president and later as president of the National Housewives League, Fannie Peck maintained a reputation as a businesswoman. In a 1933 letter to an officer of the National Negro Business League, DHL vice president E. L. Hemsley described Fannie Peck as a "woman of a business concern" and "a woman leading a business organization."[36]

Other DHL members were business partners with their spouses or worked in family-owned businesses. For example, Charles C. Diggs Sr. was a prominent Detroit businessman (and later politician) known for running a successful funeral business. The Diggs Funeral Home would grow to be the largest funeral business in Michigan. Though the business was associated with Charles Diggs, his wife, Mamie Diggs, was actively involved in running it. Recognizing Mamie Diggs's role in building the family business, their son Charles Diggs Jr. recalled, "My father came [to Detroit] from Mississippi, with my mother, and built the largest Black business in the city with nothing but their bare hands."[37] Furthermore, a 1924 profile of the funeral business stated that Mamie Diggs "acts as a woman assistant to her husband and is thoroughly interested in the business." The same article reported, "In the making of the remarkable success which he now enjoys, Mr. Diggs attributes as much to the sagacity and foresight of Mrs. Diggs, as he does to any contribution which he himself has made."[38] Although such public acknowledgment of women's labor in family businesses was rare, scholarship on women's business history shows that women have always been deeply involved with family businesses and businesses legally owned by their spouse.[39] The Diggses were greatly involved in the Booker T. Washington Trade Association and the

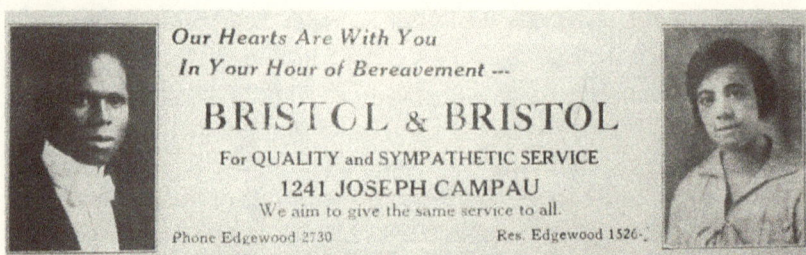

Figure 7. Bristol & Bristol advertisement featuring photographs of Vollington and Agnes Bristol. *Second Baptist Herald*, July 1, 1928, page 3, Roll 9, Publications 1913–1989, Second Baptist Church (Detroit, Mich.) Records, Bentley Historical Library, University of Michigan.

Detroit Housewives League, and Mamie Diggs was just one of many Black women who had business experience prior to organizing with the DHL.

In some cases, women appear to have been the driving force behind family business ventures. Long-term DHL member Agnes Bristol, for example, co-owned the Bristol & Bristol Funeral Home with her husband, Vollington Bristol, and both were active members of the Booker T. Washington Trade Association. However, it seems that it was actually Agnes Bristol who had the initial experience and qualifications in the mortuary field. She apprenticed under a Scottish undertaker for several years before passing the state board exam and receiving her license for embalming in 1922, becoming the first Black woman in Michigan to be a licensed mortician and the first Black mortician to receive a Special Diploma in Mortuary Sciences from the University of Michigan.[40] Although her husband began his mortuary studies in 1920 and applied to take the state examination for an embalmer's license in 1922, the same year as his wife, he worked as a shoe shiner until 1918.[41] It is plausible that Agnes Bristol entered the mortuary field prior to her husband, if not at the same time, and was central in facilitating the start of the family business. Going into business with their husbands was one way for Black women to advance in the business commercial world, where racial capitalism created limitations around not only race but also sex.

Agnes and Vollington Bristol were also involved with many other Black businesses in Detroit, particularly those in the financial and insurance sectors. Agnes Bristol served as a director of the Great Lakes Mutual Insurance Company in the 1930s.[42] After Vollington's death, Agnes maintained the Bristol & Bristol Funeral Home until her additional work as vice president and secretary of the Great Lakes Mutual Insurance Company began to take up too much of her time.[43] She approached Willis Eugene Smith, another funeral director and her late husband's close friend, and asked him to manage the day-to-day operations of her mortuary business. Smith initially declined, seemingly unwilling to have a female boss, saying he "couldn't get along with her at first because she was a woman." In an attempt to dissuade her, Smith made Agnes Bristol an offer: "I said, I'll tell you what I'll do. If you buy me a Cadillac, give me 25 percent off the top, then I'll do it. But I thought I was getting rid of her." About three days later, Smith received a call from Ed Davis, a local African American car dealer, informing him that Mrs. Bristol "came in and gave me six thousand dollars and told me she was buying [the car] and to give you the keys."[44] Smith took the job and the business continued until 1975.[45] This story says a great deal about Agnes Bristol's acumen as a businesswoman; she made smart business decisions and knew how to get what she wanted. Surely she brought this entrepreneurial savvy to her ongoing participation in the Detroit Housewives League.

While women were not always the face of the businesses in which they were involved, the DHL was committed to acknowledging their business expertise. For example, the organization held a "Get Acquainted Tea" that featured "women in business and women who are contributing largely to the success of their husband's business."[46] One such woman was Helen Malloy, a key Detroit Housewives League organizer who served as the group's "chairman of publicity," writing articles and overseeing the production of all DHL bulletins.[47] Malloy became involved with the DHL and BTWTA as a result of her experience at Malloy's Shoe Repair, a family business established by her husband, Lorenzo Malloy. Helen Malloy was initially reluctant to accept his marriage proposal because "shoemaking was not much of a business," in her opinion. But after she began working in the shop and helping Lorenzo run the business, her opinion changed. Helen realized that Lorenzo "made good" and earned much more money than she had as a schoolteacher in Alabama, where she was from originally. She gained significant business experience participating in the shop's day-to-day affairs, maintaining the inventory, and dealing with customers and applied her expertise to her work with the DHL.[48] Malloy made a reputation for herself as a businesswoman. In the BTWTA and DHL's 1935 directory, she was listed as a "stockings" sales agent.[49] She was also featured working in the family business in the organizations' *Picture Book of Business*.[50]

Likewise, Bertha Gordy was a DHL member who operated a business associated with her husband. She and her husband, Berry Gordy Sr., migrated

to Detroit in 1922 from Sandersville, Georgia. The couple's business experience began there, as Berry Gordy Sr. owned a farm and sold livestock, cotton,
and produce.[51] It is likely that Bertha Gordy was involved with these ventures,
since farmwork required family effort and women were often responsible for
selling farm goods to peddlers and merchants.[52] Additionally, Bertha's father
was a business owner, and she may have gained some of her entrepreneurial
acuity through his mentorship.[53] Berry Gordy Sr. described Bertha this way:
"My wife was a very intelligent girl, smart. . . . I'd tell a joke and have people
laughing all the time. She kinda broke me from that, kinda made me more
intelligent."[54] When Gordy Sr. went to Detroit and saw that there were many
opportunities to launch a successful business in this northern city, he wrote
to his wife asking her to join him. He later recalled, "I told her to sell out
everything."[55] His instructions indicate that Bertha Gordy was probably
handling the family's business affairs in Georgia while her husband was in
Detroit. According to Gordy Sr., "I meant for her to sell the cows, our home,
the chickens, mules, horse, wagon, and buggy, sell everything! But she didn't
sell nothin'!!"[56] Instead, Bertha Gordy took matters into her own hands and
decided to leave the farm under the care of family members when she went to
Detroit. Her decision would prove to be a critical one once the Great Depression was under way.

In Detroit, Bertha Gordy was a deciding factor in the family's economic
success. After working for wages for a time, Berry Gordy Sr. established a
contracting business doing plastering and carpentry and also purchased a
grocery store.[57] In his memoir *Movin' Up: Pop Gordy Tells His Story*, Gordy
describes the family grocery store as his business.[58] However, it was Bertha
Gordy who actually operated the store with the help of their children, who
would arrive after school.[59] And advertisements for the grocery store listed
Bertha Gordy as the proprietor.[60] Working in the family business and learning much of their business acumen from their mother, many of the Gordy
children went on to become successful entrepreneurs, most notably Motown
Records founder Berry Gordy Jr.[61]

The Gordys' businesses continued to grow until the Great Depression.
Berry Gordy Sr. began receiving fewer contracts and those he could secure
were for small jobs. He ultimately had no choice but to close the contracting
business.[62] As the Gordys' income dwindled, their family connections in the
South were crucial, as was Bertha Gordy's decision not to sell all of their property when she migrated to Detroit. One day, the family received one hundred
dollars in the mail. Bertha Gordy's father had sold two of the cows the family

had left in Georgia. Gordy Sr. remembered, "We was so happy! I wish he'd sold all of 'em! We got that hundred dollars; seemed like *five hundred* dollars at that time. But then again, I thought anything was big money in the Depression years." In addition to the money from the cows, the Gordys received a steady stream of income from renting the property they still owned in Georgia.[63] Bertha Gordy's keen business sense had saved the family. Furthermore, her connections with the BTWTA and DHL likely also helped the family business survive during this difficult time. Bertha Gordy was a member of the BTWTA and she also served as the BTWTA corresponding secretary.[64]

As these examples demonstrate, even though they were not always the public face of the operation, entrepreneurial DHL women had business experience and expertise. They did not only see themselves as housewives, nor did others in the Black business community. Importantly, they used their business knowledge to help the Detroit Housewives League and the Booker T. Washington Trade Association formulate strategies for boosting Black-owned business.

One such strategy was for DHL women to act as intermediaries between consumers and entrepreneurs, as researching consumers' attitudes was necessary for Black businesses to better appeal to their clientele. As business "boosters," DHL members went door-to-door to solicit information from Black consumers and explain the benefits of supporting Black-owned businesses. Because their position as respectable women allowed them to enter strangers' homes, they had access to the community's main purchasers: Black women.[65] And as Black women themselves—consumers who also wanted the best for their households—their message likely engendered a sense of trust that enabled people to reveal what they felt were the problems with certain Black businesses or why they preferred to go to a white-owned enterprise. DHL women then took this information back to merchants to help them improve and grow their businesses. The DHL's role of interlocutor between consumers and business owners was key to the organization's importance in cultivating Detroit's Black business community. According to DHL president Fannie B. Peck, "Bringing the producer and consumer into closer relationship cannot but bring about an understanding that will be beneficial to all. Working together, trying to solve our many problems, will go a long way toward helping us to attain our goal—an equal opportunity to take our place in the economic life of this nation."[66]

The Detroit Housewives League also studied and compiled information about Black commercial institutions in the city. The March 14, 1931, issue of the *Detroit Economist* reported that the Housewives League was planning a "survey of Negro business of every kind in Detroit."[67] Conducting business research would serve the DHL and BTWTA's mission—namely, to build and boost Black-owned businesses—and indeed the DHL's survey provided valuable insight into the economic situation of African American entrepreneurs in the city. In 1933, the DHL again planned a "complete survey of Negro business of every kind in Detroit." The survey was designed to serve the community by gathering knowledge about existing businesses; business owners "expressed great satisfaction in learning that the housewives have undertaken this work." Collecting information on every Black-owned business in the city was a massive assignment. But according to the DHL, "That the task is a hard one all agree and this is perhaps why the housewives are better fitted to do the job than any other group."[68] Black entrepreneurial women in the Detroit Housewives League occupied a unique position as both business and consumer experts.

The league published the findings from their consumer surveys in an article titled "Why Do We Buy What We Buy?" The author, Gertrude J. Tolbert, laid out several factors that governed Black women's consumer decisions: (1) quality, (2) quantity, (3) price, (4) brand, (5) confidence in merchant, and (6) attractiveness of wrappers and containers. The article advised women shoppers to test different brands and consult circulars and newspaper advertisements for the best prices. Tolbert also opined, "Buying regularly of one merchant is an advantage to the dealer and customer as a better understanding is derived between the two."[69] Speaking to both consumers and business operators, this article exhibits the DHL's position as a go-between for these two groups. Moreover, the data they gathered and distributed about Black business was no doubt useful for understanding Black entrepreneurs' representation in specific business sectors and for planning conferences and other events to benefit the Black business community. The DHL's interlocutor role continued throughout the organization's history. In the late 1930s, the DHL offered a list of tips "to improve business," which included: "Offer slow moving stock at reduced prices or combination sales"; "Shelf arrangements for quick and efficient service"; "Notice all special radio offers in your line of goods and demand them from your wholesaler"; "Polite sales people, with good memory, both of stock placements and customers [*sic*] needs"; and "Offer specials every three months."[70] Thus, the DHL's astute initiatives produced valuable information for both business owners and consumers.

By the interwar era, white business infrastructures were well-developed. There was a national network of business schools and public relations firms doing market research, advertising, and advising for white businesses. However, for the most part, white companies ignored Black business and the Black consumer market through the 1930s. In 1928, the National Negro Business League had undertaken a national survey of Black business, but the business environment had shifted greatly with the onset of the Great Depression. In the late 1920s and 1930s, H. A. Haring published two articles on Black consumers that appeared in the trade journal *Advertising & Selling*, and the 1940s, David J. Sullivan, a pioneering African American market researcher, published key information about Black consumers. The Detroit Housewives League stepped in and conducted the market research necessary for Detroit's Black business owners to survive and grow in the 1930s and 1940s.[71]

When DHL members felt that their work was unappreciated by male entrepreneurs, they made their role in developing Black businesses explicit. An article in the *Detroit Economist* stated that the Housewives League "accused some of our businesses and professional men of being a bit indifferent to the interests of the League and its members." The DHL wondered "how some men in business (we shall not call them business men) think they can bite the hand that is feeding them and expect to be fed very long." The organization warned, "One thing is certain. Any Negro business or professional interest who thinks it [can get] very far without the support of Negro housewives and the influence they have is a plum fool."[72] Nannie Black, who served as DHL president after Fannie B. Peck, reiterated the point, stating, "Women [hold] the key to economic success or failure, it may be turned right or left."[73] The DHL understood the magnitude of their influence on Black business success in Detroit and threatened to remove their support if male business owners did not respect their leadership and cooperate with them. Making their position clear, a 1935 publication claimed, "It can be said that the life of the Trade Association is really found in the Housewives League."[74] It can only be assumed that some male business owners had trouble accepting the women's authority. It is certainly possible that Black businessmen resisted Black women acting as business leaders, as women in business with spouses were often expected to play a supportive role and not be too assertive with male colleagues. In general, Black business leadership was imagined as a masculine endeavor.[75] It is also possible that some businessmen minimized DHL women's contributions. As Detroit Housewives Leaguer Helen Malloy indicated, DHL members did not like being thought of or treated as auxiliary to the BTWTA.[76]

However, many male proprietors did recognize and respect the DHL's positive impact on Black business growth. As mentioned at the beginning of this chapter, Black entrepreneur Lincoln Gordon recognized the DHL's power as "business makers" and asked for the group's assistance. The Detroit Housewives League did end up supporting Gordon's product. In the September 1940 issue of the *Voice of Negro Business*, an advertisement for Gordon's Quality Cleanser stated that it was "endorsed by the Housewives League of Detroit."[77] This exposure and endorsement undoubtedly resulted in increased sales for Lincoln Gordon. Gordon's Quality Cleanser was just one business that the DHL and BTWTA assisted during the 1930s and 1940s. Richard Austin, who struggled to establish his practice as Michigan's first Black certified public accountant, later remembered the Detroit Housewives League as an effective "band of non-violent militants" who promoted patronage of Black-owned businesses like his.[78] Many other enterprises founded or expanded during the 1930s found success because of the proprietors' close ties with the DHL and BTWTA, and these businesses would go on to impressive success in the 1940s and 1950s.[79]

Job Creation and Business Education: Beauty Schools, Commercial Institutes, and Business Colleges

DHL women worked to create business opportunities for all, but their business leadership and networks especially aided Black women. The institutions they established to train the next generation of Black entrepreneurs especially supported one of the Detroit Housewives League's key objectives: to improve the career prospects of young African Americans.[80] Scholars have shown that early civil rights activism in urban Great Migration sites in the 1930s and 1940s was often linked to job opportunities for Blacks in white-owned companies.[81] In Detroit, too, Black women's organizations promoted an integrationist approach to expanding economic opportunities.[82] For the women of the Detroit Housewives League, Black employment was an important concern. However, they did not focus on integrating white-owned businesses; rather their vision of freedom enterprise centered on growing Black enterprises as a way to expand job opportunities for African Americans. This strategy was no doubt shaped by the organization's mission to increase Black business but also by DHL women's own experiences as business owners and personal beliefs that enterprise was the most promising avenue for improving the economic conditions of African Americans. As key promoters of Black business and creators of business education venues, entrepreneurial DHL women illuminate another facet of Black women's contributions to the goal of Black economic development in this era.

In 1933, the Detroit Housewives League stated: "The problem of getting on in the progressive age is largely centered about commercial developments. Opportunities to earn a livelihood, to secure an education and to do everything worthwhile come in the final analysis through jobs." They continued, "Jobs are essential for our group. These jobs can be acquired in proportion to our ability to mobilize the dollars we earn and spend. Spending these dollars intelligently, we will create places for our boys and girls in the commercial world."[83] The DHL approached the matter of Black youth partly through their endeavors to strengthen Black businesses, working to ensure that growing enterprises could provide more employment opportunities for Black workers in Detroit. They sought "to encourage many in business to improve their businesses, and instill in our youth the fact that all work well done is honorable."[84] The league adopted the slogan "Find a job, or make one and make your dollar do Triple duty." A dollar "doing triple duty" would "get you what you need, give the Race what it needs—Employment, and bring what all investments should bring—Dividends."[85]

The beauty industry provided the best opportunities for Black women entrepreneurs; by the 1930s it was one of the strongest business sectors in Black Detroit.[86] Because Black women contended with both race and sex discrimination and had even fewer opportunities for lucrative employment than Black men in the 1920s, they often chose entrepreneurship to gain economic benefits and autonomy not possible through other jobs, where they often faced long hours, violence, sexual harassment, and meager wages. These challenges were particularly acute for Black women who worked as domestic servants, and working-class southern migrants longed to escape the degrading aspects of domestic labor.[87] The 1930s saw an explosion in the number of Black women who established beauty culture businesses in Detroit as a survival strategy during the depression.[88] Despite economic hardship, the demand for cosmetologists' services increased during this period. Beauty salons in northern migration cities like Detroit were important venues in which southern migrant women could shed the stigma of being "rural folk" and reconstruct themselves as sophisticated and modern. Donning the latest hairstyles (such as waved or dyed hair) enabled them to become "modern women" and "New Negroes."[89] Additionally, the high demand for beauty culture created opportunities for entrepreneurs to manufacture hair and cosmetic products to sell to burgeoning salons and their patrons.

One such cosmetics entrepreneur was Vivian Nash, founder of Bee Dew Laboratories. Nash was a southern migrant from Locust Grove, Georgia. Her father was a prosperous farmer and, having grown up on a farm, young Vivian developed an interest in canning produce, a skill she learned from her grandmother.[90] After attending Spelman College and completing her training as a nurse at Grady Hospital in Atlanta, Nash worked in public health.[91] In 1920, she migrated to Detroit because of the many job opportunities she heard were available.[92] However, after settling in the city, Nash was disappointed to find that there were few prospects for African Americans in the field of nursing, and she had trouble obtaining permanent work in her profession. The field of beauty culture seemed to be a lucrative alternative, and Nash saw great possibilities in manufacturing cosmetics for African American consumers. Since cosmetics involved preparing vegetables and chemicals in various combinations, she decided to merge her canning skills and training as a nurse to create cosmetic products.[93]

Nash established her business in 1924.[94] After the U.S. Patent Office rejected her applications for more than a dozen possible names, she finally hit upon an acceptable tag in "Bee Dew." She sold her products door-to-door until she rented her first basement office, and later purchased the entire building at 615 East Forest Street. She hired two staff members and trained them to "sell, sell, sell."[95] A firm believer in the value of advertising in Black newspapers, Nash consistently placed advertisements promoting the benefits of Bee Dew products in leading Black periodicals. By advertising in the Black press, she built up an international mailing list of almost one hundred thousand names, which drastically increased her mail-order business.[96] By 1934, ten years after founding Bee Dew Laboratories, Vivian Nash had the largest Black-owned manufacturing business in the State of Michigan. At the company's Detroit headquarters, 47 employees manufactured and sold Bee Dew products, while 452 agents and representatives were employed throughout the United States, the Canal Zone, and South Africa. Most of Bee Dew's sales agents were Black women.[97]

The DHL and BTWTA were key to Vivian Nash's continued success throughout the 1930s. She was a lifelong member of the Booker T. Washington Trade Association and was deeply involved in the organizational work from the start. In a 1935 joint publication, the BTWTA and DHL thanked several people, including Nash, for being "outstanding men and women who have contributed their part in the development of this work."[98] Nash regularly advertised in the publications and directories of the DHL and BTWTA.

Figure 8. Bee Dew Cosmetic Company photograph. Exhibition Collections–Black
Bottom and Paradise Valley: Help Us Collect Your Past PH148, Folder 1/16.
Charles H. Wright Archives & Research Library, Charles H. Wright Museum of
African American History.

A 1935 advertisement for Bee Dew Laboratories stated: "Together we work
for a common cause—Employment and Economic Security."[99] Bee Dew and
the Detroit Housewives League shared a common goal: increasing Black economic development by creating job opportunities within the Black business
community. In 1938, Vivian Nash hosted "Beauticians Night" for the DHL
and BTWTA's Eighth Annual Trade Exhibition. In this program, beauticians
from all over the city displayed their skills for a chance to win a prize. This
event also provided exposure for beauty shop owners.[100] Thus, Vivian Nash
was not only a successful entrepreneur herself but also exemplified the DHL's
mission of creating jobs and economic opportunities for others in order to
uplift the Black community in the context of racial capitalism.

In addition to encouraging job creation through business development,
the DHL thought it vital for Blacks to get not just an academic education but
also a professional and business education to acquire the necessary skills to
establish successful enterprises. In addition to identifying as businesswomen,
many DHL women identified with their role as mothers and took seriously the need to create business opportunities for their children and future

generations. The DHL established Junior Units of the DHL for boys and girls from the ages of six to sixteen, designed to develop an interest in establishing future businesses and fostering economic security among Black youth.[101] At the 1940 National Housewives League annual meeting, one of the program highlights was a discussion led by DHL member Gertrude Tolbert. Women who were "housewives and business women" served as discussants, including DHL member and future DHL president Nannie Black, who operated a real estate company. Discussants debated the meeting theme, "A Business Educational Program the Negro's Need," from the standpoints of merchants, professionals, parents, and youth.[102] In addition, a DHL informational pamphlet from the early 1940s included in a list of the organization's purposes "to develop opportunity for our youth" and espoused the slogan "Forward Today for Tomorrow Through Youth, Service, Education and Business."[103] Creating educational opportunities was a primary strategy for the organization, and entrepreneurial DHL women led the charge. By establishing successful Black-owned business and commercial colleges in Detroit, they furthered their reputation as "a body of noble women working unselfishly to increase the opportunities of the youth of tomorrow."[104]

Black women's success in the beauty industry led to the establishment beauty colleges in Detroit, some of the city's first institutions for business training. By 1937, African American women ran eight cosmetology or beauty schools in Detroit.[105] One of them was the Bee Dew Beauty College, which Vivian Nash started in 1936 to instruct trainees in the proper methods of using Bee Dew merchandise.[106] She purchased a building at the corner of Hastings Street and Forest Avenue, which in addition to the college housed the manufacturing plant, the Bee Dew Beauty Shop, and the company's general offices.[107] Nash embraced (and likely shaped) the DHL's goal of encouraging young Black women to pursue business as a road to racial and economic uplift. An advertisement for the Bee Dew Beauty College exclaimed, "Girls! Women! Men! Learn a Profession, Become Independent, Own Your Own Business."[108] By creating schools to train Black women to become professionals in the beauty industry, Nash and other women entrepreneurs helped them expand their own careers and further enhanced Detroit's Black business community.[109]

The onset of World War II in the 1940s saw an expansion of Black women's economic opportunities. The war carried the United States out of the grips of the Great Depression and also spurred a second wave of the Great Migration that brought tens of thousands of Black southerners to Detroit. The rapid expansion of wartime production drastically reduced unemployment in the city.[110] Moreover, as men joined the military and created an industrial labor shortage, women were able to enter the defense industries in a meaningful way.[111] The shifting nature of women's work and increased financial independence opened up a discussion among DHL women about the changing economic landscape for women entrepreneurs. In 1942, DHL founder and National Housewives League president Fannie Peck wrote a piece for *Service Magazine* titled, "Negro Housewives What Now?" Peck pointed out, "Because of world conditions, women find doors of opportunity for participation open to them," and asked, "Will we be wise enough to take advantage of the many opportunities that are being made available to us at this time?"[112] Relatedly, in 1944, Iota Phi Lambda, a sorority for Black businesswomen, held its northern regional meeting in Detroit. Discussion topics at the meeting included "Opportunities for Negro Women in the Post-War Business World" and "What Business Women Can Do to Retain Present Employment."[113]

The DHL's vision for economic advancement through education came to fruition when women entrepreneurs established a business school and two commercial institutes in Detroit. The founders of these institutions, Rosa Slade Gragg, R. Louise Grooms, and Violet T. Lewis, all had strong ties to the Detroit Housewives League and the Booker T. Washington Trade Association. These schools—the Slade-Gragg Academy of Practical Arts, the Detroit Institute of Commerce, and Lewis Business College—significantly boosted the local Black business community by providing crucial skills to future entrepreneurs and training workers who went on to secure jobs as bookkeepers, typists, and secretaries in Detroit's expanding Black enterprises. By the end of the 1940s, Detroit's business community was larger and more prosperous than ever in large part due to the work of DHL women.

Prior to establishing these Black business institutions, African Americans did not have the opportunity to attend business school in the State of Michigan. However, recognizing the strengthening economy and influx of new migrants, women entrepreneurs saw the writing on the wall. They understood that there would be greater opportunities for Black entrepreneurship and as Black businesses grew, so too would the demand for African Americans trained to work in business offices. Rosa Slade Gragg explained that she founded the Slade-Gragg Academy in 1947 to provide displaced and uneducated persons opportunities for careers beyond unskilled labor after the war ended.[114] She envisioned Slade-Gragg Academy graduates who were poised, confident, and able to achieve financial independence and dignity.[115]

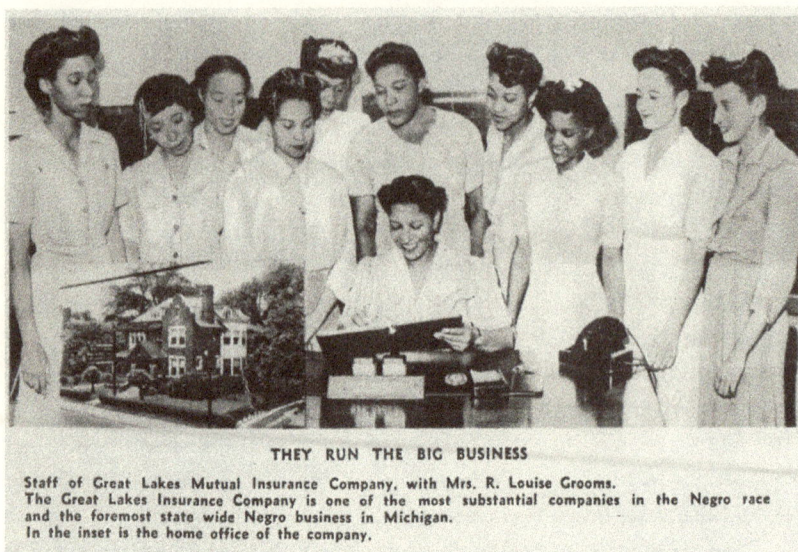

THEY RUN THE BIG BUSINESS

Staff of Great Lakes Mutual Insurance Company, with Mrs. R. Louise Grooms.
The Great Lakes Insurance Company is one of the most substantial companies in the Negro race
and the foremost state wide Negro business in Michigan.
In the inset is the home office of the company.

Figure 9. R. Louise Grooms and the staff of the Great Lakes Mutual Insurance
Company that she trained in 1944. Walter P. Reuther Library, Archives of Labor and
Urban Affairs, Wayne State University.

Likewise, according to R. Louise Grooms, founder of the Detroit Institute of Commerce, "When we started even the public schools discouraged
Blacks from taking business courses on the theory that there was no point
in it. But I always urged our students to be prepared for the opportunity that
would come."[116] Grooms had a long career before opening the Detroit Institute of Commerce in 1941, working for more than twenty years in business
administration in some of Detroit's most prominent Black-owned businesses.
Grooms was the longtime bookkeeper and cashier for the Great Lakes Mutual
Insurance Company and had served as the BTWTA's auditor.[117] She also spent
six years as a public school teacher and decided to use her knowledge and
experience in both business and education to prepare young Black women
and men to earn a livelihood.

The Detroit Institute of Commerce had a modest start, residing in two
rooms in the Tobin Building in downtown Detroit, but throughout the 1940s
grew to occupy the entire sixth and eighth floors. R. Louise Grooms was no
doubt aided by the Detroit Housewives League and the Booker T. Washington Trade Association in her efforts to establish the institute. Grooms was
an active DHL member. In December 1943, the DHL and BTWTA held a

Better Business Conference with the theme "Doing More with Less," and Grooms was on the planning committee and also gave the conference's closing remarks. She was a member of the BTWTA's Executive Committee, serving as the recording secretary, and the Detroit Institute of Commerce was a member of the BTWTA as well.[118] The Detroit Institute of Commerce offered stenography, executive secretarial, finishing secretarial, junior accounting, and business administration courses. The institute was licensed by the Michigan State Board of Education and authorized to train World War II veterans under the GI Bill. After ten years of operation, Grooms considered her school a success, declaring, "Negroes now own more, larger, and better organized businesses."[119]

Lewis Business College (LBC) was the largest and most successful of Detroit's Black business schools. It was also the first, established by Violet T. Lewis in 1939, and paved the way for both the Slade-Gragg Academy and the Detroit Institute of Commerce. Like Rosa Slade Gragg and R. Louise Grooms, Lewis had a strong business background, which undoubtedly contributed to the success of her college. After graduating from the secretarial program at Wilberforce University in her home state of Ohio, she obtained her first professional job as secretary to the president of Selma University in Alabama. While there, she also taught secretarial classes in the university's business department. Lewis eventually landed a job as a bookkeeper at the Madam C. J. Walker Company in Indianapolis and also operated several small businesses on the side. She enjoyed her work, but after she noticed an abundance of unemployed local young people, Lewis got the idea to start her own secretarial school to train African Americans for business careers. In January 1928, Lewis opened the Lewis Business College in Indianapolis.[120]

After operating the school for almost ten years, Lewis decided that she needed to increase her income in order to send her two daughters to college. She reasoned that opening another school in a nearby city would be a viable solution. A family friend and distant cousin, Cortez Peters, suggested Detroit, noting that there were more Black-owned businesses there than in any other major city. Moreover, Detroit had a large Black community but no business schools that accepted African Americans.[121] Lewis decided to visit Detroit to explore this option and with the help of some local family found a suitable location for the college. She signed a one-year lease on an administrative building at West Warren and McGraw Avenues.[122]

However, it was not just her family's help that enabled Lewis to set up the Detroit branch of her school. Assistance from Black entrepreneurs and organizations proved crucial to her success in breaking into the Detroit market, particularly the Detroit Housewives League and the Booker T. Washington Trade Association. Lewis had researched Detroit's Black community and learned of the BTWTA and DHL's significance for local Black enterprises and community belonging. She met with the organizations to discuss her plans for a new business college and solicited their advice before establishing the school. Members of both organizations pledged to support her, and DHL women promised to help promote the new Lewis Business College.[123]

The DHL made good on their promise. After the State of Michigan approved her educational program and issued her a license to operate a business school, Lewis got to work advertising to Detroit's Black youth. She ran full-page ads in all three Black local newspapers; members of the Detroit Housewives League canvassed neighborhoods distributing flyers; and pastors of Detroit's major Black churches (many of whom were associated with the BTWTA) placed inserts in their Sunday bulletins.[124] When the doors of Detroit's LBC opened in September 1939, Lewis was surprised and delighted to see that more than fifty students had showed up and registered for classes—more than the number of students enrolled for an entire year at the Indianapolis campus.[125] Lewis Business College became a member of the BTWTA.[126]

LBC originally educated women who wanted to gain the necessary skills to work in "businesses careers," which typically meant being a secretary or stenographer. These skills could also be used in operating one's own enterprise. The college offered nine-month courses on topics such as typewriting, shorthand and stenography, bookkeeping, filing, and office machines, and later expanded its curriculum with programs in business administration and accounting.[127] Demand for the school's services was so high that after the first year that Lewis Business College had to move from its original Detroit location and eventually occupied three adjacent properties. While those first fifty students in 1939 gave Lewis a tremendous sense of affirmation that her Detroit venture would be a success, by 1942 the college had grown to almost 300, and attendance would continue to increase.[128] Between September 1942 and August 1943, the college enrolled 514 students and registration for the 1944–45 school year totaled 626.[129] LBC also became coeducational when World War II veterans wanted to take advantage of the GI Bill; the college added more class sessions to keep up with increased enrollment. On average, 350 students attended classes daily.[130]

LBC's expansion did not come without challenges and failures. For example, in the first year of operating the Lewis Business College in Detroit,

Violet Lewis trusted a manager who ended up embezzling money from the college.[131] There were other difficult situations as well. In the early 1940s, racial tensions in Detroit were growing and the city would ultimately erupt into a race riot in 1943. A story Violet Lewis relayed to her daughters provides insight on the racial climate that DHL entrepreneurs had to navigate when pushing boundaries in the business world. When Lewis expanded the Detroit college from its original location and moved into the historic East Ferry Avenue District in 1940, Lewis chose to move into the building at night. She framed this story as having to do with money being tight and being unable to afford to hire a moving company. She gathered a group of family and friends who brought their cars and trailers to transport the school's equipment and furniture. They supposedly chose to do this in the middle of the night so that Lewis's elegant new neighbors would not see the caravan of cars pulling trailers.[132] While there were certainly times when money was tight and Lewis Business College's working capital was minimal, the act of moving at night likely reflected Lewis's fears that relocating to a majority-white neighborhood would be met with resistance. Violet Lewis was not the only Black entrepreneur in Detroit to use this strategy. In his memoir, Sunnie Wilson, who operated the Forest Club in Detroit, mentioned that he too moved into his property at night when he started the business in 1941. According to Wilson, "My acquiring the Forest Club upset my white competitors who owned established bars on adjacent corners. In an effort to block my purchase, the local [white] businessmen signed petitions in protest against me. I told my friend Police Inspector Edwin Morgan about the situation and he told me to move in at night."[133] The threat of violence directed toward Black business owners remained tangible for those pushing against the hierarchical boundaries of racial capitalism.

Violet Lewis did experience antagonism from whites in the neighborhood once she moved into the new building. One day when she was sitting in the college's office, Lewis received a registered letter containing a summons from the city of Detroit instructing her to "cease and desist the operation of Lewis Business College at 5450 John R Street, Detroit, Michigan in the County of Wayne, within 24 hours."[134] White neighbors had filed a petition against her for violating a zoning ordinance (the area where the school was located was a residential zone). However, Lewis and others in Detroit's Black community believed that the petition was racially motivated and white neighbors simply did not want Black people in the neighborhood. Violet Lewis described the moment she received the summons: "I felt as if the whole world had caved in upon me. . . . Here I was, riding this wave of prosperity and success, and 'bang' its [sic] all wiped away in one crushing moment."[135] Lewis met with Reverend Horace White of Plymouth Congregational Church, who was able to draw on his political connections and obtain a ten-day extension. Then Lewis called on Herbert Dudley and Carleton Gaines, board members of the Great Lakes Mutual Insurance Company. Dudley was a Black attorney and Gaines had a real estate business and was president of Detroit's Victory Loan and Investment Company. Gaines was also a charter member of the Booker T. Washington Trade Association and served as BTWTA president in the 1940s.[136] Dudley's research found that a for-profit business could not operate in the neighborhood. From there, Lewis worked with Gaines and Dudley to incorporate Lewis Business College as a nonprofit organization so that Lewis could avoid eviction and the college could continue to operate.[137]

Violet T. Lewis recognized a lucrative untapped market for the training she could offer, and Lewis Business College provided bookkeepers, typists, and secretaries that enhanced the Black business community in Detroit.[138] While white companies refused to hire African Americans as office workers, Detroit's Black professionals wanted Black secretaries and bookkeepers but had a hard time finding them prior to the founding of the school. Now they sought out and employed Lewis Business College graduates, acquiring the staff they needed to expand their businesses, which they did throughout the 1940s.[139] Moreover, the school provided hundreds of young African Americans with qualifications for career success. In March 1943, Lewis Business College was happy to report, "We have young men and women scattered throughout the city of Detroit, able to make their living, and to hold their own in the business world."[140] By the early 1950s, graduates were working as personal secretaries to executives, doing administrative work for the government and private companies, and operating their own small businesses.[141] In establishing Lewis Business College, Violet Lewis advanced the Ellioto-rians' vision to encourage young women to enter business careers and the Detroit Housewives League's efforts to grow Black-owned business in Detroit through education.

*   *   *

Despite the devastation of the Great Depression, Detroit gained a reputation for having one of the strongest Black-owned business communities in the 1930s and 1940s in the United States. This was due in large part to the work of the Detroit Housewives League and the Booker T. Washington Trade Association, partner organizations committed to boosting and building local Black business. A deeper investigation into the lives of key organizational leaders reveals that DHL women were not traditional "housewives," nor did they only offer supplementary support to the BTWTA. Rather, they were businesswomen and entrepreneurs in their own right, drawing on their business knowledge and experience to implement essential strategies to improve Black-owned businesses. Entrepreneurial DHL women conducted research that produced valuable business information for their community, and Black entrepreneurs relied on the DHL, recognizing the organization's importance for generating business success.

DHL women's work not only boosted business in the Black community as a whole but also resulted in boosting their own businesses, whether individual enterprises such as Vivian Nash's Bee Dew Cosmetics or family businesses they operated with their husbands. Moreover, the DHL's commitment to business education and job creation inspired Black women entrepreneurs to establish beauty schools and commercial institutes. Black women with ties to the DHL and BTWTA established all of the major institutions for business education in Detroit in this period. Institutions such as Lewis Business College not only provided their proprietors with income but also were crucial for training the next generation of Black entrepreneurs in the city. The DHL's instructive and community-focus "boosting" ensured that Detroit's Black business community expanded rapidly in the 1940s and would continue to flourish into the next decade.

CHAPTER 6

Booming: The Apex of Black Business
in Paradise Valley

In 1940, Detroit attorney Herbert Dudley reported on the progress of Detroit's
Black business community, claiming that "Negroes own and operate perhaps
more business of their own in Detroit, than in any other of the large Metropolitan cities."[1] Corroborating this claim, a 1941 publication produced by the
Works Progress Administration (WPA) observed that "Detroit has a greater
per-capita volume of business controlled and patronized by Negroes than
any other city in the United States." According to the WPA report, Detroit
African Americans had "built businesses and laid the foundations for a few
major industries, their enterprises ranging from the nondescript barbershop
to the well-equipped hospital, summer resort, and finance corporation . . .
a thriving insurance company and a large cleaning and dyeing plant compete successfully with similar establishments owned by whites. There are
seven Negro hospitals in Detroit alone."[2] In the decade that followed the
Great Depression, Detroit's Black business community, made up mostly
of southern migrants, boomed and grew to become one of the strongest
in the country. This period was the height of migrant entrepreneurs' business community in Detroit and when they seemed to be making the most
progress toward their freedom enterprise goals. Yet, the impending white
backlash to the city's 1943 race riot would have long-term consequences for
the community.

Increases in the Black population in the city due to World War II era
migration coupled with the shifting racial geography of the city created new
possibilities for Black entrepreneurs; yet all was not rosy. The 1941 WPA publication mentioned above indicated that Blacks had established themselves
in Michigan's business and professional life *despite* the racial hostility that

existed. During the first wave of the Great Migration in the 1910s and 1920s, "white people regarded the influx of Black workers with alarm and hostility," and the preexisting Black community feared the influx would increase "anti-Negro feeling."[3] African Americans were restricted to a "sharply defined 'Negro district,'" and over time they continued to be "barred from many areas."[4] These racialized residential patterns would have a profound impact on the trajectory of Black-owned business in Detroit. In 1943, racial tensions in the city boiled over, sparking an unprecedented race riot, which became a catalyst for the geographic expansion of Black-owned businesses in the 1940s. White-owned businesses, which were vandalized and looted during the riot, fled from Detroit's east-side neighborhoods. The majority-Black area of the city expanded north and Black entrepreneurs took over the businesses of white entrepreneurs who moved out. Black-owned businesses thrived, especially in the Paradise Valley area bisected by Hastings Street.

It might seem contradictory that new "opportunities" for Black business owners were opened up through the 1943 race riot when traditionally the inherent violence of U.S. racial capitalism has benefited whites economically. However, the backlash that would come through urban redevelopment began almost immediately after the riot. Even though the Black business community was booming in the 1940s and it seemed African Americans were making progress in their freedom enterprise, in reality the demographic changes that took place in Paradise Valley following the riot made the area a target for destruction.

World War II–Era Boom and Black Business Organizing

With the onset of World War II, Detroit emerged from the Great Depression as "Detroit the Dynamic" and the "Arsenal of Democracy." Automobile factories adapted to produce tanks, airplanes, and other military goods to meet the demand created by the war. As a result, employment opportunities in the city increased drastically. With Detroit's economy flourishing again, Black workers experienced new gains in industrial employment. Southern Blacks again migrated to Detroit seeking high-wage jobs.[5] The World War II wave of migration was much larger than the one that took place during the 1910s and 1920s and brought unprecedented increases in Detroit's Black population. Between 1940 and 1950, the number of Blacks living in Detroit would increase from 150,000 to 300,000.[6]

The influx of Black southerners and high employment rates and wages created new opportunities for Detroit's entrepreneurs to establish or expand their businesses. Blacks already operating in Detroit as well as those who migrated to the city during this period enjoyed economic gains. The Black-owned *Detroit Tribune* noted that there had been an "influx of progressive business[people] who have come into the area since [the] end of World War II."[7] However, entrepreneurial conditions were somewhat different during the second wave of the Great Migration than during the first wave around World War I. During the second wave an established Black business community already existed in Detroit. This likely made it more difficult for new migrant entrepreneurs to enter fields that were already fairly saturated (such as the hair care and barbering industries). On the other hand, more Black residents created a higher demand for goods and service, which was an opportunity for new migrant entrepreneurs.

Established enterprises such as local insurance companies found increased business in the war wages of thousands of workers and new migrants. Gloster B. Current, head of the Detroit chapter of the NAACP, wrote in 1944: "Until recently the average Negro worker did not earn enough to have something left over which could be invested in life insurance. When he did buy insurance he bought it from a certain large white eastern insurance company. Not so in Detroit today. The answer to what the Negro worker is doing with his increased earnings can be found in the increased assets of local companies like the Great Lakes Mutual Insurance Company, the Superior Life Insurance Company and Western Union Mutual."[8] Besides Detroit-based Black companies, Chicago's Supreme Liberty Life Insurance Company and several southern Black insurance companies also saw increased patronage from Black Detroiters during the war years. According to Current, there were hundreds of agents in Detroit "selling post-war security to the Negro" on behalf of Black-owned companies.[9]

The 1940s also saw a diversification in the types of businesses Black women engaged in. One new field Black women entrepreneurs entered during the 1940s was the real estate and resort business. A 1945 publication profiling successful African Americans highlighted a "New Field for Women" when featuring Ella F. Towns. Towns, who migrated to Detroit from Atlanta, was a pioneer in the field of summer resort management when she opened Kelsonia Inn in Woodland Park Resort at Bitely, Michigan. Her vision was to cater to Black Detroiters who were overworked and needed rest and relaxation outside of the city. According to the profile Towns had "made an unusual effort to provide good food, swimming, boating and fishing facilities for tired city dwellers." For the safety of bathers, the resort also had a lifeguard on duty. Cottages could be rented during the summer and for game hunting in the winter.[10] Similarly, Detroit Housewives League president Nannie Black entered into the real estate business selling property in Michigan's resort towns during the 1940s.[11]

However, wartime rationing created challenges for businesses. Forty-eight-hour workweeks in Detroit's factories had "put a surplus of money in workers' pockets," but there were also limits on what they could buy. Consumer goods were in short supply, and items such as meat, butter, sugar, coffee, and gasoline were rationed. This impacted grocery stores and gas stations. Many people traveled to Canada to buy items that were hard to find in the United States. Additionally, automobile production practically ceased.[12] Wartime rationing created financial challenges for Ed Davis, who owned an automobile dealership and Standard Oil gas station. Detroit's assembly lines were producing trucks, tanks, and planes instead of cars. The cars that were being built were mostly intended for military use. Car rationing began in the spring of 1942, and any cars still in stock at dealerships could only be sold to "essential people" at 1941 prices. According to Davis, "Soon, like that of most dealerships, the survival of my business depended largely on servicing cars that were getting older and older."[13]

In spite of the challenges of operating in a war economy, those involved in the Booker T. Washington Trade Association and the Detroit Housewives League were still "eager to build bigger, better and more serviceable businesses among our group, although we have less."[14] In 1944 the BTWTA established a company that provided loans from $10 to $300. Instrumental in this venture were Carleton Gaines and Louis C. Blount. Gaines had experience in banking, as he was previously an officer in a Black-owned bank in Georgia. He was also the past president of the BTWTA and served as the president of the loan company. Louis Blount was born in Washington, D.C., attended Howard University for his undergraduate work, and then specialized in life insurance when studying at Temple University before moving to Detroit. Blount served as executive secretary of the Great Lakes Mutual Insurance Company and was the president of the Booker T. Washington Trade Association. The loan company was just one of the many enterprises the organization established in the 1940s. According to Gloster Current, the Booker T. Washington Trade Association was the factor that "holds Negro business together in Detroit." He praised the organization's work of hosting special lectures on improving

Black businesses, charting the latest economic trends, and planning postwar activity to increase the amount of Black business in Detroit.[15]

The Booker T. Washington Trade Association and the Detroit Housewives League continued assisting numerous entrepreneurs in establishing and developing their businesses throughout the 1940s, and their activities were also key in cementing Detroit's reputation as a hub for Black business organizing on the national level. The partner organizations leveraged their national reputation to host the annual convention of the National Negro Business League (NNBL) in Detroit from August 27 to 30, 1940.[16] The convention's theme was "Trends and Opportunities for the Negro in Business." There were panel discussions on the topics "How do present Negro consumers' attitudes affect Negro businesses"; "Should united efforts be made to integrate Negroes into general business"; "What are some effective methods for building strong local Negro trade associations"; "How may cooperative efforts strengthen Negro business"; and "What improved business techniques are needed in Negro business today." According to A. L. Holsey, secretary of the NNBL, advance enrollment for the 1940 convention exceeded that of any previous year. Holsey also reported that more local chapters of the NNBL had been organized or revived in 1940 than during the previous five years.[17] Clearly, Black entrepreneurs in Detroit and across the country were taking advantage of new opportunities for Black business growth.

Detroit was also a leader when it came to organizing Black "unofficial mayors," who were often business owners and leaders.[18] The 1940 NNBL's meeting overlapped with the inaugural National Colored Mayors Convention, which also met in Detroit. Held August 29–31, 1940, the convention was intended to bring together the more than 300 Black "mayors" from around the country to form the National Association of Colored Mayors (NACM) and elect the organization's officers. Similar to the way the Detroit Housewives League was a model for the National Housewives League in the 1930s, the 1940 National Association of Colored Mayors conference in Detroit was organized by the Michigan Colored Mayor's Association, which served as an inspiration for the national organization. These "mayors" descended on Detroit from larger cities like Chicago and New York and other locales because Detroit was a recognized hub for Black business and political organizing.[19]

The next year the National Negro Business League convention was held in Memphis, Tennessee, where Detroit was awarded the 1941 Robert R. Moton cup for being the city with the largest attendance at the NNBL convention. The annual meeting of the National Housewives League (NHL) was held in conjunction with the NNBL and according to a newspaper report, the address by Fannie Peck and the report on the work of the Detroit Housewives League were "the outstanding features of the meeting." Peck was reelected as the president of the NHL. Detroiters reelected to leadership positions in the NNBL included Fred A. Allen, second vice president; Louis C. Blount, regional vice president; Carlton Gaines, member of the steering committee; and Reverend William H. Peck, member of the Executive Committee. Although the city for the 1942 convention had not been selected, Detroit was "already making plans to double its attendance."[20] Clearly Detroit was maintaining its reputation as a leading city when it came to Black business organizing and freedom enterprise.

In December 1943, the BTWTA and DHL held a Better Business Conference, "Doing MORE with Less," which had national attendance. The conference's program stated, "These are busy times. The war has added to an already complicated situation, especially for the proprietors of small business. Naturally, all business owned and controlled by Negroes are in this class."[21] There were several speakers and sessions on various topics, including: "Post-War Planning for Small Business" by S. D. Fuller, president of Fuller Products of Chicago; "U.S. Chamber of Commerce and Its Aid to Small Business" by Emmer M. Lancaster, head of Negro Affairs for the U.S. Department of Commerce; "Who Should Go into Business" by Fred Allen, proprietor of Supreme Linen and Laundry; "The Proper Locations for Business Establishments and How to Select Them" by W. D. Morison, real estate broker; "The Relationship of the Housewives' League to Business" by Christina Fuqua, president of the Detroit Housewives League; and "Negro-Jewish Relations" by Dr. Donald C. Marsh, assistant professor of sociology, Wayne University. There were also talks devoted to thinking ahead to economic opportunities that would be available after the war ended.[22]

The Detroit Race Riot of 1943

It was no accident that the 1943 Better Business Conference held a session titled "Negro-Jewish Relations." Six months earlier the city had been rocked by a riot that saw wartime racial tensions boil over. Racial conflicts stemmed from an acute housing shortage, social strains caused by the city's growing population, and whites' opposition to working alongside African Americans in Detroit industrial plants.[23] The riot also shined a light on tensions between

African Americans and Jewish business owners in the Black Bottom and Paradise Valley neighborhoods. Here, African Americans' response to whites'
anti-Black violence was linked to economic exploitation (for example, they
looted exploitative white-owned stores, particularly pawn shops). While the
social and economic dynamics of the urban North differed from those of the
Jim Crow South, the race riot demonstrated that racial capitalism maintained
through violence was very much a reality in Detroit.

On June 20, 1943, Detroit exploded. It was a hot Sunday, and one hundred thousand people visited Detroit's Belle Isle park. Throughout the day,
there had been minor fights between Black and white youths. Late on Sunday night racial tensions escalated as rumors spread in the Black community that whites had thrown a Black woman and her baby over the Belle Isle
Bridge. Meanwhile, in the white community another rumor spread: people
said that a white woman had been raped by a Black man. Enraged by these
rumors, white and Black Detroiters converged on the streets near downtown
and began throwing rocks at bystanders and property. The violence spread
throughout the city during the early morning hours of Monday, June 21.
Reminiscent of southern white mobs' reactions to accusations of Black men
assaulting white women, a throng of over ten thousand whites descended
on Paradise Valley and attacked African Americans at random. Blacks also
assaulted whites and looted white-owned stores in Paradise Valley.[24] The rioting did not subside until Wednesday after federal troops were brought in to
restore order. At the riot's end 34 people had died, 675 were injured, and
1,893 had been arrested. Most of the dead were Black, and all of the 17 who
were killed by police were African American. The riot also caused two million
dollars' worth of property damage. This was one of worst race riots the United
States had ever seen.[25]

Black Detroiters' migrant identity and familiarity with southern Jim
Crow shaped their understanding of their experiences in Detroit. Many felt
as though the racial dynamics of the South had followed them north to some
extent. The second wave of the Great Migration saw a parallel influx of southern whites to the city.[26] Detroit police officials blamed the "economic situation" as well as the flood of southern whites and Blacks as underlying causes
of the 1943 riot.[27] African Americans also believed the presence of southern
white migrants contributed to the tense atmosphere that led to the 1943 riot.[28]
In oral histories, Blacks point to racial animosity from white southerners or
"hillbillies" as the main factor that sparked the 1943 riot, though certainly
African Americans had conflicts with other groups as well, such as Polish

immigrants.[29] Marcena Taylor, one of the first Black firefighters for the city of Detroit, was with his wife at a Paradise Valley club when the riot broke out. On the way to their home on the west side on Sunday, Taylor and his wife encountered trouble with white southern transplants. As they crossed through "the area going out Warren, Forest, out in the area of Grand River, where those hillbillies lived at the time," they attracted the attention of some whites, who "got in cars following us, and harassing us." Fortunately, the Taylors made it home safely.[30] Likewise, factory worker Charles Denby remembered, "My chief steward, a hillbilly, asked me what I thought about the riot. He asked me if it was the fascists that caused it. Did the Germans plant people to start the riot? I said, 'Hell, no. Some of them Goddamned hillbillies from the South started the whole thing.' He looked real sad about my statement, 'I don't know, I'm from down South.' He felt pretty bad. At first I was sorry for speaking so sharp, I had forgotten he was a hillbilly. But I thought, hell, he knows how they treat us down there."[31] Walter White of the NAACP reported that the white workers recruited chiefly in the South not only gravely complicated the housing, transportation, educational, and recreation facilities of Detroit but also "brought with them the traditional prejudices of Mississippi, Arkansas, Louisiana, and other Deep South states against the Negro."[32] According to Detroit Urban League director John C. Dancy, "The urgency of war production had accelerated the upgrading of Negroes in factories; it had also resulted in importation of white labor from the more backward sections of the South. Many people had felt that some sort of explosion was inevitable and the only question was when."[33]

Black laborers' elevated status in the automobile industry angered white workers, as did African Americans' push for access to affordable housing and the city's recreational sites.[34] The close working conditions of Black and white southerners, coupled with the fact that whites resented Black economic progress, strained race relations so much that a confrontation was almost inevitable. According to one Detroit journalist, "It did not take a prophet to know the riot was coming. . . . Detroit has been building steadily for three years towards a race riot."[35] Less than a year before the riot *Life* magazine had predicted trouble in the city because of wartime racial tensions: "Detroit can either blow up Hitler or it can blow up the U.S." The article also lamented that "too many of the people of Detroit are confused, embittered and distracted by factional groups that are fighting each other harder than they are willing to fight Hitler."[36] Similarly, in 1942 Black journalist Elmer H. Carter had predicted: "There is something highly disturbing in the repetition of racial clashes in Detroit, something ominous like the low rumble of distant thunder before a storm. The clouds gather. And the storm will eventually break unless the constructive forces of racial amity in Detroit take aggressive and positive action to quell those irresponsible and vicious elements in the population who are intent on fastening the pattern of race relations of Mississippi and Florida on that municipality."[37] Not all white southern migrants held racist attitudes or were hostile to Blacks living in Detroit. Walter White opined, "Here and there among these Southern whites were members of the UAW-CIO and other labor unions, churchmen and others who sloughed off whatever racial prejudices they had brought with them from the South." Nevertheless, White concluded, "the overwhelming majority retained and even increased their hostility to negroes."[38] It seems these white Detroiters could not abide changes to the racial and economic hierarchy.

Overpolicing and police brutality were key instruments whites used to maintain the racial order in Detroit, and police practices in the city became a major issue of discussion related to the 1943 riot. According to business owner Sunnie Wilson, "Traditionally, the police had always been cruel in their treatment of Detroit's Black folks. Racial animosity within the police department emerged out of a leftover southern hatred for Blacks. These patrolmen, many of them southern born, were raised on hatred for Black people and they fought to maintain a sense of superiority."[39] Black Detroiters also complained about the southern origins of the federal troopers brought in to end the disturbance. According to Denby, "The Negroes said that all the white troopers were hillbillies. 'Why weren't there some Negro soldiers?' was the question everybody asked. 'Why aren't these guys overseas fighting Hitler?' We felt we'd have a better chance with Negro soldiers. They wouldn't shoot us as quick as white soldiers would."[40] While Black Detroiters linked police and military violence to whites' southern origins (which indeed may have been a factor), in reality the dynamics of racial capitalism in the North were constantly shifting, and police violence had long been an issue in Detroit. Racial segregation was an important aspect of white supremacy in both the South and North, but it was just one tool for maintaining racial capitalism.[41] Racial violence, in various forms, was also intrinsic to U.S. racial capitalist development. There were certainly regional differences; the threat of lynching and the extralegal violence Blacks faced in the Jim Crow South was not the same as the threat of violence and murder at the hands of the police force and military in Detroit. These differences provide insight into the inner workings of U.S. racial capitalism, which is a transforming and adaptable system.

And a different approach to maintaining economic white supremacy through violent action (the destruction of Black property and wealth through urban redevelopment) would emerge in the wake of the 1943 riot.

Black Detroiters associated most of the racial hostility they experienced with white southern migrants, but Jewish merchants in their neighborhoods were the targets of Blacks' frustrations with racial capitalism during the riot. At the time, the majority of Detroit's Black residents lived in an east-side area bounded by Jefferson on the south, John R on the west, East Grand Boulevard on the north, and Russell on the east. This area covered approximately sixty square blocks.[42] Hastings Street ran south to north through this area and was the main commercial thoroughfare. The white-owned businesses on Hastings were mainly owned and operated by Jewish merchants. Future Detroit mayor Coleman Young recalled, "By the late 1920s the [Black Bottom] neighborhood was entirely Black, except for some of the merchants on St. Aubin and Hastings streets."[43] According to Detroit pharmacist Sidney Barthwell, "At the time there were a lot of drugstores on Hastings, but all except one were operated by people of the Jewish faith. They didn't seem interested in hiring a Black pharmacist at the time."[44] Sunnie Wilson recalled that in the early 1940s, "Hastings remained a center of Jewish business."[45] Similarly, artist Leroy Mitchell remembered, "We [Blacks] didn't live on Hastings. Jews still lived on Hastings, over the stores. We lived on the cross streets that cut across Hastings. That's the way it was. . . . All of the [business] activity was taking place on Hastings . . . they owned the drugstores, chili parlors, a lot of chili parlors . . . a lot of small [businesses], all Jewish."[46] According to Mitchell, on Sunday night of the riot, Blacks were very angry when they came across the Belle Isle Bridge. When they arrived at the Hastings Street area, "that's when they started venting their anger against white businesses. They started tearing up things, going up and down Hastings."[47] Black rioters began to stone and destroy shops; the destruction spread until practically all the white-owned businesses in the Black section of town had been attacked.[48]

Still, Charles Denby remembered that Black rioters were somewhat sympathetic toward their Jewish neighbors. According to him, African Americans at the time put Jewish people in a different category than other whites because they tended not to participate in white mob violence against Blacks in the South and were not part of the police force. Denby recalled, "If a difference arose between a Negro and a Jewish person to the point of a fight we were not expecting a lynch mob to come to our home or for a Jewish man to act in the same way as the rest of the whites." According to Denby, during the riots some Black people would say, "I don't give a darn if I beat the hell out of a Jew, but I don't want to kill them. They're not in on everything. There aren't many of them on the police force. But they deserve a beating because they've been robbing us too."[49]

African Americans had a long and complicated relationship with the Jewish community and Jewish business owners in Detroit. Blacks and Jews had always lived close to each other in Detroit's east-side neighborhoods, and they had worked together to fight discrimination that affected both groups. Additionally, Frederick Butzel, a Jewish lawyer, businessman, and philanthropist, worked closely with Black institutions to improve the social circumstances of Blacks in Detroit from the 1910s through the 1940s.[50] Moreover, Jews had provided some of the first opportunities for Black southern migrant entrepreneurs and laborers during the first wave of the Great Migration. For example, when future funeral home owner Willis Eugene Smith first moved to Detroit from Alabama in 1919, a Jewish merchant employed him to sell fur coats.[51]

Yet, Blacks had long felt that Jewish merchants were exploiting them.[52] In 1933, ten years before the race riot, Theodore R. Barnes wrote in the Black-owned *Detroit Tribune*: "Some of the best friends of the Negroes have been Jews, and for this type of Jewry I have the deepest respect and admiration. . . . Such men as Julius Rosenwald, who gave millions for the education of Negroes, and Fred Butzel, was and are all high-minded and high-class men, all the Jewry of this type deserve the admiration of the Negro race."[53] However, Barnes lamented the fact that some Jewish-owned businesses exploited the Black community:

> The average Jew on Hastings Street at the present time, when he is financially independent, will move into a neighborhood far detached from the Negro Race and will do nothing to turn back into the hands of the Negro any of the business profits reaped from his business. Not only that, but he will do nothing to aid in the elevation of the Negro. He wishes to keep him unenlightened in order that he might be more easily exploited. . . . [This exploitation] is sapping, from the Negro race, its very economic backbone and livelihood.[54]

In fact, by 1943 most of the city's Jewish population had moved from the east-side to the "'Herring Belt' in the Twelfth Street and Dexter neighborhoods" yet still operated businesses in the Black eastside neighborhoods.[55]

Not all African American Detroiters held anti-Jewish attitudes when it came to business. In the 1930s the Reverend H. H. Williams of the Metropolitan Baptist Church attempted to facilitate cooperation with Jews, Syrians, and others operating businesses in neighborhoods where Blacks lived. Williams met with three hundred members of the Booker T. Washington Trade Association and the Detroit Housewives League in November 1934. He posited that Jews were "brothers in distress"; therefore, African Americans should be more tolerant of those operating in the community. Conversely, Williams encouraged Jewish business owners to work to "bridge the gap and promote good relations between the two peoples." That is, they should "promote the economic welfare of the black community."[56]

In January 1941, Samuel Lieberman, a merchant in Paradise Valley, led the effort to found the Eastside Merchants Association. This group organized "brotherhood dinners" at the local YWCA to ease racial tensions and reduce anti-Jewish sentiment among Blacks. The association also funded scholarships for Black and Jewish graduate students to research Black-Jewish relations in Detroit. Together the Jewish Community Council and the NAACP sponsored a study called *Some Aspects of Negro-Jewish Relations in Detroit, Michigan.*[57] The study explored topics such as Jewish "commercial establishments," "prices charged," "attitudes of Jews toward Negroes," "attitudes of white Gentiles toward Negroes," "attitudes of Negro youth toward Jews," and "economic data on the Negro consumer and Negro adult attitudes toward Jews in commercial relationships."[58] However, the efforts of the Eastside Merchants Association and Jewish individuals were often overshadowed by "Black perceptions of Jewish slumlords" and Jewish merchants' economic exploitation.[59]

In discussing the Detroit riot, NAACP leader Walter White admitted, "There is no question that shameful and inexcusable looting of stores operated by whites in the east side Negro area, particularly on Hastings and John R Streets was perpetrated by Negroes." However, White also illuminated the causes of Black attacks on white-owned businesses during the riot. According to White, looting was "a form of vengeance . . . against the prejudice in Detroit from which Negroes had suffered" and a response to news of an anti-Black riot in Beaumont, Texas, less than a week earlier on June 15–16, 1943.[60] There, whites had looted Black homes and businesses. Blacks across the country were outraged by these events, and southern migrants who settled in Detroit were no exception.

When the Detroit riot first broke out, Blacks vandalized white-owned businesses largely to vent their frustration with whites in Detroit, and perhaps subconsciously with the system of racial capitalism. Walter White reported that when the windows in the stores on Hastings Street were first broken on Sunday night, there was no looting. An officer of the Merchants Association had walked the length of Hastings Street around 7:00 a.m. on Monday and noticed that none of the stores with broken windows had been looted.[61] Likewise, Charles Denby, who lived on Harper Street, remembered going outside on Monday morning: "Every store that was white-owned, in that block, was completely smashed. Many things were in the street, groceries, druggist equipment, dry goods, everything." However, Denby stated, "Nobody was touching the stuff."[62]

That would not last long. Soon people began looting and, in doing so, took financial revenge on white merchants who exploited them. Leroy Mitchell recalled, "It just really caught on. It was like anger that had been pent up and had come to the boil. There were lots of people, but mainly youngsters. . . . The youngsters were the ones doing the most destruction. Of course once the youngsters started destroying the stores, the older people were helping themselves to things in there."[63] Black Detroiters especially targeted pawnshops, which were seen as a particularly exploitative business. According to Mitchell, "Boy, they were cleaning out those. Hastings was just full of pawnshops. That used to be a major business in the Black neighborhoods. That's where you got money. You'd take your things and then you'd try to get them back. They just took over those pawnshops. They just took everything. That's what they wanted mainly. They weren't so much worried about the stores and the food and things, but those pawnshops . . . that was the main thing they were hitting."[64] Local Black businessman Ed Davis also remembered that pawnshops were particularly targeted by rioters.[65] Sidney Barthwell remembered driving over to Hastings Street to check on his drugstore during the riot: "It made my flesh crawl. Where you'd see all those steel bars [on the windows], the guys had just put a tow chain on the back of the truck and drove off and pulled them off. All of Hastings Street was just wide open, full of people just looting all of the stores."[66] When the riot was over, there were hardly any white-owned businesses that were intact on Hastings Street between Canfield and Medbury.[67]

Some sources suggested that the looting was worsened by the actions (or inactions) of Detroit police and federal troopers. Barthwell noted, "I think there was some racism, because the police department had a large percentage of Southerners. I think they were almost as much against the Jewish people as they were against Blacks. Two and three police were on each side of the street, and they did absolutely nothing to try to stop these things."[68] Other witnesses' accounts seem to support Barthwell's claim that the police did not protect Jewish businesses from looting during the riot.[69] Walter White reported that throughout Monday, June 21, instead of placing policemen in front of the stores to protect them from looting, Detroit police contented themselves with driving up and down Hastings Street and from time to time stopping in front of the stores, jumping out of squad cars with drawn revolvers and riot guns to shoot anyone who might be in a store.[70] Police indifference to the destruction of Jewish businesses points to the gradations of whiteness within racial capitalism.

Jewish business owners suffered immense property damage during the 1943 riot.[71] This fact had profound implications for the trajectory of Black business for the rest of the decade. A wave of "white flight" to the city's west side followed the disturbance, including businesses that relocated to Twelfth Street and Dexter Avenue, where the number of Jewish merchants increased dramatically.[72] This is also the area where many African American businesses

Figure 10. A boarded-up storefront after Detroit's 1943 race riot. Courtesy of the Burton Historical Collection, Detroit Public Library.

displaced by urban renewal in the 1950s and 1960s would relocate, as well as the commercial area most affected by Detroit's 1967 urban rebellion (discussed in the Epilogue). Jewish merchants were unable to attain property insurance after the riot, and this was a deal breaker for many. They were "unwilling to tie their economic future to a Black neighborhood."[73] In the system of racial capitalism proximity to Blackness was costly.

The destruction of white-owned businesses during Detroit's 1943 race riot temporarily opened up space for Black business expansion. Even as the riot was taking place Black entrepreneurs suspected that damage to their white competitors would benefit them. Sidney Barthwell remembered, "I had a friend who told me that when they were tearing out the Jewish stores across the street from him he stood and laughed, because he thought, 'It's good they're gone, then my business will be better.'"[74] After the riot most white business owners sold their establishments and property to Black entrepreneurs. As Leroy Mitchell remembered, "After the '43 riot, that's when the Blacks started getting businesses on Hastings. That was the major change, because most of the Jews, they just packed up and left." Mitchell continued,

> We replaced them. We took over the drugstores . . . we didn't have
> that many drugstores on Hastings, chili shops, restaurants, things
> like that. A lot of those things, Blacks took them over. Which they
> hadn't had before. You had more professionals there. They were
> upstairs, over some of the stores: medical doctors, dentists. The pro-
> fessionals moved in and had more of their offices down on Hastings
> . . . of course we had businesses before, but not on Hastings. . . . In
> fact, all through the area I'd say, east of Woodward, the Blacks took
> over much of the businesses in there after the '43 riot.[75]

According to Charles Denby, even after the riot violence played a role in driving white merchants out of the east side. "Some of the White businessmen tried to go back to their stores when the riot was over and many were killed," he recalled. "There was a drugstore on the corner of Hastings and Henrie Streets. When they opened up, they lasted one week and were killed. The store was closed up and later sold to a Negro."[76] Eastsider Justine Wylie remembered, "The riot of 1943 sparked the beginning of changes that affected the demographics of the neighborhood. This was perhaps the beginning of 'White Flight.' Following the riot, businesses were rebuilt and flourished on the near eastside of Detroit."[77]

The post-riot white flight in the 1940s did not benefit all Black entrepreneurs, including Ed Davis. His car dealership was in an advantageous location being next to a large Black-occupied area on the east side yet also close to downtown Detroit. Almost 60 percent of his customers were white, which meant a "wider customer base and more moneymaking opportunities." Davis recalled, "This changed drastically after June 20, 1943. A terrible race riot broke out. When it was over the service traffic to my dealership from white customers dropped off."[78] Davis never regained the same level of patronage from the white community following the riot. According to Davis, "I continued to serve some white customers, but the majority of my business was now with my fellow Blacks."[79] Post–1943 riot white flight and decreased white patronage had a negative impact on Davis's business as well as that of other Black entrepreneurs in the area who had both white and Black clients.

Still, many African American entrepreneurs saw white flight as creating business opportunities for them. One of Leroy Mitchell's friends bought a record shop from a white owner who was ready to leave Hastings Street.[80] Likewise, James E. Cummings's first opportunity to own a business was a result of the post-riot exodus of white-owned business from the east side. Cummings was born in 1908 in Greenville, Alabama, and migrated to Detroit in late 1918 where he later became a successful businessman. For years Cummings had saved up money as he worked as a bellhop in some of Detroit's white-owned hotels. However, after the 1943 riot, Cummings owned several businesses, including a Standard Oil gas station. According to Cummings, "The way the buildings were bought was because we had a riot in 1943. . . . The owners of the property became afraid, and they began to sell all of this property right from Harper Hospital [Alexandrine Street] north and sold it almost on your terms. They thought it would break out again."[81] Cummings began purchasing property right after the war. Having served in the military for two years, he converted an insurance policy into enough money to make a down payment on his gas station. Cummings's assessment that white owners sold their property "almost on your terms" was an important breakthrough for Blacks who previously had been barred from purchasing certain properties or who had no choice but to pay exorbitant prices to white owners. Though it came through violence, the flight of white business created possibilities for Black entrepreneurs to acquire property at manageable prices. In this way, the riot changed the racial geography of the city and economic landscape for Black entrepreneurs. However, these "opportunities" would be short-lived, as the 1943 riot was also a catalyst for

the city to look to urban planning to push Blacks out of the area and ultimately destroy Black business.

Proliferation of Black Business in Paradise Valley

African Americans had settled primarily on Detroit's east side, mostly in the
Black Bottom and Paradise Valley neighborhoods. This area would continue
to be a destination for the numerous Black migrants who came to the city
during the second wave of the Great Migration during and after World War II.
The Paradise Valley area became the commercial center of Black Detroit and
Black businesses filled Hastings Street and the surrounding area to cater to
new customers arriving from the South. According to Leroy Mitchell, during
the mid-1940s, "Hastings was a classic street for the whole [business] situation. Up and down Oakland, too, we had more restaurants. . . . Most of the
Jews had left."[82] Detroiter Alice Cain Newman noted that in the 1940s Paradise Valley "was a thriving Black business community, probably one of the
most thriving in the United States that was owned by Blacks, not just fronted
by Blacks but it was owned."[83] This differed from cities such as Chicago, where
whites predominantly owned the businesses in the "Stroll," Black Chicago's
commercial amusement and business district.[84] The number of Black-owned
businesses on Hastings increased so much that entrepreneurs were able to
establish a softball league of teams representing different Black-owned enterprises. Heavyweight champion Joe Louis had a team representing his restaurant, the Brown Bomber's Chicken Shack. So did Bender's Fish Market and
Swanson's Barbershop.[85]

In 1941, entrepreneur Sunnie Wilson established the Forest Club, which
became a popular spot for nightlife entertainment in Paradise Valley. He
rented a building at the corner of Hastings and Forest that ran the entire
block. The building formerly had three white owners, one of whom was Leo
Adler, a wealthy white businessman who loaned Wilson $25,000 to buy out
the lease. In the 1920s the building had been an amusement park and Wilson transformed it into an entertainment space that had a banquet hall, a
dance floor, a two-level roller-skating rink, twenty-six lanes for bowling, and
a famous 107-foot-long bar.[86] Because the Forest Club was located at a streetcar stop, Wilson's business benefited from the steady flow of people arriving
and departing from the street. Wilson put up a big sign outside reading "Stop
in and Get Your Morning Nip" to attract customers in the daytime. The Forest

Club was so popular Wilson was able to hire nearly three hundred employees, including clerks, bartenders, cooks, waiters, and bouncers.[87] This was just one of many Black-owned businesses that thrived in Paradise Valley during the 1940s and was able to offer dignified employment to African Americans, a key aspect of many African Americans' freedom enterprise.

Community-focused cooperation and instruction were other key aspects of Black Detroiters' vision of freedom enterprise. Many business owners gave back to their community in the ways they could and had socially minded as well as financial goals. According to Sunnie Wilson, "In the [Forest] club we set up a school for poor Black people to learn to read and write. Watching these women and men learn to write their names was an emotionally moving experience. They had tears running down their cheeks." Having the skills to read and write could be economically beneficial for Black southern migrants. Wilfred E. Little came to Detroit in 1940 and began selling furniture at a white-owned company called Cut Rate Department Stores in 1941. The store was located on Hastings and Livingstone in the mostly Black neighborhood. Little recalled the ways white business owners exploited Black customers. According to Little, "When they'd write up their contract, they'd write an altogether different price. Sometimes they'd add as much as one hundred dollars or more to their bill, and the person wouldn't even know it. . . . You had people coming from the South and other places. Some of them couldn't read too well. They hadn't gone to high school . . . and many of them couldn't even count their money too well."[88] Wilfred Little's insider view on the schemes white companies used to exploit Black customers highlight why it was important for Black businesses to serve multiple functions in their neighborhoods. The school at the Forest Club provided new arrivals with the tools to combat economic exploitation.

The Hastings Street area remained the economic epicenter of the Black community through the early 1950s and earned a "world-wide reputation."[89] Dorothy Elizabeth Lawson remembered, "During the war my husband and my brother were both stationed in Illinois . . . every time I would go there, we would go out or meet somebody and they would say, 'Where are you from?' I would say, 'Detroit.' And they would say, 'Where, on Hastings Street?' Everybody thought everybody from Detroit was from Hastings Street or Black Bottom; and then it was changed to Paradise Valley."[90] Paul B. Shirley worked as waiter at the Downtown Club and Penobscot Club, and as a singer, dancer, and stand-up comedian in clubs such as Lark's Grill, Turf Bar, and Flame Show Bar. According to Shirley, "Hastings Street—there will never be another like it, and it is known all around the world. Hastings Street in Detroit."[91]

Figure 11. A 1940s photograph of a "typical Negro business district" in
Detroit. Library of Congress, Prints & Photographs Division, FSA/OWI Collection,
LC-DIG-fsa-8d25381.

Hastings Street was particularly known for its clubs and nightlife. One
reason Hastings was so well-known was because it was mentioned in popular
blues and jazz songs. For example, Big Maceo and Tamps Red's 1945 song
"Detroit Jump" included a reference to Hastings Street. Pianist Detroit Count
recorded "Hastings Street Opera," which contained colorful and humorous
descriptions of Hastings Street bars. This song included a reference to Sunnie
Wilson's Forest Club:

> Forest and Hastings!
> Sunnie Wilson,
> longest bar in town.
> That's the onlyst bar you can walk in when you get ready to buy a
>   bottle beer
> you have to walk a mile after you get in the joint.[92]

Additionally, blues legend John Lee Hooker's 1948 hit song, "Boogie Chillen,"
described the thriving club scene in Detroit and on Hastings Street:

When I first come to town, people,
I was walkin' down Hastings Street
Everybody talkin' 'bout, Henry's Swing Club,
I decided to drop in there that night.
When I got there,
I said "Yes, people, yes,"
They were really havin' a ball.
Yes, I know . . .
Boogie chillen![93]

Hooker, whose recording career began in Detroit, explained what drew him and others to Hastings Street: "Oh that was *the street, the street* in town. Everything you lookin' for on that street, *everything*. Anything you wanted was on that street. Anything you *didn't* want was on that street. Stores, pawnshops, clothing stores, winos, prostitutes. . . . Everybody was talking about Hastings Street, and everybody was talking about Henry's Swing Club. That was a famous place. A famous street. Best street in all the world. Too bad they tore it down."[94] However, not everyone was so nostalgic about Hastings Street. One woman insisted, "Oh Hastings Street. There was a lot of guys on the street, a lot of hanging out. Hastings was one of the predominant places where most families wouldn't allow their children to go. Hastings was a rough street, that was the understood thing. . . . That's what Hastings was like. If you had any type of respect, you stay off Hastings."[95] Conversely, Charleszetta Waddles, who lived on Hastings and Wilkins, had this to say about the area: "Hastings Street was supposed to be the bad street and you could leave your door open. You could go to the store and come back." Waddles continued: "They had all-night movies up on Hastings. You could take your child at nine o'clock at night when it was too hot and just go to the movies. I did that many a time. You pass down the street, you might find somebody playing three-card molly, but you just walk around them. Or a prostitute was in the door and, you know, you just kept walking. But you didn't have this violence, and you didn't have the apprehension about even being on the streets. It wasn't that kind of feeling."[96] Similarly, club owner Sunnie Wilson recalled: "At that time, the Black population of the east side was a closely knit community. Relations among our people were fine. There was very little violence. If someone got robbed, the criminals would leave him a dollar to get home."[97]

PARADISE VALLEY DISTRIBUTORS—A Successful Negro Business

Figure 12. Paradise Valley Distributing Company photo. Courtesy of the Burton Historical Collection, Detroit Public Library.

While some Black Detroiters looked down on Paradise Valley's rowdy scene, its clubs and bars facilitated the growth of related businesses. This included the Paradise Valley Distributing Company (PVDC). Founded in 1937, PVDC boasted that it was the "first and only fully owned and operated Negro beer distributing agency in the entire United States. Everything Negro from the FRONT OFFICE to the porter."[98] The company was the exclusive supplier of beer brands such as Koppitz, Friars Old Stock Ale, Hi-Brau, and Koerbers Pilsner to the Black sections of Detroit.[99] In 1941, the gross income of the company was $500,000 (more than $10 million in 2023 dollars).[100] By 1943, PVDC owned ten trucks and had forty-two employees.[101] In 1944 the company sponsored three Detroit youths with $1,500 in scholarship money to attend college.[102] Most Black business owners in Paradise Valley put money back into the community in order to uplift the race.[103]

Although the east side became well-known for its nightlife, Black entrepreneurs established a wide variety of businesses in the 1940s.[104] For example, in 1943 three Black entrepreneurs (Irving Roane, John White, and Walter Norwood) joined together to purchase the magnificent Gotham Hotel.[105] Located at 111 Orchestra Place (near John R Street), the Gotham boasted nine stories and more than two hundred rooms, several penthouses, an elegant lobby, a restaurant, a flower shop, and a drugstore on the first floor.[106] The Ebony Room restaurant's kitchen was run by Arthur Madison, "former *chef de cuisine* of Boston's Latin Quarter," and served impressive meals including lobster. However, the hotel's Ebony Room did not have a bar because the "liquor license was refused because of opposition of nearby white hospital."[107] As the Black business community seemingly blossomed there continued to be racial conflicts and opposition from whites.

The Gotham Hotel was widely considered the best Black-owned hotel in the country. Leroy Mitchell remembered, "[John] White had the Gotham, which was huge, one of the best hotels. Was the best hotel Blacks had in the whole of the United States. Guys would come up from New York, [and] they were startled. It was nothing but a bunch of dumps in Harlem."[108] Similarly, Langston Hughes—who traveled extensively and was a good judge—marveled at the quality of the Gotham Hotel. In 1945 Hughes wrote a glowing piece on the hotel in the *Chicago Defender* where he indicated, "This miracle I speak of is the Hotel Gotham, owned, managed, and staffed by Negroes."[109] A 1947 profile on the Gotham in *Ebony* magazine called the Gotham the "undisputed holder of the title of best Negro hotel in America."[110] Additionally, while working as the NAACP's chief legal counsel Thurgood Marshall stated: "I travel approximately 70,000 miles a year, and the Gotham Hotel is the finest hotel operated by Negroes in this country and one of the finest hotels operated by any. I believe this to be true not only because of service, but the apparent desire of the owners and the manager to keep the place up."[111] The Gotham's managers had a "Courtesy Code" that all employees were expected to follow. Among other things, the code emphasized that "A cheerful 'Glad to see you, sir,' or 'It's nice to have you back with us madam,' has made many a hotel cash register ring with repeat business." The Gotham Hotel was illustrated on a postcard, which was mailed across the country by those visiting Detroit. This symbolized the hotel's reputation as a prominent establishment in the city. The Gotham would remain a popular business in Paradise Valley until the early 1960s, when it was demolished by the city.

A. W. Curtis Laboratories, established by Austin W. Curtis, was another new type of business established in the Paradise Valley area. Curtis was a migrant entrepreneur who was impressed by the business prospects in Detroit. Born in 1911 in Institute, West Virginia, he graduated with a DSc in chemistry from Cornell University in 1932. After teaching at the Agricultural and Technology College in Greensboro, North Carolina, for two years, Curtis moved to Tuskegee, Alabama, in 1935 to become the assistant of

Figure 13. The Gotham Hotel depicted in an E. C. Kropp Company postcard. The back states: "200 rooms all with private bath tub or shower; popular priced restaurant. Irving Roane & John J. White, Props."

Dr. George Washington Carver at the Tuskegee Institute. After Carver's death in 1943, Curtis moved to Detroit and established the A. W. Curtis Laboratories at 454 Farnsworth. There, he manufactured and distributed eighty different products, including cosmetics such as face powder, vanishing and cleansing creams, shampoos, cough medicine, rubbing oils, and peanut cooking oil.[112] According to Curtis, he chose to migrate to Detroit to establish his laboratory because "Detroit had a reputation of being the leading city in the nation for Black business development and progress."[113] Curtis had a particular interest in creating job opportunities for Black youth and economic opportunities for numerous Black workers as dealers of his products.[114] Curtis encouraged Black Detroiters to become dealers of Curtis products as a way to gain economic independence and claimed that A. W. Curtis Laboratories "swings wide open the door of financial independence for you. It is the organization that will never cease in its desire to help you realize the utmost profit and happiness." Additionally, the company touted: "You own your own business when you become a Curtis dealer . . . and you will never find an easier way to be your own boss!"[115] A. W. Curtis Laboratories' promises spoke to one of the key desires of migrant entrepreneurs and Black freedom enterprise.

The 1940s also saw the expansion of Black professional entrepreneurship. By the early 1950s there were 18 Black-owned hospitals, 8 medical-dental labs, more than 150 physicians and 50 dentists, 15 accountants, and 75 Black lawyers serving the city's 361,000 African American residents.[116] Though Black professionals are not typically included in the traditional definition of business owners or entrepreneurs, historical sources on Detroit's Black business community provide a wealth of examples of professionals who were clearly entrepreneurial and had profitable practices. For the most part, Black professionals in Detroit could not hope to be hired at white institutions or in public positions. Throughout the first half of the twentieth century, white-owned law and architecture firms refused to hire African Americans. It was rare for Black doctors and lawyers to be hired by the state to work at public hospitals or in public health fields, or as public defenders or judges. Some Black professionals would likely have preferred this route, but it was simply not an option for the vast majority of African Americans due to racial discrimination.[117] Certainly not all of Detroit's Black professionals were entrepreneurs; some worked as employees of Black-owned enterprises. However, the proprietors of for-profit hospitals, legal offices, architecture firms, dental practices, and so forth were widely considered to be business men and women.

The case of Black-owned hospitals provides a clear example of Black professional entrepreneurship. Longtime Detroit Urban League director John Dancy noted that "at one time there were more Negro hospitals in Detroit than in any other city in the United States."[118] The number of Black-owned hospitals expanded with the influx of migrants into the city. The 1952 Booker T. Washington Trade Association/Detroit Housewives League business directory listed seventeen such hospitals: Barlow Hospital, Bethesda Hospital, Erskine Medical Center, Fairview Sanatorium, Good Samaritan Hospital, Haynes Memorial Medical Hospital, Kirkwood Hospital, Maywood Hospital, Mercy General Hospital, Mercy Hall Hospital, Parkside (Dunbar) Hospital, Resthaven Hospital, Sumby Hospital, Edyth K. Thomas Memorial Hospital, Trinity Hospital, Warren Diagnostic Hospital, and Wayne Diagnostic Hospital.[119] Most of these hospitals were founded by physicians and were for-profit ventures.[120]

Mercy Hospital, the city's first Black-owned hospital, was established in 1917 by Drs. David and Daisy Northcross after they became fed up with racist treatment at a white hospital.[121] Next, Dunbar Hospital was incorporated in 1918 (it was later renamed Parkside Hospital after moving from its original location).[122] In 1931 the Detroit Housewives League reported that Dunbar Memorial Hospital (located at Brush Street at Illinois) was considering an addition to its already "magnificent building." According to the DHL: "This institution aside from being a sound business organization is one of the most elaborate and complete hospital[s] of its kind in the country. The equipment that make up the Dunbar furnishings represent many thousands of dollars and the well trained personnel together with an ideal architectural arrangement has given this great institution such remarkable public support until the new addition seems inevitable according to Mr. W. C. Osby, Business Manager."[123] As with other enterprises, women played an important part in the operation of Detroit's Black hospitals, even though they faced sex discrimination and glass ceilings in the medical field. For example, Dr. Daisy Northcross operated Mercy General Hospital with her husband and continued as the administrator after his death. Similarly, Dr. Luetta T. Boddie moved to Detroit from Georgia after her husband's death and established a practice with her son, Dr. Arthur Boddie, in the early 1940s.[124]

Dr. Alfred E. Thomas was one of the most successful Black professional entrepreneurs in Detroit. Thomas migrated to Detroit from Birmingham, Alabama, and established a pair of hospitals.[125] According to a 1938 pamphlet produced by the hospital, "Edyth K. Thomas Memorial Hospital and its sister institution, Bethesda Hospital, being both under one ownership, constitute one of the largest privately owned Negro businesses in America." The pamphlet continued, "These hospitals distribute many thousands of dollars annually to their ninety-two employees and to various Negro business houses which supply them with food products, fuel, linen supply services, and other commodities. Edyth K. Thomas Memorial Hospital and Bethesda Hospital are assets to the Race in Detroit economically as well as scientifically."[126] Clearly Dr. Thomas viewed the hospital as a business and himself as entrepreneurial. A 1944 *Color* article titled "The Detroit Negro Leads the World" stated that Thomas was "alleged to be one of Detroit's most wealthy Negroes."[127] In addition to the hospitals, Dr. Thomas was the sole owner of a 120-acre lake resort called the Mid-West Country Club, which was located sixty miles west of Detroit. This club was open to the public and housed a "modern and spacious hotel with forty private rooms, besides a beautiful club house with facilities for dining, dancing and gaming." Guests could relax on the wide sweeping verandas overlooking Little Pleasant Lake.[128] Dr. Thomas passed on considerable wealth to his children when he died, and an oral history interview with a prominent Black businessman in Detroit also recalled that Dr. Thomas was "a very rich man," one of the wealthiest African Americans in Detroit.[129] In the context of Great Migration Detroit (and likely other Great Migration cities), Black professionals were indeed entrepreneurs. And the expansion of Black professional entrepreneurship in the 1940s was indicative of the World War II–era Black business boom.

*　*　*

Since the 1930s, Detroit had a reputation for having more Black-owned businesses than any other major city, and its reputation was further consolidated in the 1940s. As the Black business community expanded rapidly in the 1940s, many migrant entrepreneurs had achieved their dream of operating an enterprise that provided them and members of the race with more economic freedom and self-determination. Businesses such as Sunnie Wilson's Forest Club, the Gotham Hotel, Paradise Valley Distributing Company, Violet T. Lewis's Lewis Business College, and A. W. Curtis Laboratories not only provided the proprietors with wealth but also helped other Blacks secure dignified employment and prepared many to be their own boss. Black business owners, most of them southern migrants, saw Detroit as a mecca for Black business and freedom enterprise. As Austin W. Curtis, a leading scientist and inventor with a national standing, put it, "Detroit had a reputation of being the leading city in the nation for Black business development and progress."[130] As the 1940s came to a close, Black entrepreneurs looked forward to the prospect of Black business continuing to boom along with the U.S. economy.

In fact, Detroit's Black business community did continue to flourish into the next decade. According to future Detroit mayor Coleman Young, "Throughout the fifties, Detroit had more Black homeowners and more Black-owned businesses than any other city in America."[131] Since the early decades of the Great Migration, the Black business community had grown in both size and variety by the early 1950s. In 1926, a report on Blacks in Detroit counted 720 business establishments in Detroit "conducted by Negroes and depending for the most part on Negro patronage."[132] Twenty-five years later, the diversity and size of Black business in Detroit had grown tremendously.

By 1952, Black professionals and business owners numbered at least 2,500 in Detroit and their enterprises employed thousands of Black workers. The greatest growth of Black business had taken place after 1930.[133]

In addition to the professional entrepreneurship already discussed in this chapter, other businesses that served Detroit's Black residents in the early 1950s included 68 real estate firms, 18 insurance companies, and 3 savings and loan associations. There were 59 Black engineers of various types, 45 general contractors, 85 electricians, 50 carpentry contractors, 10 plastering contractors, 8 masonry contractors, 8 plumbing concerns, and 1 architect. Other Black-owned businesses included 100 barbershops, 200 beauty shops, 75 hotels, 53 drugstores, and 200 dry cleaning and tailoring establishments. There were 2 new car dealerships, 100 gasoline stations, 100 groceries, 6 wholesale meat companies, 50 moving and cartage companies, 100 restaurants, 27 funeral homes, 18 florists, and 4 furriers. There were 7 appliance stores with TV franchises, 3 wholesale beer distributors, 60 taverns and bars, 2 advertising businesses, 3 Black newspapers, 4 hardware stores, 20 printing shops, 20 radio and TV servicing businesses, and 100 confectioneries. Other businesses operated by Blacks included 20 coal companies, 20 commercial photography studios, 6 commercial art studios, 6 manufacturing plants, 2 cemeteries, 100 billiard halls, and 2 bowling alleys. Additionally, there were 50 garages, 6 taxicab companies, 20 apparel businesses, 5 slipcover and drapery factories, and 2 furniture factories.[134] These businesses, and others not accounted for here, were the manifestation of southern migrants' and second-generation Detroiters' freedom enterprise.

By the early 1950s, Detroit also had numerous Black business organizations. The Booker T. Washington Trade Association and Detroit Housewives League were open to all Black entrepreneurs, and there were also industry- and location-specific organizations as well. One of the city's largest was the Detroit Real Estate Brokers Association, founded in 1933. Others included the Paradise Valley Businessmen's Association, the Michigan Council of Insurance Executives, the United Beauty School and Teachers Association, the Wolverine Funeral Directors Association, the Association of Fashion and Accessory Designers, the Wolverine Bar Association, the Detroit Association of Electricians, the Pharmacists Guild, the East Side Tavern Owners, the Detroit Technical Association, the Detroit Medical Society, the Elliotorian Business Women's Club, and the Cotillion Club.[135]

Detroit's Black business community, concentrated along Hastings Street, was undeniably booming in the early 1950s. Eastsider George D. Ramsey Sr.

summed up the importance of Hastings Street in Paradise Valley in this way: "Hastings Street was the corridor that Black businesses thrived on."[136] The Booker T. Washington Trade Association, while proud of the record of achievement of Black business owners, noted that it "expected a far greater advance in the second quarter century than it had seen in its first."[137] Unfortunately this was not to be. The proliferation of Black-owned business following the 1943 race riot violated the laws of racial capitalism, and the city's white stakeholders would seek to tilt the scales back toward economic white supremacy. The next decade would usher in postwar urban planning initiatives that would shake Detroit's Black business community to its core and threaten to destroy all the progress Black entrepreneurs had made during the previous three decades.

CHAPTER 7

Falling: Urban Planning and the Destruction of Black Business

Willis Eugene Smith was one of the most well-known and successful entrepreneurs in Detroit's Black funeral industry during the first half of the twentieth century. Originally from Eufaula, Alabama, Smith opened his funeral home in 1929 after ten years of living in Detroit and saving money. A few years later he moved to 611 East Canfield near St. Antoine and Hastings Streets. This was a prime location for a Black entrepreneur, since both Hastings and St. Antoine were main thoroughfares of Detroit's Black business community. Everything went well initially; Smith made money and lived a good life. But his stint as a business owner was cut short; as he recounted later, "I had the Smith Funeral Home until the expressway came in." Smith lost his property in the early 1960s due to construction of the Walter P. Chrysler Freeway and did not reestablish his business in a new location. Instead, he worked for another funeral home until his retirement in 1983.[1] Smith's story of moving from the South, establishing a successful business, and then losing it through urban planning initiatives was a familiar story among Black entrepreneurs in post–World War II Detroit.

Though they faced obstacles, Black migrant entrepreneurs who left the South during the Great Migration built a thriving business community in Detroit between the 1920s and 1940s, particularly in Black Bottom and Paradise Valley (see Figure 1). The city's Black population was highly concentrated in these east-central neighborhoods due to discriminatory real estate practices, and even Black entrepreneurs who lived elsewhere often established their businesses there to serve Black clientele.[2] In the 1950s and 1960s, this flourishing business community was bulldozed as part of city planners' and politicians' vision of a modern urban space for white citizens.

Hastings Street was paved over for the Walter P. Chrysler Freeway (a section of I-75 and I-375), and city planners selected other Black business areas for additional expressway construction and redevelopment projects. Detroit's selection of urban renewal sites was racially motivated. One urban planner recalled that the city chose the Black-occupied area over comparably "blighted" ones for urban renewal. He surmised, "I guess the practical difference was that the east side was predominantly Black." With nonwhites comprising up to 98 percent of the families living in some locations slated for urban renewal, these efforts displaced thousands of Black residents and destroyed countless businesses. Urban renewal so plainly disproportionately affected African Americans that Black Detroiters often referred to it as "Negro Removal."[3]

This chapter explores the destructive and racist impact of postwar expressway construction and urban renewal projects on Black entrepreneurship in Detroit. It begins by exploring the city's plans for the postwar city and white stakeholders' desire to maintain economic white supremacy, that is, racial capitalism, by sacrificing Black homes and businesses for their vision of a new, modern downtown.[4] Targeting Black neighborhoods with fewer resources to challenge redevelopment, city planners and officials campaigned to purchase devalued property, launch building projects intended for middle-class white consumers, and turn a vast profit. Urban planning tore apart the Black business community, and migrant entrepreneurs' gains in obtaining economic security, independence, and upward mobility through business came crashing down.

The chapter also discusses how postwar redevelopment projects led many migrant entrepreneurs in Detroit's Black business community to lose the establishments they had spent decades building. Some started over and continued on in business but experienced severe financial setbacks as a result of forced relocation and inadequate compensation. Others who closed their businesses and went to work for someone else lost the ability to be their own boss—a key aspect of the self-determination, economic independence, and financial security many migrant entrepreneurs desired. Automobile dealership owner Ed Davis recounted, "In just the area around my business, where houses and stores and apartment buildings were destroyed to make way for the Fisher Freeway and the Medical Center, it was almost as though a city had been lost within a city." He lamented, "In truth, a community had been broken up and a whole way of life had been torn apart and lost forever."[5] Davis's assessment was not mere nostalgia. The destruction wrought by urban planning initiatives was a devastating blow to the Black business community and Black entrepreneurs' economic trajectory in Detroit.

Silences in the archive make it impossible to know precisely how many businesses were displaced by urban renewal and freeway construction, what percentage of them reopened in new locations, and the true financial impact on business owners. What is clear, however, is that freeway construction and other postwar redevelopment projects significantly influenced the decline of Detroit's once-thriving Black business community, its spectacular rise offset by a swift fall over which proprietors had no control. As Coleman Young lamented, "Looking back I can see that Black Bottom had everything but a fighting chance. . . . It was red-tagged by the government as a sort of Yankee Doodle sacrifice, a trespasser upon somebody's sacred bureaucratic vision of America, a sociological trouble spot for which keepers of the dream had no real solution but to lay it to waste."[6] The literal falling of this community marked the traumatic end of many southern migrant entrepreneurs' freedom enterprises and demonstrated the nature of racial capitalism in an urban context.

Postwar Urban Planning and White Visions for the City

In the 1940s, many cities began strategizing about how to regenerate urban spaces that had deteriorated due to industrial use and lack of upkeep during the Great Depression. Postwar deindustrialization and suburbanization also generated significant economic and demographic shifts and as Black employment declined and middle-class whites fled to the suburbs, cities like Detroit suffered a loss in their tax base. Those concerned with cities' economic fate, including elected officials, urban planners, downtown corporations, retailers, banks, and realtors, promoted a vision of urban redevelopment that economically benefited whites at the expense of African Americans and other marginalized communities. With the goal of luring the white middle class back to the core city, this vision prioritized clearing "slums" and "blighted areas" and revitalizing these districts with new middle- and upper-income private housing, commercial centers, parks, and recreational facilities.[7]

In November 1946, Mayor Edward Jeffries introduced the Detroit Plan, a master redevelopment blueprint designed to address both the conditions of urban slums and suburban white flight. During the depression there had been practically no construction of private dwellings, and the World War II

influx of workers followed by the baby boom created a severe housing shortage for postwar Detroiters, even as middle- and upper-income families fled to
the suburbs.[8] The Detroit Plan intended to replace deteriorated housing with
new affordable housing. The city would identify redevelopment zones, condemn and purchase the lots from their owners, raze the sites, and then sell the
cleared land to private developers at a fraction of the acquisition cost.[9] However, the initial goal of utilizing redevelopment zones for affordable housing
was soon abandoned. In short, private developers did not want to build low-
cost accommodations primarily for African Americans and others objected
to the loss in tax revenue from the nearby business district.[10] Once Albert
Cobo was elected mayor in 1949, any wide-ranging plans for public housing
largely fell by the wayside, and throughout the 1950s and 1960s the city used
its power to clear "blighted" areas and resell the land to private parties to
redevelop downtown Detroit.[11]

Throughout this process, urban leaders made it clear that they viewed
Black neighborhoods as a threat to their vision of a white city core.[12] Walter Reuther, president of the United Auto Workers union, sent a telegram to
Mayor Cobo and the Detroit Common Council in 1954, declaring, "It is economically stupid and morally wrong for an industrial community with the
wealth, power, and the know-how of Detroit to tolerate the social cesspools of
our slums, which breed crime and disease."[13] That same year, Cobo appointed
a Detroit-Tomorrow Committee comprised of business, civic, labor, church,
and industrial leaders, charged with the responsibility of "saving the core
city."[14] This 250-person committee was cochaired by Selden B. Daume, president of Detroit Bank & Trust Company, and Walker L. Eisler, president of
Detroit Edison Company.[15] One of the main objectives was to map out a long-
term program for redeveloping downtown and the Black Bottom area. Given
Cobo's propensity for policies that supported private redevelopment at the
expense of public housing, Coleman Young later reflected, "[Cobo's] obvious
priority was to wipe out the lower east side," that is, remove African Americans from the area.[16] As one *Detroit Free Press* writer put it in 1954, the "target
is 160-Block Area South of Vernor."[17]

A racially coded emphasis on "slums" and "blight" permeated the discussion on postwar urban redevelopment. African Americans like Young recognized that slum clearance was "tantamount to the evacuation of Blacks from
a given area," concluding, "Somebody had thought up another way to screw
Black people."[18] Indeed, urban planners acknowledged that targeting Black
neighborhoods was optimal, in part because Blacks had fewer resources to

challenge redevelopment. George Emery, who was the city's planning director in the mid-1940s, admitted as much, stating that in "colored sections" of
the city "there may be less likelihood of organized opposition."[19]

Coded language or not, officials, planners, and other interested parties
plainly exhibited their belief that creating a modern and renewed city required
minimizing the Black population adjacent to the downtown central business
district. Building properties that would entice more desirable urban residents—that is, the white middle class—was also a vital component of their
vision. Planners essentially wanted to swap out "slums" for, as one *Architectural Forum* article put it, "a green suburb of houses and apartment buildings inside the city ... gracious squares like Rittenhouse in Philadelphia and
Gramercy in New York." Highlighting hopes for a demographic shift, the
author asked, "Can traffic be reversed on the motor city's new superhighways
to bring people and money back into midtown? Detroit will try by replacing a
slum with a midtown suburb."[20] Likewise, when the Citizens Redevelopment
Committee unveiled its plan for the Gratiot renewal zone in 1954, the proposal emphasized that a successful redevelopment program was dependent
upon the ability to "attract back to the heart of the city people who are finding
their housing in the outlying sections of the city and its suburbs." Comprised
of "bankers, merchants, and chiefs of industry," and led by Walter J. Gessel, a
real estate broker; Walter Gehrke, a mortgage broker; Walter P. Reuther; and
Foster K. Winter, a merchant, the Citizens Redevelopment Committee was
formed to expedite the sluggish Gratiot redevelopment project.[21] The committee insisted, "Anything short of attaining that objective would be of dubious
value from both an economic and social point of view."[22] Understanding the
monetary value of whiteness within the system of racial capitalism, officials
and white business owners worked to reverse Detroit's trend of becoming an
increasingly Black city.

Their efforts not only proved detrimental to Black Detroiters but also
directly and explicitly benefited whites. White-owned companies greatly
influenced the course of urban redevelopment in Detroit, especially during
Cobo's tenure as mayor from 1950 to 1957. According to historian Thomas
Sugrue, "The roster of housing officials in Detroit in the Cobo years reads
like a Who's Who of the city's real estate and construction industries." Upon
his election, Cobo appointed Harry J. Durbin as head of the Detroit Housing
Commission (DHC). Durbin was a well-known developer (former president of Durbin Builders, Inc., in Detroit) and previously served as president
of the National Association of Home Builders. Cobo also appointed "real

estate magnate" Walter Gessell, property manager George Isabell, and Ed Thal and Finlay C. Allan, both officers of the Detroit Building Trades Council of the American Federation of Labor. These individuals "represented the interests of private industry and the building trades in their government positions."[23]

Accordingly, white officials, urban planners, and business owners advocated for "putting public subsidy to work for private capital."[24] Using public funds for the expansion of white-owned enterprises, the city sold land seized from Blacks through eminent domain at rock-bottom prices to private white developers who constructed luxury high-rises, middle-income housing units, and massive commercial upgrades to the downtown central business district. Throughout the 1950s and 1960s, Detroit awarded millions of dollars in contracts to white-owned businesses for demolition and construction redevelopment projects. For instance, the Gratiot site, which was 90 percent demolished by mid-1954, needed further work before "improvements" could begin. This included relocating utility, water, and sewer lines and tearing up "obsolete streets," alleys, and sidewalks in the area. An estimated $1.13 million (over $12 million in 2023 dollars) would be paid for the work, going to companies such as Cooke Contracting, which won a contract to install and pave approximately one-quarter of the streets in the Gratiot renewal zone.[25] In March 1962, the city awarded Arrow Wrecking Company $586,800 (almost $6 million in 2023 dollars) to raze two hundred buildings in the area bounded by Cass, Lafayette, the Lodge Expressway, and Bagley.[26] A year later, the city paid S. Weissman Excavating Company $108,700 (more than $1 million in 2023 dollars) for the demolition of 175 buildings, site clearance, and related work in the Elmwood Park renewal zone.[27] With these contracts, the urban planning projects that devastated Black Detroiters' livelihoods and communities put hundreds of thousands of dollars into white business owners' pockets.

Some redevelopment projects, such as the medical center and midtown cultural center, benefited whites from outside the region as well. The state's expanding freeway network created a "route to the arts," allowing its target audience (middle-class whites) in far-off communities to access Detroit's cultural heart in mere hours. Attractions on the "art route" included Wayne State University's campus, the McGregor Memorial Community Conference Center, the Detroit Public Library, the Detroit Institute of Arts, the Detroit Historical Museum, Rackham Memorial, and Wayne Theatre. In 1963, an article quoted WSU president Clarence B. Hilberry as saying, "Until recently, few visitors to Detroit would have thought to associate this city with a modern cultural rebirth. Today, the artistic upsurge is one of the City's most striking features."[28] That this cultural transformation was the result of dislocating Black businesses and residents from the city center remained unsaid.

Some whites did express concerns about uprooting the Black community in the name of progress. In 1956, Mel J. Ravitz, a sociology professor affiliated with the City Plan Commission and who would go on to serve on the Detroit Common Council, contended, "Perhaps the most serious problems churned up by the urban renewal endeavor is the problem of dislocation of people and their consequent relocation. This is a problem few people are willing to face squarely; all too many of us become easily intoxicated with the alluring visions of modern apartments and a network of expressways nestled among wide parks and playgrounds, all replacing the rotten and rotting slums."[29] Although communities living in "blighted" neighborhoods were supposed to be relocated to other parts of the city and/or rehoused in newly constructed public housing, officials found ways to skirt regulations and abandon plans for subsidized housing and other forms of assistance.[30] Recognizing this negligence, Ravitz continued, "The slums must go; everyone is agreed that this must happen. . . . But where shall the people displaced go? Were it possible to obliterate them along with the houses in which they lived, many might breathe a sigh of relief; but these people do exist and they cannot be lightly dismissed or made to disappear."[31] However, it seems that most whites who stood to benefit from the displacement of African Americans did not share this opinion and tried their best to simply ignore the crisis facing the Black community. By 1962 Ravitz concluded that urban renewal had become an "instrument primarily for the economic advantage of certain citizens and businesses who profit from investments, or who may benefit from residence in the c[o]re of the city."[32]

Indeed, whites' vision of a renovated postwar city, complete with new cultural and medical centers, high-end commercial districts, and private housing geared toward white consumption, came at a high cost to Black Detroiters. As Ed Davis put it, people were "often being bulldozed out for some urban redeveloper's quick profit," and "the urban renewal dream of bright new cities [was] often built on a nightmare of human destruction."[33] Through the use of eminent domain and public monies, Detroit's highway and urban renewal projects essentially functioned as state-sponsored wealth redistribution programs. In short, postwar urban planning initiatives helped maintain the economic white supremacy inherent in U.S. racial capitalism.

The Impact of Expressways

The postwar construction of freeways drastically changed the landscape of urban America. Enormous interchanges and ramps produced large areas of empty and unusable space, and expressways slashed through inner-city neighborhoods, dislocating tens of thousands of residents who were "overwhelmingly poor and Black."[34] This pattern was not an accident. Although the federal funds provided for highway construction were not intended to clear "slums," state and federal officials promoted new highways as a means of eliminating "blighted" neighborhoods. Decades of discriminatory practices including restrictive covenants and redlining had forced Blacks into the oldest areas—such as Black Bottom—and white urban leaders saw new expressways as an expedient method for bulldozing Black neighborhoods, redeveloping coveted inner-city land, and reviving central business districts for white citizens.[35] This is one example of how the social aspects of Jim Crow (racial segregation) fed into the economic hierarchies of racial capitalism. Transportation planners could create a seemingly credible case for designating Black areas as blighted, even when there were so many businesses present, because the architecture was some of the oldest in the city. Perhaps the wealth these businesses generated for African Americans was simply not legible to white planners and politicians.[36] Or, maybe they did not view Black business as worthy of being preserved and simply chose to ignore the impact expressway construction would have on Black-owned businesses.

This destruction of Black-owned businesses was not a new phenomenon in Detroit. Since the 1930s, Black entrepreneurs had been adversely affected by modifications to the city's landscape, particularly those in smaller communities located in pockets beyond the east side where most Blacks lived. One such community developed in the late 1910s and early 1920s near 8 Mile Road at Detroit's northern boundary. In 1921, there were approximately one hundred Black migrant families living there. These migrants purchased large lots on which they built their own houses.[37] According to Alice Cain Newman, who grew up in the area, "They were frame houses. It was very nice. It was safe, it was clean, and the businesses were Black-owned. . . . We were right on Eight Mile Road, because my dad had a business. On both sides of Eight Mile was a Black-owned commercial strip."[38]

The Cain family moved to Detroit during the first wave of the Great Migration and settled in the 8 Mile neighborhood when it first developed. There, Alice's father, Jimmy Cain, established a hot dog stand called Jimmy's, which became a popular spot for young people. Cain also co-owned a pool hall in the area, and Alice Cain Newman recalled that "my dad made a lot of money" from these enterprises. He was in good company; there was also a candy manufacturer, a theater, and several restaurants owned by African Americans along 8 Mile.[39] Most were family-run businesses, and neighborhood customer loyalty was essential for their success.

But when the city decided to widen 8 Mile Road in the 1930s, business owners in the area were required to move. Believing they were being treated unfairly, Black entrepreneurs advocated for themselves and hired an attorney to fight the forced removal.[40] They faced an uphill battle, however, as officials employed the constitutional mechanism of eminent domain, which granted governments the right to confiscate private property for public use.[41] Business owners like Jimmy Cain were eventually forced to sell and were displaced from the neighborhood they had built. As Alice Cain Newman put it, "They broke up the community. They broke up the business."[42] New roads and expressways destroyed Black-owned enterprises in other small African American enclaves throughout the city.[43] However, it was the larger Black business community in Black Bottom and Paradise Valley that would bear the brunt of expressway construction in a devastating and unprecedented way.

Highway construction expanded on a national scale in the 1940s and 1950s. Recognizing the need for a national and regional highway network, Congress passed the Federal-Aid Highway Act of 1944 authorizing the National System of Interstate Highways. The system was an essential component of a Cold War strategy known as decentralization, which included efforts to make the defense industry less vulnerable by moving factories away from urban centers. This industrial relocation moved many jobs out of the city proper, spurring the postwar growth of suburban residential and shopping subdivisions and, conversely, making it easier for suburbanites to commute to and from Detroit for work.[44] The highway system accelerated suburbanization and caused large cities to abandon public transportation (which would prove harmful to minority communities). Detroit's white-owned auto industry profited most directly from the Federal-Aid Highway Act of 1944, which made the United States and Americans more reliant on car travel than ever before.

The suburbanization resulting from highway expansion facilitated the rise of what historian Lizabeth Cohen calls a postwar "consumers' republic." By buying homes, automobiles, furniture, and household appliances, white middle-class suburban families would maximize employment, production,

and purchasing power, their consumption working to maintain a flourishing postwar economy for all.[45] In Detroit, however, Blacks were not simply
excluded from the rewards of postwar economic citizenship. Rather, the prosperity that white suburbanites enjoyed was *made possible* through the destruction of Black property and wealth.

Highway construction and its accompanying devastation increased significantly with the Federal-Aid Highway Act of 1956, also known as the
National Interstate and Defense Highways Act. The act authorized $27 billion
to complete 41,000 miles of highways spanning the United States by 1972.
Approximately 20 percent of the system's mileage was designated to provide
alternative interstate service into, through, and around urban areas. With
the federal government shouldering 90 percent of the costs and leaving only
10 percent to the states, the Highway Act of 1956 led to a mammoth effort to
construct new highways in the late 1950s and 1960s, including in and around
the Motor City.[46]

Michigan's highway commissioner, John C. Mackie, spearheaded these
efforts with an aggressive plan for expanding the state's system of highways
and expressways—an unsurprising move considering the strength of Michigan's automobile industry and car culture. Under Mackie's direction, Michigan led the nation in interstate freeway construction with 89 new interstate
miles under contract by June 1960, surpassing larger states such as California and Texas. Mackie proudly noted in September 1960, "In the last three
years, the amount of freeway in Michigan has more than quadrupled, from
101 miles on July 1, 1957, to 408 miles today."[47]

Both prior to and as a result of the state's aggressive interstate expansion efforts, a staggering amount of highways were built through Detroit.[48]
This created a housing crisis for Black and low-income residents and proved
disastrous for businesses located in the paths of proposed expressways.[49] The
Walter P. Chrysler Freeway, also known as the Hastings-Oakland Expressway during this time, had the most widespread and damaging effect on
Detroit's Black business community. It was constructed directly over the
city's foremost Black commercial thoroughfare: Hastings Street.[50] At the
time the highway's path was announced, Hastings was home to Black business establishments stretching from Adams Avenue all the way to Medbury
Street. As Detroiter Leroy Mitchell put it, "That was a long way. It must have
been about four miles. That was almost half of Detroit."[51] But as politicians
and urban planners saw it, Hastings Street passed through some of the city's
"worst slums." Paving over it for a new freeway would aid in their efforts

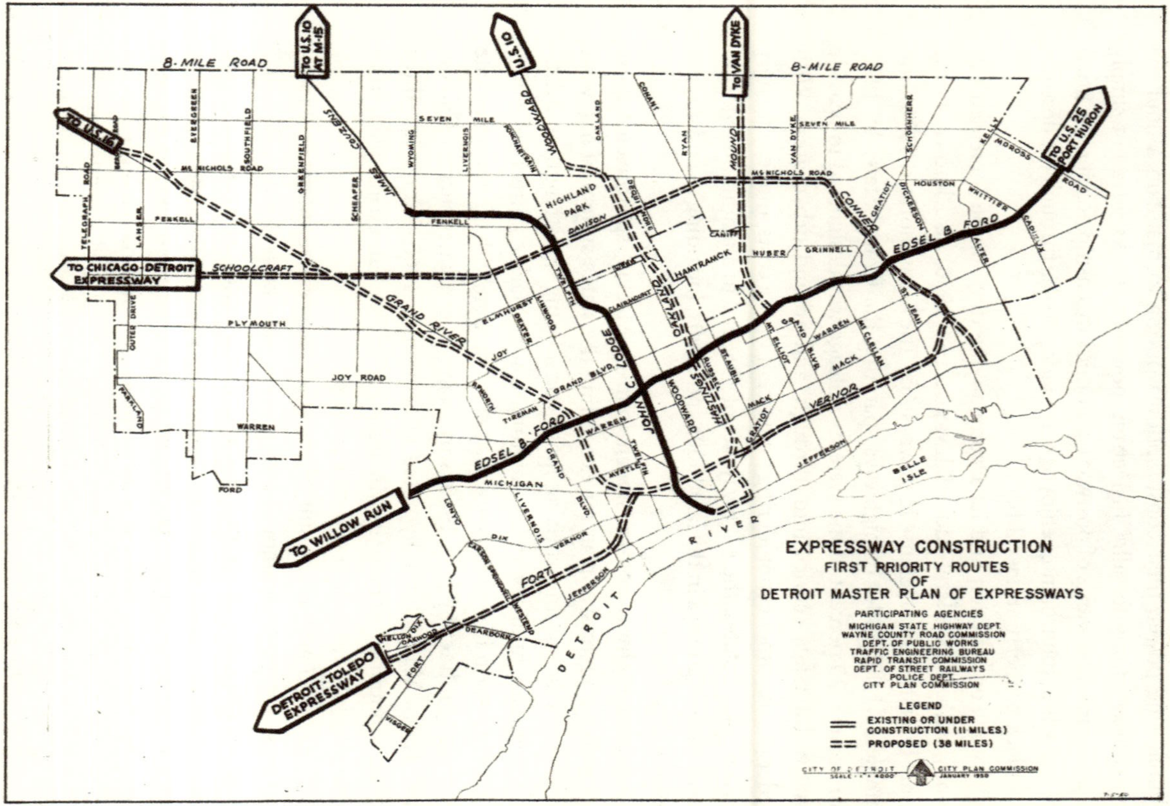

Figure 14. Map showing the proposed route of the Hastings-Oakland Expressway (dashed line in center), 1950. Walter P. Reuther Library, Archives of Labor and Urban Affairs, Wayne State University.

to eliminate "blight" on the east side and redevelop the downtown area for whites.[52] By March 1955, the Hastings-Oakland Expressway had been constructed through Black Bottom, from Jefferson Avenue up to Gratiot, and by the spring of 1958 planners confirmed that it would extend to the city's northern limit at 8 Mile Road.[53]

Expressway construction was a gradual process during which proposed routes often remained unverified and subject to change, leaving residents and business owners in anxious limbo. A proposed route could shift within a few blocks, and residents did not want to relocate prematurely only to later learn that their existing property now circumvented the finalized path. Moreover, since most people displaced by expressway construction moved relatively nearby, they ran the risk of their new location ultimately being on the final route. The *Detroit Tribune* reported that the unpredictability of the expressway route was "keeping the residents, business[owners] and home owners in a state of confusion."[54] This uncertainty made it incredibly difficult to plan a possible relocation strategy and conduct regular business, and undoubtedly caused much distress within the community.

One such area was Clay Street between Cameron and Russell, which passed through Hastings Street. The neighborhood housed a variety of businesses, nearly all of which were part of the fifty-member Clay-Oakland Merchants Association. Establishments such as "Foots" Wilson's barbershop at 8065 Russell, the Knight Beauty Shop operated by Katie Knight at 1306 Clay, and the relatively new La Bonita Drive-In located at 8319 Oakland were all at risk of forced removal by the Hastings-Oakland Expressway. La Bonita was co-owned by Sarah Williams and Beulah Green and had been in operation for only ten months when they learned of the impending construction. The businesswomen had gotten off to a promising start; they prided themselves on being the cleanest business in the area and had courteous waitstaff and a circle drive for serving delicious hamburgers and light lunches. The prospect of having to relocate was daunting for the nascent establishment. There were long-standing businesses likely to be forced out as well. Rivers Barber Shop at 1308 Clay had been in operation for ten years. The proprietor, Mr. Rivers, was satisfied with his business, noting, "The neighborhood has been good to me." Similarly, entrepreneurial couple Mr. and Mrs. Stallings co-owned Northend Lunch at 914 Holbrook for sixteen years—according to a profile in the *Detroit Tribune*, "If you try their bar-be-cue then you will never stop wanting it"—as well as a record store called the Northend Music Company.

Figure 15. A section of Hastings Street before demolition (1959). In view are several businesses. Courtesy of the Detroit Historical Society.

Mr. S. Check had been operating King's 5¢ to $5.00 Store at 8719 Oakland for twenty years and viewed his neighbors as "very congenial and wonderful as customers."[55] This tight-knit community had deep roots, and the prospect of losing businesses into which proprietors had invested their life savings was undoubtedly demoralizing.

Transportation planners seemed to view Black communities like this one as easy targets for expressway routes. Elected officials were met with more forceful opposition when proposed paths had the potential to affect white middle- and upper-income residents, and the unpopularity of destroying white-owned businesses appears to have influenced their decision making.[56] For example, there is evidence that local administrators and policymakers were reluctant to build an expressway over Grand River Avenue, fearing resistance to the possibility of damage to the value of white-owned commercial properties that lined the street.[57] It appears no such consideration was given to

Figure 16. The same section of Hastings Street after demolition for the Chrysler Freeway (1961). Courtesy of the Detroit Historical Society.

how the Hastings-Oakland Expressway would affect Black-owned businesses, since African Americans had less political power than white Detroiters.

Postwar urban planners' disregard for Black communities in the name of transportation efficiency was not limited to Detroit. Expressway construction destroyed urban Black neighborhoods and businesses across the country.[58] But while the wreckage of Detroit's Black business community was not unique, as a national leader in expressway construction the city proceeded with particular audacity. As Coleman Young put it, "The emphasis on freeway construction after the war was not limited to Detroit, but nowhere else was it administered with the same reckless abandon, and nowhere else did it carve up and mortify a municipality as it did Detroit. . . . For Detroit, the fallout from the urban highway craze was nothing short of devastating."[59] Throughout the 1950s and 1960s, much of what was left of the east side's Black business community would also crumble as a result of urban renewal.

The Destruction of Urban Renewal

Coleman Young, who would be Detroit's mayor from 1974 to 1994, had personal experience with the destruction wrought by postwar urban redevelopment. His family migrated to Detroit in 1923 with hopes of starting over in a city where they could conduct a solid business without the fear of white retaliation. Young came from a long line of Black entrepreneurs in Alabama who managed to make a decent living from their enterprises. His grandmother operated a successful restaurant in Faunsdale, and his grandfather was a barber who also "hustled around to supplement his income in any way he could." This included owning a small market, catering events with his famous barbeque, and selling wood and coal out of the family's home.[60] Coleman Young's father, William C. Young, was also a barber and sold Black newspapers like the *Pittsburgh Courier* and *Chicago Defender* in Tuscaloosa—an activity that attracted the ire of local whites. When a kindly white man recommended that he get out of town, William Young heeded the advice; he "wasn't a fool." The Young family understood the very real threat of racial violence in Alabama. They had an ancestor who was murdered when a mob set fire to his house with him and his wife locked inside.[61]

The Youngs settled in Black Bottom, joining family members who had migrated to the city in 1920. They lived with Young's maternal grandmother on Antietam Street.[62] Coleman Young "loved that old neighborhood. . . . As one of the largest and boomingest Black neighborhoods in the North, Black Bottom was a thrilling convergence of people, a wonderfully versatile and self-contained society."[63] Maintaining their entrepreneurial spirit, Young's parents eventually opened a dry cleaning business and a tailor shop on St. Aubin Avenue, which afforded the family a comfortable life.[64] Like many migrant entrepreneurs, the Youngs appeared to have found what they were looking for in migrating north. However, the ground beneath their feet was already beginning to shift, and postwar urban redevelopment projects would result in the destruction of countless Black businesses over the next two decades.

Detroit's redevelopment efforts acquired a wealth of new resources with funding made available through two significant pieces of federal legislation: the Housing Acts of 1949 and 1954. Declaring the necessity for a national housing policy to realize the lofty goal of a "decent home and a suitable living environment for every American family," the 1949 act authorized federal loans and grants to assist localities in slum clearance and urban redevelopment.[65] Although the act stipulated that renewal sites be "predominantly residential" (either before or after redevelopment), it did not specify that cleared areas be replaced with public housing.[66] The Housing Act of 1954 further eschewed the issue of affordable housing, instead broadening slum clearance and redevelopment and providing federal aid for rehabilitation and conservation efforts.[67] The act also introduced the phrase "urban renewal"—a concept that would shape decades of urban planning and policy and ultimately deepen structural inequality and racial segregation in ways that continue to resonate.[68] Urban renewal included both redevelopment—the wholesale clearance of areas deemed to be "structurally worn out beyond repair"—and conservation—attempts to prevent blight by improving a neighborhood's general environment and encouraging homeowners to maintain their properties at high standards.[69] What's more, the federal government resolved to fund two-thirds of renewal projects' net costs, leaving only one-third to local municipalities.[70]

The Housing Acts of 1949 and 1954 were game-changers for urban redevelopment in Detroit and other cities across the nation. Though Detroit began its renewal efforts before federal assistance was available for slum clearance, the city took full advantage of the opportunity to obtain federal financing once the 1949 act passed.[71] The City of Detroit filed a request for a capital grant reservation of around $4.3 million on January 16, 1950, just six months after the first law was enacted, and was awarded the requested amount on February 3, 1950.[72] Detroit was thus one of the earliest cities to participate in the federal urban renewal program.[73]

The city zealously introduced redevelopment/renewal projects throughout the 1950s and 1960s, particularly in areas with a high concentration of Black residents. In 1950, 16.2 percent of Detroit's population was Black. In 1960, that figure had increased to 28.9 percent and by 1970, it reached 43.7 percent.[74] Yet by the late 1960s, 67 percent of an estimated 8,231 families displaced by urban renewal projects in Detroit were people of color.[75] Some redevelopment zones, such as the Gratiot Redevelopment Project and Elmwood Park, were almost completely Black areas (95 percent and 98 percent, respectively).[76] These numbers correspond with broader trends that saw cities targeting minority and working-class neighborhoods for redevelopment.

As Table 1 shows, various urban renewal and redevelopment projects impacted minority neighborhoods in the city. The ones that most affected the Black business community were Gratiot, Lafayette, the Elmwood Park projects, and the Medical Center projects (Figure 17). Gratiot—the first urban redevelopment project in Detroit (and in Michigan)—covered 129 acres of

Table 1. Select Urban Renewal Projects in Detroit

Redevelopment project	Planning stage	Year "actively executing"	Year completed	Families displaced	Families of color displaced	White families displaced	Federal funding
Gratiot Project		1950	1964	1,958	1,860 (95%)	98 (5%)	$456,876
Lafayette	1952	1957	1973	561	474 (84%)	87 (16%)	$4,980,752
Elmwood Park		1960	1970	837	820 (98%)	17 (2%)	
Elmwood Park 1		1961	1974				$7,969,604
Elmwood Park 2		1965	1974	528	480 (91%)	48 (9%)	$8,545,676
Elmwood Park 3	1965	1969	1974				$11,127,393
Medical Center No. 1		1960	1967	626	503 (80%)	123 (20%)	$4,582,139
Medical Center No. 2		1963	1974	608	547 (90%)	61 (10%)	$4,221,041
Medical Center No. 3	1964	1968	1974				$8,241,325
Central Bus Dist 1	1956	1959	1974	77	6 (8%)	71 (92%)	$4,569,976
Central Bus Dist 3	1956	1959	1973	120	67 (56)	53 (44%)	$3,085,035
Distribution Ctr 1		1965	1974	158	156 (99%)	2 (1%)	$2,633,016
Research Park West		1965	1974	243	81 (33%)	162 (67%)	$2,067,759
University City		1963	1970	645	270 (42%)	375 (58%)	$5,209,546
Westside Industrial	1953	1957	1973	864	128 (15%)	736 (85%)	$4,404,459
Wyoming-Eight Mile		1960	1973	142	5 (4%)	137 (96%)	$3,141,024

Data source: Digital Scholarship Lab, "Renewing Inequality," *American Panorama*, ed. Robert K. Nelson and Edward L. Ayers, https://dsl.richmond.edu/panorama/renewal/#view=0/0/1&viz=cartogram&text=sources&city=detroitMI&loc=12/42.3830/-83.0850.

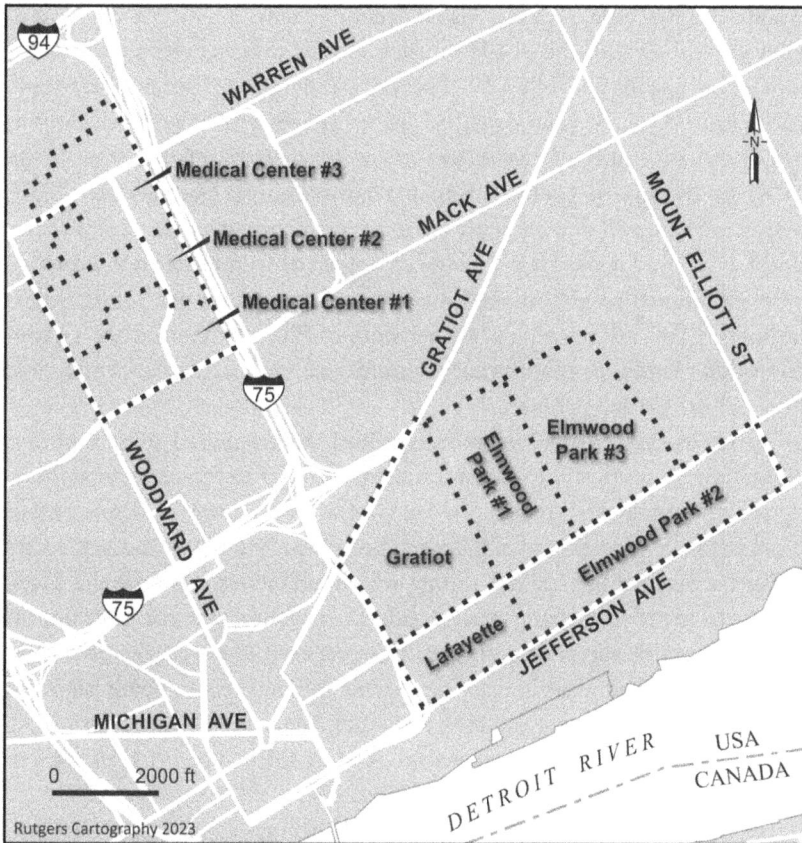

Figure 17. The urban renewal projects that most impacted the Black business community in Black Bottom and Paradise Valley.

land and 43 blocks just northeast of the central business district in Black Bottom. The city announced its plans for the project in 1946, began executing it in 1950, and completed it in 1964.[77] Alongside paving over Hastings Street to build the Chrysler Freeway, the Gratiot project did some of the most significant damage to Detroit's Black business community.[78]

The Gratiot site no doubt could have benefited from improvements. The area was crowded; there were nearly twice as many dwelling units as there were structures in the area (1,355 dwelling units within 705 structures). Additionally, the buildings themselves were old, with 51 percent of dwelling units built before 1900 and only 5 percent since 1920. But beyond the physical condition of the area, race was also a deciding factor in officials' decision to redevelop the Gratiot site. A 1945 survey showed that 90 percent of the site's population was Black, while a 1950 survey estimated 98 percent.[79] This made sense, since African Americans had been funneled into the Black Bottom area at the start of the Great Migration and largely prohibited from living elsewhere through restrictive covenants and redlining. Decades later, Black Detroiters were still dealing with the long-term consequences of this structural racism, and it was clear that the city's goal of "completely rebuilding an entire residential neighborhood" meant creating a brand-new white neighborhood.[80] This vision came at the expense of Black citizens, as the Gratiot Redevelopment Project significantly diminished homes, churches, and a wide array of vital Black businesses.[81]

To offset this dislocation, municipalities were required to submit and obtain federal approval for relocation plans in order to receive federal funding for urban renewal projects. In the Gratiot zone, however, displacement began before a relocation plan had even been filed.[82] In other words, the City of Detroit decided to pick and choose which guidelines to follow and made excuses to justify displacing Black residents without a plan for their relocation. By the time the relocation plan was prepared in February 1951, close to 400 families had already been dislocated. When the city finally signed a contract with the Housing and Home Finance Agency (HHFA) in April 1952, over 1,000 families had been displaced. And by the end of 1952, all but 196 families had been removed from the project site.[83]

It was the responsibility of the Detroit Housing Commission (DHC) to prepare a relocation plan for the Gratiot site. Since the agency did not have one when the city began removal on September 18, 1950, the DHC Relocation Office received orders to simply move residents to "decent, safe and sanitary" dwellings. Staff were given no indication of where they might actually find such dwellings.[84] Moreover, once a relocation plan was drafted, there was little effort to connect it to what was taking place on the ground. What's more, the plan was classified as confidential and staff were not even permitted to know its contents.[85] As a result of this apathy and lack of direction, relocation assistance at the Gratiot site was haphazard at best. Some displaced families moved to public housing, while others were forced to fend for themselves on the private market. To add insult to injury, the city did not erect any public housing near the Gratiot site, preventing the many displaced residents who needed affordable housing from resettling in their own neighborhood.[86] In early 1952, the fate of 35 percent of processed families was "unknown," and by the fall, the Division of Slum Clearance and Urban Redevelopment of the HHFA still had very little information about how the relocation process was being implemented.[87]

During this time, Detroit was experiencing a severe housing shortage following a lack of home construction during the Great Depression, the World War II influx of workers, and the postwar baby boom.[88] Yet although Blacks were excluded from white neighborhoods and the expanding suburbs as well as some public housing, the city recklessly proceeded with redevelopment projects without plans for where displaced communities would live. In some cases, as with the Gratiot project, clearance commenced rapidly and without following federal regulations, leaving residents and business owners with few opportunities to dispute the injustice. Still, Black Detroiters criticized the city's negligence. Longtime Detroit Urban League director John C. Dancy asserted, "Even at its best . . . the housing and slum-clearance projects were an imperfect answer to the problems that existed. When they tore down the places around Brewster Street to make way for the Brewster project, the question was 'Where are these people going?' No provision had been made to resettle them."[89] Arthur Johnson, executive secretary of the Detroit Branch of the NAACP, described the issue this way: "What urban renewal actually does is relocate Negroes from one blighted area into one that is already overcrowded, thus eventually transforming it into a slum."[90]

Detroit's urban renewal program was irrefutably harmful for Black residents.[91] Yet, in some ways it had an even more catastrophic impact on Black entrepreneurship. Displaced business owners relocated if they could, but the core of the city's Black business community, which entrepreneurs had established over the previous three decades, was completely obliterated.[92] Urban redevelopment also created unique challenges for Black entrepreneurs, as many faced the prospect of losing not only their homes and communities but also their entire life savings while they struggled to keep their businesses afloat.

Black Entrepreneurs and the Hardships of Urban Redevelopment

Scholarship analyzing the effects of postwar urban planning tends to focus on housing and residential segregation rather than small businesses.[93] In some ways, however, Black business owners were more adversely affected by urban planning initiatives than residents. Examining this impact is challenging,

in part due to the imprecision of official records. Contemporaneous surveys conducted by the Detroit Housing Commission focused on residential
relocation and did not ask questions related to businesses in redevelopment
sites.[94] And with little state assistance for dislocated businesses prior to 1956,
business owners displaced by early urban renewal projects often fell through
the cracks. As sociologist Harriet Saperstein noted in her 1964 study of business relocation in Detroit's Elmwood Park 1 redevelopment site: "One of the
major problems involved in an attempt to study the effects of urban renewal
and its consequent displacement of business establishments is that of finding the original business [owner]. . . . Using the Detroit Housing Commission files as a basic listing also meant that businesses that moved out before
acquisition began were lost. Because the 'cloud of condemnation' hung over
Elmwood I for 15 years, this may have been a sizable group."[95] Other local
studies conducted after communities had already been displaced faced similar challenges locating former residents and business owners, classifying
their whereabouts as "unknown" or "unable to trace after diligent search."[96]
And when social scientists did manage to examine urban renewal's impact on
small businesses, they tended to investigate ones owned by whites.[97] It is no
surprise, then, that traditional sources provide only partial clues about the
effects of urban renewal on Black-owned businesses.

Consequently, recovering the history of Detroit migrant entrepreneurs'
business community and the impact of its destruction requires a range of
sources. The affected neighborhoods were demolished, wiping away most
evidence of the former urban landscape, and there is no reference guide
detailing what businesses existed prior to expressway construction and urban
renewal. The evidence that does exist is fragmented and scattered among
various archives and in former residents' memories. As a result, it has been
necessary to supplement traditional urban planning sources with Black publications, newspaper advertisements, memoirs, and oral histories. These are
key for piecing together the story of the true impact of mid-century urban
planning projects.

As the city continued to launch new urban renewal projects throughout
the 1950s and 1960s, communities were haunted by the threat and reality
of sudden displacement. The Elmwood Park redevelopment project, particularly the section known as Elmwood Park 1, offers a keen example of urban
renewal's impact on Detroit's Black businesses in the 1960s. Though the area
was not the center of Black economic life like the neighborhoods destroyed by
the Gratiot project, the Elmwood Park 1 zone was majority African American

and home to many Black businesses. A typical block in 1950 was described in this way: "A stretch of two-family houses was interspersed with a four-story apartment house; a grocery store shared an entrance with a church 'temporarily in a store'; a middle-sized industrial firm manufacturing some kind of automobile parts stood between several homes; a barbershop, pool hall, and dry cleaner shared an entrance way with a store bearing a 'For Rent' sign."[98] Between residents, neighborhood institutions, and business owners, the area boasted a tight-knit community prior to the disruption of urban renewal. Seventy percent of the businesses were "moderately or highly involved in their neighborhood." Entrepreneurs had developed personal relationships with their customers and provided "special services" such as offering credit, donating goods and money for local charity efforts, and serving as centers of interaction and communication for the community.[99] However, by 1965, the same block described above had become a "cleared, leveled, windswept stretch of dirt, with a hole in the northwest corner marking the beginning of construction of a completely residential development of middle-income apartments and town houses."[100]

The city began actively executing the Elmwood Park 1 project in 1961 and completed it in 1974. At its initial phase, the project saw the displacement of 837 families, 98 percent of which were Black.[101] But even using the best historical sources available, it is exceedingly difficult to track the effect of projects like Elmwood Park on small businesses. As it was often hard to locate business owners after they had been displaced (among other challenges), existing data is undoubtedly incomplete and does not fully represent the damage done to Black entrepreneurs.[102] However, Harriet Saperstein's 1964 study provides a wealth of information on the subject. As a window into Black entrepreneurs' experiences in Elmwood Park, Saperstein's findings also provide insight into what Black business owners likely underwent in other parts of the city.

When the city began acquiring property in April 1962, the Detroit Housing Commission tallied ninety-two "legitimate" businesses and institutions located in the Elmwood Park 1 zone. Saperstein's study examined sixty-four of them, half of which were Black-owned. Most of these businesses were small, owner-operated neighborhood convenience stores (69 percent). Others included food-related establishments such as restaurants, groceries, and confectioneries (24 percent); service enterprises such as beauty and barbershops and shoe parlors (24 percent); retailers such as hat shops and hardware stores (12 percent); and recreational sites such as bars and pool halls (9 percent).[103] The study included extensive personal interviews with forty-six

Figure 18. The footprint of the Elmwood Park urban renewal project. Detroit City Plan Commission, *Detroit Urban Renewal* (Detroit, Michigan, 1963).

business owners in October and November 1964, "a fairly large group" of which constituted Black women who were widowed, divorced, or separated. Overall, almost a quarter of the businesses examined were owned by women, nearly half of the entrepreneurs were born in the "Deep South," and almost all of the Black entrepreneurs were born in the South.[104]

Before urban renewal came to Elmwood Park, most of these enterprises were stable. Twenty percent had been in business for more than thirty years, 30 percent for sixteen to twenty-nine years, 30 percent for five to six years, and 20 percent for less than five years. By 1964, only thirty-two of the sixty-four businesses surveyed in Saperstein's study had survived the Elmwood Park 1 redevelopment project. Thirty-two had either definitely or probably gone out of business.[105] This data shows a racial discrepancy, as 57 percent of Black-owned businesses did not survive urban renewal, compared to 35 percent of white-owned businesses in the area. Most of the entrepreneurs whose businesses went under were convinced that they would have successfully maintained their operations had they not been displaced by urban renewal.[106]

Urban planning initiatives affected Black business owners in distinct ways. Once the city announced plans for a new urban renewal project, residents began leaving the designated area in droves. As Black neighborhoods fractured and residents sought housing in other parts of the city, business owners experienced a spontaneous loss of trade and revenue—a problem that would continue for several years while the city took its time with the acquisition process. This trend had a particularly negative impact on small businesses that relied exclusively on neighborhood patrons (as opposed to citywide customers) as well as in cases where only one side of the block was acquired. One entrepreneur displaced by the Elmwood Park 1 project explained, "There's four blocks across from me they've taken but I'm stuck. No customers. If it wasn't for some old customers who came back to deal with me, I'd be a goner."[107] As their clientele moved away, business owners watched their sales drop drastically, and many did in fact go out of business before they had a chance to obtain a settlement for their property from the city. This was one of the most demoralizing aspects of urban renewal for Black business owners, whose success depended on strong community ties and customer loyalty. If they attempted to reestablish their business in a new location, they would essentially have to build up a fresh client base from scratch. An entrepreneur who was finally able to leave their neighborhood offered this defeatist point of view: "I felt bad when I started to lose my business. When I moved I didn't feel so bad because I didn't have any business anyway."[108]

The dispersal of clients and the breakup of community connections was especially hard on businesses operated out of people's homes. The case of Ruth Ellis highlights the largely undocumented aspect of urban renewal's impact on home-based businesses. Ellis had come to Detroit in 1937 and initially went to work babysitting for a family just outside the city in Highland Park. In her hometown of Springfield, Illinois, Ellis had worked for a neighborhood man who owned a print shop and had learned how to set type and run the press machine. On her days off from working in Highland Park, she looked for a job at a printing business and finally found one with a printer named Waterfield.[109] But before long, Ellis mused, "I was working for a printer and I said to myself, if I can do this for him, how come I can't do this for myself?"[110]

Figure 19. Ruth Ellis working at her printing press in her home-based printing business. Ruth Ellis photograph, c. 1940s, Box 2, Ruth Ellis Papers, Bentley Historical Library, University of Michigan.

She decided to open a shop of her own. In 1942, Ruth Ellis and her girlfriend, Ceciline "Babe" Franklin, took their savings, along with $500 they borrowed for a down payment, and bought a two-family home at 10335 Oakland Avenue.[111] The couple lived upstairs and rented out four of the five downstairs rooms. Ellis used the fifth, the front room, for her printing shop.

Soon Ellis and Franklin Printing Company was open for business. Though it was a family business that the couple ran together, Ruth Ellis did all the printing work and Babe Franklin kept her job as a cook.[112] Ellis recalled, "I printed anything small, not books or things like that where it had to be linotyped. I did all printing by hand . . . I would just take the walk-in trade."[113] Her store policies included: "A deposit is required on all work," "state tax must be paid on all work," and, "no credit." Several churches in the neighborhood were her clients, so she printed a large number of coin envelopes and raffle tickets.[114]

Ruth Ellis's printing business did not make her rich, but it did provide her with economic independence. As she affirmed, "I made enough money to live off of. I didn't save too much, but I could pay my bills and eat what I wanted." Ellis was her own boss, set her own hours, and chose which jobs to take.[115] She operated Ellis and Franklin Printing out of her home for two decades—until "the city had it torn down during urban renewal . . . to help improve Oakland Avenue" in the 1960s.[116] Forced to leave her home, Ellis closed the printing business and never reestablished it, "retiring" at the age of sixty-five.[117] Since all of Ellis's clients had been in her north Detroit neighborhood and were dispersed by urban renewal, it did not make sense to try to establish a new business. She subsequently moved into the Wolverine senior citizen housing project on Elizabeth Street in downtown Detroit.[118] Years later, reflecting on postwar urban planning, Ellis concluded, "I saw that progress was making the poor classes of people move, keep moving, on the move. If they decide they want your property, they take it. That's what you call progress."[119] Ruth Ellis is just one example of the many home-based entrepreneurs who were displaced from residential properties, saw their communities disperse across the city, and were unable to reestablish their businesses.

As with freeway construction, urban renewal was notorious for long periods of inaction between the city announcing a project and the process of actually acquiring property in a renewal zone. Disagreements among urban officials, changes in plans, lawsuits, and the sluggishness of bureaucratic procedure all caused delays in the proceedings.[120] For example, it took the City of Detroit almost five years to acquire the 129 acres for the Gratiot Redevelopment Project.[121] Completing the project took even longer. As Coleman Young remembered, "Black Bottom lay in ruins for six years before the first new building went up."[122] From 1946 to 1958, the city crawled through the processes of condemning properties at the Gratiot site, relocating almost two thousand Black families, preparing and obtaining federal approval for four different sets of redevelopment plans, selling the land to a developer, and constructing a high-rise apartment building.[123] By 1954, the press was referring to the vacant Gratiot zone as "Ragweed Acres" due to the fact that the area was lying fallow.[124] The project remained incomplete for the next ten years.

The city's delayed acquisition haunted business owners like Dr. Austin W. Curtis, who established A. W. Curtis Laboratories in 1945 at 454 Farnsworth, which manufactured and distributed eighty different cosmetic and personal care products. Over the next decade, Curtis built A. W. Curtis Laboratories into a thriving enterprise; in 1950, the company's gross profit was $45,926 and when he was considering incorporating the business in 1953, he valued its assets at $51,000 (approximately $584,000 in 2023 dollars).[125] However, by the late 1960s, the company was experiencing financial troubles because of urban renewal. A. W. Curtis Laboratories was in the proposed Medical Center #3 Redevelopment Project area but as usual, the city was dragging its feet.[126] Of the delay in acquiring his property, Curtis said, "It almost creates a situation where a business folds up. . . . It's impossible to do any planning." He estimated that the delay would cost his business $15,000–20,000 (approximately $137,000–183,000 in 2023 dollars).[127]

Some Black business owners took out loans to stay afloat during the long process of urban renewal. This strategy came with its own problems, however, as was the case with the proprietor of a small cleaning business. Like many Black entrepreneurs, the proprietor had thought based on his income and savings that he was pretty well set. But as urban renewal chased his customers away, his business started going downhill. He dipped into his savings, waiting for the city to purchase his property. When that was no longer enough, he was forced to borrow money—an ill-fated prospect since Detroit's white-owned financial institutions did not give loans to Blacks. This reality of U.S. racial capitalism compounded the problems created by urban renewal. The only way to get the $3,000 he needed was to borrow it from loan sharks who demanded 30 percent interest, as opposed to the 5.5 percent that banks and other loan institutions charged at the time. Unable to repay his debt without the patronage of his former customers, the entrepreneur ultimately had to sell his cleaning business. Had he been paid for his land—which was worth around $10,000—within a reasonable amount of time after the area was slated for urban renewal, the enterprise could have survived. Instead, like so many others, he saw his financial independence and the fruits of a lifetime of labor slip away.[128]

Delayed acquisition made it impossible to plan for the future and as time ticked on, business owners in renewal zones watched the value of their properties plummet due to a process known as "blight by announcement."[129] Mel Ravitz, a sociologist and member of the Detroit Common Council, summed up the pattern: "We announce a project years in advance and cast a shadow over the whole neighborhood. Owners stop improving their property, tenants move out and vandals do the rest."[130] Residents and entrepreneurs across the city complained that the years between announcing a project and the appraisers' arrival caused accelerated deterioration, vacancies, loss of rentals and business, increases in insurance rates and cancellations, vandalism, fires, and crime.[131] This was the case even when redevelopment projects were ultimately discarded. In 1949, for example, the city announced plans for a federal housing project on the St. Aubin extension, yet the neighborhood remained untouched until 1960, when the plan was finally abandoned. As Coleman Young affirmed, "Just the rumor of urban renewal was enough to ruin an area."[132]

When the city finally acquired property in a renewal zone, officials did not offer owners a settlement based on the market value prior to redevelopment. Instead, they presented condemnation awards after the value of the property had decreased significantly due to blight by announcement. Following the city's 1950 announcement that their neighborhood was slated for urban renewal, one east-side couple saw their property value drop from $12,500 in 1954 to a condemnation value of only $5,200 in 1963.[133] Black business owners were understandably frustrated with delayed acquisition and the financial repercussions of blight by announcement. As one entrepreneur remarked, "It took absolutely too long. It works a real hardship. Ninety days is long enough; why wait 10 to 15 years? Soon as the rumors started people started to move out. The only ones that stay is the ones that owns their own property and then the vandals move in and start destroying the property and they don't get their money nohow."[134] While residents could at least try to find housing elsewhere—no small task given Detroit's postwar housing shortage—business owners in long-term leases or who owned their properties were stuck. They could not simply sell privately and start over in a new neighborhood; no one would buy in a renewal zone.[135]

That said, some lucky entrepreneurs were able to obtain compensation from the city for their property and relocate their business during urban renewal. Ed Davis was one of them. Davis was born in 1911 in Shreveport, Louisiana, and moved to Detroit in the 1920s. Believing that he would get a better education in Detroit, his family allowed young Ed to join an aunt and uncle who had already migrated north to work at the Ford Motor Company.[136] Davis loved cars, and once in the Motor City found a job washing cars at a gas station and then as a used car salesman. He eventually enrolled in the Alexander Hamilton Institute's two-year correspondence course in modern business. In 1939, Davis established his own new car dealership—Davis Motor Sales, at 421 East Vernor Highway on the city's east side. Davis operated at this location for the next twenty years and built Davis Motor Sales into a thriving Studebaker dealership.[137]

However, by the mid-1950s, sales for both new and used cars were down throughout the neighborhood. Davis remembered:

The area just north of downtown Detroit had been a busy and fairly
prosperous Black district in the 1940s, but by the mid-1950s it was
turning into a no-man's-land. Those who could afford to move were
getting out. Those who couldn't (property owners, mostly) stayed
on from day to day, hoping to sell and get out themselves. Such were
the effects of the new expressway programs, industrial parks, and
urban redevelopment plans on the people in this area and others like
it. About a mile in each direction from my location—east, west, and
north, but excepting south, toward downtown Detroit—had been
condemned or was soon to be condemned. The people who were still
there were disgusted and wanted to leave.[138]

Like other entrepreneurs and property owners, Ed Davis suffered financially
as the entire area deteriorated, economically and physically. Yet his only
option was to continue working to keep his business afloat. Getting a different
job would not have solved his problem; he still owned a commercial property
and anything he earned would have gone to mortgage payments. If he did not
keep up with the taxes and the mortgage, he would have lost everything he
had accumulated over the years. Davis confessed, "It was a terrible position to
be in. Five or six years before I had been earning $25,000 or so a year [about
$285,000 in 2023 dollars]; by 1959 I was struggling just to survive."[139]

In late 1962, the city paid Davis $75,000 for his property (approximately
$760,000 in 2023 dollars). This was about half of what it had been worth
before the urban renewal announcement. Even though Davis considered the
government's payment unsatisfactory, he decided to accept it and get out of
the area. It is telling that Davis considered himself one of the lucky ones. As a
member of the Detroit Housing Commission's Relocation Advisory Committee and leader in the Black business community, he had a thorough understanding of how Black entrepreneurs in the city were being affected by urban
renewal.[140] The fact that Davis felt fortunate to receive half the value of his
property meant that even the best-case scenario for Black entrepreneurs in
renewal zones was abysmal. Some had to live with urban renewal much longer than five years, others received less than half of the value of their property,
and many lost everything.

In the Elmwood Park 1 project area, 58 percent of business owners felt
that the amount of money they received for their property was unreason-
able.[141] Explaining how the ongoing decline in property values shaped their
final settlement, one entrepreneur protested:

It was unfair. I got $40,000 and had expected $60,000. I felt the property was worth more. . . . We first heard about the city taking over in 1947. They came down and looked the place over and told us they were coming through later and wanted to look at the property. I asked them how much we would get from the city and they said somewhere between $80,000 and $85,000. We brought it up in court, but it didn't mean a thing. Why didn't they take it when they first declared it instead of waiting so long and then not doing what they promised to do—pay me a fair price? They practically steal the property from you and then you try to buy that property now and you can't.[142]

This assessment—that they were essentially victims of theft—was at the heart of Black entrepreneurs' critique of urban renewal's approach to property acquisition. Besides being unethical, inadequate condemnation payments from the city often precluded both business owners and residents from purchasing a new home or commercial space at market value. Harriet Saperstein clarified, "With the increases in the cost of labor and property, [business] owners cannot buy anything comparable to the original investment. The owners were now ten to twenty years older than when the property was purchased, and often new, higher payments could not be handled."[143] Likewise, according to Ed Davis, "Even after the government condemned a property and paid what they thought was a good price for it, many businesses couldn't afford to set up shop in a new location and win new customers. So they closed."[144] For entrepreneurs who managed to maintain their businesses through years of declining profits *and* eventually obtain a condemnation payment, inadequate compensation from the state was a bitter pill to swallow. It was also frequently the final nail in the coffin for their enterprises.

Some Black business owners made it through these obstacles, but their urban renewal troubles were far from over. Proprietors faced numerous challenges in relocating and transitioning their enterprises to a new area of the city. With redevelopment projects' shifting timelines, the circulation of inaccurate information, and convoluted government procedures, the whole process was fraught with confusion, unknowns, and additional financial hardships. In the end, many businesses did not survive the change.

The government only began providing compensation funds for moving expenses for displaced families, individuals, and businesses as a result of the Housing Act of 1956.[145] Moreover, it was not until 1964 that the Housing Act added a requirement that cities track available commercial spaces to refer to business owners forced to relocate due to urban redevelopment. City officials boasted that the Detroit Housing Commission had worked out such an arrangement with the local Small Business Administration as early as February 1961, before the 1964 mandate.[146] Still, assistance made available in 1961 or 1964 was too late for the many businesses already displaced by urban planning initiatives.[147]

Left largely to their own devices, Black entrepreneurs embarked upon the often futile task of finding a new, appropriate commercial space—a logistical nightmare in postwar Detroit. In the Elmwood Park 1 redevelopment area, for example, half of the business owners surveyed expressed having considerable trouble finding a site that was not only affordable but also in an area either zoned for their business or where they could obtain a license.[148] In addition to zoning and licensing considerations, entrepreneurs had to track down a space with a physical layout suitable to their needs that was not in a white neighborhood and did not have excess competition in their field.[149] Finding a location that checked all the boxes was virtually impossible, as almost all newly constructed postwar real estate was built in areas where Blacks were restricted from purchasing property—white middle-class urban neighborhoods and the suburbs. This racialized landscape exacerbated overcrowding and real estate shortages for Blacks in Detroit.[150] Faced with limited options, most displaced Black business owners had no choice but to compromise on adequate facilities and relocate to other overcrowded areas where they could serve Black customers.[151]

Some entrepreneurs did try to make relocation arrangements when their neighborhoods were slated for urban renewal. This was the case for "Mrs. B," a sixty-two-year-old Black woman displaced from the Elmwood Park 1 zone. Mrs. B had operated a grocery store there for eighteen years and shared a close relationship with her neighborhood customers. The grocery was "a thriving small business" that provided its owner with an above-average income and supported an additional three employees. Mrs. B rented the building, which was in fair condition, and had purchased her own equipment and fixtures. When the city began surveying the area in 1948, Mrs. B decided to be proactive. Expecting to be dislocated, she planned for the future by buying a building in a nearby area. However, the "cloud of condemnation" would hang over Elmwood Park 1 for the next fifteen years. By the time Mrs. B received the official notice to move, the neighborhood where she had preemptively purchased a building had deteriorated. Mrs. B. was forced to move into the building anyway because, as she put it, "I had no capital. . . . The rent was too high everywhere I looked."[152]

In 1964, Mrs. B was running her business alone in its new location, working twelve to fourteen hours a day, seven days a week. Although her income was adequate, she could no longer afford her employees because she was still in debt from the expenses incurred during relocation. Overworked and out of options, Mrs. B pressed on, explaining, "At my age getting a job is difficult and I'm single and this is my only support." Unfortunately, Mrs. B's troubles persisted, as rumors that her new business location would also be slated for urban renewal began to circulate. She had no plans to cope with this possibility and said simply, "I'll just have to stay on and struggle and suffer." Dejected, Mrs. B lamented the injustice against her community: "They run them from one slum to another slum and they'll always be renewing areas so there's no place to go to fix up. . . . They'll be renewing forever this way."[153]

The unpredictability of urban renewal meant that Mrs. B's strategy of promptly arranging her business relocation backfired. However, many entrepreneurs who also wanted to quickly leave a renewal zone did not have that option due to the hoops through which they had to jump to access government funds. To qualify for a federal relocation payment, business owners had to meet onerous requirements, including having all their relocation arrangements in place (new address, moving dates, and costs) but remaining in the renewal zone until the city officially broke ground or purchased the property. Other stipulations further confused the process. If a business owner's claim exceeded $10,000, they had to obtain additional approval from the Urban Renewal Administration Regional Office. The maximum commercial relocation payment available for expenses incurred through moving and/or the direct loss of property was $25,000.[154] Such limits and hurdles led to further financial losses for dislocated business owners. For example, one entrepreneur in Elmwood Park 1 spent $77,000 in moving costs yet only received $23,000 in compensation.[155] Of their relocation payment, another business owner remarked, "It didn't cover my expenses. I took a loss in money because it costs money to start over to find a new place and relocate yourself. They didn't pay for this."[156]

In addition to reimbursement for moving expenses and direct loss of property, the 1964 Housing Act included a provision for displacement payments of $1,500 for small businesses.[157] The Housing Act of 1965 increased this amount to $2,500 for certain enterprises displaced by urban renewal activities.[158] If a commercial establishment met the requirements for relocation reimbursement, it might be also be eligible for a small business displacement payment. But again, the requirements were complicated and onerous.[159]

Unsurprisingly, small business owners frequently found these processes convoluted and did not have adequate time to gather the required documentation and approvals before their move. Many lost out on the opportunity to recover moving costs because they were unaware of these procedures, misinformed, disqualified based on a technicality, or simply did not possess the skills needed to apply for these benefits. For example, to qualify for federal relocation assistance, business owners in a renewal zone were required to obtain bids from three moving companies and then hire the one with the lowest bid. Many entrepreneurs found this prerequisite problematic because companies' estimates often did not cover the full cost of the move.[160] Never having relocated their business before, some entrepreneurs likely did not know how to estimate the true cost of a commercial move. And since the government would only provide compensation based on the lowest bid, Black business owners were left in dire straits. In addition, some displaced entrepreneurs incurred incidental moving costs that were not eligible for relocation and small business displacement payments. For instance, proprietors who had to obtain a license to operate at their new location or pay inspection fees related to reinstalling equipment would not be reimbursed for these expenditures because they were not defined as moving expenses or direct loss of property.[161] Finally, the stipulation that business owners could not receive financial assistance until *after* the enterprise had already moved from the renewal zone was a major flaw.[162] The federal requirements to qualify for funds—such as committing to a new address and moving date—essentially demanded that entrepreneurs spend quite a bit of money in preparation to relocate. Since the nature of racial capitalism meant many Black establishments experienced undercapitalization, shouldering the costs of moving in the hopes of getting reimbursed later was just not feasible for many proprietors. This sizable and sudden expense caused a number of Black businesses to go under.

Some entrepreneurs managed to clear these sizable hurdles and ultimately received relocation payments. Saperstein's study found that the median amount for businesses displaced from the Elmwood Park 1 area was $875 (almost $8,900 in 2023 dollars). However, the payments were very unevenly divided. About 22 percent of proprietors received less than $300 (less than about $3,000 in 2023 dollars), while 15 percent received between $300 and $999 (approximately $3,000 to $10,000 in 2023 dollars). Nearly 20 percent received over $3,000 (about $30,500 in 2023 dollars), but almost all of these business owners were white. And close to 30 percent of the Elmwood Park entrepreneurs received no financial assistance at all.[163] In addition, those who were allotted funds complained that there was a significant delay between paying their moving costs and being reimbursed by the government. Again, this posed a considerable problem for business owners saddled with an array of unanticipated expenditures. If the state had provided reimbursement in a timely fashion (or simply up front), they could have used the money for necessary expenses, such as a security deposit for their new location. Instead, these funds remained inaccessible while displaced entrepreneurs struggled to survive the transition.[164]

To stay in business, many Black proprietors needed to obtain loans to pay for their moving expenses. This was the case for almost one-quarter of entrepreneurs surveyed in the Elmwood Park 1 area.[165] However, with limited access to credit from white-owned financial institutions, most took out "informal" loans from family and friends or "secondary" loan agencies that charged higher interest rates. Only one business owner from the Elmwood Park survey reported securing a loan from a bank, and despite a program established by the 1964 Housing Act that provided 3 percent rehabilitation loans to business owners in urban renewal areas, none mentioned contacting the local Small Business Administration (SBA).[166] This was no doubt because, based on past experiences with banks and government agencies' racist practices, Black proprietors did not expect the SBA to work with them. Indeed, Saperstein noted that small businesses in Elmwood Park 1 were unlikely to attain an SBA loan even if they tried "because of poor records of collateral, past profits, and potential earnings."[167] Moreover, as Austin Curtis of A. W. Curtis Laboratories observed, "You can't even get a loan from the Small Business Administration to enable you to move to another place until it reaches the stage where the city is acquiring the land."[168] Thus, even if the SBA did approve a Black-owned business for a loan, the proprietor would still have been stuck until relatively late in the urban renewal process. The value of their property would have already drastically declined and the longer they waited to move, the fewer options they would have in terms of available commercial spaces in other parts of the city. But the state worked according to its own timeline, not based on what was best or necessary for Black entrepreneurs in urban renewal zones.

Black business owners' inability to receive government assistance took a massive toll. Small business displacement payments were not approved until 1964, after Elmwood Park 1 proprietors had already been displaced. They were understandably upset to have missed out on the opportunity; 45 percent could think of specific ways they would have used the money, including "for working capital—to pay the costs of having things reconnected 'properly,' for decoration, or to compensate for the loss of money while they couldn't operate." Some highlighted that if they had received a displacement payment, they would not have had to take out a loan. Others would have bought necessary equipment and merchandise or could have afforded a better location. One entrepreneur whose enterprise had shut down lamented, "I could have reopened my business" had the dislocation payment been available.[169]

Black entrepreneurs who were able to move to new locations continued to experience financial difficulties related to the disruption of urban renewal. A common complaint among those whose businesses survived the Elmwood Park 1 project was the loss of revenue between closing their original establishment and reopening in their new space. According to one business owner, "We lost four months' business before starting up again. Customers and employees we had [were gone]. In effect, we started up a new business in a new location."[170] Moreover, many of the existing structures available to Black entrepreneurs were not up to code and the expense of making needed repairs to meet the city's requirements fell completely on dislocated proprietors. They also had to pay for necessities such as new flooring and the disposal of debris created through renovations. Lack of capital after these expenditures made it difficult for some entrepreneurs to buy enough stock for their new establishment.[171] In general, entrepreneurs found that they had higher overhead costs in their new locations as well. This included heat and electricity and significantly higher rents. For the Elmwood Park 1 entrepreneurs, the median rent doubled from $68 to $150.[172] Taken together, the physical renovations needed to open in their new location, becoming familiar with a new area, and building up a new clientele amounted to essentially establishing a new business.

Moreover, as redevelopment drove Black Detroiters into different areas of the city, there was a good chance their new neighborhoods would also become targets for urban renewal. Like Mrs. B the grocer, another owner displaced from the Elmwood Park 1 site reestablished his business in a new location but after a couple of years complained, "They put me in the streets and they're thinking of doing it again to this place."[173] Others learned of impending urban renewal projects before finalizing their relocation arrangements. A man known as "Mr. C," for instance, was forced to "retire" when he could not find a new location that did not have forthcoming plans for redevelopment. A seventy-seven-year-old Black man originally from Georgia, Mr. C had operated a small candy store in the Elmwood Park 1 area for fourteen years. His family lived above the store, enjoyed a pleasant life, and made a good living. When urban renewal pushed them out of the neighborhood, Mr. C planned to reestablish his business elsewhere and even succeeded in finding a new commercial space. However, the city advised him against it, anticipating that the area would soon also become a renewal zone. Rather than continuing the search and prolonging the strain on himself and his wife, Mr. C concluded that he could not rebuild his business.

This compulsory decision decreased Mr. C and his wife's quality of life in their advanced age. They both collected old-age pensions that were "enough to get by on" and supplemented their fixed income with a small vegetable garden behind their home. Additionally, Mr. C reported that he "cuts a head of hair now and then"—something he began doing as a boy in Georgia sixty years earlier. Although falling back on his barbering skills speaks to his resilience and resourcefulness, Mr. C felt a deep sense of loss. He described his store as his "best friend," his "amusement, comfort, and joy." He also lamented the loss of his customers, who were his friends and neighbors, and regretted that "all of us have scattered like Blackbirds." Begrudgingly accepting his fate, Mr. C concluded, "Every dog has his day and I've had mine."[174]

As the experiences of proprietors like Mr. C and Mrs. B demonstrate, older business owners found it especially challenging to start over once displaced by urban renewal.[175] In Saperstein's study, a large percentage of local businesses that did not survive were owned by proprietors over the age of fifty who were compelled to close up shop and "retire." All of those interviewed were "very disturbed about their forced 'retirement.'"[176] After devoting their lives and savings to their businesses, many expressed anger; as one proprietor vented, "I scraped and saved for 32 years and the city kicked me out. I can barely get by now. They hardly paid me nothing and they're asking $1,000 a foot for my property. They put me in the streets." Others were anxious about their finances as they aged without the security of owning their business. One man confessed, "I felt pretty low because first of all, I didn't want to relocate in another small store, and we were here for 34 years. Also, at my age, where in the devil would I get a job? I was worried about the future. Wherever I went for a job, they looked at me like I was a dummy."[177] If older entrepreneurs could not start over in business, they had few other options for making a living and their quality of life likely suffered.

Being forced to shutter their businesses also generated a significant sense of grief. Displaced entrepreneurs expressed their nostalgia and sorrow in statements such as, "I felt it was a great loss. It was home. It was memories. It was a great loss. The place could have taken care of us for the rest of our lives."[178] Many lamented the collapse of a business "that brought in enough extra cash for me to save something" and "gave me something to do. . . . I miss all the people that used to come in and out."[179] Through urban renewal migrant entrepreneurs lost many valuable aspects of being part of a community, in addition to income. Black business owners experienced not only financial harm but also economic and emotional trauma due to the process and displacement of urban renewal and highway construction. For migrant entrepreneurs who had come from the South in search of economic self-determination, the end result of financial reversion was devastating and an important lesson in the feasibility of freedom enterprise in a racial capitalist system.

*　　*　　*

Joe Von Battle, a migrant from Macon, Georgia, opened a record store at 3530 Hastings Street in 1945.[180] Since there were not many places to buy Black music in Detroit at that time, Von Battle's shop was extremely popular. He kept it open almost all night long, playing records through the shop's loudspeakers so people walking by would hear the music and want to come inside. In addition to selling records, Von Battle also recorded and produced music for artists. The business was a vital part of Paradise Valley's vibrant music scene.[181]

However, Von Battle was forced to close his shop when construction began on the Chrysler Freeway. As his daughter Marsha Mickens recalled, "My first memory of Hastings [around 1957 or 1958] was that my father took me to a place near where his record shop had been. . . . He walked me across the street from the place where we were standing over to this gigantic dirt pit that was in the ground. It looked like a canyon to me. He looked at me and said . . . 'This is where Hastings used to be.'" Mickens reasoned, "What my father so graphically understood and expressed with that sentence was that a way of life had been totally destroyed by the Chrysler Freeway. The street of Hastings just no longer existed."[182] Indeed, it was not just physical structures that had been demolished. Urban planning initiatives shattered a thriving business community and wiped out the evidence of migrant entrepreneurs' hard work, the wealth they hoped to pass down to their children, and other markers of freedom they had pursued in moving north to Detroit. As eastsider Justine Wylie put it, "It took the *monster* Chrysler Freeway a very few short years to destroy what had taken the area many decades to build."[183]

Many African Americans felt that Detroit and Michigan lawmakers, public officials, and urban planners deliberately set out to sabotage Black economic development, believing that the Black business community was targeted because of its success. Speaking of the city tearing down a Black commercial neighborhood to widen 8 Mile Road, Alice Cain Newman remarked, "I've noticed a pattern. The city did the same thing in the '40s down at Paradise Valley. That was a thriving Black business community, probably one of the most thriving in the United States that was owned by Blacks, not just fronted by Blacks but it was owned. They came through and did the same darn thing and let that land stay vacant ten solid years before they put up housing down there."[184] According to Marsha Mickens, "It was a very prosperous community, because you had a number of Black business people that had serviced the community for years and were becoming affluent. This is one reason people talk about how Hastings was destroyed purposefully. That has always been the scuttlebutt within the community. That the white man decided to get rid of Hastings because that community was becoming too strong."[185] Regardless of their intentions, what remains clear is that city planners and officials sacrificed Black Detroiters' property and wealth to benefit whites, all while sabotaging Black wealth transfer to future generations.

Postwar urban planning initiatives harmed Black-owned businesses, especially in cities like Detroit where Blacks were disproportionally uprooted by these projects. Expressway construction and urban renewal efforts were used as convenient devices for razing "slums," routinely targeting Black neighborhoods for demolition. In Detroit, this included destroying successful business communities—the culmination of decades of Black migrant entrepreneurs' labor, ingenuity, and hope. Any attempts to relocate their businesses were laden with financial hardships and losses, as delayed property acquisition, inadequate compensation, and countless unforeseen costs and pitfalls made starting over a nearly impossible task. Although some of the policies that harmed Black business owners were issued at the federal level, the State of Michigan and City of Detroit were not guiltless. The decisions made by white policymakers, elected officials, and urban planners sacrificed Black Detroiters' communities, including its thriving businesses, to reclaim the core city for whites. At issue is not particular stakeholders' racist attitudes or personal motive. Whether done intentionally or inadvertently (or likely a combination of both), officials' decisions demonstrated that they had a vested interest in maintaining racial capitalism. Their actions undoubtedly led to a loss of Black property, wealth, and future financial prospects. If nothing else, the city was reckless and callous with its Black residents, as officials excluded them from their vision of urban progress.

CHAPTER 8

Fighting: The Struggle for
Economic Protection and Inclusion

In November 1943—about five months after the city's explosive race riot—the city of Detroit announced plans for a new medical center associated with Wayne State University. The redevelopment project intended to establish a comprehensive medical center, new housing, commercial facilities, a sports field, and a junior high school. The earmarked site's proximity to the university, art center, and existing Children's Hospital and its potential for easy accessibility without blocking main thoroughfares made it a desirable location to revitalize the core city. Due to the site's considerable size—237 acres covering the area bounded by Mack, Woodward, Hastings, and Kirby—the City Plan Commission recommended that clearance be undertaken in three stages, or subprojects, over a period of approximately ten years.[1] The project was to be located right in the middle of Black Detroit's Paradise Valley. The 1943 race riot had drastically altered the racial geography of the city and economic landscape for Black entrepreneurs. White flight opened up possibilities for Black business owners to expand into new territory, which contributed to Paradise Valley's boom (as discussed in Chapter 6). Yet, in response to the riot, the city turned to urban planning as a way to push Blacks out of the area. As Black business exploded in the 1940s, African American business owners' freedom enterprise was being undermined by the city.

The site proposed for the medical center redevelopment project (Mich. R23 GN) was home to over ten thousand Black Detroiters as well as "a large segment of Negro business and two of the largest Negro churches—Bethel AME and Scott Methodist."[2] Upon hearing news of the project, a group of local property and business owners called a meeting at Bethel AME Church on December 2, 1943. Intending to determine the shape of their opposition,

Black stakeholders at the meeting raised their concerns about the medical center project, considered their legal options to prevent the condemnation of property within the area, and selected a committee to consult with city officials and urge them toward a different location. At the meeting Jasper Adams, owner of Adams Standard Service at Beaubien and Farnsworth, pointed out that the project would disrupt long-established Black businesses in the area and leave displaced entrepreneurs in the difficult position of trying to obtain another suitable commercial space.[3] Business owners recognized not only that the medical center would break up communities but also that displaced residents and businesses would face restrictive covenants and other racist limitations that would severely curtail their ability to resettle elsewhere in the city. In voicing these concerns, Adams and others essentially forecasted the destruction that would accompany urban redevelopment in the 1950s and 1960s as early as 1943.

It seemed that white urban planners and city officials viewed Black-owned businesses as expendable. However, Detroit's Black entrepreneurs did not take threats to their community lying down; they actively defended their economic interests early on in the process of postwar urban redevelopment. They organized against urban renewal and highway construction, utilizing the press, the courts, and other forms of protest to make their grievances known and attempted to halt efforts to raze their communities in the name of urban progress. However, Black entrepreneurs' and property owners' objections to projects like the medical center did not mean that they were opposed to urban redevelopment in principle. African Americans who fought against such endeavors underscored that their intention was not to limit urban development but rather to challenge the racist discrimination in the city's decisions about which neighborhoods to demolish and communities to remove. With a shrewd understanding of racial capitalism at work in their city, Black entrepreneurs saw that officials' vision for the future of Detroit did not include them, or their economic stability. In response, they articulated their own visions for the city, fought for inclusion in that process, and struggled to maintain the economic self-determination that brought them there in the first place.

This chapter examines Black business owners' and community leaders' fight for unbiased treatment and inclusion in urban redevelopment. Black Detroiters protested private development because it led to the unjust loss of their homes, businesses, and financial security. But they also protested urban planners' and administrators' vision for Detroit, which insisted that redevelopment could attract white middle-class suburban families—and their money—back to the city. Black business owners and residents adopted a different view on urban renewal's purpose: improving the quality of life for the preexisting community.[4] Black Detroiters objected to the utilization of public funds to expand private enterprises that discriminated against African Americans and tried to minimize urban renewal's negative impact on their communities. While this activism did lead to some victories, they unfortunately came too late for Black entrepreneurs who had already been forced to shutter their businesses.

Speaking Out Against Economic Injustice

Black Detroiters watched as the city demolished their neighborhoods and commercial districts and displaced thousands without adequate plans for relocation, but they did not stand idly by. Rather, Detroit's Blacks recognized that the city's postwar redevelopment plans would lead to the destruction of the communities they had labored to build, and they challenged these efforts immediately. A fierce determination to protect their economic well-being was central to their protest. Black entrepreneurs and leaders fought to safeguard their livelihoods—both individual and collective—and openly condemned the racial discrimination that infused postwar urban planning. Yet while they denounced their exclusion from the processes and profits of redevelopment, they maintained that their critiques did not signify hostility toward urban progress. On the contrary, Black Detroiters were eager to participate in creating a modern city in ways that benefited rather than harmed their communities. In doing so, they expressed their own vision for Detroit's future—one that regrettably would not come to pass.

The formal announcement of the Wayne University Medical Center in November 1943 created instant controversy. Black entrepreneurs' and property owners' December meeting at Bethel AME Church was just the beginning of their crusade to halt the project. By the fall of 1944, they had established the Warren-Ferry Property Owners Association to lead the battle.[5] The group's organizers included many migrant entrepreneurs who had worked for decades to build up Detroit's Black business community. The Reverend William H. Peck, pastor of Bethel AME Church and founder of the Booker T. Washington Trade Association (BTWTA), was appointed president of the organization; the Reverend Robert L. Bradby of the Second Baptist Church was vice president; Moses L. Walker of the Great Lakes Mutual Insurance Company took on the role of secretary; A. G. Wright, owner of Wright Funeral Home, was selected as treasurer; and drugstore owner Aaron C. Toodle was chairman of the executive committee.[6]

Mostly business owners themselves, the group's officers recognized the damage the medical center would inflict upon the commercial district already on the project's chosen site. The neighborhood was home to an array of Black businesses, including the Paradise Distributing Agency, Porters Cleaners, Adams Standard Service, Fairview Sanitarium, and Great Lakes Manor, an apartment house owned and operated by the Great Lakes Mutual Insurance Company.[7] The Warren-Ferry Property Owners Association defended and advocated for these economic interests early on in the process of urban renewal and would inspire Black entrepreneurs in other neighborhoods to follow their example when redevelopment plans threatened their communities.[8]

In 1945, the Warren-Ferry Property Owners Association reformed as the United Housing Committee on Medical Center.[9] Although the name emphasized housing, Black entrepreneurs' continued involvement ensured that business interests were also central to the organization's efforts.[10] The United Housing Committee on Medical Center made this intention plain in a resolution issued in March 1945, declaring, "We are absolutely opposed to the proposed location for the center which involves the destruction of one of our best sections in Detroit for homes, business enterprises, churches and cultural centers, unless definite relocation that meets our satisfaction within the city limits is guaranteed before the condemnation is started." Highlighting the economic losses of such a project and members' experiences as migrant entrepreneurs, the statement continued, "This area for 25 years has been the battlefield of our struggles and sacrifices, through which we have succeeded in building our finest business enterprises with a gross receipt of more than a million dollars per year [close to $17 million in 2023 dollars] and giving employment to nearly 400 Negroes. In this area there are also five Negro churches . . . whose doors are opened every night for religious, social, civic, political and business activities. To destroy all of these without satisfactory relocation robs us of that, which makes us poor indeed." The resolution concluded:

> Our committee, without malice and hate, in a spirit of human justice, is pledged and determined to oppose and fight this condemnation through all the courts of our land. We invite every right thinking

person regardless of race, creed or color who believes that all human beings, Black and white, are justly entitled to decent homes and all kinds of places and opportunities to work out their destiny and take their places under the sun, to join us in this holy crusade and help us to fight until a glorious victory for simple justice has been won.[11]

In moving north to Detroit, migrant entrepreneurs had doggedly pursued the ability to control their economic destiny as a matter of "simple justice." Decades later, after having successfully built a thriving business community in their new home, they still had to fight for self-determination within the confines of racial capitalism.

The organizers faced an uphill battle. The City Plan Commission, Wayne University County Hospital trustees, the Medical Science Center Corporation board of directors, and university administration all endorsed the proposed project site, and plans for the medical center moved forward.[12] However, three months after the United Housing Committee on Medical Center released their statement, university officials and other supporters of the project sought "absolute assurance" from the city that the site they selected would "ultimately be theirs without resistance."[13] It seems that after four years of research and consultations to develop their plans with urban officials, the outcry of Black residents and business owners had become a thorn in the side of the medical center designers. Powerful resistance had continued to grow in the neighborhood chosen for the project. This opposition would postpone condemnation proceedings for local buildings and delay medical center construction for several years.

Local Blacks expressed their apprehension about the proposed site in various ways. Understandably, they questioned the logistics of where displaced communities should go considering Detroit's acute housing shortage and the racial restrictions already in place. But they also called attention to the financial burdens of displacement. Clarence Anderson of the *Michigan Chronicle* inquired: "Are Negroes in this instance to be ruthlessly treated as expendables in the war on disease and death? Where in the city of Detroit could four to six thousand colored citizens find new homes? Where are the five big churches and the four little ones in this area to relocate even if condemnation paid them a fair sum with which to start over? What about the colored brothers [and sisters] who have spent the best years of their lives building a business in the area? Where can they start anew?"[14] This line of questioning raised several concerns. Anderson addressed the near impossibility of finding adequate

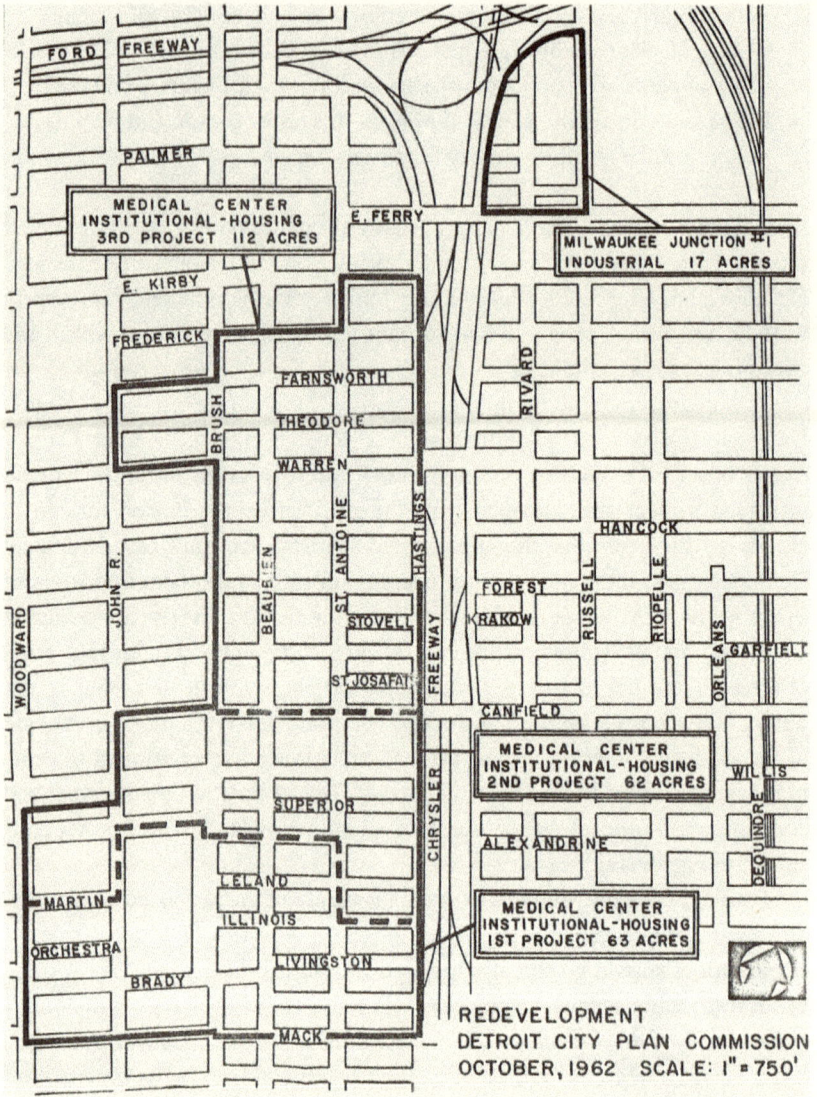

Figure 20. The medical center urban renewal project area, showing subprojects #1, 2, and 3. Detroit City Plan Commission, *Detroit Urban Renewal* (Detroit, Michigan, 1963).

housing and commercial space in the city as well as the sorrow of dividing
up neighborhoods and their key institutions. He also highlighted the area's
business community, lamenting that entrepreneurs could both lose the fruits
of their substantial labor and likely not receive a fair price for their properties.
Finally, Anderson acknowledged the sad truth underlying the project: that in
order to achieve their vision of urban progress, whites viewed African Americans as disposable.

Although Black Detroiters had misgivings about the city's urban renewal
projects, opponents made it clear that they did not inherently have a problem
with urban renewal itself but the way such plans were implemented. Most
of the entrepreneurs displaced from the Elmwood Park 1 redevelopment
zone, for example, criticized the city's methods, the laws enabling the project,
and the personal and communal harm resulting from it but did not challenge the idea of modernizing Detroit.[15] Arthur Johnson, Detroit NAACP
executive secretary, articulated the organization's stance on the city's urban
renewal program: "In principle we heartily endorse urban renewal, but until
these programs can be carried out with[out] discrimination of any kind, we
cannot totally embrace them in their present form."[16] Likewise, the United
Housing Committee on Medical Center agreed that a new medical facility
was a worthwhile objective and even asserted, "We are compelled to welcome a Medical Center and it is a matter of record in the Board of Education
that Negroes have offered to help raise funds and make other contributions
toward its success."[17] The group specified that it was not the project to which
members objected; it was the proposed site and the damage that would result
from building there, including the real possibility that Blacks displaced from
the area would become homeless.[18]

Such critiques often subsumed the problem of housing within larger arguments about the economic injustice of demolishing Black neighborhoods.
As Anderson wrote in his *Michigan Chronicle* article: "To criticize as short-
sighted the Negroes who have an interest in the area and who are leading the
opposition is, it seems to me, to indicate ignorance of the need of Negroes for
housing in Detroit. It also indicates lack of understanding of the way human
beings organize in any community when they recognize a threat to their hard-
won economic gains. For certainly on the basis of human experience we may
assume that the opposition to the site is not entirely due to sentimental attach-
ments to the neighborhood or fear of a place to go. There are economic interests."[19] By highlighting economic losses, this line of argumentation framed

concerns about the medical center's location as commonsensical rather than needlessly emotional. The fourteen-block area chosen for the project contained over one hundred different types of businesses ranging from shoeshine stands to a modern dry cleaning plant. The majority of these enterprises were grocery stores, followed by cleaning shops, beauty parlors, restaurants, and barbershops.[20] It was only reasonable for Black migrant entrepreneurs who had spent decades building up this business landscape to fight to protect their community, properties, and livelihoods.

Even so, Blacks recognized the necessity of urban redevelopment, particularly in the Black Bottom area, which was the oldest part of the city. Detroit contained one hundred thousand dwellings built before 1915 and many were unacceptable by modern standards. Built prior to contemporary building codes, older structures often lacked masonry foundation and modern plumbing, heating, and electrical wiring. Narrow lots were common, leaving buildings' interiors devoid of natural light and fresh air.[21] Acknowledging these conditions, the Booker T. Washington Trade Association stressed, "No responsible private citizen, or business organization, could in good conscious [sic]] adopt a position which is adverse to the eradication of slum conditions and factors which produce neighborhood decay."[22]

However, the BTWTA and other African American organizations urged the city to recognize that to effectively rid Detroit of slums and blight, it must get to their root cause: racial discrimination.[23] As the United Housing Committee on Medical Center noted in a formal statement, "Negroes are more restricted than any other group in Detroit. They are denied places to work out their destiny on the basis of color. These restrictions increase daily. To destroy the homes of 6,000 Negroes who have no place to go is not only un-American but pushes us beyond tragedy." Addressing those who criticized their opposition to the medical center as retrograde, the statement continued:

If color were not the signal for prejudice and restriction, if Negroes enjoyed the liberty to live and develop like all other groups in Detroit, we would be the last to oppose the location of a Medical Center in our section. The Negro has never been guilty of willfully obstructing progress in America. Our opposition to the center is the natural outcome of injustices heaped upon our defenseless heads. We must protest or lose our self-respect. Every man should fight for a decent place for his wife and children to live and an opportunity to work out his destiny. This spells our opposition to the location

of the Medical Center. Destroy the restrictions against us because
we are black and our opposition will fade away like a dream. In this
condemnation these are the terrible facts of injustice and crushing
losses. Destroy the home, business, church and cultural centers of
any race in Detroit except Negroes, give them money and they are
free to go any place in Detroit and relocate or rebuild. Everyone
knows that Negroes cannot do likewise because they are hedged in
everywhere by damnable restrictions. With less than we need, we
have none to spare even for a Medical Center.[24]

With this statement, the United Housing Committee on Medical Center joined
other detractors in condemning the racism that hindered African Americans'
economic autonomy.

In addition, critics of the project site pointed out that although Africans
Americans would benefit substantially from greater access to medical services, they were unlikely to receive it at the proposed center. The research of
the Detroit Urban League demonstrated that Detroit's white-operated hospitals discriminated against African Americans—both patients and medical
professionals.[25] A *Michigan Chronicle* article inquired in 1948:

When you think of the medical benefits that the community will
derive from the proposed medical center, how will the Negroes
fare? Will Negro Doctors be permitted to practice there? Will Negro
medical students be allowed to intern and serve as residents? Will
Negro girls be accepted as nursing students? Will there be, or is there
now a quota system used on the admission of Negro students to the
Wayne College of Medicine? These are all important questions to
an important element of Detroit's citizenry. Negroes have had much
difficulty in years past in finding places to train for the medical
profession. The majority of young Negro girls and men who desire to
be doctors or nurses have had to leave Detroit to find a place to train
or intern. If Detroit gets a medical center, let us see that the situation
will be better.[26]

As the battle over the medical center site dragged on into the 1950s, organizers continued to call attention to Detroit hospitals' ongoing racial inequity
in terms of patient admittance, staff appointments, and training opportunities for Black nurses and doctors. When the Detroit Medical Committee

submitted an updated project proposal to the City Plan Commission in May 1956, the Booker T. Washington Trade Association responded with a four-page letter outlining its objections.[27] One of the group's primary reservations was the fact that the city would be using public money to fund a project that discriminated against African Americans. The BTWTA acknowledged that developing a state-of-the-art medical, teaching, research, and service facility that was "beneficial to all the citizens of the Detroit community" was a desirable goal. However, the group concluded that these praiseworthy objectives were "inconsistent with their present hospital practice." The letter continued, "Therefore, we believe there is sufficient justification for being apprehensive of promised equal benefits until there has been immediate modification of present hospital policy in the areas of training, service and employment." The BTWTA further asserted, "We are of the opinion that a governmental expenditure for the establishment or expansion of a privately owned hospital facility which racially discriminates in its service to the community is an improper object to which to devote money belonging to all people. Therefore, we submit that there should be assuring proof in advance that the policy and practice of the hospitals which are represented by the Detroit Medical Center Committee will be such that the improved facilities and services will be available to all of the people equally."[28]

In addition to concerns about equitable access to the medical center, the BTWTA emphasized the implications for Black businesses in the area. The group stated, "It is estimated that approximately ten thousand people, 80% of whom are Negroes, will be displaced and an undetermined number of business, and organizations, many of whom are members of our Association, face possible relocation or disestablishment in the development of the proposed medical center."[29] Here too they protested the city's biased practices, explaining that racial discrimination prevented free mobility and would certainly "restrict the occupancy of commercial properties" for entrepreneurs dislocated by the medical center. The association concluded that the project represented "a misuse of the slum clearance program," maintaining, "We withhold endorsement of this plan and any other urban renewal-public improvement proposal where public funds are involved, until we are assured that the potentiality for human accomplishment inherent in the Urban Renewal Program in the areas of housing, medical services, training and employment, and business opportunity is given parallel consideration with that of physical change and engineering accomplishment."[30] By calling out the misapplication of eminent domain, the BTWTA argued that redevelopment projects that flouted the true meaning of public use violated African Americans' property rights.

Other Black Detroiters, including individual business leaders, also challenged the use of public funds to expand private enterprises that discriminated against Blacks. They cried foul at their property rights being trampled in the name of public use when really their homes and businesses were taken to make way for white-owned ventures. Wallace Tyler of the *Detroit Courier* called out the "one-sidedness" of the city's redevelopment program, declaring that those who stood to "benefit most by urban renewal, or more accurately, 'Negro Relocation,' are the individuals in the upper-middle class bracket."[31] Likewise, Ernest Shell, vice president and agency director of Great Lakes Mutual Insurance Company, wrote a piece about the expansion of several Detroit hospitals, asserting, "When the above hospitals gave as one of their main reasons why the expansion was needed—to increase their facilities and services to the public—they were on 'high ground' with a noble purpose. We seriously question their motivation as well as the city's."[32] Referencing a report compiled by the Detroit Urban League documenting the discrimination African Americans faced in these facilities, Shell questioned how the hospitals could ask "for the city to use its power of 'eminent domain' to condemn land (chiefly occupied by Negroes) for their expansion." He maintained that neither the city nor the federal government should subsidize a project that had been publicly condemned for practicing discrimination.[33]

In addition, Shell directly criticized the city's urban renewal program for targeting Black neighborhoods. Employing the same statistics as the BTWTA, he wrote, "There are areas where hospitals could be built without displacing approximately 10,000 people, 80% or more being Negroes. I seriously doubt if this area had 20% Negroes instead of 80% whether this expansion program would be considered, and if considered, approved by government agencies."[34] Shell demanded that the city make an effort to redress the problems created by urban renewal, such as giving dislocated business owners precedence to repurchase cleared land if they desired. He also called for hospitals to correct all discriminatory practices prior to receiving state approval for expansion. If the facilities and governmental agencies did not take steps to remedy the injustices of urban redevelopment, Shell warned, "They will create serious doubt in the minds of the people presently living in that area . . . whether they are getting (1) equal protection of the laws. (2) That the use of public funds, to which they contribute as tax payers, are not being used against their best interests; or 'taxation without

Figure 21. Members of the Detroit Urban League meet with the Detroit City Plan Commission, Mayor Edward Jeffries, and the city's Common Council to discuss the issue of urban renewal, ca. 1950s. Bentley Historical Library, University of Michigan.

representation.'" He continued, "These are things in which America believes. It must believe them strong enough to apply to all Americans regardless of race, creed, religion or national origin."[35]

By the early 1960s, about 15 percent of the city—approximately ten thousand acres—had been razed due to urban renewal. The majority of those displaced by the clearance were African American. Unwilling to accept Black Detroiters being disproportionately forced to forfeit their homes and businesses, community leaders continued to condemn the negative effects of urban renewal and fight for fairer treatment. The Reverend Albert B. Cleage Jr., leader of the Shrine of the Black Madonna church, adamantly called out these injustices in the *Detroit Illustrated News*, consistently characterizing urban renewal as "Negro Removal" and denouncing the city for using Blacks' tax dollars to finance the destruction of their own communities. In 1962, Cleage, together with brothers Milton and Richard Henry, established the Group on Advanced Leadership (GOAL), an all-Black organization to challenge racial bias in Detroit. Alongside other groups, GOAL took the fight to federal court. Filing a suit that claimed the Urban Renewal Redevelopment Program was unconstitutional, they argued that the government did not have the right to demolish private properties to benefit private enterprise that practiced racial discrimination.[36]

However, the prospect of a successful lawsuit was not good. The Michigan Supreme Court had already issued a decision on the legality of condemning "slum" property for private resale in December 1951 (331 Mich. 714, 50 N.W. 2d 340). Addressing the site between Hastings, Gratiot, Dequindre, and Mullet Streets, the plaintiff argued that condemning the area for slum clearance was unconstitutional because the property, while taken for a public purpose, was to be used for private redevelopment. The court ruled against this argument and upheld the city's actions. The decision made it clear that defining a project as "slum removal" was enough to justify condemnation and clearance at taxpayers' expense.[37] Additionally, in 1954 the U.S. Supreme Court found in *Berman v. Parker* that it was constitutional for the government to seize property through eminent domain and then transfer the cleared land to privately owned companies.[38] Still, filing the lawsuit was one way Black activists tried to bring attention to the injustices of urban renewal.

GOAL also filed a lawsuit regarding the 8 Mile Road conservation site—a plan that included razing an entire strip of Black businesses and replacing it with a new shopping center. The suit argued that by destroying Black institutions and businesses and threatening Black political and economic power, the project was in violation of African Americans' rights. Knowing that the displaced businesses were unlikely to gain access to the new commercial space, the lawsuit demanded the city grant them the right to return to the area once it was redeveloped and provide financial assistance to aid in their relocation process. Further, GOAL insisted, "The government must guarantee through operable law and administrative measures, that no business, institution, apartment, person or persons in [an urban renewal] area may practice racial discrimination in any form, including its economic guise."[39]

Individual entrepreneurs also sought legislative justice for the damages inflicted by urban renewal. However, taking the city to court was an arduous process, and one in which they were unlikely to emerge victorious. Several dislocated business owners from the Elmwood Park 1 redevelopment site took this route, to no avail. One entrepreneur reported that he "disagreed with the authorities and refused to go back [to court]," while seven others either attempted to file a claim and were unsuccessful or gave up after investigating the procedures involved. A typical comment was, "I felt there was no use; I was pushed from one fellow to another."[40] Moreover, many felt that suing the city was simply not worth the trouble and expense; as one business owner explained, "We took their offered payment in disgust after having talked to others who went to court." And in fact, the experiences of those who managed to win their cases revealed that lawyers' fees ate up a significant portion of any additional compensation.[41]

Still, Blacks with financial interests in urban renewal sites wanted to make their voices heard and protest the injustices they experienced. To that end, appearing at public hearings and meetings to deliver testimony was a common alternative to filing an expensive, laborious lawsuit. According to C. L. Farris of the federal Division of Slum Clearance and Urban Redevelopment, this was the case in many cities. In a 1952 letter to Harry Durbin, director-secretary of the Detroit Housing Commission, Farris reported that people who were about to be displaced from renewal areas "frequently make appearances at public hearings to object to programs formulated by Local Public Agencies for their relocation."[42] In Detroit, a group of forty Hastings Street business owners appeared before the City Council in 1961 to protest what they deemed "unnecessary delays in building a service drive on the [Chrysler] expressway." The merchants, whose businesses were on the west side of a fifteen-block stretch of Hastings from Brewster to Alexandrine, informed the city council of the problems caused by these recurring delays in construction. In order to make deliveries, vendors had to back up their trucks a block or more, and the number of holdups and robberies in the area had increased since the police were unable to quickly reach the scene of a crime. In response to this public protest, city officials offered promises of a work speed-up in the construction of the Chrysler Freeway as well as "adequate police protection."[43] It is unclear whether the city upheld these promises.

Some business owners protested particular redevelopment projects altogether. A group of citizens opposed to the 8 Mile renewal plan jammed a Detroit Common Council hearing in 1960. The council heard two hours of testimony from area residents and merchants. Dr. Richard McGhee, who had lived in the neighborhood for fourteen years, voiced his disapproval of the entire plan. He was especially critical of the city's intention to eliminate Black-owned businesses on the south side of 8 Mile Road and replace them with "outside"—that is, white-owned—businesses. The council also heard from entrepreneurs such as James H. Smith, who claimed, "Their plans don't make sense." Telling the council, "There is a plot of 26 acres, without anything on it in the area," Smith suggested, "Why not locate the park there[?]" Ernest Cockfield, a seventy-nine-year-old funeral director in danger of being displaced, simply asked, "What else can I do, if I have to relocate at my age?"[44]

Many Black Detroiters hoped that publicly voicing their painful experiences with urban redevelopment would help convince the city to change course. Mildred Smith, the Research Park Relocation Council delegate to the West Central Organization (WCO), conveyed the significance of such testimonies in a 1966 letter to the Detroit Housing Commission. From approximately 1965 to 1967, the WCO contested the injustices of urban renewal through picketing, meeting with state officials, distributing newsletters, and showering the city council and media with protest statements.[45] Smith's letter condemned the Housing Commission's "inhuman relocation practices," asserting that they had resulted in "too many broken promises and too many broken people." She urged the members of the Housing Commission to visit the Research Park area and hear from residents themselves about the true experience of urban renewal. Smith wrote, "We would like the Commissioners to talk with homeowners about their difficulty getting enough for their homes to buy a new house." The letter did not overlook affected entrepreneurs, also imploring the commission, "Listen to the voices of owners of neighborhood businesses that are losing everything they have worked for. Nobody pays them for the years it has taken them to build up a trade."[46] Harriet Saperstein's 1964 study of the Elmwood Park 1 redevelopment zone also revealed an underlying need among dislocated business owners to express their suffering under urban renewal. Saperstein noted that most of her subjects seemed to react "positively" to the interview, even thanking the interviewer for the chance to "get things off my chest" and "let the people upstairs know."[47]

However, articulating their grievances was simply not enough, especially when at times it seemed that the only people concerned about the devastation of urban renewal were those being displaced. As a pool hall owner who refused to participate in Saperstein's study put it: "If you had been interested to listen the many times we had meetings on the lower east side the 10 years or more before, maybe it would have had some meaning: I was not paid enough to start over into anything. If you wish to pass any information on you may say I feel very bitter over the way people in general were treated. It will not help to say any more. I tried for many years and many meetings with people that lived in the area to get a better consideration. We did not get it. So there is nothing more to say."[48] Similarly, the Booker T. Washington Trade Association never received an adequate response to the detailed letter they submitted to the City Plan Commission outlining their objections to the medical center project site. Yet the letter was preserved in the city's archive (it did not get lost or thrown away). Thus, state agents were aware of Black business owners' opinions but remained unconcerned with addressing them.[49] Car dealer Ed Davis, who was deeply involved with organizing for better treatment for Detroit's Black business owners, also concluded that no one in power listened or cared about the hardships urban planning inflicted upon African Americans. He reported, "I went to the state capitol in Lansing several times to talk to legislators. I even made a couple of trips to Washington, DC, trying to get some laws passed which would alleviate some of the problems of people caught in the web of urban renewal."[50] Davis continued, "Those of us who knew what urban renewal was doing, because we were also caught in its trap, were virtually the only ones trying to solve some of these problems. Sometimes it seemed like an impossible struggle. Sometimes it seemed as though no one else in the whole country knew, or cared, what was happening."[51]

As regional vice president of the National Business League (formerly National Negro Business League) and a BTWTA member, and having served on the Detroit Housing Commission's Relocation Advisory Committee as well as the mayor's Community Relations Commission, Ed Davis had intimate knowledge of the urban renewal program, its impact on the Black business community, and the challenges of attempting to resolve its injustices. His experiences illustrate the difficulties of working with leadership that often remained indifferent to Black struggles. In early 1963, for example, a federal bill passed that authorized the federal government to remunerate the moving expenses of an individual or business owner forced to relocate due to the federal highway program. However, in order for Detroit residents to benefit from this act the Michigan State Legislature needed to pass a law approving the reimbursement of moving expenses. According to Davis, the Relocation Committee worked endlessly to get the law through but had to fight "against the lack of interest of the state highway department and the lethargy of many of our elected representatives in Lansing" all the while. Gradually and in a "piecemeal fashion," the state enacted some of the measures Black entrepreneurs called for, providing some payments for moving expenses and financial assistance to relocating businesses. But as Davis concluded, "It still took a lot of effort from the affected citizens."[52] Black business owners were simply not a priority in the city's vision of a modern Detroit. Treated as second-class economic citizens, Black entrepreneurs learned once again that America's system of racial capitalism was not designed or intended for their preservation—and certainly not for their success.

A Different Vision: Black Detroiters' Fight for Equitable and Inclusive Urban Planning

In addition to speaking out against the detrimental aspects of urban planning, Black Detroiters offered comprehensive strategies to rectify existing damages and prevent further harm. Central to these efforts was fighting for their own inclusion in the process—an objective to which white urban officials remained unwilling to acquiesce. Even so, Black entrepreneurs and residents persevered in this struggle throughout the postwar period, providing their own vision for Detroit that included both their participation and sustained economic autonomy for the Black community.

As a prominent Black business organization in Detroit, the Booker T. Washington Trade Association's response to the proposed medical center site articulated an image of urban change that aligned issues of housing and entrepreneurship under the larger matter of economic self-determination. The letter they sent to the City Plan Commission suggested strategies to make the project less damaging to the Black community, requesting that the City of Detroit withhold official approval until taking the following steps:

1. All of the families which are scheduled for immediate or subsequent relocation have the unencumbered and racially unrestricted opportunity to be rehoused in private or public dwellings better than those from which they were displaced consistent with their economic status.
2. Negro owned business concerns which face possible relocation from urban renewal sites have opportunity equal to that of other business establishments to relocate themselves in areas zoned for commercial uses instead of having to relocate in other residential areas of the community.
3. Proof be established that the four hospitals involved have corrected their present racially discriminatory practice in training, service, and employment.

4. All of the affected interests primarily involved in the proposed
   Urban Redevelopment sites be included at the planning level
   in order that the fullest cooperation and participation may be
   realized. Certainly, with 80% of the people being affected being
   Negroes, there should be competent representation from this
   group at the planning level.[53]

Again calling attention to the structural racism shaping Black Detroiters'
lives, these terms prioritized unbiased access to commercial and residential
properties for those displaced by the medical center as well as to the facility's
professional opportunities and clinical care. If opponents could not prevent
the project from proceeding in the proposed location, the BTWTA hoped
to at least alleviate the hardships of forced removal. Moreover, their call for
inclusion in the planning stages of redevelopment reveals a vision for the city
that would allow Blacks to contribute to and benefit from urban renewal in
ways that would safeguard their economic well-being.

Black entrepreneurs also urged elected officials to pass measures to
assuage the impact of dislocation, such as allowing business owners to secure
relocation funds and fairer compensation for their properties. Ed Davis presented suggestions developed by the National Business League to the Detroit
Common Council. Addressing the frequent drop in property values due to
"blight by announcement," the league asked that the city appraise real estate
soon after areas were marked for redevelopment; this would allow property
owners to be paid more equitably. They also insisted that business owners
receive either full or partial payments promptly, to allow them to plan their
relocations as soon as possible. As for entrepreneurs who did not own property, the league wanted the government to assume responsibility for reimburs-
ing long-term leaseholders who had invested money in rented commercial
properties in areas designated for redevelopment. Finally, they requested that
all dislocated businesses be given relocation assistance and financial compensation for income lost during the moving process.[54]

Davis and other Black entrepreneurs also pursued measures that would
involve Black Detroiters in urban planning. They urged the Common Council to recruit retired executives to serve on committees with current Black
business owners to evaluate their needs and determine both federal and local
governments' financial responsibilities to business owners displaced by urban
renewal. They further requested that once these responsibilities were designated, payments be issued within six months. Significantly, entrepreneurs

specified that all of these steps be taken fairly, without bias, charging the state with the "moral and legal responsibility" to ensure that all banks, savings associations, the Small Business Administration, and other organizations that dealt with government funding cease discrimination on the basis of race, creed, color, or social position. According to Davis, the council responded to these demands with promises for improvements but as he well knew, "Promises were not enough in Detroit or in the other cities around the nation with areas marked for urban renewal."[55] Still, Black business owners and residents appealed to their elected officials to address their grievances and create a more equitable Detroit.

Their cries did not fall on completely deaf ears. By 1960, African Americans were approximately 29 percent of Detroit's population; this increase gave Blacks almost double the voting power than they had a decade before.[56] In 1957, attorney William T. Patrick Jr. was the first African American elected to the Detroit Common Council, and he was joined by Reverend Nicholas Hood in 1965.[57] They along with white council member Mel Ravitz worked tirelessly to change the discrimination within postwar urban planning initiatives.[58] In council meetings, Patrick asserted that the purpose of urban renewal was to upgrade the city for existing residents—not to attract the white middle class back from the suburbs at Blacks' expense.[59] To address specific issues, Reverend Hood called a special Common Council meeting to discuss the problems faced by small business owners in the medical center redevelopment area. The meeting revealed that Black entrepreneurs' main concern was finding out exactly when the city would take possession of their properties because their property values were dropping and they were losing money.[60] Regarding that problem, Ravitz demanded legislative changes that would permit the city to acquire property in renewal zones soon after announcing a project, arguing that it would help reduce neighborhood deterioration.[61]

The efforts of Black entrepreneurs, community leaders, and residents to challenge the injustices of urban renewal did lead to some victories. Pressure from the Black community and the Detroit Medical Society led hospitals in the proposed midtown medical center to sign nondiscrimination pledges in 1960, and in October 1963 the Detroit Common Council passed a widespread hospital antidiscrimination ordinance. In addition, access to training opportunities and staff appointments for Blacks increased in most major Detroit hospitals; between June 1960 and September 1963, the number of Black physicians at Harper Hospital rose from zero to eleven.[62] At the

federal level, the 1964 Housing Act included a new stipulation that no demolition project begin "until the Housing and Home Finance Agency determined that the same goals could not be realized through rehabilitation." A
year later, the Housing Act of 1965 established a "uniform land-acquisition
procedure for property seized through eminent domain under the renewal
program."[63]

Another legal breakthrough came soon after. In 1966, U.S. District Judge
Fred W. Kaess ruled that a property owner should be paid the "fair market
value immediately before the city took active steps to carry out the work on
the [urban renewal] project," not the depreciated value after years of delay
had blighted the neighborhood.[64] Judge Kaess's ruling pertained to the case
of Thomas E. Foster and Georgia Lee Foster. The couple's east-side property,
which was worth $12,500 in 1954, had by 1963 slipped to a condemnation
value of just $5,200. After earmarking the neighborhood for urban redevel-
opment in 1950, the city delayed property acquisition for more than a decade,
during which time the area rapidly deteriorated. There were a few reasons
for this. First, the city had warned owners to avoid making any improvements to their properties, as those costs would not be factored into eventual
condemnation awards. Second, the neighborhood suffered from blight by
announcement—when the mere news of a renewal project generated property depreciation. Finally, the city's decision to demolish additional houses
and remove welfare tenants from the area only exacerbated the neighborhood's decline by increasing vacancies and causing prices to drop further.
Whether or not the city deliberately intended to depress property values, that
was certainly the result of its actions.[65]

The city appealed Judge Kaess's ruling but the Sixth Circuit Federal
Court of Appeals upheld the decision, concluding that the city's drawn-out
condemnation process had lowered the Fosters' property value. Like Judge
Kaess, the court of appeals also ruled that all property owners in the designated renewal zone were entitled to have their land reappraised and be paid
according to its value in 1950, when the project was first announced.[66] This
was a substantial victory. Yet it came eighteen years after Detroit's urban
renewal program had begun dislocating Black communities. By then, countless Black entrepreneurs had already shuttered their businesses. Considering
Black entrepreneurs' past experience with the courts, it is unlikely that many
benefited from this ruling.

Alongside efforts to right the wrongs of urban redevelopment, Black
Detroiters sought access to its economic benefits. Urban planning projects

offered abundant opportunities for contractors and others in the building trades. However, Detroit's building and construction industries had a
long history of racial discrimination; in the early 1960s African Americans
"remained locked out of nearly every building trade union." Blacks had
formed "parallel craft associations," but these associations did not provide
union affiliation for Black workers; therefore, they still could not access the
city's most well-paid jobs.[67] After decades of being excluded from the financial
rewards of city contracts, they decided to organize. In 1969, fifty of Detroit's
Black contracting businesses founded the Metropolitan Builders and Home
Improvement Association to ensure that "Black contractors have equal access
in rebuilding the inner city."[68]

George Walker of Walker Brothers Building Contractors became president of the Metropolitan Builders and Home Improvement Association.
According to Walker, Black contracting businesses had difficulty obtaining
large city contracts in part because "banks and other financial institutions
have systematically discriminated against us." He noted, "Many bankers still
automatically consider a Black contractor a bad risk." In addition, as Henry
McClendon, associate vice president and owner of the McClendon Home
Improvement Association, explained, "Trade unions, by their attempts to
limit their number, have created a severe labor shortage in the building trades."
While this shortage would seem to illustrate the inefficiency of discrimination, McClendon made it clear that racism informed unions' decisions: "This
shortage is especially in the inner city where Blacks are becoming more insis-
tent in demands that they contribute a major share to its rebuilding." As John
Bingham, president of Hi-Fashion Homes, concluded, "Up to now, the Black
contractor has been largely ignored. However, I want to emphasize our eager-
ness and our ability to get the job done."[69]

Finally, in rare cases, prosperous Black entrepreneurs tackled their vision
for Detroit head-on, offering their own redevelopment plans that would
enable their communities to profit rather than perish. In 1959, businessman
and civic leader Charles C. Diggs Sr. sought to purchase a 410-by-650-foot
tract of land in the Woodward-Mack area and build a $2 million business
complex for the city's medical center. Diggs and his family owned several
businesses, including the Detroit Metropolitan Mutual Assurance Company and Diggs Enterprises, an undertaking and funeral home, and he was
renowned as one of the most successful Black entrepreneurs in Michigan.[70] In
fact, just a year before Diggs submitted his proposal to the city, Martin Luther
King Jr. sent a letter to Diggs's son, Congressman Charles C. Diggs Jr., after

a recent visit to Detroit. Expressing how impressed he was with the family's business empire, King wrote, "It was a great privilege to have you escort me through the Diggs Enterprises. Although I knew the Diggs Enterprises represented an important business set-up, I had no idea it was so extensive until the other day. You and your father are doing a marvelous job in the world of business."[71]

Understandably, the Diggs family wanted to maintain their economic success. Thus, when they learned that the city's medical center project would force their businesses out of their existing locations, Diggs set to work on a plan that would allow Black businesses to return to the redeveloped area. Diggs proposed taking over a portion of the city's project to build a business complex called the Diggs Center. He requested that once the land designated for the medical center was condemned, the city permit him to purchase the southwest tract for construction. Located only five blocks from the family's existing commercial locations, their enterprises would be the complex's primary tenants, while they would lease the remaining space to medical professionals. For the family's insurance company, Detroit Metropolitan Mutual, architectural plans submitted with the proposal depicted a five-story, textured concrete panel structure completely surrounded by reflective pools. The facility would include retail and office space for physicians, medical suppliers, and other health-related services. A landscaped shopping mall would connect the insurance building to the complex's other structures, including a two-story building housing Diggs Enterprises, several community meeting rooms, and a concealed off-street parking lot for more than two hundred cars. As a particularly striking design element, the plan boasted two circular chapels adorning the House of Diggs funeral home.[72]

In putting forth his plan for the Diggs Center, Charles C. Diggs Sr. expressed his desire for Blacks to be included in the urban renewal process, declaring, "We believe very deeply that that program we hope to achieve will inspire more Negroes to make major contributions to Detroit's commercial betterment."[73] Diggs's proposal for redeveloping the tract was no doubt thorough and viable, as he was an astute entrepreneur and successful politician. Yet the City of Detroit rejected Diggs, sold the land to white-owned companies, and continued to shut African Americans out of the processes and rewards of urban redevelopment. Hinting at the limitations of Black business success under a racial capitalist system, Elijah Muhammad described Diggs Sr. this way: "Old man Diggs had the mind, the drive and the ambition.

He cut over everything and went right to his goal. At one time, he was a millionaire. If he had been white, he would have been a multimillionaire."[74] Diggs's experience with urban renewal demonstrates that even the most successful Black business owners were still vulnerable to capriciousness of U.S. racial capitalism.

*   *   *

From 1943 to 1962, Detroit's Gotham Hotel was considered one of the finest Black-owned hotels in the country.[75] The hotel was advertised as "A Monument to Our Race," offering "every convenience" as well as proximity to the city's shopping centers, theaters, movie houses, and night clubs.[76] Notable hotel guests included Langston Hughes, U.S. congressman Adam Clayton Powell, Billie Holiday, Sammy Davis Jr., and others. The Gotham's primary owner, John White, was at one time the city's leading numbers banker. According to Detroit businessman Sunnie Wilson, "For years the Gotham stood as a proud example of Black entrepreneurship. . . . [It was] known from coast to coast."[77]

In July 1963 the hotel was torn down to make way for the Wayne State University Medical Science Center. Like other businesses, the Gotham suffered from the sluggish acquisition process, seemingly complicated by the FBI's raid of the hotel related to numbers gambling.[78] In 1947, the Gotham's owners had refused offers of $400,000 for the hotel.[79] Yet, in the early 1960s, the city valued the property at much less. According to Sunnie Wilson, "In 1962 the neighboring medical center offered to buy the Gotham. The hospital offered $350,000, but its owner John White wanted $450,000 and a fierce disagreement ensued. With the eventual consummation of the deal, the hotel was slated for demolition."[80] Clearly the announcement of urban renewal for the area had negatively affected the market value of the property. A worker involved in the hotel's demolition attested to the quality of the building. One foreman for Arrow Wrecking, which was clearing the site, observed: "All that's left is 500 loads of rubble. It must have been real nice one time. Up on the roof, even the walls were padded. This building was solid, I'll tell you that." He concluded, "It's coming down hard."[81]

In the year leading up to its demolition, the community mourned the loss of a great African American institution. In August 1962, Joe Ziggy, one of the hotel's longtime tenants, wrote, "Closing of the Gotham won't be a

Figure 22. The
Gotham Hotel during
demolition in July
1963. Courtesy of
Detroit Free Press,
USA Today Network.

picnic. . . . For what had been considered the best Negro owned hotel in the country, will be no more. Some of the greatest and finest people in the world have been guests in the Gotham, and I don't think there will ever be another hotel, Negro-owned, and personally managed that will come close to what John J. White established for Detroit and world visitors."[82] In early September 1962, several hundred people attended a farewell party held at the Gotham. And the day it was torn down, hundreds turned out to pay their last respects to the hotel. Sunnie Wilson remembered, "That day John [White] asked me to drive him by the Gotham. When I looked over at his face, John had tears running down his cheeks."[83] The destruction of the Gotham Hotel marked the end of an era.

The obliteration of the Gotham Hotel, and the Black business community more broadly, was traumatic for Detroit's Black community. The dynamiting of African Americans' businesses no doubt brought to mind the racial and economic violence migrant entrepreneurs had been subjected to in the Jim Crow South. As discussed in Chapter 1, Black communities like that in Blue-field, West Virginia, experienced terrorism at the hands of local whites. Here, every Black business owner had received letters from the "Lynching Commit-tee," on September 10, 1912, "ordering them to move from Raleigh street by

Saturday, or their places would be dynamited."[84] Black migrant entrepreneurs had left their southern homes where they worried about white mobs taking away their lives, property, and wealth through violence. However, forty and fifty years later, Detroit's business owners in the city had to worry about the state condemning their property, bulldozing it, and clearing away the businesses they spent decades building.

Ed Davis lamented the damage caused by Detroit's postwar redevelopment efforts in his 1979 memoir, *One Man's Way*. As a southern migrant, a prominent Detroit entrepreneur for over thirty years, and an activist in the local fight against urban renewal, Davis witnessed the destruction of countless Black businesses and communities. Davis opined, "I think that the people . . . who were caught in urban renewal areas in the early years are entitled to some kind of consideration even now for what they suffered. They were mistreated by their own government. Their own tax money was being used to harm them, if not destroy them." He asserted, "Urban renewal—often rightly called 'Negro removal'—was discrimination at its worst. People who had spent their lifetimes in buying a home or building a business lost everything they had." Many property owners in renewal zones had never heard of eminent domain, he explained: "They were not aware that some unknown bureaucrats could decide that the public needed their land more than they did, and they didn't know that, if these men made the decision, then the government could legally condemn their land, paying what these faceless men said was a fair price, and force them to give it up."[85] This left Black entrepreneurs with "no control over their own destinies"—the very reason many of them had left the Jim Crow South for Detroit in the first place, for economic self-determination. Years later, urban renewal "destroyed their sense of security. . . . They knew that a lifetime of hard work and saving could be swept away by government edict." Davis concluded, "Urban renewal showed them that they did not even have power over their own property and funds."[86]

Detroit's officials may have had a bright vision for the postwar city but for African Americans, urban planning's critical outcome was the loss of Black wealth, economic stability, and self-determination. However, Black Detroiters did not surrender to whites' vision for their city. On the contrary, they offered their own vision for the future of Detroit—one that included their input and safeguarded their people. Against the odds of white supremacy and racial capitalism, migrant entrepreneurs had taken their economic destinies into their own hands and built a thriving business community in their new home. When faced with postwar urban planning, they proposed alternate strategies that would redress existing injustices, help rather than harm African Americans, and enable their own economic participation. Their efforts exhibit Black Detroiters' vision for a more equitable modern city, revealing an underlying hope that redevelopment held the potential for evolution rather than destruction.

Epilogue

Although post–World War II urban planning initiatives had devastating consequences for Black business in Detroit, not all was destroyed. Detroit's most famous Black-owned business—Motown Records—was founded in 1959, when freeway construction and urban renewal projects were well underway. Motown's iconic record label featured a map with a red star bringing attention to the city of Detroit.[1] Numerous expressways going through and around the city were also depicted. The establishment of "Hitsville, U.S.A." on West Grand Boulevard on the city's west side, not on Hastings Street, was significant. Perhaps Berry Gordy Jr. watched the changing landscape on the east side and decided to locate his business elsewhere. What is clear is that Motown represented a new era for Black business, breaking from the tradition of Black business life in Black Bottom and Paradise Valley.[2]

According to Juliet E. K. Walker, Motown Records "symbolized a distinct era in twentieth-century American business history." Between 1973 and 1983, Motown was the most successful Black-owned business in the United States; the company had annual sales of over $50 million in the 1970s and $100 million by the early 1980s.[3] Yet, Berry Gordy Jr. left Detroit for Los Angeles during the height of Motown's success (and portions of Gordy's empire also became increasingly managed and/or owned by whites in the 1970s and 1980s).[4] Motown's decision to leave Detroit was "simply a matter of sound business judgment, economics, and logistics," according to the company's general manager, Amos Wilder.[5] Changes to the city after the racial unrest in 1967 and following Martin Luther King's assassination in 1968 would also influence the decision to leave Detroit.[6]

Meanwhile, in Paradise Valley and Black Bottom, numerous Black businesses had been lost by the late 1960s, either from declining sales as business owners' neighborhood customers moved to other sections of the city or because the payments they received from the city for their property were inadequate to reestablish their enterprise. East-side entrepreneurs who were not stuck with long-term leases or mortgages in areas slated for redevelopment or in the path of a proposed highway dispersed to other sections of the city. Most businesses ended up on the west side of Detroit along Twelfth Street, which was already a major commercial street when Blacks moved in, though Jewish merchants owned most of the businesses. As the area was rapidly becoming Black, many white business owners sold their homes and moved their families out of the area while continuing to operate their businesses along Twelfth Street.[7]

For Black entrepreneurs who survived displacement and moved over to the west side, the consequences of highway construction and urban renewal projects continued to haunt them in 1967. The overcrowding of the west side caused by displaced eastsiders contributed to the explosive urban rebellion that further destroyed Black (and white) businesses.[8] On July 23, 1967, the Detroit police raided a blind pig after-hours drinking establishment, sparking the most destructive urban rebellion of the 1960s. It lasted for five days and 17,000 men from the U.S. Army, Michigan National Guard, Michigan State Police, and Detroit Police Department were called in to restore order. Overall, the disturbance claimed 43 (mostly Black) lives and resulted in nearly 700 injuries. Over 7,000 individuals were arrested, and property damage was estimated at over $75 million (almost $690 million in 2023 dollars).[9] More than 400 buildings were destroyed, including 20 percent of the ones on Twelfth Street near the Virginia Park area.[10]

Overcrowding created by urban renewal and the continued southern migration to the city was a major factor that contributed to the rebellion. Postwar urban redevelopment had displaced thousands of Blacks from the east side and exacerbated the housing shortage. George Romney, who was governor of Michigan from 1963 to 1969 and deeply involved with the state's reaction to the disturbance, had sought federal assistance to squash the 1967 rebellion. According to Romney: "What triggered the riot in my opinion, to a considerable extent, was that between urban renewal and expressways, poor Black people were bulldozed out of their homes. They had no place to go in the suburbs because of suburban restrictions. They settled along 12th Street. The concentration of people on 12th Street was too great. So when that incident occurred, it was a spark that ignited the whole area."[11]

Businessman Ed Davis also reflected on the conditions of the west side in the late 1960s: "As the bulldozers moved in the people were pushed out, with no consideration given to where they were going." Davis recalled,

No provision was made for them at all. Consequently many moved
into areas that were already heavily populated. . . . Older areas
around the city were therefore jammed with newcomers until there
was nearly four times the population that was planned for when the
areas were built. Single-family homes were sheltering three or four
families. Duplexes, flats, and apartments had families in each room.
The streets became crowded with cars parked bumper to bumper
along each curb; others lined up in front of driveways or in alleys;
some were even parked in front yards to get them out of the way.[12]

Davis concluded, "As much as anything else, urban renewal created the urban
ghetto."[13]

When the disturbance began, the main concerns of business owners
located in the Twelfth Street area were looting and arson. During the uprising,
Black entrepreneurs placed signs in their windows in an attempt to save their
businesses from looting. William Lowell Hurt recalled, "We started writing
a phrase on the side of the house, on the windows; and all the store owners
who wised up to what was happening would put the signs in their windows
that said, 'Soul Brother,' or 'I'm a Soul Brother,' or something like that."[14] Ollie
Foster recounted, "I guess the word got out that they weren't going to burn
any Black guy's establishment because they said you were supposed to write
on there 'soul brother.' I remember a Chinese had on his window, 'Me soul
brother too.'" Similarly, William Hines remembered, "a Chinese laundry
put on his door, 'Me colored too.'"[15] In some cases this seemed to work and
those who looted targeted white-owned stores. According to Hurt, "That was
almost like painting the blood over the top of the house to let death pass over,
because they didn't mess with the houses that had those signs or the stores
that had the signs."[16] But these signs could not guarantee that entrepreneurs
would not lose all that they had worked for. As Ed Davis put it, "Store fronts
around the city bore hastily lettered signs: *Soul Brother*, or just *Soul*. They
were fire insurance for some, but not for others. Blacks and whites alike were
burned out. The rioters did not discriminate."[17]

Not all damage to Black-owned businesses came from civilians. Police
destroyed Vaughn's Book Store, the only Black bookstore in Detroit. Vaughn's
was most likely targeted because it was a meeting place for Black radical
activists. When the uprising started, Edward Vaughn felt sure that "nothing would be wrong with my store, at least from the people, and of course I
was correct."[18] However, after two days police wrecked the bookstore. They

firebombed the shop, damaged artwork and books, and left water running, which destroyed the remaining books. African Americans viewed the attack on Vaughn's as a hate crime (the police claimed that they needed to raid the bookstore because allegedly there were guns in the building).[19] Either way, the loss of inventory was detrimental for Ed Vaughn's business.

The loss of property through looting, arson, and police attacks was devastating for all businesses in the rebellion zone. It was especially so for entrepreneurs who had already been displaced by urban renewal and had started over again on the west side. The 1967 rebellion was the last blow for many. This was certainly true for Joe Von Battle, who had migrated from Georgia and opened a successful record store at 3530 Hastings Street in 1945.[20]

Like many other entrepreneurs displaced from the east side, Joe Von Battle relocated to Twelfth Street. While the process of reestablishing his business was difficult, Von Battle managed to build up the Twelfth Street record shop. The new store had pop, rhythm and blues, and gospel sections and was soon a key part of the area's nightlife.[21] Things went well for Von Battle until the summer of 1967. While at his home in Highland Park, just a few miles from his shop, Von Battle looked over the trees and saw smoke coming from Twelfth Street. From news reports Von Battle knew something was brimming, but during the first day of the disturbance it seemed like it might easily be contained.[22] Von Battle closed down the store thinking that the police would contain the unrest and everything would blow over. He tried to assure himself that looters were not going to bother the shop.[23]

When it became clear that the disturbance was going to be a multiday upheaval, Joe Von Battle thought about putting a "Soul Brother" sign in his shop window even though he was "an old school Black that didn't believe in this soul brother stuff." After the second day, Von Battle decided he would take a pistol and protect his record store from looters. He sat in the doorway and dared anybody to come in. However, as the days went on, it became obvious that his record shop was going to be caught up in the looting. According to his daughter Marsha, "He knew he could not save it."[24] At the end of the rebellion, Von Battle took his children to the record shop to assess the damage. It looked like a war zone with glass all over the street; the shop was torn apart. When he saw his business he just said, "Oh, Lord."[25]

Von Battle had feared arsonists had completely burned down the shop; thankfully they had not. Still, it was completely looted and his merchandise was strewn everywhere. Tape recordings that Von Battle had owned for a generation were destroyed. Marsha Mickens remembered the terrible feeling she had witnessing her father observe the damage at the store, "of seeing him powerless over the situation."[26] His whole life's work had been destroyed; he was "bereft and adrift after the loss of his shop."[27] After the rebellion, Von Battle managed to pull things together and briefly reopened his record store. However, it never flourished and he ended up losing it shortly afterward.[28]

Though the Black business community had experienced major setbacks due to mid-twentieth-century urban planning and the 1967 uprising, they continued to fight to attain greater economic and political power in the civil rights and Black Power eras. While African Americans in Detroit would gain more political power in the late 1960s and 1970s, at the same time the city's economic strength was also declining.

As a consequence, Black Detroiters' business activism in the 1960s saw a return to the Black self-help and uplift strategies emphasized in earlier periods. Consumer boycotts are traditionally associated with the southern civil rights movement, but this type of protest also took place in northern cities like Detroit. As African Americans were displaced from the east-side of Detroit and resettled in west-side neighborhoods where whites owned most of the businesses, they experienced increased hostility, humiliating treatment, and economic exploitation from white business owners. In the early 1960s, Black activists and political leaders organized selective-buying campaigns to protest discriminatory behavior from white business owners and to urge Black Detroiters to support and create more Black-owned businesses.[29]

For example, in the spring of 1962, the Robert Oakman Neighborhood Association joined with other block clubs to boycott the white-owned Cabot Grocery located at 3709 Pasadena Street near Dexter Avenue on Detroit's west side. The boycott was initiated as a result of the attitude and behavior of the owner toward his Black customers. In one instance, the storeowner drew a gun on a Black woman while small children, who were not involved in the dispute, were in the store. Customers' other complaints included short-changing children, refusing to exchange unsatisfactory merchandise, over-priced merchandise, discourteousness toward female customers, and having a "don't care attitude." The neighborhood association asked for the cooperation of everyone to make the boycott a success. They contended, "If the selective buying means walking or driving a few extra blocks, consider the extra blocks the price of self-respect and dignity."[30] Likewise, in 1962 the *Detroit Illustrated News* printed a piece titled "Selective Patronage" to promote the development of Black-owned business in the city. Speaking of rising unemployment caused by automation, the author, Reverend Albert B. Cleage Jr., wrote, "Neither Henry Ford nor unions can help [Black workers]. The time has come for the Negro to help himself, and to help himself in the City of Detroit the Negro must collectively utilize his consumer power through the intelligent use of 'Selective Patronage.'"[31]

The next year, African Americans boycotted and picketed a Kroger supermarket that discriminated against Blacks in hiring. There was a similar action against A & P grocery store that lasted for seven weeks. These actions led both Kroger and the A & P store to promise to cease discriminatory practices.[32] Also in 1963, Detroit-based congressman Charles C. Diggs Jr., the first African American U.S. representative from Michigan (1955–80), spearheaded a "buy-in" campaign at Detroit's Community Supermarket, which had been purchased by a group of African Americans. Diggs worked with groups including the Detroit Housewives League, the Booker T. Washington Trade Association, the NAACP, the Nation of Islam, and the Trade Union Leadership Council to organize support for the store. The buy-in campaign was a success, attracting unprecedented numbers of customers to the store.[33] Selective-buying campaigns were a product of the larger climate of civil rights activism taking place around the nation and in Detroit.[34] Additionally, 1960s consumer activism also reflected a long history and politics of Black economic self-help in Detroit.[35]

Perhaps after seeing how urban renewal was destroying the Black business community in Detroit Charles C. Diggs Jr. came to believe that renewing business-boosting strategies could be an effective strategy for generating Black economic development. Diggs was acutely aware of the negative effects urban planning initiatives in Detroit were having on Black entrepreneurs because his family business had been directly affected. Diggs's family operated one of the largest Black funeral homes in the country, and he had been taught the importance of racial unity throughout his life. Diggs's mother and father had been active leaders in the Black business community since the 1920s when they established Diggs Funeral Home, which expanded into the House of Diggs. In addition to the funeral home, the family operated a florist shop, an ambulance service, and a mutual insurance company. The Diggses' business was located at Mack Avenue and at its peak employed five hundred people. Though the Diggs family were some of the most successful Black business owners in Detroit, they, like so many others, were affected by postwar urban planning. When the Chrysler Freeway came along, it cut through the neighborhood where the House of Diggs was located. The junior Diggs recalled, "The city took that property, because of the extension of the freeway. We had to move out of there."[36] Without significant political power to protect their interests, Black entrepreneurs operating in Detroit's segregated market were vulnerable to the whims of white politicians and industry leaders.

Additionally, the encroachment of white-owned chains into Black residential areas also threatened Black entrepreneurs. The disappearance of independent small businesses was a wider trend during the 1960s, as chain stores expanded and put local, family-owned stores out of business.[37] But this trend also illuminates the possibilities and promises of Black capitalism. The fate of Black-owned chains such as Barthwell's Drug Stores is telling. Sidney Barthwell was born in Cordele, Georgia, in 1906 and came to Detroit in 1920 to join his father, who worked at Ford Motor Company. After graduating from Wayne State University with a degree in pharmacy and with $500, Barthwell opened his first drugstore at 8640 Russell Street in 1933. By 1945 he had six stores with over seventy employees. With his wife, Gladys, Sidney Barthwell expanded the chain to ten retail drugstores in the Detroit area. The stores also had soda fountains and sold ice cream, and Barthwell operated his own ice cream plant to supply the various locations. By 1957 Barthwell's Drugs employed more than one hundred men and women and was worth millions.[38] However, Barthwell was negatively impacted by urban renewal; for example, his 8640 Russell location was demolished for the Chrysler Freeway. Though his business took a hit, Barthwell held on, not closing his last store until 1987. Yet, for Barthwell and so many Black entrepreneurs, the development of their businesses was hindered by urban planning policies, and they never had the chance to pursue their potential uninhibited by structural racism. Without the effects of racial capitalism, perhaps Barthwell's Drugs could have grown to become a national pharmacy chain.

African American activism in the 1960s did lead to important political changes in Detroit. Black activists founded the Freedom Now Party in 1963, which was the first all-Black political party in the nation.[39] According to Reverend Albert B. Cleage Jr., one of the founders, "The Freedom Now Party advocates that you vote Black and buy Black. That's something you can do. It's no dream."[40] The push for Black economic and political power also saw African Americans' chances of being elected in Detroit improve in the late 1960s and early 1970s. In the 1969 mayoral election, Richard H. Austin, a Black accountant considered to be moderate in his political views, ran but lost to the white "law-and-order" candidate Roman S. Gribbs.[41] Four year later in 1973, left-leaning Colman Young won the election for Detroit mayor, becoming the city's first Black mayor in 1974. Young would serve as mayor of Detroit for twenty years.[42]

By the time Blacks were able to gain significant political power in the 1970s, Detroit's economic strength was declining. The city was experiencing an economic crisis shaped by deindustrialization, white flight to the suburbs (taking taxes and businesses with them), and larger economic downturns affecting the entire nation.[43] Shifts in the auto industry undermined the economic basis for Black entrepreneurship in the city, as Detroit's increasingly Black workforce faced high unemployment. In the 1970s, Detroit was experiencing an economic crisis, and by 1977 Black unemployment in the city reached 25 percent.[44] According to Thomas Sugrue, "Detroit's postwar urban crisis emerged as the consequence of two of the most important, interrelated, and unresolved problems in American history: that capitalism generates economic inequality and that African Americans have disproportionately borne the impact of that inequality."[45] With Black workers and the city as a whole severely economically disadvantaged, Black business suffered as well.

In response, Mayor Coleman Young turned to urban revitalization plans, most notably along the Detroit riverfront, with the hope of bringing about a renaissance of the city.[46] Young's administration supported Black enterprise, giving preference to Black-owned businesses for government contracts. However, this emphasis on Black capitalism failed to bring economic recovery for Detroit or equity for the Black business community.[47] In 2013, Detroit filed for chapter 9 bankruptcy, becoming the largest U.S. city to file for bankruptcy.[48] Efforts to redevelop and "revitalize" Detroit continued throughout the twentieth and into the twenty-first centuries (often in ways that continue to shortchange the city's Black residents).[49]

*   *   *

Following emancipation and Reconstruction, the southern system of Jim Crow was maintained through violence and the disenfranchisement of African Americans. When Black entrepreneurs left the South for Detroit during the Great Migration, they fled a long-standing norm of Black economic subjugation. Yet, American capitalism was racial capitalism. The mechanisms of economic white supremacy that upheld racial capitalism in the twentieth century were not the same in the North and South. Still, the end result for Black migrant entrepreneurs operating in the North was the same as it had been in the South: the suppression of Black economic advancement and the perpetuation of economic white supremacy.

The losses Black business owners experienced during the era of postwar freeway construction and urban renewal demonstrate the limitations of African Americans' efforts to attain self-determination through business. Black migrant entrepreneurs were not able to participate in a system of fair competition and an "invisible hand" of the market did not decide their fate. Rather, the decisions of city officials, urban planners, and white business owners regarding urban redevelopment led to the downfall of a thriving business community. Detroit's reputation as the epitome of the "urban crisis" and scholarship's focus on inner-city poverty obscure the Black wealth that existed prior to the urban renewal era. The derailment of migrant entrepreneurs' quest for economic empowerment and self-determination through business had long-term consequences for Black economic development in Detroit.

The destruction of the Black business community in Paradise Valley and Black Bottom would continue to reverberate for generations. When I first started researching the history of Black-owned business in Detroit while I was an undergraduate student at Wayne State University, almost everyone I talked to brought up the destruction of Black Bottom and Paradise Valley—this was fifty to sixty years after the fact. People would tell me anecdotes about the business their grandparents had owned or the stories they had heard about what Paradise Valley was like in its heyday. There was a sense of pride, but there was always a sense of sadness, and incredible loss. After all these decades, the effects of this community trauma—this economic trauma—were clearly still being felt. This is one reason I felt this story needed to be documented. I hope this history will be taken into consideration in the development of future urban policies.

NOTES

Archives and Libraries

AM   Archives of Michigan, Lansing
BHL   Bentley Historical Library, University of Michigan, Ann Arbor
CHWA   Charles H. Wright Archives & Research Library, Charles H. Wright
        Museum of African American History, Detroit
DPL   Burton Historical Collection, Detroit Public Library
WPRL   Walter P. Reuther Library, Archives of Labor and Urban Affairs,
        Wayne State University, Detroit

Manuscript Collections

AEC   Applicants for Embalmer's Certificates, 1901–1933, Board of Mor-
            tuary Science, Michigan Department of Licensing & Regulation, RG
            93-45, AM
AWCP   Austin W. Curtis Papers, BHL
DCCR   Detroit Commission on Community Relations/Human Rights Depart-
            ment Collection, WPRL
DUL   Detroit Urban League Papers, BHL
DUL-M   Detroit Urban League Papers Microfilm, DPL
EBWCP   Elliotorian Business Women's Club Papers, DPL
HLDP   Housewives' League of Detroit Papers, DPL
HLDAP   Housewives' League of Detroit, Additional Papers, DPL
HLDAP89   Housewives' League of Detroit, Additional Papers 1989, DPL
JCDP   John C. Dancy Papers, BHL
JPC   Jerome P. Cavanagh Papers, WPRL
LBC   Lewis Business College and Violet T. Lewis Collection, CHWA
MSACWC   Michigan State Association of Colored Women's Clubs Collection, AM
NHLAR   National Housewives' League of America Records, BHL
REP   Ruth Ellis Papers, BHL
SBCR   Second Baptist Church (Detroit, MI) Records, BHL

Introduction

1. Jerome Hansen, "Negro Faces Rough Fight in Business," *Detroit Free Press*, June 20, 1957.

2. Hansen, "Negro Faces Rough Fight in Business"; Fifteenth Census of the United States, 1930, Detroit, Wayne, Michigan, Enumeration District: 0073, page 2B; Snow F. Grigsby, *Ambitions That Could Not Be Fenced In* (Detroit: Research Bureau for Negroes and Minority Groups, Post War Economic Security, 1945), 38.

3. Hansen, "Negro Faces Rough Fight."

4. "Express Thanks," *Detroit Tribune*, March 21, 1936.

5. Hansen, "Negro Faces Rough Fight"; Fifteenth Census of the United States, 1930, Detroit, Wayne, Michigan, Enumeration District: 0073, page 2B; *Detroit Economist*, March 14, 1931, HLDP, Box 5, Folder: LMM; H. L. Dudley, "Detroit's Outstanding Lawyer Writes on 'Negroes in Detroit,'" *Pittsburgh Courier*, March 30, 1940; Sunnie Wilson with John Cohassey, *Toast of the Town: The Life and Times of Sunnie Wilson* (Detroit: Wayne State University Press, 1998), 46–47; Sixteenth Census of the United States, 1940, Detroit, Wayne, Michigan, Enumeration District: 84-140, page 9B; Seventeenth Census of the United States, 1950, Detroit, Wayne, Michigan, Enumeration District: 85-1071, page 10.

6. "Thousands Attend Opening of New $60,000 Laundry," *Detroit Tribune*, January 4, 1936.

7. Hansen, "Negro Faces Rough Fight"; Booker T. Washington Trade Association, *Directory*, 1933, HLDAP, Box 5, Folder: BTWTA Directories; "Among Detroit's Leaders," *Color*, September 1944, CHWA, Joe P. and Valma (Glenn) Branam Collection, Box 1, Folder 1.

8. Richard W. Thomas, *Life for Us Is What We Make It: Building Black Community in Detroit, 1915–1945* (Bloomington: Indiana University Press, 1992), 204–5; Roberta Hughes Wright, *Detroit Memorial Park Cemetery: The Evolution of an African American Corporation* (Southfield, MI: Charro Book Company, 1993), 116–17; "The Detroit Elections: Problem in Reconversion," *The Crisis* (November 1945): 320–21.

9. Dreck Spurlock Wilson, *African American Architects: A Biographical Dictionary, 1865–1945* (New York: Routledge, 2004), 600–604.

10. The origin of the name "Black Bottom" is unclear. While many believe it refers to the dark, fertile soil on the city's Lower East Side, Detroit historian Thomas Klug has found no historical basis for this claim. According to Klug, there is no evidence of the term before the 1920s and "Black Bottom" likely emerged alongside the Great Migration. Thomas Klug, email to author, July 13 and 20, 2023; Detroit Bureau of Governmental Research and Detroit Mayor's Inter-racial Committee, *The Negro in Detroit* (Detroit, 1926). A 1920 report claimed that this area was known as the "St. Antoine Street District" up until 1915. Forrester B. Washington, *The Negro in Detroit: A Survey of the Conditions of a Negro Group in a Northern Industrial Center During the War Prosperity Period* (Detroit: Research Bureau Associated Charities of Detroit, 1920), sec. "Environment."

11. Clyde McGrady, "Bruce's Beach Was Hailed as a Reparations Model. Then the Family Sold It," *New York Times*, February 19, 2023.

12. California Task Force to Study and Develop Reparation Proposals for African Americans, *The California Reparations Report*, June 29, 2023, https://oag.ca.gov/ab3121 /report; Tim Arango, "Can Reparations Bring Black Residents Back to San Francisco?" *New York Times*, May 16, 2023; Rachel Treisman, "In Likely First, Chicago Suburb of Evanston Approves Reparations for Black Residents," National Public Radio, March 23, 2021, sec. "Code Switch."

13. "Reparations Task Force," City of Detroit, https://detroitmi.gov/government /city-council/city-council-president-district-5/reparations-task-force.

14. Cedric J. Robinson, *Black Marxism: The Making of the Black Radical Tradition* (1983; repr., Chapel Hill: University of North Carolina Press, 2000), 2–3. Racial capitalism as a concept was initially developed in South Africa by "Marxist activists and radical members of the Black Consciousness movement . . . to understand the resilience of Apartheid rule." Cedric Robinson popularized this concept in the American context. Donna Murch, "History Matters," Forum Special Issue: Race Capitalism Justice, *Boston Review* (2017): 35.

15. For more on the debates that surround racial capitalism, see Justin Leroy and Destin Jenkins, eds., *Histories of Racial Capitalism* (New York: Columbia University Press, 2021), 1–15.

16. Robinson, *Black Marxism*; Eric Eustace Williams, *Capitalism and Slavery* (Chapel Hill: University of North Carolina Press, 1944). See also Walter Rodney, *How Europe Underdeveloped Africa* (1972; repr., New York: Verso, 2018).

17. Jacquelyn Dowd Hall uses the concept of racial capitalism in a narrower time frame than others. Of the Jim Crow era, Hall notes, "What we think of as the age of segregation might better be called the age of 'racial capitalism,' for segregation was only one instrument of white supremacy, and white supremacy entailed not only racial domination but also economic practices." Additionally, Hall proposes that there were similarities between racial capitalism in the North and the South. I build on this idea to examine Black business in a racial capitalist system across the Great Migration. Jacquelyn Dowd Hall, "The Long Civil Rights Movement and the Political Uses of the Past," *Journal of American History* 91, no. 4 (2005): 1243. For more on U.S. racial capitalism in an international context, see Peter James Hudson, *Bankers and Empire: How Wall Street Colonized the Caribbean* (Chicago: University of Chicago Press, 2017).

18. Robin D. G. Kelley, "What Did Cedric Robinson Mean by Racial Capitalism?" Forum Special Issue: Race Capitalism Justice, *Boston Review* (2017): 7.

19. Exceptions include Nathan Connolly and Pedro Regalado, who have examined Black and Latinx businesses within the context of racial capitalism. Nathan D. B. Connolly, *A World More Concrete: Real Estate and the Remaking of Jim Crow South Florida* (Chicago: University of Chicago Press, 2014); Pedro A. Regalado, "'They Speak Our Language . . . Business': Latinx People and the Pursuit of Wealth in New York City," in *Histories of Racial Capitalism*, ed. Justin Leroy and Destin Jenkins (New York: Columbia

University Press, 2021), 231–50. Some histories that engage labor related to racial capitalism include Walter Johnson, *Soul by Soul: Life Inside the Antebellum Slave Market* (Cambridge, MA: Harvard University Press, 1999); Jennifer L. Morgan, *Laboring Women: Reproduction and Gender in New World Slavery* (Philadelphia: University of Pennsylvania Press, 2004); Stephanie E. Smallwood, *Saltwater Slavery: A Middle Passage from Africa to American Diaspora* (Cambridge, MA: Harvard University Press, 2007); Seth Rockman, *Scraping By: Wage Labor, Slavery, and Survival in Early Baltimore* (Baltimore: Johns Hopkins University Press, 2009); Daina Ramey Berry, *The Price for Their Pound of Flesh: The Value of the Enslaved, from Womb to Grave, in the Building of a Nation* (Boston: Beacon Press, 2017); Stephanie E. Jones-Rogers, *They Were Her Property: White Women as Slave Owners in the American South* (New Haven: Yale University Press, 2019); and Caitlin Rosenthal, "Capitalism When Labor Was Capital: Slavery, Power, and Price in Antebellum America," *Capitalism: A Journal of History and Economics* 1, no. 2 (Spring 2020): 296–337.

20. Jacquelyn Dowd Hall, "'The Mind That Burns in Each Body': Women, Rape, and Racial Violence," in *Powers of Desire: The Politics of Sexuality*, ed. Ann Barr Snitow, Christine Stansell, and Sharon Thompson (New York: Monthly Review Press, 1983), 331.

21. Joseph A. Schumpeter, *Capitalism, Socialism and Democracy* (1943; repr., London: Routledge, 2010), chaps. 7 and 8.

22. "Free enterprise" is a loaded term championed by anti-union, anti–New Deal business leaders in the twentieth century as a mode of achieving democracy in the workplace, often discussed uncritically and ignoring the issue of race. In naming my book *Freedom Enterprise*, I do not aim to associate my historical subjects' actions with these ideas. For more on this history, see Elizabeth A. Fones-Wolf, *Selling Free Enterprise: The Business Assault on Labor and Liberalism, 1945–60* (Urbana: University of Illinois Press, 1995); Kim Phillips-Fein, *Invisible Hands: The Businessmen's Crusade Against the New Deal* (New York: W. W. Norton, 2009); and Lawrence B. Glickman, *Free Enterprise: An American History* (New Haven: Yale University Press, 2019).

23. Additionally, as scholars such as Nathan Connolly have demonstrated, African Americans could not escape the inherently exploitative nature of capitalism—not that all Black entrepreneurs had the desire to—and many profited at their own community's expense. Nathan D. B. Connolly, *A World More Concrete*.

24. Census tract 553, Detroit, Wayne, Michigan, Sixteenth Census of the United States, 1940; Census tract 603, Detroit, Wayne, Michigan, Seventeenth Census of the United States, 1950; Hansen, "Negro Faces Rough Fight."

25. Hansen, "Negro Faces Rough Fight."

26. Hansen, "Negro Faces Rough Fight."

27. Hansen, "Negro Faces Rough Fight."

28. Hansen, "Negro Faces Rough Fight."

29. "Caldwell Confesses Laundry Murder," *Detroit Tribune*, March 14, 1936; "Caldwell Pleads Guilty," *Detroit Tribune*, March 21, 1936.

30. "Allen Gets New Death Threat Note," *Detroit Tribune*, March 28, 1936.

31. "Caldwell Confesses Laundry Murder."

32. For more on infrapolitics in the Jim Crow era, see Robin D. G. Kelley, "'We Are Not What We Seem': Rethinking Black Working-Class Opposition in the Jim Crow South," *Journal of American History* 80, no. 1 (1993): 77–79.

33. Tiffany M. Gill, *Beauty Shop Politics: African American Women's Activism in the Beauty Industry* (Urbana: University of Illinois Press, 2010); Leslie Brown, *Upbuilding Black Durham: Gender, Class, and Black Community Development in the Jim Crow South* (Chapel Hill: University of North Carolina Press, 2008); Connolly, *A World More Concrete*; Brandon K. Winford, *John Hervey Wheeler, Black Banking, and the Economic Struggle for Civil Rights* (Lexington: University of Kentucky Press, 2020); Tanisha Ford, *Our Secret Society: Mollie Moon and the Glamour, Money, and Power Behind the Civil Rights Movement* (New York: Amistad, 2023).

34. Suzanne Smith has demonstrated that Detroit-founded Motown Records was one example of how "Black capitalism, in practice, did not always guarantee racial, social, or economic justice for African Americans." Suzanne E. Smith, *Dancing in the Street: Motown and the Cultural Politics of Detroit* (Cambridge, MA: Harvard University Press, 1999), 16, 15, 214, 246, 253–56.

35. Merah S. Stuart framed "race businesses" that were owned by and catered exclusively to members of a particular group as devices of racial prejudice. Stuart argued that while the policy of segregation in the market was "in conflict with the fundamental logic of commerce, of trade, which thrives the more by expansion and suffers under constriction," U.S. economic leaders "approve—or at least tolerate—this barrier, this doctrine of a separate economy for the Negro; and grant the assumption that the Negro can accomplish that which under similar circumstances no other group has accomplished, viz., a separate 'race' business by the side of, and in competition with, the general business of the nation." Merah S. Stuart, *An Economic Detour: A History of Insurance in the Lives of American Negroes* (New York: Wendell Malliet, 1940), xvii–xviii.

36. For more on the politics of Black capitalism, see Robert E. Weems Jr. and Lewis A. Randolph, "The National Response to Richard M. Nixon's Black Capitalism Initiative: The Success of Domestic Detente," *Journal of Black Studies* 32, no. 1 (2001): 66–83; Mehrsa Baradaran, *The Color of Money: Black Banks and the Racial Wealth Gap* (Cambridge, MA: Harvard University Press, 2017), chap. 6.

37. For more on how (Black) capitalism has failed to raise Blacks' quality of life, see Manning Marable, *How Capitalism Underdeveloped Black America: Problems in Race, Political Economy, and Society* (Cambridge, MA: South End Press, 1983); Robert L. Allen, *Black Awakening in Capitalist America: An Analytic History* (1969; repr., Trenton, NJ: Africa World Press, 1990); Earl Ofari Hutchinson, *The Myth of Black Capitalism* (1970; new edition, New York: Monthly Review Press, 2024).

38. For an excellent discussion of African American business historiography, see Shennette Garrett-Scott, "A Historiography of African American Business," *Business and Economic History On-Line* 7 (2009), http://www.thebhc.org/publications/BEHonline/2009/garrett-scott.pdf.

39. Walker writes, "In African American history, the period from 1900 to 1930 marked the first of three waves in the rise of Black corporate America. This was the golden age of Black business, which saw the emergence of leading Black capitalists who achieved millionaire status and established million-dollar enterprises. . . . But while Black business activity expanded from 1900 to 1930, most Black businesses established during this period, with the exceptions of banks, insurance companies, and the hair care industry[,] did not survive the Great Depression." Juliet E. K. Walker, *The History of Black Business in America: Capitalism, Race, Entrepreneurship* (New York: Twayne, 1998), 182–83.

40. U.S. Bureau of the Census, *Negroes in the United States, 1920–1932* (Washington, DC: Government Printing Office, 1935), 55, table 10.

41. Kenneth L. Kusmer, *A Ghetto Takes Shape: Black Cleveland, 1870–1930* (Urbana: University of Illinois Press, 1976); William H. Harris, *The Harder We Run: Black Workers Since the Civil War* (New York: Oxford University Press, 1982); Joe William Trotter Jr., *Black Milwaukee: The Making of an Industrial Proletariat, 1915–45* (Urbana: University of Illinois Press, 1985); Peter Gottlieb, *Making Their Own Way: Southern Blacks' Migration to Pittsburgh, 1916–30* (Urbana: University of Illinois Press, 1987); James R. Grossman, *Land of Hope: Chicago, Black Southerners, and the Great Migration* (Chicago: University of Chicago Press, 1989); Carole Marks, *Farewell—We're Good and Gone: The Great Black Migration* (Bloomington: Indiana University Press, 1989); Kimberley Louise Phillips, *AlabamaNorth: African-American Migrants, Community, and Working-Class Activism in Cleveland, 1915–45* (Urbana: University of Illinois Press, 1999); Isabel Wilkerson, *The Warmth of Other Suns: The Epic Story of America's Great Migration* (New York: Vintage, 2010); Luther Adams, *Way Up North in Louisville: African American Migration in the Urban South, 1930–1970* (Chapel Hill: University of North Carolina Press, 2010); Bernadette Pruitt, *The Other Great Migration: The Movement of Rural African Americans to Houston, 1900–1941* (College Station: Texas A&M University Press, 2013); Leah Platt Boustan, *Competition in the Promised Land: Black Migrants in Northern Cities and Labor Markets* (Princeton: Princeton University Press, 2016).

42. Lee argues that every act of migration involves an origin, a destination, and an intervening set of obstacles. The positive and negative perceptions of "factors associated with the area of origin" and "factors associated with the area of destination" translate into "push" and "pull" factors. Everett S. Lee, "A Theory of Migration," *Demography* 3, no. 1 (January 1, 1966): 49–52. Works that utilize this socioeconomic push-pull framework of Black population movement include: U.S. Department of Labor, *Negro Migration in 1916–1917* (Washington, DC: Government Printing Office, 1919); Carter G. Woodson, *A Century of Negro Migration* (Washington, DC: Association for the Study of Negro Life and History, 1918); Emmett J. Scott, *Negro Migration During the War* (New York: Oxford University Press, 1920); Louise Venable Kennedy, *The Negro Peasant Turns Cityward: Effects of Recent Migrations to Northern Centers* (New York: Columbia University Press, 1930); E. Franklin Frazier, *The Negro Family in Chicago* (Chicago: University of Chicago

Press, 1932); St. Clair Drake and Horace R. Cayton, *Black Metropolis: A Study of Negro Life in a Northern City* (1945; repr., Chicago: University of Chicago Press, 1962), 58–64; and Gunnar Myrdal, *An American Dilemma: The Negro Problem and Modern Democracy* (New York: Harper & Row, 1944).

43. Earl Lewis, "Expectations, Economic Opportunities, and Life in Norfolk, Virginia, 1920–1945," in *The Great Migration in Historical Perspective: New Dimensions of Race, Class, and Gender*, ed. Joe William Trotter Jr. (Bloomington: Indiana University Press, 1991), 25. Push factors that influenced southerners' decisions to migrate included an agricultural depression, widespread flooding and a boll weevil infestation that ruined cotton crops, Black tenants and sharecroppers being kicked off white-owned land due to a decline in cotton prices, and a discriminatory job market in the South that limited most African Americans to service positions such as domestic servants, laundresses, janitors, or waiters. Grossman, *Land of Hope*, chap. 1; and Eric Arnesen, *Black Protest and the Great Migration: A Brief History with Documents* (New York: Bedford/St. Martin's, 2002), 1–3.

44. Lewis, "Expectations, Economic Opportunities, and Life in Norfolk, Virginia," 25; Joyce Shaw Peterson, "Black Automobile Workers in Detroit, 1910–1930," *Journal of Negro History* 64, no. 3 (1979): 177; Beth Tompkins Bates, *The Making of Black Detroit in the Age of Henry Ford* (Chapel Hill: University of North Carolina Press, 2012).

45. Twenty-first-century scholarship on the Great Migration tends to offer a wider view of the Black experience that includes commercial activity in migration sites. James N. Gregory, *The Southern Diaspora: How the Great Migrations of Black and White Southerners Transformed America* (Chapel Hill: University of North Carolina Press, 2005); Davarian L. Baldwin, *Chicago's New Negroes: Modernity, the Great Migration, and Black Urban Life* (Chapel Hill: University of North Carolina Press, 2009); Marcia Chatelain, *South Side Girls: Growing Up in the Great Migration* (Durham: Duke University Press, 2015); Brian McCammack, *Landscapes of Hope: Nature and the Great Migration in Chicago* (Cambridge, MA: Harvard University Press, 2017); Judith Weisenfeld, *New World A-Coming: Black Religion and Racial Identity During the Great Migration* (New York: New York University Press, 2017); Beatrice Juanita Adams, "African Americans Who Remained in and Returned to the American South During the Great Migration" (PhD diss., Rutgers University, 2021).

46. Thomas, *Life for Us*, 27.

47. Some key works on Black Detroit include Thomas, *Life for Us*; Thomas J. Sugrue, *The Origins of the Urban Crisis: Race and Inequality in Postwar Detroit* (Princeton: Princeton University Press, 1996); Smith, *Dancing in the Street*; Victoria W. Wolcott, *Remaking Respectability: African American Women in Interwar Detroit* (Chapel Hill: University of North Carolina Press, 2001); Heather Ann Thompson, *Whose Detroit? Politics, Labor, and Race in a Modern American City* (Ithaca: Cornell University Press, 2004); Kevin Boyle, *Arc of Justice: A Saga of Race, Civil Rights, and Murder in the Jazz Age* (New York: Holt, 2004); Angela D. Dillard, *Faith in the City: Preaching Radical Social Change in*

Detroit (Ann Arbor: University of Michigan Press, 2007); and Bates, *The Making of Black Detroit in the Age of Henry Ford.*

48. Coleman Young and Lonnie Wheeler, *Hard Stuff: The Autobiography of Mayor Coleman Young* (New York: Viking, 1994), 146.

49. Ed Davis, *One Man's Way* (Detroit: E. Davis Associates, 1979), 96.

50. However, I am currently working on a digital project that will provide more quantitative information about the numbers and types of businesses operated by Black Detroiters. Bringing together historical maps, oral histories, census data, directories, and digitized print media such as photographs and newspaper advertisements, this interactive website will recreate the vibrant business landscape of key Black Detroit neighborhoods prior to the 1960s. Visit https://freedomenterprise.org.

51. For example, Walter B. Weare, *Black Business in the New South: A Social History of the North Carolina Mutual Life Insurance Company* (Urbana: University of Illinois Press, 1973). Early analyses of Black business, such as Abram Harris's 1936 study on Black banks and Merah Stuart's 1940 study on Black insurance companies, influenced this trend. Abram Lincoln Harris, *The Negro as Capitalist: A Study of Banking and Business Among American Negroes* (Philadelphia: American Academy of Political and Social Science, 1936); Stuart, *Economic Detour.*

52. Arthur S. Siegel, "Detroit, Michigan. Back View of a Negro Dressed in a Zoot Suit, Walking in the Business District," 1942, photograph, Library of Congress, Prints and Photographs Division, FSA/OWI Collection, LC-DIG-fsa-8d25384. While this February 1942 photograph does not specify the location as Hastings Street, the image shows Ace Bar, which in 1942 was located at 3878 Hastings Street. "Ace Bar Signs Contract with Local for Wage Increases," *Michigan Chronicle*, April 11, 1942.

53. Following the lead of scholars like Brittney Cooper, I have chosen to decenter the Washington-Du Bois paradigm for understanding ideologies of Black business and economic advancement in the early twentieth century. By "moving beyond the great race man narrative," this book makes space for the voices of Black migrant entrepreneurs. Brittney C. Cooper, *Beyond Respectability: The Intellectual Thought of Race Women* (Urbana: University of Illinois Press, 2017), 23–26.

54. I have chosen not to foreground the stories of Detroit's most well-known Black entrepreneurs. While it is they for whom adequate historical sources are most available to reconstruct multidecade narratives, doing so would highlight these more privileged business owners and overshadow those who were more obscure. In other words, I would reproduce the biases of the archive and, consequently, center mostly elite and male experiences.

55. For instance, I do not dive into colorism or class tensions within Black Detroit, though they certainly existed. There were also likely political clashes between Black entrepreneurs and Detroiters in radical groups such as civil rights organizations and labor unions. Other areas that do not receive thorough analysis in the text include how the southern context changed across the Great Migration, urban renewal projects in the South, and the complexity of white politicians' and city planners' motivations.

Chapter 1

1. "Business," *Detroit Contender*, November 13, 1920.

2. The economic thought of Black leaders such as W. E. B. Du Bois and Booker T. Washington received the most attention and was influential prior to the Great Migration. Many accepted Washington's influential philosophy of pursuing racial uplift through accumulating wealth in the years leading up to the first wave of the Great Migration and took this philosophy with them as they migrated. John Sibley Butler, *Entrepreneurship and Self-Help Among Black Americans: A Reconsideration of Race and Economics* (Albany: State University of New York Press, 1991), 70.

3. Eric Arnesen, *Black Protest and the Great Migration: A Brief History with Documents* (New York: Bedford/St. Martin's, 2002), 2, 6; Douglas A. Blackmon, *Slavery by Another Name: The Re-Enslavement of Black Americans from the Civil War to World War II* (New York: Doubleday, 2008); Talitha L. LeFlouria, *Chained in Silence: Black Women and Convict Labor in the New South* (Chapel Hill: University of North Carolina Press, 2015).

4. For more on the racial caste system that followed Jim Crow, see Michelle Alexander, *The New Jim Crow: Mass Incarceration in the Age of Colorblindness* (New York: New Press, 2012).

5. According to historian Juliet E. K. Walker, "even during slavery leading Black entrepreneurs accumulated wealth in the hundreds of thousands of dollars from their business activities." Juliet E. K. Walker, *Encyclopedia of African American Business History* (Westport, CT: Greenwood Press, 1999), xiii–xiv.

6. Juliet E. K. Walker, *The History of Black Business in America: Capitalism, Race, Entrepreneurship* (New York: Twayne, 1998), 169, 176; Robert E. Weems Jr., *Desegregating the Dollar: African American Consumerism in the Twentieth Century* (New York: New York University Press, 1998), 7–11.

7. Butler, *Entrepreneurship and Self-Help*, 41.

8. Walker, *The History of Black Business in America*, 150–210; Leslie Brown, *Upbuilding Black Durham: Gender, Class, and Black Community Development in the Jim Crow South* (Chapel Hill: University of North Carolina Press, 2008); Walter B. Weare, *Black Business in the New South: A Social History of the North Carolina Mutual Life Insurance Company* (Urbana: University of Illinois Press, 1973).

9. For more on the Exodusters, Black westward migration, and all-Black towns, see Nell Irvin Painter, *Exodusters: Black Migration to Kansas After Reconstruction* (1977; New York: W. W. Norton, 1992); Robert G. Athearn, *In Search of Canaan: Black Migration to Kansas, 1879–80* (Lawrence: Regents Press of Kansas, 1978); Norman L. Crockett, *The Black Towns* (Lawrence: University Press of Kansas, 1979); Kenneth Marvin Hamilton, *Black Towns and Profit: Promotion and Development in the Trans-Appalachian West, 1877–1915* (Urbana: University of Illinois Press, 1991); Sundiata Keita Cha-Jua, *America's First Black Town: Brooklyn, Illinois, 1830–1915* (Urbana: University of Illinois Press, 2000); Leslie A. Schwalm, *Emancipation's Diaspora: Race and*

Reconstruction in the Upper Midwest (Chapel Hill: University of North Carolina Press, 2009); Kendra T. Field, *Growing Up with the Country: Family, Race, and Nation After the Civil War* (New Haven: Yale University Press, 2018); Karla Slocum, *Black Towns, Black Futures: The Enduring Allure of a Black Place in the American West* (Chapel Hill: University of North Carolina Press, 2019); and Warigia M. Bowman, "Connections Between Black Wall Street and Oklahoma's All-Black Towns," *Tulsa Law Review* 57, no. 1 (Winter 2021): 293–302.

10. Stewart E. Tolnay and E. M. Beck, *A Festival of Violence: An Analysis of Southern Lynchings, 1882–1930* (Urbana: University of Illinois Press, 1995), 70. For more on lynching and economic competition, see Tolnay and Beck, *A Festival of Violence*, 69–75.

11. Tolnay and Beck, *A Festival of Violence*, 252.

12. Crystal N. Feimster, *Southern Horrors: Women and the Politics of Rape and Lynching* (Cambridge, MA: Harvard University Press, 2011), 87–90.

13. Mia Bay, *To Tell the Truth Freely: The Life of Ida B. Wells* (New York: Hill and Wang, 2009), 82–86, 88; "The Mob's Work Done with Guns, Not Rope," *Memphis Commercial*, March 10, 1892.

14. Walter White, *A Man Called White*, reprint ed. (New York: Arno Press, 1969), 10–12, as cited in Herbert Shapiro, *White Violence and Black Response: From Reconstruction to Montgomery* (Amherst: University of Massachusetts Press, 1988), 102.

15. Reverdy Cassius Ransom, "The Atlanta Riot: A Philippic on the Atlanta Riot, Delivered in Faneuil Hall, Boston, Massachusetts, September 28, 1906," in *The Spirit of Freedom and Justice: Orations and Speeches* (Nashville, TN: A.M.E. Sunday School Union, 1926), 117–21; and Shapiro, *White Violence and Black Response*, 102–3.

16. Ransom, "The Atlanta Riot"; Shapiro, *White Violence and Black Response*, 102–3; Davarian L. Baldwin, *Chicago's New Negroes: Modernity, the Great Migration, and Black Urban Life* (Chapel Hill: University of North Carolina Press, 2009), 5, 32, 54; Walker, *The History of Black Business in America*, 216.

17. "A Negro's Tale of Woe," *Austin American-Statesman*, January 1, 1898.

18. "He Was Fired Upon," *Daily Arkansas Gazette*, December 31, 1897; "Reward Offered," *Austin American-Statesman*, January 4, 1898.

19. "A Negro's Tale of Woe."

20. "If It Be True," *Arkansas Democrat*, January 29, 1898.

21. "Warned to Leave," *Daily Arkansas Gazette*, January 29, 1898; Nancy Snell Griffith, "Lonoke County Race War of 1897–1898," in *Encyclopedia of Arkansas*, September 13, 2012, https://encyclopediaofarkansas.net/entries/lonoke-county-race-war-of-1897-1898-7459/.

22. "Reign of Terror," *Journal and Tribune*, January 30, 1898; "Leaving in Droves," *Chattanooga Daily Times*, January 30, 1898; "The Governor Seems Quiet," *Montgomery Advertiser*, January 30, 1898.

23. "Reign of Terror"; "Leaving in Droves"; "The Governor Seems Quiet."

24. Emmett J. Scott, ed., "Letters of Negro Migrants of 1916–1918," *Journal of Negro History* 4, no. 3 (July 1919): 299.

25. Berry Gordy Sr., *Movin' Up: Pop Gordy Tells His Story* (New York: Harper & Row, 1979), 84–85.

26. Gordy, *Movin' Up*, 130, 133–35.

27. Richard Wormser, *The Rise and Fall of Jim Crow* (New York: St. Martin's, 2003), 82–83.

28. For more on the Wilmington Riot, see David S. Cecelski and Timothy B. Tyson, eds., *Democracy Betrayed: The Wilmington Race Riot of 1898 and Its Legacy* (Chapel Hill: University of North Carolina Press, 1998); Shapiro, *White Violence and Black Response*, 65–79.

29. Quoted in Wormser, *Rise and Fall of Jim Crow*, 86.

30. John C. Dancy, *Sand Against the Wind: The Memoirs of John C. Dancy* (Detroit: Wayne State University Press, 1966), 68–70.

31. "Race War Probable," *Day Book (Chicago)*, September 11, 1912.

32. This demographic evolution was spurred by a coal rush and industrialization in the region. According to Trotter, "In 1888, Bluefield, Mercer County, was merely a flag station on a local farm; a year later it was incorporated, with a population of 600, and it increased to over 11,000 by 1910." Joe William Trotter Jr., *Coal, Class, and Color: Blacks in Southern West Virginia, 1915–32* (Urbana: University of Illinois Press, 1990), 14–24; 15.

33. Quoted in Trotter, *Coal, Class, and Color*, 29, 31.

34. Trotter, *Coal, Class, and Color*, 31.

35. Trotter, *Coal, Class, and Color*, 26.

36. Trotter, *Coal, Class, and Color*, 27.

37. For more on the 1921 Tulsa massacre, see Lee E. Williams, *Anatomy of Four Race Riots: Racial Conflict in Knoxville, Elaine (Arkansas), Tulsa, and Chicago, 1919–1921* (Hattiesburg: University and College Press of Mississippi, 1972); R. Halliburton, "The Tulsa Race War of 1921," *Journal of Black Studies* 2, no. 3 (1972): 333–57; Butler, *Entrepreneurship and Self-Help*, 207–37; Scott Ellsworth, *Death in a Promised Land: The Tulsa Race Riot of 1921* (Baton Rouge: Louisiana State University Press, 1992); Oklahoma Commission to Study the Tulsa Race Riot of 1921, *Tulsa Race Riot: A Report by the Oklahoma Commission to Study the Tulsa Race Riot of 1921* (2001), https://digitalcollections .tulsalibrary.org/digital/collection/p15020coll6/id/447; Alfred L. Brophy, *Reconstructing the Dreamland: The Tulsa Riot of 1921: Race, Reparations, and Reconciliation* (New York: Oxford University Press, 2002); James S. Hirsch, *Riot and Remembrance: The Tulsa Race War and Its Legacy* (Boston: Houghton Mifflin, 2002); Tim Madigan, *The Burning: Massacre, Destruction, and the Tulsa Race Riot of 1921* (New York: Thomas Dunne Books/ St. Martin's Griffin, 2003); Randy Krehbiel, *Tulsa 1921: Reporting a Massacre* (Norman: University of Oklahoma Press, 2019); Victor Luckerson, *Built from the Fire: The Epic Story of Tulsa's Greenwood District, America's Black Wall Street* (New York: Random House, 2023).

38. Ellsworth, *Death in a Promised Land*, 8–15.

39. Ellsworth, *Death in a Promised Land*, 45–52.

40. Ellsworth, *Death in a Promised Land*, 2–5, 55, 57.

41. Ellsworth, *Death in a Promised Land*, 63–66, 69–70, 89.

42. Appendix, "Black Businesses Establishments and Business Persons as Listed in Tulsa City Directories," in Ellsworth, *Death in a Promised Land*, 115–16.

43. Ellsworth, *Death in a Promised Land*, 17.

44. "Mob Burns Courthouse to Lynch Negro; Store His Funeral Pyre," *Austin American*, May 10, 1930; "Negro Dies as Texas Mob Fires Court House," *Morning Herald*, May 10, 1930.

45. Ellsworth, *Death in a Promised Land*, 18.

46. For example, Elmore Bolling was lynched in 1947 in Lowndes County, Alabama, because a white competitor was jealous of Bolling's business achievements. Josephine Bolling McCall, *The Penalty for Success: My Father Was Lynched in Lowndes County, Alabama* (Montgomery, AL: McQuick Printing Company, 2015).

47. For example, see the discussion on intimidation and threats against Black business in Richmond, Virginia, in Shennette Garrett-Scott, *Banking on Freedom: Black Women in U.S. Finance Before the New Deal* (New York: Columbia University Press, 2019), 93–99.

48. Jacquelyn Dowd Hall, "'The Mind That Burns in Each Body': Women, Rape, and Racial Violence," in *Powers of Desire: The Politics of Sexuality*, ed. Ann Barr Snitow, Christine Stansell, and Sharon Thompson (New York: Monthly Review Press, 1983), 330.

49. Carter G. Woodson, *A Century of Negro Migration* (Washington, DC: Association for the Study of Negro Life and History, 1918), 99.

50. Scott, "Letters of Negro Migrants of 1916–1918," 299.

51. Scott, "Letters of Negro Migrants of 1916–1918," 279.

52. Scott, "Letters of Negro Migrants of 1916–1918," 302.

53. Scott, "Letters of Negro Migrants of 1916–1918," 334.

54. Scott, "Letters of Negro Migrants of 1916–1918," 303.

55. Scott, "Letters of Negro Migrants of 1916–1918," 303.

56. The northern press and institutions like the Urban League were key sources of information for southern Black migrants. The *Chicago Defender* was a crucial vehicle for facilitating migration to places across the nation. Since they are in such close proximity, the Chicago and Detroit Urban League offices were in constant communication with each other regarding southern migrants. For more information on the *Chicago Defender*'s influence among migrants, see James R. Grossman, "Blowing the Trumpet: The *Chicago Defender* and Black Migration During World War I," *Illinois Historical Journal* 78, no. 2 (1985): 82–96; and James R. Grossman, "The White Man's Union: The Great Migration and the Resonance of Race and Class in Chicago, 1916–1922," in *The Great Migration in Historical Perspective: New Dimensions of Race, Class, and Gender*, ed. Joe William Trotter Jr. (Bloomington: Indiana University Press, 1991), 88, 91–92.

57. Forrester B. Washington, "Report of Director," March 8, 1917, DUL-M, Reel #1.

58. Emmett J. Scott, ed., "Additional Letters of Negro Migrants of 1916–1918," *Journal of Negro History* 4, no. 4 (October 1919): 451.

59. Scott, "Additional Letters of Negro Migrants of 1916–1918," 441.

60. Beatrice Juanita Adams, "African Americans Who Remained in and Returned to the American South During the Great Migration" (PhD diss., Rutgers University, 2021).

61. Kevin Boyle, *Arc of Justice: A Saga of Race, Civil Rights, and Murder in the Jazz Age* (New York: Holt, 2004), 83–87. This trend was also indicated in a May 13, 1917, letter from Rome, Georgia, in Scott, "Letters of Negro Migrants of 1916–1918," 333; see also Dancy, *Sand Against the Wind*, 68.

62. Scott, "Letters of Negro Migrants of 1916–1918," 308.

63. Richard W. Thomas, *Life for Us Is What We Make It: Building Black Community in Detroit, 1915–1945* (Bloomington: Indiana University Press, 1992), 39.

64. Scott, "Letters of Negro Migrants of 1916–1918," 311–12.

65. For more on the noneconomic motives that propelled Black female migration, see Darlene Clark Hine, "Black Migration to the Urban Midwest: The Gender Dimension, 1915–1945," in *The Great Migration in Historical Perspective: New Dimensions of Race, Class, and Gender*, ed. Joe William Trotter Jr. (Bloomington: Indiana University Press, 1991), 127–46.

66. Scott, "Letters of Negro Migrants of 1916–1918," 308.

67. Scott, "Letters of Negro Migrants of 1916–1918," 308.

68. Scott, "Letters of Negro Migrants of 1916–1918," 291.

69. Arthur Turner and Earl R. Moses, eds., *Colored Detroit: A Brief History of Detroit's Colored Population and a Directory of Their Businesses, Organizations, Professions and Trades* (Detroit, 1924), 104.

70. Scott, "Additional Letters of Negro Migrants of 1916–1918," 450.

71. Scott, "Letters of Negro Migrants of 1916–1918," 337.

72. Scott, "Letters of Negro Migrants of 1916–1918," 339–40.

73. Scott, "Additional Letters of Negro Migrants of 1916–1918," 439–40.

74. Scott, "Additional Letters of Negro Migrants of 1916–1918," 436.

75. Scott, "Additional Letters of Negro Migrants of 1916–1918," 437.

76. Scott, "Letters of Negro Migrants of 1916–1918," 329.

77. Boyle, *Arc of Justice*, 101.

78. Boyle, *Arc of Justice*, 85, 99–101.

79. Dancy, *Sand Against the Wind*, 69.

80. Scott, "Additional Letters of Negro Migrants of 1916–1918," 465.

81. Scott, "Additional Letters of Negro Migrants of 1916–1918," 457–58.

82. Forrester B. Washington, *The Negro in Detroit: A Survey of the Conditions of a Negro Group in a Northern Industrial Center During the War Prosperity Period* (Detroit: Research Bureau Associated Charities of Detroit, 1920), sec. "The Identification of the Negro in Detroit."

83. Boyle, *Arc of Justice*, 136.

Chapter 2

1. Francis H. Warren, "Business Among Colored People," *Detroit Contender*, November 13, 1920.

2. U.S. Bureau of the Census, *Negroes in the United States, 1920–1932* (Washington, DC: Government Printing Office, 1935), 55, table 10.

3. Robert L. Boyd, "Great Migration, Black Entrepreneurship," in *Encyclopedia of African American Business History*, ed. Juliet E. K. Walker (Westport, CT: Greenwood Press, 1999), 279–81.

4. Forrester B. Washington, *The Negro in Detroit: A Survey of the Conditions of a Negro Group in a Northern Industrial Center During the War Prosperity Period* (Detroit: Research Bureau Associated Charities of Detroit, 1920), sec. "Identification," part "Social Classes Among the Negroes of Detroit."

5. Washington, *The Negro in Detroit*, sec. "Renaissance of Negro Industrially: War and Reconstruction, 1915 to 1920"; see also Karen R. Miller, *Managing Inequality: Northern Racial Liberalism in Interwar Detroit* (New York: New York University Press, 2015), 34–35.

6. These are not the only characteristics of northern racial capitalism; I am simply highlighting some aspects that are featured in my narrative of Detroit's historical Black migrant business community's rise and fall.

7. George Edmund Haynes, *Negro New-Comers in Detroit, Michigan: A Challenge to Christian Statesmanship, a Preliminary Survey* (New York: Home Missions Council, 1918), 3–4, 8; U.S. Bureau of the Census, *Negroes in the United States, 1920–1932*, 55, table 10. For more on Black migrants and industrial work in Detroit, see Beth Tompkins Bates, *The Making of Black Detroit in the Age of Henry Ford* (Chapel Hill: University of North Carolina Press, 2012).

8. Richard W. Thomas, *Life for Us Is What We Make It: Building Black Community in Detroit, 1915–1945* (Bloomington: Indiana University Press, 1992), 27–29.

9. Thomas J. Sugrue, *The Origins of the Urban Crisis: Race and Inequality in Postwar Detroit* (1996; Princeton: Princeton University Press, 2005), 23, table 1.1.

10. U.S. Bureau of the Census, *Negroes in the United States*, 55, table 10.

11. Walter White and Thurgood Marshall, *What Caused the Detroit Riot? An Analysis* (New York: National Association for the Advancement of Colored People, 1943), 5; Kurt Metzger and Jason Booza, "African Americans in the United States, Michigan and Metropolitan Detroit," *Center for Urban Studies Working Paper Series*, no. 8 (February 2002): 9, http://www.cus.wayne.edu/media/1356/aawork8.pdf.

12. Ulysses W. Boykin, *A Hand Book on the Detroit Negro* (Detroit: Minority Study Associates, 1943), 68; David M. Katzman, *Before the Ghetto: Black Detroit in the Nineteenth Century* (Urbana: University of Illinois Press, 1973), 105–10. For more on live-in domestic service, see Elizabeth Clark-Lewis, *Living In, Living Out: African American Domestics in Washington, D.C., 1910–1940* (Washington, DC: Smithsonian Institution Press, 1994).

13. This differs from Great Migration cities that experienced less dramatic increases in their Black populations. For example, in Milwaukee, the Black community was small compared to that of northern cities such as Detroit or Chicago. In 1920, only about 2,200 Blacks lived in Milwaukee, less than 1 percent of the city's total population. By 1930, the city's Black population had only reached 1.2 percent of Milwaukee's total population, and 1.5 percent of the total population by 1940. By 1950, the Black population had grown to 21,772 (3.4 percent of the city's total). Out of necessity, Milwaukee's Black community had to integrate more with the mainstream white community, since it was not large enough to support a sizable Black business community operating across a wide variety of industries. Crystal Moten, "'More than a Job': Black Women's Economic Citizenship in the Twentieth Century Urban North" (PhD diss., University of Wisconsin-Madison, 2013), 5–6, 78.

14. Sugrue, *Origins*, 23.

15. Katzman, *Before the Ghetto*, 79–80.

16. Kevin Boyle, *Arc of Justice: A Saga of Race, Civil Rights, and Murder in the Jazz Age* (New York: Holt, 2004), 105; Washington, *The Negro in Detroit*, sec. "Environment."

17. See Helen Nuttall Brown oral history in Elaine Latzman Moon, *Untold Tales, Unsung Heroes: An Oral History of Detroit's African American Community, 1918–1967* (Detroit: Wayne State University Press, 1994), 37.

18. Moon, *Untold Tales, Unsung Heroes*, 49.

19. Coleman Young and Lonnie Wheeler, *Hard Stuff: The Autobiography of Mayor Coleman Young* (New York: Viking, 1994), 16–17.

20. Sugrue, *Origins*, 23.

21. Katzman, *Before the Ghetto*, 79–80.

22. "Tom Collins Cartage and Moving Advertisement," *Detroit Herald*, November 23, 1916; "C. D. Clinton Advertisement," *Detroit Contender*, November 13, 1920; "Super Six Taxi Co. Advertisement," *Detroit Contender*, November 13, 1920.

23. According to the 1910 census, there were 5,741 Blacks in Detroit out of a total population of 465,766. U.S. Bureau of the Census, *Negroes in the United States*, 55, table 10.

24. Katzman, *Before the Ghetto*, 106.

25. D. Augustus Straker, "Greater Opportunity for the Civic Development of Mankind," *Colored American Magazine* (Boston, MA) 2, no. 3 (January 1, 1901): 19, as cited in Katzman, *Before the Ghetto*, 107.

26. See the discussion on Black professional entrepreneurship in Chapter 6.

27. Francis H. Warren, *Michigan Manual of Freedmen's Progress* (Detroit: Freedmen's Progress Commission, 1915), 53–54, 299.

28. Warren, *Michigan Manual*, 123; Katzman, *Before the Ghetto*, 97–98. For more on the Black barbering business, see Douglas W. Bristol, *Knights of the Razor: Black Barbers in Slavery and Freedom* (Baltimore: Johns Hopkins University Press, 2009); and Quincy T. Mills, *Cutting Along the Color Line: Black Barbers and Barber Shops in America* (Philadelphia: University of Pennsylvania Press, 2013).

29. Detroit Bureau of Governmental Research and Detroit Mayor's Inter-racial Committee, *The Negro in Detroit* (Detroit, 1926), sec. "Thrift and Business," 20–21.

30. Warren, *Michigan Manual*, 127, 301; listing for undertaker W. H. Howard at 302 St. Antoine, in *Detroit City Directory 1910* (Detroit: R. L. Polk, 1910), 3266; "Marriage Record for William H. Howard and Carrie C. Watson" (record number 44167, Detroit, Wayne County, MI, October 26, 1904), Ancestry.com.

31. Washington, *The Negro in Detroit*, sec. "The Housing of the Negro in Detroit."

32. Arthur Turner and Earl R. Moses, eds., *Colored Detroit: A Brief History of Detroit's Colored Population and a Directory of Their Businesses, Organizations, Professions and Trades* (Detroit, 1924), 28.

33. Katzman, *Before the Ghetto*, 77, 131; Warren, *Michigan Manual*, 114–15; "Cole's Express Moving and Cartage Co. Advertisement," *Detroit Herald*, November 23, 1916.

34. State of Michigan, *The Compiled Laws of the State of Michigan, 1915*, vol. 2, comp. Edmund C. Shields, Cyrenius P. Black, and Archibald Broomfield (Lansing, MI: Wynkoop Hallenbeck Crawford Co., State Printers, 1916), 2503.

35. Willis Eugene Smith, interview by Margaret Ward, October 28, 1980, 1 audio-cassette, DPL; Fred G. Marshall & Son Listing in *Detroit City Directory 1910*, 3266.

36. "James H. Cole, Jr.," *Detroit Contender*, November 13, 1920.

37. Jerome Hansen, "Negro Faces Rough Fight in Business," *Detroit Free Press*, June 20, 1957.

38. Willis Eugene Smith, interview by Monroe Walker, December 27, 1984, 2 audio-cassettes, DPL.

39. Len Shaw, "Detroit's New Housing Problem," *Detroit Free Press*, June 3, 1917.

40. Shaw, "Detroit's New Housing Problem."

41. Washington, *The Negro in Detroit*, sec. "The Housing of the Negro in Detroit." For more information on the ways Black landlords and entrepreneurs exploited Black renters, see Nathan D. B. Connolly, *A World More Concrete: Real Estate and the Remaking of Jim Crow South Florida* (Chicago: University of Chicago Press, 2014).

42. Washington, *The Negro in Detroit*, sec. "The Housing of the Negro in Detroit."

43. Katzman, *Before the Ghetto*, 74–76; Sugrue, *Origins*, 34.

44. Washington, *The Negro in Detroit*, sec. "The Housing of the Negro in Detroit."

45. "Food Conservation Is," *The Baptist Item*, December 8, 1917, SBCR, Microfilm roll #9, Publications 1913–1989 series, Weekly 1913–1989 subseries.

46. "High Cost of Living Hits the Theaters Forces Raise in Price at Dudley's Vaudette," *Detroit Herald*, November 30, 1916.

47. "Clubs Reopened," *Detroit Herald*, November 30, 1916.

48. Berry Gordy Sr., *Movin' Up: Pop Gordy Tells His Story* (New York: Harper & Row, 1979), 107–9.

49. John C. Dancy, *Sand Against the Wind: The Memoirs of John C. Dancy* (Detroit: Wayne State University Press, 1966), 141. The Detroit branch of the Urban League was established in 1916 to help acclimate rural African American migrants to life in the industrial city. Forrester B. Washington (who would eventually direct the Atlanta School

of Social Work) served as the first director of the Detroit Urban League from 1916 to 1918. Washington was succeeded by John C. Dancy, who served as the organization's director until his retirement in 1960. Frederica H. Barrow, "Forrester Blanchard Washington and His Advocacy for African Americans in the New Deal," *Social Work* 52, no. 3 (July 2007): 202; Boykin, *Hand Book*, 25.

50. Dancy, *Sand Against the Wind*, 141.

51. Thomas, *Life for Us*, 27; Elizabeth Anne Martin, *Detroit and the Great Migration, 1916–1929* (Ann Arbor, MI: Bentley Historical Library, 1993), 4; William Haber, "Fluctuations in Employment in Detroit Factories, 1921–1931," *Journal of the American Statistical Association* 27, no. 178 (1932): 143.

52. John C. Dancy, "Urban League Report Covering July and August," September 1920, DUL-M, Reel #1.

53. Washington's study was cited in Monroe Nathan Work, ed., "Savings by Negroes Help to Tide Over Industrial Depression," in *Negro Year Book: An Annual Encyclopedia of the Negro, 1921–1922* (Tuskegee, AL: Negro Year Book Co., 1922), 36.

54. Washington, *The Negro in Detroit*, sec. "Thrift and Savings Among the Negroes of Detroit."

55. Work, "Savings by Negroes," 36.

56. Tanzy was sometimes spelled Tanzey. "Hotel Tanzy Advertisement," *Detroit Contender*, November 13, 1920.

57. "Tanzy Hotel Advertisement," *Detroit Contender*, May 7, 1921.

58. Thomas, *Life for Us*, 180–81; and Work, *Negro Year Book*, 371.

59. W. E. B. Du Bois, ed., *Economic Co-Operation Among Negro Americans*, Conference for the Study of the Negro Problems (Atlanta: Atlanta University Press, 1907).

60. Robert E. Weems Jr., *Desegregating the Dollar: African American Consumerism in the Twentieth Century* (New York: New York University Press, 1998), 58.

61. For more on Black cooperative economics, see Jessica Gordon Nembhard, *Collective Courage: A History of African American Cooperative Economic Thought and Practice* (University Park: Pennsylvania State University Press, 2014).

62. Thomas, *Life for Us*, 174.

63. Thomas, *Life for Us*, 178, 180.

64. Thomas, *Life for Us*, 213.

65. Van B. Cannon, "'Fat' Greek Restaurants Versus 'Lean' Colored Restaurants, and Why?" *Detroit Contender*, November 13, 1920. For more on white competition in Black business districts, see Juliet E. K. Walker, *The History of Black Business in America: Capitalism, Race, Entrepreneurship* (New York: Twayne, 1998), 213–17.

66. Deborah Gray White frames the National Association of Colored Women (NACW) as "allied, not united" to push beyond a narrative of altruism and account for class and cultural differences within the NACW. These women's "alliance was based on race and sex sameness and the sentiments that flowed from this kinship—not on social or cultural unity." Deborah Gray White, *Too Heavy a Load: Black Women in Defense of Themselves, 1894–1994* (New York: W. W. Norton, 1999), 78.

67. Lawrence Levine, "Marcus Garvey and the Politics of Revitalization," in *The Unpredictable Past: Explorations in American Cultural History* (New York: Oxford University Press, 1993), 123. For more on women's role in the UNIA, see Keisha N. Blain, *Set the World on Fire: Black Nationalist Women and the Global Struggle for Freedom*, Politics and Culture in Modern America (Philadelphia: University of Pennsylvania Press, 2018).

68. "Objectives of the Universal Negro Improvement Association," in Robert A. Hill, ed., *The Marcus Garvey and Universal Negro Improvement Association Papers, Volume I, 1826–August 1919* (Berkeley: University of California Press, 1983).

69. David Allan Levine, *Internal Combustion: The Races in Detroit, 1915–1926* (Westport, CT: Greenwood Press, 1976), 101.

70. Charisse Burden-Stelly notes that "Garvey's Black Nationalism was a powerful critique of Capitalist Racist Society. . . . Garvey's emphasis on race first, race pride, self-reliance, and the autonomous development of the Black race was considered radical agitation" in the context of racial capitalism. Charisse Burden-Stelly, *Black Scare/Red Scare: Theorizing Capitalist Racism in the United States* (Chicago: University of Chicago Press, 2023), 8.

71. Marcus Garvey, "West Indies in the Mirror of Truth," *Champion Magazine*, January 1917.

72. Marcus Garvey, "Editorial Letter," June 4, 1919, in Hill, *Marcus Garvey . . . Papers, Volume I*, 413–14; "Biltmore Hotel Group Profile," *Detroit Contender*, November 13, 1920.

73. Booker T. Washington Trade Association, *Directory*, 1935, HLDAP, Box 5, Folder: BTWTA Directories; "Biltmore Hotel Group Profile."

74. Garvey, "Editorial Letter."

75. Robert A. Hill, ed., *The Marcus Garvey and Universal Negro Improvement Association Papers, Volume IX: Africa for the Africans, June 1921–December 1922* (Berkeley: University of California Press, 1995), 556n2; Levine, "Marcus Garvey and the Politics of Revitalization," 134–35; Levine, *Internal Combustion*, 101–2. For information on the "Garvey Must Go" campaign, see Harry H. Pace et al., "Letter to Harry M. Daugherty, United States Attorney-General," in *The Philosophy and Opinions of Marcus Garvey: Africa for the Africans*, ed. Amy Jacques Garvey (London: Routledge, 1978), 294–99; Sheldon Avery, *Up from Washington: William Pickens and the Negro Struggle for Equality, 1900–1954* (Newark: University of Delaware Press, 1989), 68–71; and D'Weston Haywood, *Let Us Make Men: The Twentieth-Century Black Press and Manly Vision for Racial Advancement* (Chapel Hill: University of North Carolina Press, 2018), 57–96. For more information on the Black Star Line and its failure, see Judith Stein, *The World of Marcus Garvey: Race and Class in Modern Society* (Baton Rouge: Louisiana State University Press, 1986).

76. Contemporary rivals such as Reverend Robert W. Bagnall, a Detroit NAACP activist and minister, likened Garvey to Judas Iscariot and once described him as "cunning, shifty, smooth and suave, avaricious . . . prolix to the 'nth degree in devising new schemes to gain the money of poor ignorant Negroes; gifted at self-advertisement . . .

promising ever, but never fulfilling, without regard for veracity . . . a sheer opportunist and a demagogic charlatan." Robert W. Bagnall, "The Madness of Marcus Garvey," *The Messenger*, March 1923. Historian Judith Stein has also compared Garvey's tactics to those of con man Charles Ponzi and others. Stein, *World of Marcus Garvey*, 102–4, 161–69.

77. Stein, *World of Marcus Garvey*, 61–97.

78. Unfortunately, the papers of the Detroit UNIA have not been preserved. According to Judith Stein, "The absence of a full set of raw materials . . . makes sound scholarship on Garvey and the UNIA a difficult task. The Justice department seized, and subsequently destroyed, UNIA records in 1922 when it indicted UNIA leaders. The UNIA's factional wars led to the destruction and scattering of organizational papers" (*World of Marcus Garvey*, 2). While the available evidence is limited, it suggests that the Detroit UNIA played an important role in uniting Black entrepreneurs and fostering an ethos of business cooperation in the city. The organization also helped generate a network of entrepreneurs that outlasted the organization's decline after Garvey's imprisonment.

79. Victoria W. Wolcott, *Remaking Respectability: African American Women in Interwar Detroit* (Chapel Hill: University of North Carolina Press, 2001), 127.

80. Levine, *Internal Combustion*, 101.

81. Robert A. Hill, ed., *The Marcus Garvey and Universal Negro Improvement Association Papers, Volume IV: September 1921–September 1922* (Berkeley: University of California Press, 1985), 804n1; Thomas, *Life for Us*, 194–98.

82. Stein, *World of Marcus Garvey*, 87; list of contributors and amounts of contribution to "Rehabilitation and Expansion Fund," *Negro World* (New York), July 3 and September 4, 1926, as cited in Levine, *Internal Combustion*, 101.

83. Stein, *World of Marcus Garvey*, 230–31; Robert A. Hill, ed., *The Marcus Garvey and Universal Negro Improvement Association Papers, Volume V: September 1922–August 1924* (Berkeley: University of California Press, 1987), 245.

84. "Classified Detroit Negro Business Directory," 1927, HLDP, Box 4, Folder: Awards and Certificates, Advertising Agreements.

85. Jeannette Smith-Irvin, *Footsoldiers of the Universal Negro Improvement Association: Their Own Words* (Trenton, NJ: Africa World Press, 1989), 47.

86. Detroit Bureau of Governmental Research and Detroit Mayor's Inter-racial Committee, *The Negro in Detroit*, sec. "Community Organization," 6–7.

87. Boykin, *Hand Book*, 44–45; and Thomas, *Life for Us*, 194–201.

88. The UNIA's newspaper, the *Negro World*, highly commended the Postons for using the *Detroit Contender* to gain local support for the organization. Thomas, *Life for Us*, 197.

89. The most thorough accounts of the Postons' lives and activities are provided in Tony Martin, *Literary Garveyism: Garvey, Black Arts, and the Harlem Renaissance* (Dover, MA: Majority Press, 1983); Kathleen A. Hauke, *Ted Poston: Pioneer American Journalist* (Athens: University of Georgia Press, 1998); and Ted Poston, *The Dark Side*

of Hopkinsville, ed. Kathleen A. Hauke (Athens: University of Georgia Press, 1991), xvii–xviii.

90. Hauke, *Ted Poston*, 16.

91. Jack Glazier, *Been Coming Through Some Hard Times: Race, History, and Memory in Western Kentucky* (Knoxville: University of Tennessee Press, 2012), 141; Martin, *Literary Garveyism*, 71.

92. Martin, *Literary Garveyism*, 70–73.

93. Martin, *Literary Garveyism*, 71.

94. "And Yet We Smile," *Detroit Contender*, November 13, 1920.

95. "Business," *Detroit Contender*, November 13, 1920.

96. Robert L. Bradby, "Rev. R. L. Bradby Hits the Nail on the Head Again," *Detroit Contender*, November 13, 1920.

97. Bradby, "Rev. R. L. Bradby Hits the Nail on the Head Again."

98. The Postons' newspaper continued to thrive until they decided to close the *Contender* and accept the opportunity to become Garvey's associates in the New York City UNIA. The brothers rose quite high in the organization, particularly Robert, and both contributed to the UNIA publication the *Negro World*. Glazier, *Been Coming Through Some Hard Times*, 141; Martin, *Literary Garveyism*, 71–72.

99. Bates, *The Making of Black Detroit*, 7–8; Angela D. Dillard, *Faith in the City: Preaching Radical Social Change in Detroit* (Ann Arbor: University of Michigan Press, 2007), 64–68.

100. Bradby, "Rev. R. L. Bradby Hits the Nail on the Head Again."

101. Bradby, "Rev. R. L. Bradby Hits the Nail on the Head Again."

102. John C. Dancy, "Director's Report," June 10, 1920, DUL-M, Reel #1.

103. "Urban League Board Report," September 14, 1922, DUL-M, Reel #1.

104. Martin, *Detroit and the Great Migration*, 4.

105. Phyllis Vine, *One Man's Castle: Clarence Darrow in Defense of the American Dream* (New York: Harper Collins, 2004), 207; Thomas, *Life for Us*, 26.

106. Turner and Moses, *Colored Detroit*, 40–41.

107. Turner and Moses, *Colored Detroit*, 55–56.

108. Turner and Moses, *Colored Detroit*, 55–56; Washington, *The Negro in Detroit*, sec. "The Health of the Negro in Detroit."

109. Detroit Bureau of Governmental Research and Detroit Mayor's Inter-racial Committee, *The Negro in Detroit*, sec. "Thrift and Business," 13–17, 25.

110. Although the report says "business men" were surveyed, there was at least one woman entrepreneur included in the study. Detroit Bureau of Governmental Research and Detroit Mayor's Inter-racial Committee, *The Negro in Detroit*, sec. "Thrift and Business," 17–18.

111. Turner and Moses, *Colored Detroit*, 16.

112. "The Best Apron Shop," advertisement, Turner and Moses, *Colored Detroit*, 16.

113. Detroit Bureau of Governmental Research and Detroit Mayor's Inter-racial Committee, *The Negro in Detroit*, sec. "Thrift and Business," 13–14.

114. Detroit Bureau of Governmental Research and Detroit Mayor's Inter-racial Committee, *The Negro in Detroit*, sec. "Thrift and Business," 15, 19.

115. Thomas, *Life for Us*, 184–85; Detroit Bureau of Governmental Research and Detroit Mayor's Inter-racial Committee, *The Negro in Detroit*, sec. "Thrift and Business," 7.

116. Michigan People's Finance Corporation Application for a Mortgage from the Detroit Savings Bank, February 6, 1929, DUL, Box 9, Folder 13.

117. Detroit Bureau of Governmental Research and Detroit Mayor's Inter-racial Committee, *The Negro in Detroit*, sec. "Thrift and Business," 3; "Michigan People's Finance Corporation" advertisement, Turner and Moses, *Colored Detroit*, 5.

118. John C. Dancy, director of the Detroit Urban League, served as president and treasurer of the Michigan People's Finance Corporation for several years. It is likely that he wrote some of the information that appeared in the financial review section. Thomas, *Life for Us*, 214, 83.

119. Clark-Lewis, *Living In, Living Out*, 108–13, 123–25, 166.

120. Washington, *The Negro in Detroit*, sec. "The Negro Woman in the Industries of Detroit."

121. Wolcott, *Remaking Respectability*, 88–89. Forrester Washington reported that prior to 1910, about 98 percent of Black working women in Detroit were employed in some form of personal service while about 2 percent were employed as teachers. He divided personal service into categories of "skilled" and "unskilled." Skilled personal service included occupations such as manicuring, hairdressing, dressmaking, cooking, etc., but some women categorized as "skilled personal service" workers were in fact entrepreneurs who operated independent enterprises. Washington, *The Negro in Detroit*, sec. "The Negro Woman in the Industries of Detroit."

122. Warren, *Michigan Manual*, 37–38; "Eleanora DeVere Listing," in *Detroit City Directory, 1910*, 3025; "Eleanora DeVere Classified Business Listing," in *Polk's Detroit City Directory, 1916* (Detroit: R. L. Polk & Company, 1916), 3555.

123. DeVere's dressmaker listing in a business directory provides the same address (230 Bagg Street) recorded as her home address in the 1920 U.S. census. This is different from the address of the salon that she operated from 1919 to at least 1932 (2509 St. Antoine Street). "Eleanora DeVere Listing" (1910); "Eleanora DeVere in the 1920 United States Federal Census" (United States of America, Bureau of the Census, 1920); "Eleanora DeVere Listing," in *Polk's Detroit City Directory, 1932* (Detroit: R. L. Polk & Company, 1932), 2226.

124. "Eleanora DeVere Listing," in *Polk's Detroit City Directory, 1915* (Detroit: R. L. Polk & Company, 1915), 3195; "Eleanora DeVere Profile," *Detroit Contender*, November 13, 1920.

125. "Eleanora DeVere Profile"; Turner and Moses, *Colored Detroit*, 21.

126. "Eleanora DeVere Profile."

127. Boyle, *Arc of Justice*, 7.

128. Boyle, *Arc of Justice*, 8–9.

129. Vine, *One Man's Castle*, 79–80; Boyle, *Arc of Justice*, 8; Kenneth T. Jackson, *The Ku Klux Klan in the City, 1915–1930* (New York: Oxford University Press, 1967), 129.

130. "Michigan Is Engulfed in Klan Wave," *Fiery Cross* (Indiana State Edition), August 17, 1923.

131. Kathleen M. Blee, *Women of the Klan: Racism and Gender in the 1920s* (Berkeley: University of California Press, 1991), 151–53. Additionally, Blee states that Women of the Ku Klux Klan (WKKK) joined the KKK in promoting local Klan members' businesses and often boycotted businesses they did not perceive as "100 percent American" (147–51).

132. Calvin W. Enders, "Under Grand Haven's White Sheets," *Michigan Historical Review* 19, no. 1 (1993): 48.

133. Jackson, *The Ku Klux Klan*, 133.

134. Boyle, *Arc of Justice*, 101.

135. Vine, *One Man's Castle*, 2; Boyle, *Arc of Justice*, 146.

136. Sugrue, *Origins*, 34. For more information on racial discrimination and residential segregation in Detroit, see Sugrue, *Origins*; Reynolds Farley, Sheldon Danziger, and Harry J. Holzer, *Detroit Divided* (New York: Russell Sage Foundation, 2000); David M. P. Freund, *Colored Property: State Policy and White Racial Politics in Suburban America* (Chicago: University of Chicago Press, 2007); Richard Rothstein, *The Color of Law: A Forgotten History of How Our Government Segregated America* (New York: Liveright, 2017), 58, 74, 80, 104, 128–29, 214, 223.

137. Boyle, *Arc of Justice*, 9. Boyle discusses the exploitative lending arrangement the Sweets had to enter in order to buy their home on page 146.

138. Vine, *One Man's Castle*, 7–10; Boyle, *Arc of Justice*, 67–69. This is just one example of the ways the migrant identity was persistent, and Black migrant entrepreneurs' experiences in Detroit were shaped by their participation in the Great Migration in ways that resonated long after they arrived.

139. Vine, *One Man's Castle*, 56.

140. Boyle, *One Man's Castle*, 35–41.

141. For more information on the case of Ossian Sweet, see Kenneth G. Weinberg, *A Man's Home, A Man's Castle* (New York: McCall Publishing, 1971); Vine, *One Man's Castle*; Boyle, *Arc of Justice*; Donald McRae, *The Old Devil: Clarence Darrow: The World's Greatest Trial Lawyer* (New York: Simon and Schuster, 2009).

142. Boyle, *Arc of Justice*, 152–53.

143. Boyle, *Arc of Justice*, 153–56.

144. Quoted in Boyle, *Arc of Justice*, 134.

145. Weinberg, *A Man's Home*, 28; Boyle, *Arc of Justice*, 39.

146. Weinberg, *A Man's Home*, 10.

147. "Report of the Urban League for the Months of June, July, and August 1929," September 1929, DUL-M, Reel #1.

148. Suzanne E. Smith, *To Serve the Living: Funeral Directors and the African American Way of Death* (Cambridge, MA: Belknap Press, 2010), 64–65.

149. Carolyn P. DuBose, *The Untold Story of Charles Diggs: The Public Figure, the Private Man* (Arlington, VA: Barton Publishing House, 1998), 5; Thomas, *Life for Us*, 265; Smith, *To Serve the Living*, 64.

150. Thomas, *Life for Us*, 196, 199.

151. Smith, *To Serve the Living*, 64–65; Roberta Hughes Wright, *Detroit Memorial Park Cemetery: The Evolution of an African American Corporation* (Southfield, MI: Charro Book Company, 1993).

152. "Memorial Park Cemetery" advertisement, *Detroit Independent*, June 10, 1927; "Memorial Park Cemetery" advertisement, *Detroit Independent*, September 16, 1927; Smith, *To Serve the Living*, 64–65.

Chapter 3

1. Bailey had witnessed the body of a "dead and rotten" Black man being fished out of a pond, presumably the victim of a lynching by local whites. This was Bailey's inauguration into what Angelou describes as "the enigma that young Southern Black boys start to unravel, start to try to unravel, from seven years old to death. The humorless puzzle of inequality and hate." Maya Angelou, *I Know Why the Caged Bird Sings* (New York: Bantam Books, 1993), 194–99.

2. Angelou, *I Know Why the Caged Bird Sings*, 199–225.

3. Coleman Young and Lonnie Wheeler, *Hard Stuff: The Autobiography of Mayor Coleman Young* (New York: Viking, 1994), 35. For more on Black survivalist entrepreneurship during the Great Depression, see Robert L. Boyd, "Survivalist Entrepreneurship Among Urban Blacks During the Great Depression: A Test of the Disadvantage Theory of Business Enterprise," *Social Science Quarterly* 81, no. 4 (December 2000): 972–84.

4. Young and Wheeler, *Hard Stuff*, 17–18.

5. These ideas were not unique to Detroit. In Harlem, the numbers business was not viewed as a major nuisance and some argued that "lotteries of any kind should not be put in the same illegal category as burglary and other major crimes." Shane White et al., *Playing the Numbers: Gambling in Harlem between the Wars* (Cambridge, MA: Harvard University Press, 2010), 219.

6. Young and Wheeler, *Hard Stuff*, 19–20.

7. Young and Wheeler, *Hard Stuff*, 17–18.

8. Kevin Mumford, *Interzones: Black/White Sex Districts in Chicago and New York in the Early Twentieth Century* (New York: Columbia University Press, 1997), 16–18.

9. Karen R. Miller, *Managing Inequality: Northern Racial Liberalism in Interwar Detroit* (New York: New York University Press, 2015), 106–7; Victoria W. Wolcott, *Remaking Respectability: African American Women in Interwar Detroit* (Chapel Hill: University of North Carolina Press, 2001), 101–6; Jayne Morris-Crowther, *The Political Activities of Detroit Clubwomen in the 1920s: A Challenge and a Promise* (Detroit: Wayne State University Press, 2013), 86–93.

10. Wolcott, *Remaking Respectability*, 101; Holly M. Karibo, *Sin City North: Sex, Drugs, and Citizenship in the Detroit-Windsor Borderland* (Chapel Hill: University of

North Carolina Press, 2015), 5; Sarah Elvins, "Lady Smugglers and Lynx-Eyed Customs Agents: Gender, Morality, and Cross-Border Shopping in Detroit and Windsor," *Canadian Historical Review* 101, no. 4 (December 1, 2020): 497–521.

11. Wolcott, *Remaking Respectability*, 102; and Forrester B. Washington, "Report of Secretary to First Meeting of Joint Committee," July 17, 1916, WPRL, Box 34, Folder 19, as cited in Wolcott, *Remaking Respectability*, 102.

12. George Edmund Haynes, *Negro New-Comers in Detroit, Michigan: A Challenge to Christian Statesmanship, a Preliminary Survey* (New York: Home Missions Council, 1918), 8; and Wolcott, *Remaking Respectability*, 102.

13. Washington, "Report of Secretary to First Meeting of Joint Committee."

14. Haynes, *Negro New-Comers*, 8.

15. Detroit Bureau of Governmental Research and Detroit Mayor's Inter-racial Committee, *The Negro in Detroit* (Detroit, 1926), sec. "Recreation," 18–19.

16. Forrester B. Washington, *The Negro in Detroit: A Survey of the Conditions of a Negro Group in a Northern Industrial Center During the War Prosperity Period* (Detroit: Research Bureau Associated Charities of Detroit, 1920), sec. "The Housing of the Negro in Detroit."

17. LaShawn Harris, *Sex Workers, Psychics, and Numbers Runners: Black Women in New York City's Underground Economy* (Urbana: University of Illinois Press, 2016), 37–39; Victoria W. Wolcott, "The Culture of the Informal Economy: Numbers Running in Interwar Black Detroit," *Radical History Review* 69 (1997): 50.

18. Beth Tompkins Bates, *The Making of Black Detroit in the Age of Henry Ford* (Chapel Hill: University of North Carolina Press, 2012), 62, 65–66, 252.

19. Charles Denby, *Indignant Heart: A Black Worker's Journal* (Boston: South End Press, 1978; Detroit: Wayne State University Press, 1989), 35–36.

20. Kevin Boyle, *Arc of Justice: A Saga of Race, Civil Rights, and Murder in the Jazz Age* (New York: Holt, 2004), 104.

21. Bates, *The Making of Black Detroit*, 288n39.

22. Roaldus Richmond, "Open All Night," Folklore Project, Life Histories, 1936–39 MSS55715: Box A738, WPA Federal Writers' Project Collection, Manuscript Division, Library of Congress.

23. Elaine Latzman Moon, *Untold Tales, Unsung Heroes: An Oral History of Detroit's African American Community, 1918–1967* (Detroit: Wayne State University Press, 1994), 140; Georgia S. Schuyler, "Negro Editor Condemns Ford's Uncle Toms: Finds Ford Propaganda Machine Eager to Divide Workers," *United Automobile Worker* 5 (March 1938), as cited in Bates, *The Making of Black Detroit*, 229–30.

24. Denby, *Indignant Heart*, 36.

25. Maurice Sugar, *The Ford Hunger March* (Berkeley, CA: Meiklejohn Civil Liberties Institute, 1980), 30–38.

26. Darlene Clark Hine, "The Housewives' League of Detroit: Black Women and Economic Nationalism," in *Visible Women: New Essays on American Activism*, ed. Nancy A. Hewitt and Suzanne Lebsock (Urbana: University of Illinois Press, 1993), 228.

27. Ernestine E. Wright quoted in Moon, *Untold Tales, Unsung Heroes*, 94; Wolcott, *Remaking Respectability*, 80–82, 170–71. For more on Black women's engagement in the urban sex economy, see Harris, *Sex Workers*, 123–66; Cynthia M. Blair, *I've Got to Make My Livin': Black Women's Sex Work in Turn-of-the-Century Chicago* (Chicago: University of Chicago Press, 2018).

28. Detroit Bureau of Governmental Research and Detroit Mayor's Inter-racial Committee, *The Negro in Detroit*, sec. "Recreation," 18–19.

29. Ulysses W. Boykin, *A Hand Book on the Detroit Negro* (Detroit: Minority Study Associates, 1943), 97.

30. Glen S. Taylor, "Prostitution in Detroit," Study for the Earhart Foundation for Community Leadership and the Department of Sociology of the University of Michigan, typewritten manuscript, 1933, as cited in Wolcott, *Remaking Respectability*, 175.

31. Wolcott, *Remaking Respectability*, 175; and Kathy Peiss, *Cheap Amusements: Working Women and Leisure in Turn-of-the-Century New York* (Philadelphia: Temple University Press, 1985), 110.

32. "Report of Director to the Joint Committee," November 9, 1916, DUL-M, Reel #1.

33. Harris, *Sex Workers*, 46.

34. Boykin, *Hand Book*, 97.

35. Richard W. Thomas, *Life for Us Is What We Make It: Building Black Community in Detroit, 1915–1945* (Bloomington: Indiana University Press, 1992), 114.

36. Matthew Vaz, *Running the Numbers: Race, Police, and the History of Urban Gambling* (Chicago: University of Chicago Press, 2020), 79.

37. Ulysses W. Boykin, "The Bulletin Board," *Detroit Tribune*, April 13, 1940.

38. Detroit Bureau of Governmental Research and Detroit Mayor's Inter-racial Committee, *Negro in Detroit*, sec. "Recreation," 1–38.

39. Thomas, *Life for Us*, 114.

40. "Inquiry Aimed at Gun Permits," *Detroit Free Press*, January 31, 1940; "Spann Denied His Men Protect Policy Houses," *Detroit Tribune*, February 3, 1940; *Charter of the City of Detroit* (The City of Detroit, 1918), 95.

41. "Owner Arrested in Cafe Slaying," *Detroit Evening Times*, September 25, 1944; "Louis Spann Kills Man in Tavern Row," *Michigan Chronicle*, September 30, 1944; "Spann to Be Sentenced on Murder Count," *Michigan Chronicle*, June 9, 1945.

42. Thomas, *Life for Us*, 113–16.

43. William J. Robinson, editor of the *Detroit Independent*, quoted in H. O. Weitschat, "Crimes by Negroes Running High," *Detroit Saturday Night*, December 24, 1927, as cited in Wolcott, *Remaking Respectability*, 101–2.

44. *Detroit Tribune*, December 28, 1940, January 4, 1941, as cited in Thomas, *Life for Us*, 115–16.

45. Davarian L. Baldwin, *Chicago's New Negroes: Modernity, the Great Migration, and Black Urban Life* (Chapel Hill: University of North Carolina Press, 2009), 51.

46. St. Clair Drake and Horace R. Cayton, *Black Metropolis: A Study of Negro Life in a Northern City* (1945; repr., Chicago: University of Chicago Press, 1962), 490–91.

47. Boykin, *Hand Book*, 94–95.

48. Charles Weber, "Honor Among Thieves? Not at the Gotham," *Detroit Free Press*, December 6, 1962.

49. Young and Wheeler, *Hard Stuff*, 35.

50. Quoted in Moon, *Untold Tales, Unsung Heroes*, 170.

51. Quoted in Moon, *Untold Tales, Unsung Heroes*, 90–91.

52. In May 1917, the state legislature passed Governor Act No. 161 (commonly called the Damon Act) and Act No. 338 (known as the Wiley Act). The latter made it unlawful to manufacture, sell or keep for sale, give away, barter, furnish, or otherwise dispose of intoxicating liquors, while the Damon Act covered bringing and carrying into the state and receiving and possessing intoxicating liquors. Both acts went into effect on May 1, 1918. Ralph W. Aigler, "Repeals by Implication: Prohibition in Michigan," *Michigan Law Review* 17, no. 6 (1919): 495–96.

53. Boyle, *Arc of Justice*, 103; Ford R. Bryan, *Henry's Lieutenants* (Detroit: Wayne State University Press, 2003), 70.

54. Young and Wheeler, *Hard Stuff*, 21–22; Karibo, *Sin City North*, 5; Lisa McGirr, *The War on Alcohol: Prohibition and the Rise of the American State* (New York: W. W. Norton, 2016), 99. See also Philip P. Mason, *Rumrunning and the Roaring Twenties: Prohibition on the Michigan-Ontario Waterway* (Detroit: Wayne State University Press, 1995).

55. Young and Wheeler, *Hard Stuff*, 21–22.

56. Detroit News Staff, "Prohibition, Smuggling, Automobiles, Lake St. Clair, Detroit, 1920s," December 10, 1929, Prohibition in Southeastern Michigan Image Gallery, Photo ID 27827, WPRL, http://reuther.wayne.edu/node/8246.

57. Moon, *Untold Tales, Unsung Heroes*, 46.

58. Detroit News Staff, "Prohibition, Smuggling, Detroit, 1920s," Prohibition in Southeastern Michigan Image Gallery, Photo ID 27832, WPRL, http://reuther.wayne.edu/node/8251.

59. Quoted in Moon, *Untold Tales, Unsung Heroes*, 46.

60. "Legal Beer Flows in 19 States . . . State Has to Wait at Least 10 Days," *Detroit Free Press*, April 7, 1933.

61. "Gold's Drug Store Advertisement," *Detroit Tribune*, May 20, 1933; "Mack's Barbecue & Beer Palace," *Detroit Tribune*, May 27, 1933.

62. "Williams' Cafe Advertisement," *Detroit Tribune*, September 9, 1933.

63. "New Café—Detroit's Finest and Best," *Detroit Tribune*, May 27, 1933.

64. "W. S. Fornay Advertisement," *Detroit Tribune*, September 30, 1933.

65. "Cotton Club Advertisement," *Detroit Tribune*, May 13, 1933.

66. For a discussion of the numbers business in Detroit during the interwar years, see Wolcott, "Culture of the Informal Economy"; and Thomas, *Life for Us*, 110–22. For more on the gambling and numbers business in New York, see White et al., *Playing the Numbers*; Harris, *Sex Workers*; and Douglas J. Flowe, *Uncontrollable Blackness: African American Men and Criminality in Jim Crow New York* (Chapel Hill: University of North

Carolina Press, 2020), 58–93. For more on the numbers business in Chicago, see Baldwin, *Chicago's New Negroes*, 45–51; Elizabeth Schroeder Schlabach, *Dream Books and Gamblers: Black Women's Work in Chicago's Policy Game* (Urbana: University of Illinois Press, 2022); and Drake and Cayton, *Black Metropolis*, 470–94. For more on the history of urban gambling and policing, see Vaz, *Running the Numbers*.

67. Boykin, *Hand Book*, 94–96; Vaz, *Running the Numbers*, 2–3; Young and Wheeler, *Hard Stuff*, 19–20. "Yellow Dog" refers to the Yazoo Delta railroad line that ran from Clarksdale to Yazoo City, Mississippi. African Americans assigned the words "Yellow Dog" to the letters "Y.D." that were painted on the freight trains. W. C. Handy, *Father of the Blues: An Autobiography*, ed. Arna Bontemps (New York: Macmillan, 1941; New York: Da Capo Press, 1991), 71–72.

68. Sunnie Wilson with John Cohassey, *Toast of the Town: The Life and Times of Sunnie Wilson* (Detroit: Wayne State University Press, 1998), 66.

69. Boykin, *Hand Book*, 111.

70. Detroit Bureau of Governmental Research and Detroit Mayor's Inter-racial Committee, *Negro in Detroit*, sec. "Recreation," 18.

71. Gustav Gunnar Carlson, "Number Gambling: A Study of a Culture Complex" (PhD diss., University of Michigan, 1940), 150.

72. Thomas, *Life for Us*, 117–18.

73. Young and Wheeler, *Hard Stuff*, 19–20.

74. Wilson, *Toast of the Town*, 67.

75. Boykin, *Hand Book*, 110–11.

76. Wilson, *Toast of the Town*, 66.

77. "Boxing?" *Atlanta Constitution*, December 21, 1941; "Louis Aspires to Leave Ring Still Champion," *St. Cloud Times*, October 7, 1937; "Joe Louis Is Ready to Quit Ring for 1939," *Santa Cruz Sentinel*, September 10, 1939; "John Roxborough, Former Numbers Racket Czar," *News-Journal*, October 9, 1946; Young and Wheeler, *Hard Stuff*, 28; Thomas, *Life for Us*, 116; and Wolcott, *Remaking Respectability*, 196.

78. Boykin, *Hand Book*, 95; Thomas, *Life for Us*, 116.

79. That one hundred forty Black women employees were arrested during a raid on one numbers bank substantiates this claim. Evidence also suggests that Ida Watson was involved in the numbers empire run by her husband, Everett Watson. Wolcott, "Culture of the Informal Economy," 64–65; "Grand Jury Starts Move to Extradite Fugitive to Detroit," *Detroit Tribune*, February 11, 1940; "Ex-Mayor Faces Five-Year Term," *Detroit Free Press*, December 16, 1941. For more on Black women entrepreneurs in the numbers racket, see Harris, *Sex Workers*, 15, 46, 54–55, 57, 68–72; and Schlabach, *Dream Books and Gamblers*.

80. Charleszetta Waddles, interview by Marcia McAdoo Greenlee, March 28, 1980, transcript, Black Women Oral History Project, Interviews, 1976–1981, Charleszetta Waddles, OH-31, Schlesinger Library, Radcliffe Institute, Harvard University; and Wolcott, *Remaking Respectability*, 122.

81. Quoted in Wolcott, "Culture of the Informal Economy," 53.

82. "Strike Called in Detroit's Policy Game," *Detroit Free Press*, December 3, 1941. Workers in Chicago's illegal gambling industry also organized and went on strike. Drake and Cayton, *Black Metropolis*, 482–84.

83. "Press Confiscated in Raid by Myers," *Detroit Free Press*, February 18, 1940.

84. Wolcott, "Culture of the Informal Economy," 56–58; Drake and Cayton, *Black Metropolis*, 474–78.

85. Carlson, "Number Gambling," 55–56.

86. "Dream Author Gets Real Cash and Ends Suit," *Detroit Free Press*, December 4, 1940.

87. Thomas, *Life for Us*, 116; and Wolcott, "Culture of the Informal Economy," 56.

88. Quoted in Moon, *Untold Tales, Unsung Heroes*, 78.

89. Wilson, *Toast of the Town*, 66–67.

90. Carlson, "Number Gambling," 148. For more on Detroit religious leaders' opposition to and acceptance of the numbers game, see Thomas, *Life for Us*, 117. Drake and Cayton noted that the majority of civic and religious leaders in Chicago also did not think of the numbers game as "vice" and could "not arouse any righteous indignation against the game." Drake and Cayton, *Black Metropolis*, 491–92.

91. Boykin, *Hand Book*, 94–95, 110–11.

92. Wolcott, *Remaking Respectability*, 169. Wolcott also discusses the ambiguity of Detroit's formal and informal economy on pp. 94–95. Davarian Baldwin examines the links between the formal and informal economy in Chicago. In describing the businesses on the Stroll, Baldwin draws attention to the mixing of legal and illegal business interests, arguing that while "the 'official' history of Chicago's black business world" credits respectable "old settler" businessmen, "in fact, it was the underworld of policy gambling that stabilized the city's black economy and social world, especially during the Depression." Policy gambling money provided capital for the development of many aspects of the "Black Metropolis," such as music clubs, films, commercial sports, banks, politicians, churches, and smaller businesses. Baldwin, *Chicago's New Negroes*, 48–50. See also White et al., *Playing the Numbers*, 19-22.

93. Wilson, *Toast of the Town*, 66–67.

94. Wolcott, "Culture of the Informal Economy," 69.

95. Detroit Bureau of Governmental Research and Detroit Mayor's Inter-racial Committee, *The Negro in Detroit*, sec. "Thrift and Business."

96. Arthur Turner and Earl R. Moses, eds., *Colored Detroit: A Brief History of Detroit's Colored Population and a Directory of Their Businesses, Organizations, Professions and Trades* (Detroit, 1924), 5.

97. Michigan People's Finance Corporation Application for a Mortgage from the Detroit Savings Bank, February 6, 1929, DUL, Box 9, Folder 13; Turner and Moses, *Colored Detroit*, 53; Michigan People's Finance Corporation Building Committee Report, January 22, 1929, DUL, Box 9, Folder 13; "To the Michigan People's Finance Corporation," January 29, 1929, DUL, Box 9, Folder 13; "Henry Stevens Is Dead at 55," *Detroit*

Free Press, February 13, 1934; Mortgage Agreement Between Henry G. Stevens and Michigan People's Finance Corporation, June 19, 1929, DUL, Box 9, Folder 13; Mortgage Agreement Between Henry G. Stevens and Michigan People's Finance Corporation, August 10, 1929, DUL, Box 9, Folder 13.

98. "Analysis of Loans," DUL, Box 9, Folder 13; "Semi-Annual Review of the Current Operations of the Michigan People's Finance Corporation, January 1–June 30, 1929," June 30, 1929, DUL, Box 9, Folder 13.

99. "Comparison of Income and Expenses for the Two Years Ending March 31, 1929, 1930," DUL, Box 9, Folder 14; Ferdinand W. Penn, untitled document, ca. 1930, DUL, Box 9, Folder 14.

100. It is unclear how long the company continued to operate. The Detroit Urban League's manuscript collection at the University of Michigan's Bentley Historical Library has three folders on the MPFC and the last document in these folders is dated June 30, 1938. I have not been able to locate any references to the company after this date.

101. Wolcott, "Culture of the Informal Economy," 52.

102. Leroy Mitchell Jr., interview by Deborah Evans, November 15, 1990, transcript, 12, DPL; Moon, *Untold Tales, Unsung Heroes*, 85.

103. Carlson, "Number Gambling," 153; Thomas, *Life for Us*, 118; Wolcott, "Culture of the Informal Economy," 55.

104. Merah S. Stuart, *An Economic Detour: A History of Insurance in the Lives of American Negroes* (New York: Wendell Malliet, 1940), 66; Thomas, *Life for Us*, 116, 204.

105. Stuart, *Economic Detour*, 66, 71; "Joe Louis Is Ready to Quit Ring for 1939."

106. Jimmy Powers, "The Power House," *Daily News*, April 25, 1940.

107. Mark Haller, "Policy Gambling, Entertainment, and the Emergence of Black Politics: Chicago from 1900 to 1940," *Journal of Social History* 24, no. 4 (1991): 739n43; Wolcott, "Culture of the Informal Economy," 52–53.

108. Carlson, "Number Gambling," 54–55.

109. Vaz, *Running the Numbers*, 3.

110. Wilson, *Toast of the Town*, 67. According to Sunnie Wilson, law enforcement also played a role in dispelling the mob: "A white mob from Cleveland tried to come and take over, but they were run out of town by my Irish friend, Police Inspector Morgan" (*Toast of the Town*, 66).

111. Young and Wheeler, *Hard Stuff*, 20–21.

112. Carlson, "Number Gambling," 57–68. For more on corrupt police and politicians' connections to illegal business, including gambling, see Haller, "Policy Gambling, Entertainment, and the Emergence of Black Politics"; Vaz, *Running the Numbers*; Flowe, *Uncontrollable Blackness*, 79–80; and Drake and Cayton, *Black Metropolis*, 473, 481–84, 486.

113. Wilson, *Toast of the Town*, 69–72.

114. "Policy Game History Told," *Windsor Star* (Ontario, Canada), September 12, 1938.

115. Mark Haller notes that "because syndicate backers had a strong interest in cultivating friendly relations with police and judges, payments to support politicians—or

to finance their own political careers—were normal business expenses. Furthermore, a policy syndicate, with perhaps a hundred sellers in friendly daily contact with bettors, constituted in itself a formidable political machine to influence voters and get out the vote. And, since many of the small neighborhood businesses—including newspaper stands, barbershops, and saloons—enjoyed a steady income from the sale of policy slips, legitimate businessmen were often allies in the protection of policy gambling. In neighborhoods where policy was popular, then, policy backers were often a significant resource linked to local political organizations" ("Policy Gambling, Entertainment, and the Emergence of Black Politics," 720).

116. Powers, "Power House."

117. The elder Roxborough served three terms as the city attorney for Plaquemine, Louisiana, and was an assistant U.S. attorney in Tennessee. Michigan Freedmen's Progress Commission, *Michigan Manual of Freedmen's Progress*, comp. Francis H. Warren (Detroit, 1915), 49; David M. Katzman, *Before the Ghetto: Black Detroit in the Nineteenth Century* (Urbana: University of Illinois Press, 1973), 64–65, 158.

118. Charles Roxborough Jr.'s election was an impressive feat because he was elected in a predominantly Polish neighborhood. Charles's law clients were mostly Polish, and he was reported to have spoken the language fluently. Prior to his election to state senate, Charles Roxborough Jr. worked as a clerk for Republican governor Chase S. Osborn from 1911 to 1913, ran the Osborn Colored Republican Club in Detroit to support Osborn leading up to the 1914 statehouse election, and served as deputy oil inspector of the City of Detroit. Michigan Freedmen's Progress Commission, *Michigan Manual*, 49; Katzman, *Before the Ghetto*, 64–65, 78, 203–4; "Louis' Climax of Career Has Tragic Moment," *Dayton Herald* (Dayton, OH), January 27, 1942.

119. "Louis' Climax of Career Has Tragic Moment"; Wolcott, *Remaking Respectability*, 196. For more on numbers operators as race leaders and philanthropists, see Carlson, "Number Gambling," 147–50; and Drake and Cayton, *Black Metropolis*, 486–87. Vas also notes, "During the 1920s, the numbers and policy games were operated by black gambling figures with profiles in business, politics and philanthropy" (*Running the Numbers*, 3).

120. Powers, "Power House."

121. Thomas, *Life for Us*, 259–60.

122. Powers, "Power House."

123. Mark Haller has demonstrated that in Chicago, political organizations were tied to the gambling business there as well. According to Haller, "blacks in the 1920s built local political organizations . . . that fostered and protected the development of gambling and entertainment in the black wards." These organizations were linked to the Republican Party. In the 1930s, "Democrats captured permanent control of the city government at the same time that the Depression brought unemployment[;] . . . soon afterward, repeal brought an end to Prohibition. These developments created a crisis for the traditionally Republican politicians of the black belt and for the gambling and entertainment enterprises linked to them. Black politicians and policy gamblers undertook

the painful process of forging new political organizations allied with the now-dominant Democratic Party" ("Policy Gambling, Entertainment, and the Emergence of Black Politics," 721). For more on Black Detroiters' switch from Republican to Democrat, see Thomas, *Life for Us*, 257–69; and Angela D. Dillard, *Faith in the City: Preaching Radical Social Change in Detroit* (Ann Arbor: University of Michigan Press, 2007), 157–62.

124. Thomas, *Life for Us*, 291. In the 1939 election Reading lost to the moderate Edward Jeffries. Dominic J. Capeci, ed., *Detroit and the "Good War": The World War II Letters of Mayor Edward Jeffries and Friends* (Lexington: University Press of Kentucky, 1996), 5–6.

125. In 1944 Charles Diggs Sr. was convicted on two counts of accepting bribes. After serving almost two years in prison he was reelected, but the senate voted to refuse him his seat and subsequently adopted a resolution that ex-convicts could not be seated. Suzanne E. Smith, *To Serve the Living: Funeral Directors and the African American Way of Death* (Cambridge, MA: Belknap Press, 2010), 121–22; "Fall Kills Charles Diggs, Sr.," *Detroit Free Press*, April 26, 1967.

126. Young and Wheeler, *Hard Stuff*, 28–29.

127. Rufus Jarmon, "Woman Scorned Bares Detroit's Bribe Ring," *St. Louis Post-Dispatch*, February 13, 1944. Relatedly, Everett Watson once threatened to "take care of" a policeman who "kept bothering" a numbers game pickup man. The officer was later transferred to another precinct. "Reading Gave Aid to Racket, Ferguson Told," *Detroit Free Press*, May 7, 1940.

128. Jarmon, "Woman Scorned"; "Suspended Police Inspector Says Reading Took $18,000 in Nine Months," *Detroit Free Press*, May 5, 1940.

129. "Suspended Police Inspector"; "Reading Gave Aid to Racket, Ferguson Told."

130. "Suspended Police Inspector."

131. Jarmon, "Woman Scorned."

132. Jarmon, "Woman Scorned."

133. Mitchell, interview, 13–14.

134. Drake and Cayton, *Black Metropolis*, 472–73.

135. Jarmon, "Woman Scorned."

136. "Policy Game History Told." For more on Black "mayors," see note 18 in Chapter 6.

137. Carlson, "Number Gambling," 56–57, plate VI.

138. "Gets Pen Term: Ex–Detroit Mayor Sentenced on Conspiracy Charge," *News-Journal*, January 7, 1942; Jarmon, "Woman Scorned."

139. Jarmon, "Woman Scorned."

140. These included Detroit Police Superintendent Fred W. Frahm, Deputy Superintendent William J. Heidt (who was in charge of anti-gambling enforcement), Sheriff Thomas C. Wilcox, prosecuting attorney Duncan C. McCrea, and John P. McCarthy, commander of Detroit's Racket Squad. Three city councilmen were also indicted as well as two members of the Wayne County Board of Auditors (a third member was dismissed from office but not prosecuted). The Reading administration graft scandal

was covered extensively in local newspapers. See: "McBride Released as Pickert Revives Graft Investigation," *Detroit Free Press*, August 11, 1939; "Grand Jury Seizes Fugitive in Illinois After Long Search," *Detroit Free Press*, February 10, 1940; "Grand Jury Starts Move to Extradite Fugitive to Detroit"; "Watson Case Before Court," *Detroit Tribune*, April 6, 1940; United Press, "Former Mayor Indicted in Policy Probe," *News-Journal*, April 24, 1940; "Suspended Police Inspector"; "Reading Gave Aid to Racket, Ferguson Told"; "Boykin-Mosley Testify in Police Graft Hearing," *Detroit Tribune*, May 11, 1940; "Bombing Comes After Operator's Testimony," *Detroit Tribune*, May 18, 1940; "Policy Payoffs to 17 Charged," *Detroit Free Press*, June 16, 1940; "Graft Figures to Be Recalled," *Detroit Free Press*, June 19, 1940; "Raid Sets Off Gaming Probe," *Detroit Free Press*, September 26, 1940; Kenneth F. McCormick, "Policy Game Is Termed Unmolested," *Detroit Free Press*, October 10, 1941; "Say Reading Was Grafter," *Windsor Star*, November 8, 1941; "Policy Graft Hotly Denied by Reading," *Detroit Free Press*, December 3, 1941; "Ex-Mayor Faces Five-Year Term"; "Reading, 22 Others Guilty in Graft Conspiracy Case," *Detroit Free Press*, December 16, 1941; "Gets Pen Term"; "Numbers Rackets Flourish Despite Police," *Detroit Free Press*, July 26, 1942; "Appeal Lost by Reading," *Windsor Star*, December 30, 1943.

141. Both men appealed their convictions but were denied. After serving slightly less than two years of his sentence, Roxborough resumed his position as president of the Great Lakes Mutual Insurance Company. "Louis' Climax of Career Has Tragic Moment"; "Appeal Lost by Reading"; "John Roxborough, Former Numbers Racket Czar," *The Mercury*, October 8, 1946; Seventeenth Census of the United States, 1950, Detroit, Wayne, Michigan, Enumeration District: 85-78, Roll: 210, page: 75.

142. Wilson, *Toast of the Town*, 72.

143. United Press, "Former Mayor Indicted in Policy Probe."

144. Wilson, *Toast of the Town*, 72.

145. "It Began by Cutting Violin Lessons," *Philadelphia Daily News*, July 24, 1978, reprinted excerpt from Joe Louis, *Joe Louis, My Life* (New York: Harcourt), 1978; and Wolcott, "Culture of the Informal Economy," 47.

146. Wilson, *Toast of the Town*, 66.

Chapter 4

1. David M. Katzman, *Before the Ghetto: Black Detroit in the Nineteenth Century* (Urbana: University of Illinois Press, 1973), 77, 131.

2. Roberta Hughes Wright, *Detroit Memorial Park Cemetery: The Evolution of an African American Corporation* (Southfield, MI: Charro Book Company, 1993), 100.

3. Sidney Fine, *Frank Murphy: The Detroit Years* (Ann Arbor: University of Michigan Press, 1975), 250.

4. John C. Dancy, interview by Marvin Petroelje, April 10, 1964, transcript, 17, JCDP, Box 1, Folder: Misc Personal and Biographical Materials.

5. "January 30, 1930 Minutes of the Urban League Board," January 30, 1930, DUL-M, Microfilm No. 1547, Reel #1.

6. Charles Denby, *Indignant Heart: A Black Worker's Journal* (Boston: South End Press, 1978; Detroit: Wayne State University Press, 1989), 37.

7. "Relief Group Is Given Boost," *Detroit Free Press*, December 30, 1930.

8. For more on migrants returning to the South during the depression years, see James N. Gregory, *The Southern Diaspora: How the Great Migrations of Black and White Southerners Transformed America* (Chapel Hill: University of North Carolina Press, 2005), 28–29.

9. Ulysses W. Boykin, *A Hand Book on the Detroit Negro* (Detroit: Minority Study Associates, 1943), 65.

10. Richard W. Thomas, *Life for Us Is What We Make It: Building Black Community in Detroit, 1915–1945* (Bloomington: Indiana University Press, 1992), 208.

11. See, for example, Van B. Cannon, "'Fat' Greek Restaurants Versus 'Lean' Colored Restaurants, and Why?," *Detroit Contender*, November 13, 1920.

12. Roland Marchand, *Advertising the American Dream: Making Way for Modernity, 1920–1940* (Berkeley: University of California Press, 1985), 2.

13. For more on African Americans and advertising, see Robert E. Weems Jr., *Desegregating the Dollar: African American Consumerism in the Twentieth Century* (New York: New York University Press, 1998); and Brenna Wynn Greer, *Represented: The Black Imagemakers Who Reimagined African American Citizenship* (Philadelphia: University of Pennsylvania Press, 2019). For a discussion on Black business and the use of advertising to attract Black urban migrants, see Davarian L. Baldwin, *Chicago's New Negroes: Modernity, the Great Migration, and Black Urban Life* (Chapel Hill: University of North Carolina Press, 2009), 55–56, 68–71, 105–6, 145–48.

14. "Ohio Barbershop Advertisement," *Detroit People's News*, December 28, 1930.

15. "Walter L. Riley, Funeral Director Advertisement," *Detroit People's News*, December 28, 1930.

16. "A. G. Wright Funeral Home Advertisement," *Detroit Tribune*, December 23, 1933.

17. "Bristol and Bristol Funeral Directors Advertisement," *Detroit Tribune*, December 30, 1933.

18. "Belle's Beauty Saloons Advertisement," *Detroit Tribune*, September 16, 1933.

19. "Mitzie-Bobette Beauty Shoppe Advertisement," *Detroit Tribune*, September 16, 1933.

20. "C. J. Cole Advertisement," *Detroit People's News*, December 28, 1930.

21. Wright, *Detroit Memorial Park Cemetery*, 100.

22. Carolyn P. DuBose, *The Untold Story of Charles Diggs: The Public Figure, the Private Man* (Arlington, VA: Barton Publishing House, 1998), 6.

23. "Despondency Causes Two Prominent Detroiters to End Lives with Guns," *Detroit Tribune*, September 9, 1933. For an informative discussion of Black Detroiters' investments and stock purchases, see Forrester B. Washington, *The Negro in Detroit: A Survey of the Conditions of a Negro Group in a Northern Industrial Center During the War Prosperity Period* (Detroit: Research Bureau Associated Charities of Detroit, 1920), sec. "Thrift and Savings Among the Negroes of Detroit."

24. "Despondency Causes Two Prominent Detroiters to End Lives with Guns"; "Undertaker Ends Life," *Detroit Free Press*, September 7, 1933.

25. "Hewitt Watson Death Certificate," September 8, 1933, Death Records, Michigan Department of Community Health, Division for Vital Records and Health Statistics, Lansing, Michigan.

26. Fine, *Frank Murphy*, 248.

27. U.S. World War II Draft Registration Cards, 1942, for William Ellis Jackson, April 27, 1942, United States, Selective Service System, Selective Service Registration Cards, World War II: Fourth Registration, Records of the Selective Service System, Record Group Number 147, National Archives and Records Administration, Ancestry.com.

28. William Ellis Jackson Application, May 24, 1920, AEC, Box 5, Folder 3.

29. U.S. World War I Draft Registration Cards, 1917–1918, for William Ellis Jackson, September 12, 1918, United States, Selective Service System, World War I Selective Service System Draft Registration Cards, 1917–1918, Washington, DC, National Archives and Records Administration, M1509, 4,582 rolls, Ancestry.com.

30. William Ellis Jackson Application, May 24, 1920.

31. "Billy Jackson Profile," *Detroit Contender*, November 13, 1920, Special Business Issue.

32. "Billy Jackson Advertisement," *Detroit Contender*, November 13, 1920, Special Business Issue.

33. For more on the African American funeral industry, see Suzanne E. Smith, *To Serve the Living: Funeral Directors and the African American Way of Death* (Cambridge, MA: Belknap Press, 2010).

34. "William Jackson in the 1940 United States Federal Census" (United States of America, Bureau of the Census, 1940), Sixteenth Census of the United States, Washington, DC, National Archives and Records Administration, 1940, T627, 4,643 rolls.

35. U.S. World War II Draft Registration Cards, 1942, for William Ellis Jackson; William Ellis Jackson Death Certificate, October 25, 1942, Texas Department of State Health Services, Texas Death Certificates, 1903–1982, Ancestry.com.

36. Berry Gordy Sr., *Movin' Up: Pop Gordy Tells His Story* (New York: Harper & Row, 1979), 86–87.

37. National Conference on Social Welfare, "Discussion of Negro Migration Panel," in *Official Proceedings of the 44th Meeting of the National Conference on Social Welfare* (Chicago, 1917), 503.

38. National Conference on Social Welfare, "Discussion of Negro Migration Panel," 501.

39. Gordy, *Movin' Up*, 86–87.

40. Gordy, *Movin' Up*, 100.

41. Gordy, *Movin' Up*, 122.

42. Gordy, *Movin' Up*, 126.

43. Gordy, *Movin' Up*, 125–26.

44. Eric Rauchway, *The Great Depression and the New Deal: A Very Short Introduction* (New York: Oxford University Press, 2008), 40.

45. Gordy, *Movin' Up*, 125–26.

46. "Relief Group Is Given Boost."

47. Gordy, *Movin' Up*, 125.

48. Gordy, *Movin' Up*, 126–27.

49. Wright, *Detroit Memorial Park Cemetery*, 38.

50. Boykin, *Hand Book*, 65.

51. Gordy, *Movin' Up*, 127.

52. Gordy, *Movin' Up*, 125.

53. Gordy, *Movin' Up*, 127.

54. "Theus Photo Service Advertisement," *Detroit People's News*, December 28, 1930.

55. John C. Dancy to John J. O'Brien, January 10, 1936, DUL, Box 32, Folder 12.

56. Deborah Gray White, *Too Heavy a Load: Black Women in Defense of Themselves, 1894–1994* (New York: W. W. Norton, 1999), 142.

57. For more on African Americans and the New Deal, see Cheryl Lynn Greenberg, *To Ask for an Equal Chance: African Americans in the Great Depression* (Lanham, MD: Rowman & Littlefield, 2009); Ira Katznelson, *When Affirmative Action Was White: An Untold History of Racial Inequality in Twentieth-Century America* (New York: W. W. Norton, 2005); John B. Kirby, *Black Americans in the Roosevelt Era: Liberalism and Race* (Knoxville: University of Tennessee Press, 1980); Mary Poole, *The Segregated Origins of Social Security: African Americans and the Welfare State* (Chapel Hill: University of North Carolina Press, 2006); Patricia Sullivan, *Days of Hope: Race and Democracy in the New Deal Era* (Chapel Hill: University of North Carolina Press, 1996); and Robert E. Weems Jr. and Lewis A. Randolph, *Business in Black and White: American Presidents and Black Entrepreneurs in the Twentieth Century* (New York: New York University Press, 2009).

58. John Sibley Butler, *Entrepreneurship and Self-Help Among Black Americans: A Reconsideration of Race and Economics* (Albany: State University of New York Press, 1991), 86.

59. Juliet E. K. Walker, *The History of Black Business in America: Capitalism, Race, Entrepreneurship* (New York: Twayne, 1998), 190.

60. Walter B. Weare, *Black Business in the New South: A Social History of the North Carolina Mutual Life Insurance Company* (Urbana: University of Illinois Press, 1973), 183.

61. Walker, *The History of Black Business in America*, 194.

62. St. Clair Drake and Horace R. Cayton, *Black Metropolis: A Study of Negro Life in a Northern City* (1945; repr., Chicago: University of Chicago Press, 1962), 430–33. For more on churches and religious leaders' connection with business in the Black community, see Weare, *Black Business in the New South*, 6–7, 87, 134, 183–95; Butler, *Entrepreneurship and Self-Help*, 86–95; Walker, *The History of Black Business in America*,

199, 207, 226–30, 233, 420n6, 444, 69; Bessie House-Soremekun, *Confronting All Odds: African American Entrepreneurship in Cleveland* (Kent, OH: Kent State University Press, 2002), 173; Shennette Garrett-Scott, *Banking on Freedom: Black Women in U.S. Finance Before the New Deal* (New York: Columbia University Press, 2019), 7, 9, 44–49, 77, 123, 131, 141, 159, 182–84; and Brandon K. Winford, *John Hervey Wheeler, Black Banking, and the Economic Struggle for Civil Rights* (Lexington: University of Kentucky Press, 2020), 7, 63.

63. Thomas, *Life for Us*, 2, 175–76. For more on African American religion and the Great Migration, see Marcia Chatelain, *South Side Girls: Growing Up in the Great Migration* (Durham: Duke University Press, 2015), chap. 2; and Judith Weisenfeld, *New World A-Coming: Black Religion and Racial Identity During the Great Migration* (New York: New York University Press, 2017).

64. Katzman, *Before the Ghetto*, 135–36. For more on the history of the Black church in Detroit, see Angela D. Dillard, *Faith in the City: Preaching Radical Social Change in Detroit* (Ann Arbor: University of Michigan Press, 2007); and Thomas, *Life for Us*, 175–80, 254–55, 273–74; and Katzman, *Before the Ghetto*, 135–47.

65. Dillard, *Faith in the City*, 51.

66. Thomas, *Life for Us*, 218–19; Victoria W. Wolcott, *Remaking Respectability: African American Women in Interwar Detroit* (Chapel Hill: University of North Carolina Press, 2001), 176; and Darlene Clark Hine, "The Housewives' League of Detroit: Black Women and Economic Nationalism," in *Hine Sight: Black Women and the Reconstruction of American History* (Bloomington: Indiana University Press, 1994), 138.

67. Thomas, *Life for Us*, 214.

68. For more on Black entrepreneurs and white competition, see Walker, *The History of Black Business in America*, 213, 226.

69. Tentative Report of the Program Committee of the BTWTA Luncheon Committee, c. 1932, NHLAR, Box 2, Folder: Related Organizations: Booker T. Washington Trade Association 1932–1987; Boykin, *Hand Book*, 114; and Booker T. Washington Trade Association, *Directory*, 1935, HLDAP, Box 5, Folder: BTWTA Directories.

70. "Supporting Negro Business," *The Voice of Negro Business*, February 1, 1936, NHLAR, Box 2, Folder: Chapters: Housewives League of Detroit: News Clippings 1931–1981.

71. "Cooperative Movers Association Members," *Detroit Tribune*, December 9, 1933.

72. "Negro Manufacturers Ass'n Organized," *Detroit Tribune*, April 22, 1933.

73. For more on religious groups' entrepreneurial impulses, see Weisenfeld, *New World A-Coming*, 95, 103, 131–32, 146, 149–50, 181, 203, 216–17, 222–26, 229–40, 268–69.

74. Walker, *The History of Black Business in America*, 234–35.

75. Beryl Satter, "Marcus Garvey, Father Divine and the Gender Politics of Race Difference and Race Neutrality," *American Quarterly* 48, no. 1 (1996): 44; Walker, *The History of Black Business in America*, 234–35; Jill Watts, *God, Harlem U.S.A.: The Father Divine Story* (Berkeley: University of California Press, 1992), 52.

76. Boykin, *Hand Book*, 39.

77. "Photograph of Ferguson Lunch Counter," HLDP, Box 4, Folder: Awards and Certificates, Advertising Agreements; "Eat with Ferguson Advertisement," *The Voice of Negro Business*, September 1940, NHLAR, Box 2, Folder: Related Organizations: Booker T. Washington Trade Association 1932–1987.

78. Satter, "Marcus Garvey, Father Divine and the Gender Politics of Race Difference and Race Neutrality," 45.

79. Erdmann Doane Beynon, "The Voodoo Cult Among Negro Migrants in Detroit," *American Journal of Sociology* 43, no. 6 (May 1938): 895.

80. Beynon, "The Voodoo Cult Among Negro Migrants in Detroit," 895. For more on the appeal of the NOI to Black women, see Ula Y. Taylor, *The Promise of Patriarchy: Women and the Nation of Islam* (Chapel Hill: University of North Carolina Press, 2017).

81. Beynon, "The Voodoo Cult Among Negro Migrants in Detroit," 897; and Wolcott, *Remaking Respectability*, 185.

82. Nation of Islam FBI file, part 1, pp. 26–27, FBI Records: The Vault, http://vault .fbi.gov/Nation%20of%20Islam/Nation%20of%20Islam%20Part%201%20of%203/view.

83. Clifton E. Marsh, *From Black Muslims to Muslims: The Transition from Separatism to Islam, 1930–1980* (Latham, MD: Scarecrow Press, 1984), 42.

84. Martha Frances Lee, *The Nation of Islam: An American Millenarian Movement* (Syracuse, NY: Syracuse University Press, 1996), 20–21; Suzanne E. Smith, *Dancing in the Street: Motown and the Cultural Politics of Detroit* (Cambridge, MA: Harvard University Press, 1999), 80–88.

85. Thomas, *Life for Us*, 199; Beynon, "The Voodoo Cult," 898; and Smith, *Dancing in the Street*, 83–84.

86. Jeannette Smith-Irvin, *Footsoldiers of the Universal Negro Improvement Association: Their Own Words* (Trenton, NJ: Africa World Press, 1989), 49, emphasis in original.

87. Boykin, *Hand Book*, 46–47.

88. Boykin, *Hand Book*. For more on Black and Japanese political alliances, see Keisha N. Blain, *Set the World on Fire: Black Nationalist Women and the Global Struggle for Freedom*, Politics and Culture in Modern America (Philadelphia: University of Pennsylvania Press, 2018), 53–56; and Yuichiro Onishi, "The New Negro of the Pacific: How African Americans Forged Cross-Racial Solidarity with Japan, 1917–1922," *Journal of African American History* 92, no. 2 (2007): 191–213.

89. "Howard Grocery Advertisement," *Detroit Tribune*, December 9, 1933.

90. Beynon, "The Voodoo Cult," 904.

91. Boykin, *Hand Book*, 46–47; Wolcott, *Remaking Respectability*, 188.

92. Beynon, "The Voodoo Cult," 894.

93. When Ulysses Boykin reported that "the so-called cult movements have not grown to any great extent in Detroit" in 1943, he was not referring to the Nation of Islam or Development of Our Own. Instead, Boykin discussed these groups as legitimate organizations, not as part of "cult" movements. Boykin, *Hand Book*, 39.

94. Some sources refer to Haywood Maben as Hayward Maben. However, his son was named Haywood Maben, Jr. so I will refer to Maben as Haywood. "Hayward

Maben Listing," in *Augusta City Directory, 1923* (Augusta, GA: R. L. Polk, 1923), 689; 1930 U.S. Census, record for Haywood Maben at 2241 Waterloo, Enumeration district 0237, page 16B, family 38, Detroit, Wayne County, MI, Ancestry.com; "Hayward Maben Listing," in *Augusta City Directory, 1921* (Augusta, GA: R. L. Polk, 1921), 655; and "Hayward Maben Listing," in *Polk's Detroit City Directory, 1930* (Detroit,: R. L. Polk, 1930), 1225.

95. Coleman Young and Lonnie Wheeler, *Hard Stuff: The Autobiography of Mayor Coleman Young* (New York: Viking, 1994), 29. For more on hair salons and barbershops as political spaces, see Tiffany M. Gill, *Beauty Shop Politics: African American Women's Activism in the Beauty Industry* (Urbana: University of Illinois Press, 2010); and Quincy T. Mills, *Cutting Along the Color Line: Black Barbers and Barber Shops in America* (Philadelphia: University of Pennsylvania Press, 2013).

96. Young and Wheeler, *Hard Stuff*, 29.

97. U.S. Congress, House of Representatives, Subcommittee of the Committee on Un-American Activities, "Communism in the Detroit Area," 81st Cong., 1st sess., July 25–27, 1951, 43, https://congressional.proquest.com/congressional/docview/t29 .d30.hrg-1951-uah-0044?accountid=13626.

98. Young and Wheeler, *Hard Stuff*, 29.

99. The 1940 census reported Haywood's income at $980. This compared to $1,000 of a skilled auto factory worker and $864 of an unskilled foundry worker. U.S. Census, 1940, record for Hayward Maben at 1836 Maple Street, Enumeration district 84-304, page 2b, household 34, Detroit, Wayne County, MI, Ancestry.com.

100. Bettie E. Parham, "What of the Negro Bourgeoisie?" *The Crisis*, July 1936; "'Miracle' Treatment for the Hair Attracts Throngs to 125th Street," *New York Age*, August 15, 1936. For information on the Black elite's anticapitalist stance, see Tanisha Ford, *Our Secret Society: Mollie Moon and the Glamour, Money, and Power Behind the Civil Rights Movement* (New York: Amistad, 2023), 56, 126, 277, 286.

101. Parham, "What of the Negro Bourgeoisie?"

102. U.S. Congress, "Communism in the Detroit Area," 55, 24–25, 92.

103. During a 1952 House Un-American Activities Committee probe, a Mr. Mikkelsen accused Haywood Maben of being a Communist Party member. "FBI Counterspy Points Finger at 30 Minor Red Officials at Detroit Hearing," *Detroit Free Press*, May 5, 1954.

104. U.S. Congress, "Communism in the Detroit Area," 33–34.

105. The three-day hearing was mostly comprised of the testimony of Richard F. O'Hair, a former member of the Communist Party U.S.A. and an FBI informant. O'Hair's testimony focused mainly on local organizing and activities of the CPUSA that related to the labor movement. U.S. Congress, "Communism in the Detroit Area," 1–5.

106. U.S. Congress, "Communism in the Detroit Area," 7–8, 60.

107. U.S. Congress, "Communism in the Detroit Area," 105–6.

108. "What the Detroit Citizens League Thinks of Candidates," *Detroit Free Press*, September 6, 1936.

109. "Campaign Flyer for Aaron Toodle, Republican Candidate for Michigan State Senate," c. 1934, MS/Toodle, Aaron C., DPL. https://digitalcollections.detroitpubliclibrary .org/islandora/object/islandora%3A142931.

110. Wright, *Detroit Memorial Park Cemetery*, iii, 21, 46.

111. "Campaign Flyer for Aaron Toodle."

112. Booker T. Washington Trade Association, *Directory*, 1935.

113. Negro History Week Program, February 15, 1931, EBWCP, Box 4, Folder: Programs—Negro History 1933-1985; Booker T. Washington Trade Association, *Directory*, 1933, HLDAP, Box 5, Folder: BTWTA Directories; Booker T. Washington Trade Association, *Directory*, 1935; Negro History Week Program, February 9, 1936, EBWCP, Box 4, Folder: Programs—Negro History 1933-1985; *Trade Week Guide*, April 1941, NHLAR, Box 2, Folder: Chapters: Housewives League of Detroit: Publications: Trade Week Guide, 1941-1947; Booker T. Washington Trade Association and Detroit Housewives' League, Better Business Conference program, December 7, 1943, HLDP, Box 3, Folder: Printed Materials by Housewives League 1934-1968.

114. "Campaign Flyer for Aaron Toodle."

115. U.S. Congress, "Communism in the Detroit Area," 33-34.

116. The lodges that conducted business in Detroit included the Knights of the Pythias, the Odd Fellows, the American Woodmen, the Masonic and Shriners Lodges, the Eastern Star, Easter Lily Society, and the Elks (IBPOEW). Detroit developed several Elk lodges, one of which was the Twelve Horsemen. Boykin, *Hand Book*, 106-8.

117. Erma Henderson, *Down Through the Years: The Memoirs of Detroit City Council President Emeritus*, Kindle ed. (Bloomington, IN: AuthorHouse, 2004), Kindle locations 1018-25.

118. Henderson, *Down Through the Years*, 1030-36.

119. Henderson, *Down Through the Years*, 1055-59.

120. Henderson, *Down Through the Years*, 1059-65.

121. U.S. Congress, "Communism in the Detroit Area," 68-70.

122. Biographical Sketches, MSACWC, Box 1.

123. Darlene Clark Hine, "Black Women in the Middle West," in *Hine Sight: Black Women and the Re-Construction of American History* (Bloomington: Indiana University Press, 1994), 73-74.

124. U.S. Congress, "Communism in the Detroit Area," 68-70.

125. Timothy B. Tyson, *Radio Free Dixie: Robert F. Williams and the Roots of Black Power* (Chapel Hill: University of North Carolina Press, 1999), 39-40.

126. For more on African Americans and the Communist Party in the United States, see Mark I. Solomon, *The Cry Was Unity: Communists and African Americans, 1917-36* (Jackson: University Press of Mississippi, 1998); Mark Naison, *Communists in Harlem During the Depression* (New York: Grove Press, 1984); Robin D. G. Kelley, *Hammer and Hoe: Alabama Communists During the Great Depression* (Chapel Hill: University of North Carolina Press, 1990); Harry Haywood, *Black Bolshevik: Autobiography of an Afro-American Communist* (Chicago: Liberator Press, 1978); Wilson

Record, *The Negro and the Communist Party* (Chapel Hill: University of North Carolina Press, 1951); Glenda Elizabeth Gilmore, *Defying Dixie: The Radical Roots of Civil Rights, 1919–1950* (New York: W. W. Norton, 2008); and Charisse Burden-Stelly, *Black Scare/Red Scare: Theorizing Capitalist Racism in the United States* (Chicago: University of Chicago Press, 2023).

127. As cited in Tyson, *Radio Free Dixie*, 39.

128. Tyson, *Radio Free Dixie*, 62.

129. "'Get the Facts on Communism' Advertisement," *Michigan Chronicle*, June 10, 1939.

130. Tyson, *Radio Free Dixie*, 39–40.

131. For more on the Scottsboro Boys case, see Dan T. Carter, *Scottsboro: A Tragedy of the American South* (Baton Rouge: Louisiana State University Press, 1969); James E. Goodman, *Stories of Scottsboro* (New York: Vintage Books, 1995); James A. Miller, Susan D. Pennybacker, and Eve Rosenhaft, "Mother Ada Wright and the International Campaign to Free the Scottsboro Boys, 1931–1934," *American Historical Review* 106, no. 2 (2001): 387–430; and Gilmore, *Defying Dixie*.

132. Dillard, *Faith in the City*, 77–78.

133. Harry Haywood, *The South Comes North in Detroit's Own Scottsboro Case: An Address Delivered in Detroit* (New York: National Office, League of Struggle for Negro Rights, 1934), 8.

134. Christopher H. Johnson, *Maurice Sugar: Law, Labor, and the Left in Detroit, 1912–1950* (Detroit: Wayne State University Press, 1988), 300.

135. Maurice Sugar, *A Negro on Trial for His Life: The Frame-Up of James Victory Exposed—Speech to Jury by Counsel for Defense, Maurice Sugar* (1935), cited in Dillard, *Faith in the City*, 78.

Chapter 5

1. Lincoln Gordon to Christina M. Fuqua, November 14, 1939, HLDP, Box 1, Folder: Correspondence 1932–1967.

2. I use the organizational name Detroit Housewives League (DHL). This organization was also at times referred to as the Detroit House Wife League or the Housewives' League of Detroit.

3. Scholarship that details the history of the DHL includes: Darlene Clark Hine, "Black Women in the Middle West," in *Hine Sight: Black Women and the Re-Construction of American History* (Bloomington: Indiana University Press, 1994), 73–85; Darlene Clark Hine, "The Housewives' League of Detroit: Black Women and Economic Nationalism," in *Hine Sight*, 129–45; Victoria W. Wolcott, *Remaking Respectability: African American Women in Interwar Detroit* (Chapel Hill: University of North Carolina Press, 2001), 176–83; Richard W. Thomas, *Life for Us Is What We Make It: Building Black Community in Detroit, 1915–1945* (Bloomington: Indiana University Press, 1992), 214–21; Monroe Friedman, *Consumer Boycotts: Effecting Change Through the Marketplace and Media* (New York: Routledge, 1999), 111–12; Megan Taylor Shockley, "We, Too, Are

Americans": *African American Women in Detroit and Richmond, 1940–54* (Urbana: University of Illinois Press, 2004), 17, 40; Tamara Barnes, "Buying, Boosting, and Building with the National Housewives' League," *Michigan History*, March 2013; and Kendra D. Boyd, "A 'Body of Business Makers': The Detroit Housewives League, Black Women Entrepreneurs, and the Rise of Detroit's African American Business Community," *Enterprise & Society* 23, no. 1 (March 2022): 164–205.

4. The various branches of the National Housewives League spent different amounts of time and effort boosting Black-owned businesses versus trying to integrate white-owned businesses. For example, the St. Louis Housewives League was founded one year after the DHL, and it seems that they made more of an effort to integrate white businesses in St. Louis than the DHL did in Detroit. The St. Louis Housewives League staged "Don't Buy Where You Can't Work" protests to win sales positions for young Black women. See Keona K. Ervin, *Gateway to Equality: Black Women and the Struggle for Economic Justice in St. Louis* (Lexington: University Press of Kentucky, 2017), 79–81.

5. Helen Malloy, interview by Monroe Walker, January 7, 1985, 2 audiocassettes, DPL.

6. Friedman, *Consumer Boycotts*, 201.

7. By-Laws, ca. 1935, HLDP, Box 1, Folder: Declaration of Purpose.

8. "The Booker T. Washington Trade Association," *Detroit Tribune*, April 14, 1933.

9. Tracey Deutsch, *Building a Housewife's Paradise: Gender, Politics, and American Grocery Stores in the Twentieth Century* (Chapel Hill: University of North Carolina Press, 2010), 109–10; Friedman, *Consumer Boycotts*, 201–12; Wolcott, *Remaking Respectability*, 180. For more on Black consumer boycotts, see Cheryl Greenberg, *"Or Does It Explode?": Black Harlem in the Great Depression* (New York: Oxford University Press, 1991), chap. 5; and Traci Parker, *Department Stores and the Black Freedom Movement: Workers, Consumers, and Civil Rights from the 1930s to the 1980s* (Chapel Hill: University of North Carolina Press, 2019).

10. Booker T. Washington Trade Association, *Directory*, 1935, 4, HLDAP, Box 5, Folder: BTWTA Directories.

11. For a biographical discussion of Fannie B. Peck, see Hine, "Housewives' League," 137–38.

12. Booker T. Washington Trade Association, *Directory*, 1935, 4.

13. Hine, "Black Women," 78.

14. Hine, "Housewives League," 138, 141.

15. Booker T. Washington Trade Association, *Directory*, 1933, 3, HLDAP, Box 5, Folder: BTWTA Directories.

16. "The General Council," ca. 1931, HLDP, Box 4, Folder: Booker T. Washington Trade Association.

17. Booker T. Washington Trade Association, *Directory*, 1935, 5.

18. "B. T. W. Trade Association Starts Spring Drive," *Detroit Tribune*, April 14, 1933.

19. Booker T. Washington Trade Association, *Directory*, 1933, 32.

20. "B. T. W. Trade Association Starts Spring Drive."

21. Booker T. Washington Trade Association, *Directory*, 1935, 6; "Luncheon Club Special," May 2, 1934, HLDP, Box 3, Folder: Printed Materials by Housewives League 1934–1968.

22. Booker T. Washington Trade Association and Detroit Housewives League, *Daily Bulletin*, May 2, 1934, HLDP, Box 3, Folder: Printed Materials by Housewives League 1934–1968.

23. "Booker T. Washington Trade Association Membership Drive," *Detroit Tribune*, April 29, 1944.

24. Wolcott, *Remaking Respectability*, 183.

25. For more on the politics of respectability, see Evelyn Brooks Higginbotham, *Righteous Discontent: The Women's Movement in the Black Baptist Church, 1880–1920* (Cambridge, MA: Harvard University Press, 1993); and Brittney C. Cooper, *Beyond Respectability: The Intellectual Thought of Race Women* (Urbana: University of Illinois Press, 2017).

26. Deborah Gray White, *Too Heavy a Load: Black Women in Defense of Themselves, 1894–1994* (New York: W. W. Norton, 1999), 37.

27. White, *Too Heavy a Load*, 44. For more information on respectability politics related to Black women's business and economic practices specifically, see Shennette Garrett-Scott, *Banking on Freedom: Black Women in U.S. Finance Before the New Deal* (New York: Columbia University Press, 2019), 112–49.

28. Phyllis Lewis Ponders and Marjorie Lewis Harris, *On Her Own Terms: A Biographical Conversation About Mommie "T. V." Violet Temple Harrison Lewis*, ed. Pamela June Anderson (Detroit: Harlo Printing, 2001), 45.

29. Ruth Wills-Clemons, "History of the Elliotorian Business Women's Club, Inc.," EBWCP, Box 1, Folder: History—Founder (Elliot, Elizabeth Nelson).

30. Wolcott, *Remaking Respectability*, 156.

31. Elliotorian Business Women's Club, Negro History Week programs for February 15, 1931, and February 9, 1936, EBWCP, Box 4, Folder: Programs—Negro History 1933–1985.

32. Malloy interview.

33. There were also women entrepreneurs in the St. Louis Housewives League's leadership. Ervin notes that café owners, a hat shop proprietor, and beauticians as well as the wives of shop owners, physicians, and insurance agents were involved with the organization. Ervin, *Gateway to Equality*, 83.

34. Thomas, *Life for Us*, 178, 186; Malloy interview. For more on Black women in the finance industry, see Garrett-Scott, *Banking on Freedom*.

35. Ulysses W. Boykin, *A Hand Book on the Detroit Negro* (Detroit: Minority Study Associates, 1943), 109.

36. E. L. Hemsley to Alvin [*sic*] L. Holsey, January 16, 1933, HLDP, Box 2, Folder: Committees.

37. Carolyn P. DuBose, *The Untold Story of Charles Diggs: The Public Figure, the Private Man* (Arlington, VA: Barton Publishing House, 1998), 5.

38. Arthur Turner and Earl R. Moses, eds., *Colored Detroit: A Brief History of Detroit's Colored Population and a Directory of Their Businesses, Organizations, Professions and Trades* (Detroit, 1924), 29.

39. Angel Kwolek-Folland, *Incorporating Women: A History of Women and Business in the United States* (New York: Twayne, 1998); Mary A. Yeager, ed., *Women in Business*, vol. 1 (Northampton, MA: Edward Elgar, 1999); Edith Sparks, *Capital Intentions: Female Proprietors in San Francisco, 1850–1920* (Chapel Hill: University of North Carolina Press, 2006).

40. Biographical Sketch of Agnes Fairfax Bristol, MSACWC, Box 1, Folder 10; "Fairfax Gift in Keeping with Tradition," *Crisis*, October 1986.

41. Vollington Bristol Application, March 19, 1923, AEC, Box 5, Folder 5; *Detroit City Directory* (Detroit: R. L. Polk & Co.), 1918, 550.

42. Booker T. Washington Trade Association, *Directory*, 1935, 35.

43. "Fairfax Gift"; "Vollington A. Bristol Obituary," *Detroit Free Press*, November 13, 1957; Biographical Sketch of Agnes Fairfax Bristol.

44. Willis Eugene Smith, interview by Monroe Walker, December 27, 1984, 2 audiocassettes, DPL.

45. "Agnes Bristol, Retired Teacher and Mortician," *Detroit Free Press*, February 17, 1985.

46. Helen Malloy and Nannie E. Black, invitation, November 9, 1953, HLDAP89, Box 1, Folder: Correspondence 1942–1976.

47. *Trade Week Guide*, April 1941, 1, NHLAR, Box 2, Folder: Chapters: Housewives League of Detroit: Publications: Trade Week Guide, 1941–1947; Housewives League of Detroit and Booker T. Washington Trade Association, *Picture Book of Business and Program of Annual Trade Week Campaign*, 1953, HLDP, Box 3, Folder: Trade Week Campaign.

48. Malloy interview.

49. Booker T. Washington Trade Association, *Directory*, 1935, 17.

50. Housewives League of Detroit and Booker T. Washington Trade Association, *Picture Book of Business*, 5.

51. Berry Gordy Sr., *Movin' Up: Pop Gordy Tells His Story* (New York: Harper & Row, 1979), 84–85.

52. For more on women's farm-based entrepreneurial activities, see Lu Ann Jones, *Mama Learned Us to Work: Farm Women in the New South* (Chapel Hill: University of North Carolina Press, 2002).

53. Gordy, *Movin' Up*, 67.

54. Gordy, *Movin' Up*, 69.

55. Gordy, *Movin' Up*, 87.

56. Gordy, *Movin' Up*, 87.

57. Suzanne E. Smith, *Dancing in the Street: Motown and the Cultural Politics of Detroit* (Cambridge, MA: Harvard University Press, 1999), 65–66, 76, 259.

58. Gordy, *Movin' Up*, 100.

59. Gordy, *Movin' Up*, 101–2.

60. Booker T. Washington Trade Association, *Program and Business Directory*, 1936, inside back cover, HLDAP, Box 5, Folder: BTWTA Directories.

61. For more on the Gordy family and Motown Records, see Smith, *Dancing in the Street*; Gerald Lyn Early, *One Nation Under a Groove: Motown and American Culture* (Hopewell, NJ: Ecco Press, 1995); Berry Gordy, *To Be Loved: The Music, the Magic, the Memories of Motown: An Autobiography* (New York: Warner Books, 1994); and Nelson George, *Where Did Our Love Go?: The Rise and Fall of the Motown Sound* (Urbana: University of Illinois Press, 1985).

62. Gordy, *Movin' Up*, 126.

63. Gordy, *Movin' Up*, 128.

64. "Officers," *The Voice of Negro Business*, September 1940, 2, NHLAR, Box 2, Folder: Related Organizations: Booker T. Washington Trade Association 1932–1987; Booker T. Washington Trade Association and Detroit Housewives' League, Better Business Conference, program, December 7, 1943, HLDP, Box 3, Folder: Printed Materials by Housewives League 1934–1968.

65. Wolcott, *Remaking Respectability*, 178.

66. Fannie B. Peck, "Greetings from Our Leader," *Housewives League News*, 1933, HLDAP89, Box 1, Folder: Printed Matter.

67. "Negro Business Survey," *Detroit Economist*, March 14, 1931, HLDP, Box 4, Folder: LMM.

68. "Negro Business Survey."

69. Gertrude J. Tolbert, "Why Do We Buy What We Buy?" *Detroit Economist*, March 14, 1931.

70. "To Improve Business," undated typescript draft, HLDP, Box 2, Folder: Organizing Committee Minutes—Reports.

71. Robert E. Weems Jr., *Desegregating the Dollar: African American Consumerism in the Twentieth Century* (New York: New York University Press, 1998), 18–20, 31. For more on the history of African Americans and market research, see Brenna Wynn Greer, *Represented: The Black Imagemakers Who Reimagined African American Citizenship* (Philadelphia: University of Pennsylvania Press, 2019); and Weems, *Desegregating the Dollar*.

72. "Consider the Housewife," *Detroit Economist*, March 14, 1931.

73. Nannie E. Black, "What Now That the War Is Over?" HLDP, Box 3, Folder: Speeches.

74. Booker T. Washington Trade Association, *Directory*, 1935, 5.

75. Shennette Garrett-Scott, "To Do a Work That Would Be Very Far Reaching: Minnie Geddings Cox, the Mississippi Life Insurance Company, and the Challenges of Black Women's Business Leadership in the Early Twentieth-Century United States," *Enterprise & Society* 17, no. 3 (September 2016): 475, 488. For information on white women's experiences as business leaders in corporate settings, see Edith Sparks, *Boss Lady: How*

Three Women Entrepreneurs Built Successful Big Businesses in the Mid-Twentieth Century (Chapel Hill: University of North Carolina Press, 2017).

76. Malloy interview.

77. "Gordon's Quality Cleanser Advertisement," *The Voice of Negro Business*, September 1940, NHLAR, Box 2, Folder: Related Organizations: Booker T. Washington Trade Association 1932–1987.

78. "Merchants Survived with Housewives' Aid," *Detroit Free Press*, December 5, 1980.

79. Boykin, *Hand Book*, 105.

80. Darlene Clark Hine has shown that in migrating north, Black women often sought better opportunities for their children, in addition to desiring more autonomy and to escape sexual exploitation and abuse by southern men. Darlene Clark Hine, "Black Migration to the Urban Midwest: The Gender Dimension, 1915–1945," in *The Great Migration in Historical Perspective: New Dimensions of Race, Class, and Gender*, ed. Joe William Trotter Jr. (Bloomington: Indiana University Press, 1991), 127–46.

81. Marcia Chatelain, *South Side Girls: Growing Up in the Great Migration* (Durham: Duke University Press, 2015), 111–29; Ervin, *Gateway to Equality*; Mary-Elizabeth B. Murphy, *Jim Crow Capital: Women and Black Freedom Struggles in Washington, D.C, 1920–1945* (Chapel Hill: University of North Carolina Press, 2018).

82. Shockley, *"We, Too, Are Americans,"* 64–65, 71–72.

83. Booker T. Washington Trade Association, *Directory*, 1933, 3.

84. Peck, "Greetings from Our Leader."

85. Typescript, "Slogan" of Housewives' League of Detroit, Box 1, cited in Hine, "Black Women," 80.

86. For more on the beauty industry during the Great Depression, see Tiffany M. Gill, *Beauty Shop Politics: African American Women's Activism in the Beauty Industry* (Urbana: University of Illinois Press, 2010), chap. 3.

87. Elizabeth Clark-Lewis, *Living In, Living Out: African American Domestics in Washington, D.C., 1910–1940* (Washington, DC: Smithsonian Institution Press, 1994), 166; Wolcott, *Remaking Respectability*, 88–89; Chatelain, *South Side Girls*, 112. For more on the conditions for Black domestic workers, see Rebecca Sharpless, *Cooking in Other Women's Kitchens: Domestic Workers in the South, 1865–1960* (Chapel Hill: University of North Carolina Press, 2010); Katherine Van Wormer, David W. Jackson, and Charletta Sudduth, *The Maid Narratives: Black Domestics and White Families in the Jim Crow South* (Baton Rouge: Louisiana State University Press, 2012).

88. Wolcott, *Remaking Respectability*, 173–74. The growth of the beauty industry also took place in other Great Migration cities such as New York, Philadelphia, and Chicago. Gill, *Beauty Shop Politics*, 63–68. For more on Black beauty salons and survivalist entrepreneurship during the Great Depression, see Robert L. Boyd, "Race, Labor Market Disadvantage, and Survivalist Entrepreneurship: Black Women in the Urban North During the Great Depression," *Sociological Forum* 15, no. 4 (2000): 647–70; and

Robert L. Boyd, "Survivalist Entrepreneurship Among Urban Blacks During the Great Depression: A Test of the Disadvantage Theory of Business Enterprise," *Social Science Quarterly* 81, no. 4 (December 2000): 972–84.

89. Davarian L. Baldwin, *Chicago's New Negroes: Modernity, the Great Migration, and Black Urban Life* (Chapel Hill: University of North Carolina Press, 2009), 61–64.

90. For more on Black women's canning efforts in the South, see Jones, *Mama Learned*, 144–45, 156–59.

91. Frank E. Bolden, "Former Nurse Finds Gold in Cosmetic Business," *Pittsburgh Courier*, October 18, 1947.

92. Boykin, *Hand Book*, 103–4.

93. Bolden, "Former Nurse."

94. "Woman Forges to Front with Largest Business in the State of Michigan," *Indianapolis Recorder*, November 24, 1934.

95. Bolden, "Former Nurse."

96. Bolden, "Former Nurse."

97. "Woman Forges."

98. "Vivian Hill; Ran Beauty School," *Detroit Free Press*, October 13, 1980, sec. Obituaries; Booker T. Washington Trade Association, *Directory*, 1935, 5.

99. Booker T. Washington Trade Association, *Directory*, 1935, 20.

100. "Souvenir Program: Eighth Annual Trade Exhibit," June 6, 1938, HLDAP89, Box 1, Folder: BTWTA Souvenir Program—8th Annual Trade Exhibit.

101. Black, "What Now."

102. "National Housewives League," *The Voice of Negro Business*, September 1940, 1, NHLAR, Box 2, Folder: Related Organizations: Booker T. Washington Trade Association 1932–1987.

103. Housewives League of Detroit, "Boosting Building Business" pamphlet, c. 1940s, NHLA, Box 2, Folder: Chapters: Housewives League of Detroit: Publications Informal c. 1930s.

104. Booker T. Washington Trade Association, *Directory*, 1933, 32.

105. Wolcott, *Remaking Respectability*, 174.

106. Bolden, "Former Nurse."

107. "Bee Dew Laboratories to Take New Building," *Afro-American* (Baltimore, MD), October 10, 1936; Bolden, "Former Nurse."

108. "Bee-Dew Beauty College Advertisement," *The Voice of Negro Business*, ca. 1935, NHLAR, Box 2, Folder: Chapters: Housewives League of Detroit: News Clippings 1931–1981.

109. Beauty culture education and training was a common strategy for increasing Black women's entrepreneurial opportunities in the urban North. However, the particulars varied from city to city. For example, Milwaukee experienced a less dramatic increase in the Black population than Detroit, and Black migration to the city began later in the twentieth century. In addition, Black women interested in launching beauty establishments had more difficulty obtaining licenses from the State of Wisconsin due to educational

requirements, which resulted in fewer Black women attending the one Black beauty school in Milwaukee. For information on beauty education in Milwaukee, see Crystal Moten, "'More than a Job': Black Women's Economic Citizenship in the Twentieth Century Urban North" (PhD diss., University of Wisconsin-Madison, 2013), 104–42.

110. Thomas J. Sugrue, *The Origins of the Urban Crisis: Race and Inequality in Postwar Detroit* (1996; Princeton: Princeton University Press, 2005), 19.

111. Sugrue, *Origins*, 28.

112. Fannie B. Peck, "Negro Housewives What Now?" reprinted from *Service Magazine*, November 1942, HLDP, Box 4, Folder: William and Fannie Peck.

113. "Iota Phi Lambdas Hold Regional in Detroit," *Detroit Tribune*, April 29, 1944.

114. Slade-Gragg Academy of Practical Arts, *Bulletin* (Detroit, 1947), 8–9, HLDP, Box 4, Folder: Slade-Gragg Academy.

115. For more on Rosa Slade Gragg, see Hine, "Black Women," 73–74; Florence Allen, "Northern 'Tuskegee Institute' Rising on City's East Side," *Detroit Free Press*, March 30, 1947, sec. 2; Boykin, *Hand Book*, 131–32; Slade-Gragg Academy of Practical Arts, *Bulletin*, 4–5; *The Slaggite 1949*, yearbook, HLDP, Box 4, Folder: Slade-Gragg Academy.

116. Lloyd R. Dewitt, "Louise Grooms Is Honored in Detroit," *Mt. Vernon (IL) Register-News*, February 22, 1972.

117. Booker T. Washington Trade Association, *Directory*, 1935, 35; "Committee Chairman Appointed by Pres. Peck for 1936," *The Voice of Negro Business*, February 1, 1936, 1, NHLAR, Box 2, Folder: Chapters: Housewives League of Detroit: News Clippings 1931–1981.

118. Booker T. Washington Trade Association and Detroit Housewives' League, Better Business Conference program.

119. Snow F. Grigsby, *Ambitions That Could Not Be Fenced In* (Detroit: Research Bureau for Negroes and Minority Groups, Post War Economic Security, 1945), 33; "Woman Teacher Aided Detroit's Business Growth," *New York Age*, May 18, 1957; "Detroit Institute of Commerce Marks Decade," *The Housewives League Bulletin*, October 1951, 5, NHLAR, Box 2, Folder: Chapters: Housewives League of Detroit: Publications: The Housewives League Bulletin 1948–1951.

120. Ponders and Harris, *On Her Own Terms*, 33.

121. Ponders and Harris, *On Her Own Terms*, 46–48.

122. Ponders and Harris, *On Her Own Terms*, 53.

123. Ponders and Harris, *On Her Own Terms*, 50–52.

124. Ponders and Harris, *On Her Own Terms*, 54–55.

125. Ponders and Harris, *On Her Own Terms*, 32.

126. Booker T. Washington Trade Association and Detroit Housewives' League, Better Business Conference program.

127. Ponders and Harris, *On Her Own Terms*, 57–58.

128. Lewis Business College, Minutes, January 10, 1942, LBC, Box 1, Folder 9: Minutes 1941–1967.

129. Lewis Business College, Agenda, August 1943, LBC, Box 1, Folder 9: Minutes 1941–1967.

130. Ponders and Harris, *On Her Own Terms*, 84; Lewis Business College, Agenda, August 1943; Lewis Business College, Agenda, August 8, 1945, LBC, Box 1, Folder 9: Minutes 1941–1967.

131. Ponders and Harris, *On Her Own Terms*, 61.

132. Ponders and Harris, *On Her Own Terms*, 73.

133. Sunnie Wilson with John Cohassey, *Toast of the Town: The Life and Times of Sunnie Wilson* (Detroit: Wayne State University Press, 1998), 103, 105.

134. Ponders and Harris, *On Her Own Terms*, 77.

135. Ponders and Harris, *On Her Own Terms*, 77.

136. Ponders and Harris, *On Her Own Terms*, 78; *Trade Week Guide*, April 1941, 1, 8; "Carlton Wilson Gaines Obituary," March 1952, HLDP, Box 4, Folder: Miscellaneous.

137. Ponders and Harris, *On Her Own Terms*, 78–79.

138. Ponders and Harris, *On Her Own Terms*, 50.

139. Al Stark, "The Real Detroit: Trailblazing Is Tough," *Detroit News*, February 24, 1966; Ponders and Harris, *On Her Own Terms*, 76.

140. Lewis Business College, Minutes, March 17, 1943, LBC, Box 1, Folder 9: Minutes 1941–1967.

141. Lewis Business College, Minutes, June 4, 1954, LBC, Box 1, Folder 9: Minutes 1941–1967.

Chapter 6

1. H. L. Dudley, "Detroit's Outstanding Lawyer Writes on 'Negroes in Detroit,'" *Pittsburgh Courier*, March 30, 1940.

2. Michigan State Administrative Board, *Michigan: A Guide to the Wolverine State*, comp. Workers of the Writers' Program of the Work Projects Administration (New York: Oxford University Press, 1941), 109.

3. Michigan State Administrative Board, *Michigan: A Guide to the Wolverine State*, 108.

4. Michigan State Administrative Board, *Michigan: A Guide to the Wolverine State*, 108–9.

5. Thomas J. Sugrue, *The Origins of the Urban Crisis: Race and Inequality in Postwar Detroit* (1996; Princeton: Princeton University Press, 2005), 19, 26; James N. Gregory, *The Southern Diaspora: How the Great Migrations of Black and White Southerners Transformed America* (Chapel Hill: University of North Carolina Press, 2005), 69; Julia Kirk Blackwelder, *Now Hiring: The Feminization of Work in the United States, 1900–1995* (College Station: Texas A&M University Press, 1997), 123.

6. Walter White and Thurgood Marshall, *What Caused the Detroit Riot? An Analysis* (New York: National Association for the Advancement of Colored People, 1943), 5; Kurt Metzger and Jason Booza, "African Americans in the United States, Michigan and

Metropolitan Detroit," *Center for Urban Studies Working Paper Series*, no. 8 (February 2002): 9, http://www.cus.wayne.edu/media/1356/aawork8.pdf.

7. "Tribune's Neighborhood of the Week," *Detroit Tribune*, October 1, 1955.

8. Gloster B. Current, "The Detroit Negro Leads the World," *Color*, September 1944.

9. Current, "The Detroit Negro Leads the World."

10. Snow F. Grigsby, *Ambitions That Could Not Be Fenced In* (Detroit: Research Bureau for Negroes and Minority Groups, Post War Economic Security, 1945), 47.

11. *Trade Week Guide*, April 1941, NHLAR, Box 2, Folder: Chapters: Housewives League of Detroit: Publications: Trade Week Guide, 1941–1947.

12. Justine Wylie, *Detroit's Near Eastsiders: A Journey of Excellence Against the Odds, 1920's–1960's* (Detroit: Detroit Black Writers Guild for the Near Eastsiders, 2008), 10.

13. Ed Davis, *One Man's Way* (Detroit: E. Davis Associates, 1979), 48.

14. Booker T. Washington Trade Association and Detroit Housewives' League, Better Business Conference program, December 7, 1943, HLDP, Box 3, Folder: Printed Materials by Housewives League 1934–1968.

15. Current, "The Detroit Negro Leads the World"; "Insurance Company Founder Dies in Detroit," *Jet*, October 19, 1967; Davis, *One Man's Way*, 85.

16. Program from the National Negro Business League's Annual Conference in Detroit, 1940, NHLAR, Box 1.

17. Richard W. Thomas, *Life for Us Is What We Make It: Building Black Community in Detroit, 1915–1945* (Bloomington: Indiana University Press, 1992), 217; "Business Aid Award Given by Spaulding," *Indianapolis Recorder*, August 24, 1940.

18. The election of unofficial Black "mayors" has previously been linked to Black Americans' political aspirations. For example, Hanes Walton observed that in the South straw elections and the election of their own mayors demonstrated a "kind of political consciousness among blacks." Hanes Walton, *Invisible Politics: Black Political Behavior* (State University of New York Press, 1985), 27. During 1939–1940, Ralph Bunche conducted research on the practice of electing "bronze mayors," which included running "regular campaigns with posters and meetings in connection with their election." Bunche noted that "this is also tied up with efforts to stimulate Negro business." Ralph J. Bunche, *The Political Status of the Negro in the Age of FDR*, ed. Dewey W. Grantham (Chicago: University of Chicago Press, 1973), xi–xiii, 87. By the 1930s, this practice existed in Great Migration cities including Detroit, New York, and Chicago. For more on the development of the practice in Chicago, see St. Clair Drake and Horace R. Cayton, *Black Metropolis: A Study of Negro Life in a Northern City* (1945; repr., Chicago: University of Chicago Press, 1962), 383. The origin story of unofficial Black mayors in Detroit is similar to what Drake and Cayton reported in Chicago. According to Sunnie Wilson, in the early 1930s Black Detroiters began electing a "mayor" of Paradise Valley, and most of the "mayors" were business owners. Sunnie Wilson with John Cohassey, *Toast of the Town: The Life and Times of Sunnie Wilson* (Detroit: Wayne State University Press, 1998), 63–65.

19. "Bronzeville Group Discusses Plans for Convention," *Journal Times*, August 14, 1940; "A Message from President Roosevelt Commending . . . the National Association of Colored Mayors," *Detroit Free Press*, August 20, 1940; and "Negro Convention in Detroit to Form a Group of Mayors," *Detroit Free Press*, August 29, 1940.

20. "Detroit Wins the Attendance Trophy at Business League Convention," *Detroit Tribune*, September 6, 1941.

21. Booker T. Washington Trade Association and Detroit Housewives' League, Better Business Conference program.

22. Booker T. Washington Trade Association and Detroit Housewives' League, Better Business Conference program. For more on the relationship between local small Black business and the U.S. Department of Commerce's Division of Negro Affairs, see Robert E. Weems Jr. and Lewis A. Randolph, *Business in Black and White: American Presidents and Black Entrepreneurs in the Twentieth Century* (New York: New York University Press, 2009), 39–66.

23. Sugrue, *Origins*, 29.

24. Sugrue, *Origins*, 29; Thomas, *Life for Us*, 161; Dominic J. Capeci Jr. and Martha Wilkerson, "The Detroit Rioters of 1943: A Reinterpretation," *Michigan Historical Review* 16, no. 1 (January 1990): 53; White and Marshall, *What Caused the Detroit Riot?*, 30–31.

25. Capeci and Wilkerson, "The Detroit Rioters of 1943," 53; Sugrue, *Origins*, 29; and Thomas, *Life for Us*, 166–72.

26. Capeci and Wilkerson, "The Detroit Rioters of 1943," 52; "Detroit Is Dynamite," *Life*, August 17, 1942, 19; and Suzanne E. Smith, *Dancing in the Street: Motown and the Cultural Politics of Detroit* (Cambridge, MA: Harvard University Press, 1999), 32–35.

27. Gregory, *Southern Diaspora*, 71.

28. Some historians have argued that the role of white southerners in racial clashes and tensions in migration sites like Detroit in the 1940s and 1950s has been greatly exaggerated. Gregory, *Southern Diaspora*, 298–99; Sugrue, *Origins*, 212. However, the sources they often cite are not representative of Black Detroiters' experiences and perception of the racial tensions that sparked the 1943 riot. Arthur William Kornhauser, *Detroit as the People See It: A Survey of Attitudes in an Industrial City* (Detroit: Wayne University Press, 1952), 3, 55, 104; Capeci and Wilkerson, "The Detroit Rioters of 1943," 56; Sugrue, *Origins*, 212. I am not suggesting that northern whites did not hold racist views or that white southerners were the sole cause of interracial tension in Detroit. However, my approach is to privilege Black epistemologies, and I think we should take seriously the experiences and perspectives of Black historical subjects.

29. Kornhauser's report did note that "people who came to Detroit from abroad, however, are more willing to accord Negroes their equal rights than are people from within the United States" (*Detroit as the People See It*, 104).

30. Marcena Taylor, interview by Monroe Walker, December 31, 1984, 2 audiocassettes, DPL.

31. Charles Denby, *Indignant Heart: A Black Worker's Journal* (Boston: South End Press, 1978; Detroit: Wayne State University Press, 1989), 118.

32. White and Marshall, *What Caused the Detroit Riot?*, 5.

33. John C. Dancy, *Sand Against the Wind: The Memoirs of John C. Dancy* (Detroit: Wayne State University Press, 1966), 196–97.

34. Sugrue, *Origins*, 27–28. Two examples are the Sojourner Truth Housing Projects riot of 1942 and the 1943 "hate strike" at Packard Motor Company when whites protested working with Blacks. Sugrue, *Origins*, 29, 73–75; Capeci and Wilkerson, "The Detroit Rioters of 1943," 52; and White and Marshall, *What Caused the Detroit Riot?*, 5.

35. James S. Pooler, "Three Years of Strife Behind Disorder: Persistent Predictions of Race Rioting Become Tragic Reality," *Detroit Free Press*, June 22, 1943.

36. "Detroit Is Dynamite," 15, 17; and Sugrue, *Origins*, 29; Smith, *Dancing in the Street*, 32.

37. Elmer H. Carter, "Detroit," *Opportunity: Journal of Negro Life*, May 1942, 130.

38. White and Marshall, *What Caused the Detroit Riot?*, 5–6. White was long familiar with racial hostilities in Detroit. Working for the NAACP, he was deeply involved with the Ossian Sweet case in 1925 and had personally persuaded Clarence Darrow to represent the defendants. Kevin Boyle, *Arc of Justice: A Saga of Race, Civil Rights, and Murder in the Jazz Age* (New York: Holt, 2004), 206–8, 228–30.

39. Wilson, *Toast of the Town*, 114.

40. Denby, *Indignant Heart*, 116.

41. Jacquelyn Dowd Hall, "The Long Civil Rights Movement and the Political Uses of the Past," *Journal of American History* 91, no. 4 (2005): 1243.

42. White and Marshall, *What Caused the Detroit Riot?*, 6.

43. Coleman Young and Lonnie Wheeler, *Hard Stuff: The Autobiography of Mayor Coleman Young* (New York: Viking, 1994), 17.

44. Elaine Latzman Moon, *Untold Tales, Unsung Heroes: An Oral History of Detroit's African American Community, 1918–1967* (Detroit: Wayne State University Press, 1994), 85.

45. Wilson, *Toast of the Town*, 104.

46. Leroy Mitchell Jr., interview by Deborah Evans, November 15, 1990, transcript, 45, DPL.

47. Mitchell, interview, 40.

48. Dancy, *Sand Against the Wind*, 198; "Mobs Rove the City to Stir Trouble," *Detroit Free Press*, June 22, 1943.

49. Denby, *Indignant Heart*, 118.

50. Wendy Rose Rice, "Fred M. Butzel: The Man Behind the Name," *Michigan Jewish History* 48, no. 5769 (Fall 2008): 9–11; Forrester B. Washington, "Report of Director to Monthly Meeting of Joint Committee of Detroit League on Urban Conditions Among Negroes," January 19, 1917, DUL-M , Reel #1; Elizabeth Anne Martin, *Detroit and the Great Migration, 1916–1929* (Ann Arbor, MI: Bentley Historical Library, 1993), 55.

51. Willis Eugene Smith, interview by Monroe Walker, December 27, 1984, 2 audio-cassettes, DPL.

52. For examples of the type of exploitation and abuse Black Detroiters contended with, see Lila Corwin Berman, *Metropolitan Jews: Politics, Race, and Religion in Postwar Detroit* (Chicago: University of Chicago Press, 2015), 52.

53. Theodore R. Barnes, "The New Deal, Exploitation," *Detroit Tribune*, September 30, 1933.

54. Barnes, "The New Deal, Exploitation."

55. Sidney M. Bolkosky, *Harmony & Dissonance: Voices of Jewish Identity in Detroit, 1914–1967* (Detroit: Wayne State University Press, 1991), 266.

56. Thomas, *Life for Us*, 220.

57. Bolkosky, *Harmony & Dissonance*, 267–68.

58. "News and Notes," *American Journal of Sociology* 49, no. 2 (September 1, 1943): 184.

59. Bolkosky, *Harmony & Dissonance*, 267–68.

60. White and Marshall, *What Caused the Detroit Riot?*, 11–12; Sugrue, *Origins*, 29.

61. White and Marshall, *What Caused the Detroit Riot?*, 30–31.

62. Denby, *Indignant Heart*, 110–11.

63. Mitchell, interview, 40–41.

64. Mitchell, interview, 40–41.

65. Davis, *One Man's Way*, 52.

66. Quoted in Moon, *Untold Tales, Unsung Heroes*, 87.

67. Wylie, *Detroit's Near Eastsiders*, 16.

68. Quoted in Moon, *Untold Tales, Unsung Heroes*, 87.

69. Denby, *Indignant Heart*, 113.

70. White and Marshall, *What Caused the Detroit Riot?*, 30–31.

71. Howard Hill et al., "Survey of Religious and Racial Forces in Detroit," September 30, 1943, p. 10, cited in Berman, *Metropolitan Jews*, 56.

72. Wylie, *Detroit's Near Eastsiders*, 16, 18; Bolkosky, *Harmony & Dissonance*, 269; Wilson, *Toast of the Town*, 163; Angela D. Dillard, *Faith in the City: Preaching Radical Social Change in Detroit* (Ann Arbor: University of Michigan Press, 2007), 201.

73. Berman, *Metropolitan Jews*, 56.

74. Quoted in Moon, *Untold Tales, Unsung Heroes*, 87.

75. Mitchell, interview, 1–2.

76. Denby, *Indignant Heart*, 119.

77. Wylie, *Detroit's Near Eastsiders*, 29.

78. Davis, *One Man's Way*, 51.

79. Davis, *One Man's Way*, 51–53.

80. Mitchell, interview, 1, 2, 15, 19.

81. Quoted in Moon, *Untold Tales, Unsung Heroes*, 34–35.

82. Mitchell, interview, 1, 2, 15, 19.

83. Quoted in Moon, *Untold Tales, Unsung Heroes*, 74.

84. Davarian L. Baldwin, *Chicago's New Negroes: Modernity, the Great Migration, and Black Urban Life* (Chapel Hill: University of North Carolina Press, 2009), 45–48.

85. Mitchell, interview, 43–44.

86. Wilson, *Toast of the Town*, 102–4, 107.

87. Wilson, *Toast of the Town*, 106.

88. Quoted in Moon, *Untold Tales, Unsung Heroes*, 273–75.

89. Wilson, *Toast of the Town*, 101.

90. Quoted in Moon, *Untold Tales, Unsung Heroes*, 118.

91. Quoted in Moon, *Untold Tales, Unsung Heroes*, 50.

92. Lars Bjorn, "From Hastings Street to the Bluebird: The Blues and Jazz Tradition in Detroit," *Michigan Quarterly Review* 25, no. 2 (Spring 1986): 258–59; Wilson, *Toast of the Town*, 101.

93. Charles Shaar Murray, *Boogie Man: The Adventures of John Lee Hooker in the American Twentieth Century* (New York: St. Martin's Press, 2000), 90.

94. As quoted in Murray, *Boogie Man*, 103.

95. Bernethia Bullock quoted in Murray, *Boogie Man*, 103–4.

96. Charleszetta Waddles, interview by Marcia McAdoo Greenlee, March 28, 1980, transcript, 31–32, Black Women Oral History Project, Interviews, 1976–1981, Charleszetta Waddles, OH-31, Schlesinger Library, Radcliffe Institute, Harvard University.

97. Wilson, *Toast of the Town*, 64.

98. "The Real McCoy!!!" *Detroit Tribune*, November 26, 1938.

99. "The Real McCoy!!!"; "The Biggest Drink Value Ever!" *Detroit Tribune*, March 23, 1940; "Hi-Brau Beer," *Michigan Chronicle*, October 31, 1942; "Koerbers Pilsner Beer," *Michigan Chronicle*, December 15, 1945.

100. "Paradise Distributing Co. Observes 10' Anniversary," *Detroit Tribune*, September 6, 1947.

101. Ulysses W. Boykin, *A Hand Book on the Detroit Negro* (Detroit: Minority Study Associates, 1943), 104.

102. Ulysses W. Boykin, "The Jumpin' Jive," *Detroit Tribune*, November 18, 1944.

103. Wilson, *Toast of the Town*, 110.

104. For more on the club scene in Paradise Valley, see Lars Bjorn and Jim Gallert, *Before Motown: A History of Jazz in Detroit, 1920–60* (Ann Arbor: University of Michigan Press, 2001); and Ernest H. Borden, *Detroit's Paradise Valley* (Charleston: Arcadia Publishing, 2003).

105. Architect Albert Kahn originally built the Gotham in 1925 at a cost of $590,000. "Hotel Gotham: Detroit's 200 Room Hostelry Is Finest in Negro America," *Ebony*, August 1947; "Negro Syndicate Buys $250,000 Gotham Hotel," *Michigan Chronicle*, October 23, 1943; Thomas, *Life for Us*, 205.

106. "Hotel Gotham"; "Gotham Hotel Operation Detailed," *Detroit Free Press*, October 11, 1963.

107. "Hotel Gotham."

108. Mitchell, interview, 3.

109. Langston Hughes, "A Minor Miracle," *Chicago Defender*, May 26, 1945.

110. "Hotel Gotham," 28.

111. "Hotel Gotham," 29.

112. "A. W. Curtis Laboratories, Incorporated Organization Prospectus," September 18, 1953, AWCP, Box 2, Folder: Organization Prospectus and Suggestions for Organized Office Procedures; Moon, *Untold Tales, Unsung Heroes*, 255; "The Housewives League Bulletin," June 1948, NHLAR, Box 2, Folder: Chapters: Housewives League of Detroit: Publications The Housewives League Bulletin 1948–1951.

113. Quoted in Moon, *Untold Tales, Unsung Heroes*, 254–55.

114. "The Housewives League Bulletin," 3.

115. "A. W. Curtis Laboratories Dealer's Manual" and "A. W. Curtis Laboratories Flyer for Dealers," AWCP, Box 2, Folder: Literature for Dealers.

116. Dean Richard, "Negro Progress: Business Owners Now Number 2,500," *Detroit Free Press*, August 10, 1952.

117. "What About a Medical Center?" *Michigan Chronicle*, October 16, 1948; Lucille Arcola Chambers, ed., *America's Tenth Man: A Pictorial Review of One-Tenth of a Nation, Presenting the Negro Contribution to American Life Today* (New York: Twayne, 1957), 75; Thomas, *Life for Us*, 180. Black professionals in Cleveland had similar experiences: Bessie House-Soremekun, *Confronting All Odds: African American Entrepreneurship in Cleveland* (Kent, OH: Kent State University Press, 2002), 141–42.

118. Dancy, *Sand Against the Wind*, 147.

119. "Booker T. Washington Trade Association Community Business, Church, and Professional Directory," 1952, HLDAP89, Box 1, Folder: Printed Matter.

120. For more on Detroit's Black-owned hospitals, see Thomas, *Life for Us*, 180–84.

121. W. Arthur Thompson and Robert Greenidge, "The Negro in Medicine in Detroit," *Journal of the National Medical Association* 55, no. 6 (November 1963): 475.

122. Thompson and Greenidge, "The Negro in Medicine in Detroit," 475.

123. *Detroit Economist*, March 14, 1931, HLDP, Box 5, Folder: LMM.

124. Thompson and Greenidge, "The Negro in Medicine in Detroit," 480; "Arthur Boddie Obituary," *Detroit Free Press*, July 16, 2008.

125. "They Live the Gentle Life," *Detroit Free Press*, March 30, 1957.

126. *Bethesda Hospital and Edyth K. Thomas Memorial Hospital* (Detroit, MI, 1938), Digital Collections Resource ID: bh022180, DPL, https://digitalcollections.detroitpubliclibrary.org/islandora/object/islandora%3A242910.

127. Current, "The Detroit Negro Leads the World."

128. *Bethesda Hospital and Edyth K. Thomas Memorial Hospital*.

129. "They Live the Gentle Life"; Smith, interview.

130. Quoted in Moon, *Untold Tales, Unsung Heroes*, 254–55.

131. Young and Wheeler, *Hard Stuff*, 144.

132. Detroit Bureau of Governmental Research and Detroit Mayor's Inter-racial Committee, *The Negro in Detroit* (Detroit, 1926), sec. 4, "Thrift and Business," 13.

133. Collins George, "Detroit Tops Nation in Negro-Owned Businesses," *Detroit Free Press*, March 3, 1953.

134. Richard, "Negro Progress: Business Owners Now Number 2,500."

135. George, "Detroit Tops Nation."

136. Quoted in Wylie, *Detroit's Near Eastsiders*, 34.

137. George, "Detroit Tops Nation."

Chapter 7

1. Willis Eugene Smith, interview by Monroe Walker, December 27, 1984, 2 audio-cassettes, DPL.

2. Detroit Commission on Community Relations, "The Negro in Detroit: Statistical Summary and Commentary," 1961, DCCR, Part 3, Box 12, Folder 48. For more on racial segregation in Detroit, see Thomas J. Sugrue, *The Origins of the Urban Crisis: Race and Inequality in Postwar Detroit* (1996; Princeton: Princeton University Press, 2005), 197–204; Reynolds Farley, Sheldon Danziger, and Harry Holzer, *Detroit Divided* (New York: Russell Sage Foundation, 2000), 144–77; David M. P. Freund, *Colored Property: State Policy and White Racial Politics in Suburban America* (Chicago: University of Chicago Press, 2007).

3. Merle Hendrickson, interview, March 9, 1987, as cited in June Manning Thomas, *Redevelopment and Race: Planning a Finer City in Postwar Detroit* (Detroit: Wayne State University Press, 2013), 58; Robert J. Mowitz and Deil S. Wright, *Profile of a Metropolis: A Case Book* (Detroit: Wayne State University Press, 1962), 28; Sugrue, *Origins*, 50; Angela D. Dillard, *Faith in the City: Preaching Radical Social Change in Detroit* (Ann Arbor: University of Michigan Press, 2007), 200; "Urban Renewal Means Negro Removal," *Detroit Illustrated News*, September 17, 1962; Wallace Tyler, "Is Urban Renewal Blight or a Boon to the Negro?" *Detroit Courier*, September 15, 1962.

4. For more on the ideals of modernity as related to urban renewal, see Samuel Zipp, "The Roots and Routes of Urban Renewal," *Journal of Urban History* 39, no. 3 (2013): 366–91.

5. Ed Davis, *One Man's Way* (Detroit: E. Davis Associates, 1979), 101.

6. Coleman Young and Lonnie Wheeler, *Hard Stuff: The Autobiography of Mayor Coleman Young* (New York: Viking, 1994), 144.

7. Mowitz and Wright, *Profile of a Metropolis*, 13; Samuel Zipp, *Manhattan Projects: The Rise and Fall of Urban Renewal in Cold War New York* (New York: Oxford University Press, 2010), 15–16; Zipp, "The Roots and Routes of Urban Renewal," 366.

8. Mowitz and Wright, *Profile of a Metropolis*, 13; Sugrue, *Origins*, 48–51; and Heather Ann Thompson, *Whose Detroit? Politics, Labor, and Race in a Modern American City* (Ithaca: Cornell University Press, 2004), 17.

9. Joe T. Darden et al., *Detroit: Race and Uneven Development* (Philadelphia: Temple University Press, 1987), 156; for more on Detroit's redevelopment policies, see chapter 5.

10. Mowitz and Wright, *Profile of a Metropolis*, 14–15, 55–59; Young and Wheeler, *Hard Stuff*, 145–46.

11. Darden et al., *Detroit: Race and Uneven Development*, 154–60; and Sugrue, *Origins*, 56, 82–86.

12. Urban redevelopment plans were politically beneficial to Detroit mayors Edward Jeffries and Albert Cobo, both of whom were clearly aware of the racial implications.

Sugrue, *Origins*, 47–88; Suzanne E. Smith, *Dancing in the Street: Motown and the Cultural Politics of Detroit* (Cambridge, MA: Harvard University Press, 1999), 34–35, 44; Heather Ann Thompson, *Whose Detroit?: Politics, Labor, and Race in a Modern American City*, 17–18, 237n56; Dillard, *Faith in the City*, 200; Roger Biles and Mark H. Rose, *A Good Place to Do Business: The Politics of Downtown Renewal Since 1945* (Philadelphia: Temple University Press, 2022), chap. 4; Mowitz and Wright, *Profile of a Metropolis*, chap. 1.

13. As cited in Mowitz and Wright, *Profile of a Metropolis*, 64.

14. "Cobo to Outline City of Tomorrow," *Detroit Free Press*, September 12, 1954; Mowitz and Wright, *Profile of a Metropolis*, 65.

15. Frank Beckman, "'Tomorrow' Group Wins Plaudits," *Detroit Free Press*, September 16, 1954. For a full list of Detroit-Tomorrow Committee members, see Detroit-Tomorrow Committee, *A Report and Review Compiled for the Information of Committee Members and Interested Citizens* (Detroit Conference on Civic Development, 1958), 30–37, https://hdl.handle.net/2027/mdp.39015071308335.

16. Young and Wheeler, *Hard Stuff*, 145.

17. James Ransom, "Cobo Names Group to Plan Detroit of 1975," *Detroit Free Press*, July 2, 1954.

18. Young and Wheeler, *Hard Stuff*, 145–46.

19. George Emery, comments on a panel discussion, "Problems of Large Cities," *Planning* 1945 (Chicago: ASPO, 1945), 4, cited in Thomas, *Redevelopment and Race*, 58.

20. "Redevelopment f.o.b. Detroit: The Motor City Plans a Midtown Suburb," *Architectural Forum: The Magazine of Building* 102, no. 3 (March 1955): 116–19.

21. "Redevelopment f.o.b. Detroit," 117, 119; "Gratiot Plan Rejected by U.S.," *Detroit Free Press*, December 30, 1954. For more on the Citizens Redevelopment Committee, see Mowitz and Wright, *Profile of a Metropolis*, 64–72.

22. Mowitz and Wright, *Profile of a Metropolis*, 68.

23. Sugrue, *Origins*, 85.

24. Zipp, "The Roots and Routes of Urban Renewal," 366.

25. "Urban Renewal and Public Housing in Detroit" (Detroit Housing Commission, 1954), 10, DCCR, Part 3, Box 29, Folder 11.

26. "Bids Sound Death Knell of Skid Row," *Detroit News*, March 13, 1962.

27. Robert D. Knox, "Letter to the Common Council Re: Elmwood Park Rehabilitation Project #1 Michigan R-40, Section 4, Demolition of Buildings and Related Work Approval Contract," January 24, 1963, JPC, Series III, Box 84, Folder 12.

28. "Freeways Provide 'Art Route' Leading to Detroit and WSU," *Detroit Tribune*, February 2, 1963.

29. Mel J. Ravitz, "Urban Renewal and Relocation," October 1956, DCCR, Box 122, Folder 4.

30. Mowitz and Wright, *Profile of a Metropolis*, chap. 1; Thomas, *Redevelopment and Race*, 64.

31. Ravitz, "Urban Renewal and Relocation."

32. Tyler, "Is Urban Renewal Blight or a Boon to the Negro?"; and Dillard, *Faith in the City*, 261.

33. Davis, *One Man's Way*, 101, 104.

34. Raymond A. Mohl, "Race and Space in the Modern City: Interstate-95 and the Black Community of Miami," in *Urban Policy in Twentieth-Century America*, ed. Arnold R. Hirsch and Raymond A. Mohl (New Brunswick, NJ: Rutgers University Press, 1993), 100–101.

35. Mohl, "Race and Space," 101, 108–110.

36. For more on illegibility and city design, see James C. Scott *Seeing Like a State: How Certain Schemes to Improve the Human Condition Have Failed* (New Haven: Yale University Press, 1998).

37. "Detroit Urban League Director's Report," March 1, 1921, DUL-M, Reel #1.

38. Quoted in Elaine Latzman Moon, *Untold Tales, Unsung Heroes: An Oral History of Detroit's African American Community, 1918–1967* (Detroit: Wayne State University Press, 1994), 72.

39. Moon, *Untold Tales, Unsung Heroes*, 72–74.

40. Moon, *Untold Tales, Unsung Heroes*, 74.

41. For more on the history of eminent domain and urban renewal, see Wendell E. Pritchett, "The 'Public Menace' of Blight: Urban Renewal and the Private Uses of Eminent Domain," *Yale Law & Policy Review* 21, no. 1 (2003): 1–52; and Zipp, "The Roots and Routes of Urban Renewal," 370–72.

42. Quoted in Moon, *Untold Tales, Unsung Heroes*, 74.

43. For example, the Willow Run Expressway ran through a west-side neighborhood, destroying Black-owned businesses including restaurants, gas stations, a shoe repair shop, and a pharmacy. Catherine Blackwell, interview by Louis Jones, June 29, 2005, transcript, Oral History Project of the WestSiders, http://thedetroitwestsiders.org/slider/catherine-Blackwell.

44. Young and Lonnie, *Hard Stuff*, 144–45, 148–50; Thomas J. Sugrue, "From Motor City to Motor Metropolis: How the Automobile Industry Reshaped Urban America," *Automobile in American Life and Society*, (Dearborn: Henry Ford Museum and University of Michigan-Dearborn, 2005), http://www.autolife.umd.umich.edu/Race/R_Overview/R_Overview4.htm; Edward Weiner, *Urban Transportation Planning in the United States: History, Policy, and Practice*, 3rd ed. (New York: Springer Science & Business Media, 2008), 16–18, 26–28. For more on plans for shopping centers in the Detroit suburbs and downtown area, see Jeffrey M. Hardwick, *Mall Maker: Victor Gruen, Architect of an American Dream* (Philadelphia: University of Pennsylvania Press, 2010), 107–11, 124–38.

45. Lizabeth Cohen, *A Consumers' Republic: The Politics of Mass Consumption in Postwar America* (New York: Knopf, 2003), 13–14, 116–29, 190.

46. Mohl, "Race and Space," 108; Weiner, *Urban Transportation Planning*, 16–18, 26–28; Mowitz and Wright, *Profile of a Metropolis*, 408.

47. "Michigan Leads Nation in New Freeway," *Detroit Tribune*, September 3, 1960.

48. Young and Wheeler, *Hard Stuff*, 150. For more on freeway planning in Detroit, see Biles and Rose, *A Good Place to Do Business*, 90–108; Mowitz and Wright, *Profile of a Metropolis*, chap. 7; and W. Earles Andrews and Detroit Transportation Board, *Detroit Expressway and Transit System* (New York: Steidinger Press, 1945).

49. Mohl, "Race and Space," 101–2.

50. Mowitz and Wright, *Profile of a Metropolis*, 410.

51. Leroy Mitchell Jr., interview by Deborah Evans, November 15, 1990, transcript, 16, DPL.

52. Mowitz and Wright, *Profile of a Metropolis*, 410–12.

53. "Redevelopment f.o.b. Detroit," 118; Mowitz and Wright, *Profile of a Metropolis*, 417.

54. "Exclusive Route of Expressway: A Tribune Service," *Detroit Tribune*, September 24, 1955.

55. "Tribune's Neighborhood of the Week," *Detroit Tribune*, September 17, 1955; "Exclusive Route of Expressway: A Tribune Service."

56. Mowitz and Wright, *Profile of a Metropolis*, 405.

57. Mowitz and Wright, *Profile of a Metropolis*, 415–16.

58. Mohl, "Race and Space," 102, 114, 134–53; Nathan D. B. Connolly, *A World More Concrete: Real Estate and the Remaking of Jim Crow South Florida* (Chicago: University of Chicago Press, 2014), 282; Bernard J. Frieden and Lynne B. Sagalyn, *Downtown, Inc.: How America Rebuilds Cities* (Cambridge, MA: MIT Press, 1991), 28; Ronald H. Bayor, "Roads to Racial Segregation: Atlanta in the Twentieth Century," *Journal of Urban History* 15, no. 1 (November 1, 1988): 3–21.

59. Young and Wheeler, *Hard Stuff*, 150.

60. Young and Wheeler, *Hard Stuff*, 12.

61. Young and Wheeler, *Hard Stuff*, 10, 13–15.

62. Young and Wheeler, *Hard Stuff*, 16.

63. Young and Wheeler, *Hard Stuff*, 144.

64. Young and Wheeler, *Hard Stuff*, 19–20.

65. U.S. Department of Housing and Urban Development, "Major Legislation on Housing and Urban Development Enacted Since 1932," September 1, 2023, https://www.hud.gov/sites/documents/LEGS_CHRON_JUNE2014.PDF; Ashley A. Foard and Hilbert Fefferman, "Federal Urban Renewal Legislation," *Law and Contemporary Problems* 25, no. 4 (1960): 635–84.

66. Digital Scholarship Lab, "Legislative History" in "Renewing Inequality," *American Panorama*, ed. Robert K. Nelson and Edward L. Ayers, https://dsl.richmond.edu/panorama/renewal/#view=0/0/1&viz=cartogram&text=defining&city=detroitMI&loc=12/42.3830/-83.0850.

67. Zipp, "The Roots and Routes of Urban Renewal," 366; Digital Scholarship Lab, "Legislative History"; U.S. Department of Housing and Urban Development, "Major Legislation on Housing."

68. Zipp, "The Roots and Routes of Urban Renewal," 366.

69. Detroit City Plan Commission, *Detroit Urban Renewal* (Detroit, Michigan, 1963), http://hdl.handle.net/2027/mdp.39015071335148; Darden et al., *Detroit: Race and Uneven Development*, 155–74.

70. Mowitz and Wright, *Profile of a Metropolis*, 24, 75; Darden et al., *Detroit: Race and Uneven Development*, 156.

71. Mowitz and Wright, *Profile of a Metropolis*, 20–21.

72. Mowitz and Wright, *Profile of a Metropolis*, 24, 26.

73. Harriet Saperstein, "Business Relocation: Owners' Views," in *Change and Renewal in an Urban Community: Five Case Studies of Detroit*, ed. Eleanor Paperno Wolf and Charles Nathan Lebeaux (New York: Praeger Publishers, 1969), 445.

74. Kurt Metzger and Jason Booza, "African Americans in the United States, Michigan and Metropolitan Detroit," *Center for Urban Studies Working Paper Series*, no. 8 (February 2002), http://www.cus.wayne.edu/media/1356/aawork8.pdf.

75. Digital Scholarship Lab, "Detroit, MI," in "Renewing Inequality," *American Panorama*, ed. Robert K. Nelson and Edward L. Ayers, https://dsl.richmond.edu/panorama/renewal/#view=0/0/1&viz=cartogram&city=detroitMI&loc=15/42.3385/-83.0281.

76. Data is drawn from the federal government's *Urban Renewal Project Characteristics*, which was issued quarterly from 1955 to 1966, as cited in Digital Scholarship Lab, "Detroit, MI."

77. Mowitz and Wright, *Profile of a Metropolis*, 48.

78. Detroit City Plan Commission, *Detroit Urban Renewal*; Mowitz and Wright, *Profile of a Metropolis*, 13; Arnold S. Goldsmith, "Urban Renewal in Detroit: A Comparison Between Elmwood I and Gratiot" (Master's thesis, Wayne State University, 1966), 29.

79. Mowitz and Wright, *Profile of a Metropolis*, 17, 28.

80. Detroit City Plan Commission, *Detroit Urban Renewal*.

81. Dillard, *Faith in the City*, 200–202.

82. Mowitz and Wright, *Profile of a Metropolis*, 33–34.

83. In April 1952, federal approval was obtained and a contract settled between the Detroit Housing Commission and the U.S. government, acting by and through the Housing and Home Finance Agency, for carrying out the Gratiot Slum Clearance and Urban Development Project, known as U.R. Mich. 1-1. Mowitz and Wright, *Profile of a Metropolis*, 34, 45, 52, 54.

84. Mowitz and Wright, *Profile of a Metropolis*, 24, 34.

85. Mowitz and Wright, *Profile of a Metropolis*, 35.

86. Thomas, *Redevelopment and Race*, 62.

87. Mowitz and Wright, *Profile of a Metropolis*, 40–41.

88. Mowitz and Wright, *Profile of a Metropolis*, 13.

89. John C. Dancy, *Sand Against the Wind: The Memoirs of John C. Dancy* (Detroit: Wayne State University Press, 1966), 223.

90. Tyler, "Is Urban Renewal Blight or a Boon to the Negro?"

91. Sugrue, *Origins*; Darden et al., *Detroit: Race and Uneven Development*; Thomas, *Redevelopment and Race*.

92. The devastating impact of urban renewal on small business occurred in other cities as well. For example, in his work on New York, Samuel Zipp details an array of small businesses that were plowed under to make way for Lincoln Square. Zipp, *Manhattan Projects*, 237–38.

93. The literature on urban renewal is too voluminous to cite in its entirety. For bibliographic information on urban renewal, see Zipp, *Manhattan Projects*, 375n5.

94. Mowitz and Wright, *Profile of a Metropolis*, 27–28.

95. Saperstein, "Business Relocation," 446.

96. Mowitz and Wright, *Profile of a Metropolis*, 40, 45.

97. Saperstein, "Business Relocation," 445. For more on the discontinuation and disappearance of small business as a result of urban renewal, see William N. Kinnard Jr. and Zenon S. Malinowski, *The Impact of Dislocation from Urban Renewal Areas on Small Business* (Storrs, CT: University of Connecticut for the Small Business Administration, 1960), 44–53; and Basil G. Zimmer, *Rebuilding Cities: The Effects of Displacement and Relocation on Small Business* (Chicago: Quadrangle Books, 1964).

98. Saperstein, "Business Relocation," 443.

99. Saperstein, "Business Relocation," 444, 494.

100. Saperstein, "Business Relocation," 443.

101. Digital Scholarship Lab, "Detroit, MI."

102. Saperstein, "Business Relocation," 446, 496n7.

103. Saperstein, "Business Relocation," 448–49.

104. It should be noted that the forty-six entrepreneurs interviewed had owned forty-eight businesses in the Elmwood Park 1 area. Two entrepreneurs had previously operated two different businesses and were able to maintain one enterprise after closing the other. Saperstein, "Business Relocation," 446–47, 451–52, 453, 455.

105. Saperstein, "Business Relocation," 447–48.

106. Saperstein, "Business Relocation," 455, 472, 491–92.

107. Saperstein, "Business Relocation," 467–68.

108. Saperstein, "Business Relocation," 465.

109. Ruth Ellis, interview by Terri Jewell, April 23, 1989, transcript, REP, Box 1, Folder: Papers, Correspondence, and Events, "Living with Pride: Ruth Ellis @ 100"; "Ruth's Story," REP, Box 1, Folder: Papers, Correspondence, and Events Biographical Information; Lesley Rogers, "Witness of 1908 Race Riots Returns to Springfield to Remember, Be Recognized," *State Journal Register*, May 12, 1998.

110. Kathleen Wilkinson, "A Hundred Years of Sisterhood: Gay Rights Are Old Hat to America's Senior Lesbian," *UTNE Reader*, no. 97 (January–February 2000): 26.

111. Ted Shen, "Film Explores Pride, Prejudice of a Lifestyle," *Chicago Tribune*, August 26, 1999.

112. While Ellis and Franklin could never marry, the couple stayed together for thirty years and raised a daughter. According to Ellis, Franklin had a child when she was seventeen before she graduated from high school. In the 1940 U.S. census, Ruth Ellis is listed

as the head of household, Ceciline Franklin as a lodger, and Shirley Draper (age thirteen) as "lodger/daughter." In the 1950 census Ellis is listed as the "head" and Franklin as her "partner." Ellis remained single after Franklin died in 1973. Ellis, interview; Sixteenth Census of the United States, 1940, Detroit, Wayne, Michigan, Roll: m-t0627-01853, page 1B, Enumeration District 84-427; Seventeenth Census of the United States, 1950, Detroit, Wayne, Michigan, Roll: 2599, Enumeration District: 85-231, page 7; Rhonda Smith, "Celebration of a Century to D.C. Black Pride," *Washington Blade*, May 28, 1999.

113. Ellis, interview.

114. Ellis, interview.

115. Ellis, interview.

116. Ellis, interview.

117. Smith, "Celebration of a Century."

118. The Wolverine Hotel at 55 East Elizabeth Street was turned into a federally subsidized senior housing complex in the late 1960s. Ruth Ellis moved there in 1970. She and other residents were then forced out of the Elizabeth Street building in 1986 because of its numerous code violations. "Ruth's Story"; "Residents Say Public Housing Still the Same," *Detroit Free Press*, December 7, 1994.

119. "'Living on Earth' Transcript," January 7, 2000, REP, Box 1, Folder: Papers, Correspondence, and Events, "Living on Earth," National Public Radio, January 7, 2000.

120. For information about delays in the Gratiot Redevelopment Project, see Mowitz and Wright, *Profile of a Metropolis*, chap. 1.

121. Mowitz and Wright, *Profile of a Metropolis*, 20.

122. Young and Wheeler, *Hard Stuff*, 146.

123. Mowitz and Wright, *Profile of a Metropolis*, 12; Darden et al., *Detroit: Race and Uneven Development*, 158.

124. Mowitz and Wright, *Profile of a Metropolis*, 65.

125. "A. W. Curtis Laboratories, Incorporated Organization Prospectus," September 18, 1953, AWCP, Box 2, Folder: Organization Prospectus and Suggestions for Organized Office Procedures; Moon, *Untold Tales, Unsung Heroes*, 255.

126. Small Business Administration, "Attention: Small Businessmen in Medical Center #3 Redevelopment Project: What Can the Small Business Development Center Do for You?," ca. 1960s, DCCR, Box 122, Folder 4.

127. William Pannill, "City Delays Purchase of Renewal Site Land, Families Hurt, Hood Charges," *Detroit Free Press*, February 1, 1967.

128. Davis, *One Man's Way*, 100. According to Sunnie Wilson, "The only way for Blacks to enter business was to borrow money from loan sharks or loan companies. These operations usually offered five-year loans at 10 percent interest a year, often adding 6 or 8 percent on top of the yearly interest rate." Sunnie Wilson with John Cohassey, *Toast of the Town: The Life and Times of Sunnie Wilson* (Detroit: Wayne State University Press, 1998), 65.

129. Young and Wheeler, *Hard Stuff*, 146.

130. Hal Cohen, "Funds Wasted? Blame U.S. Policy in Slum-Fighting Lag," *Detroit Free Press*, November 28, 1963.

131. Harry Golden, "Owner of Flat Defends Island in Sea of Urban Renewal," *Detroit Free Press*, May 16, 1966.

132. Young and Wheeler, *Hard Stuff*, 146.

133. "Justice for Property Owners," *Detroit News*, June 14, 1966.

134. Saperstein, "Business Relocation," 468.

135. Davis, *One Man's Way*, 96.

136. Davis, *One Man's Way*, 11–14.

137. Davis Motor Sales advertisement, "The Housewives' League of Detroit 25th Anniversary Banquet Program," June 10, 1955, HLDP, Box 2, Folder: Annual Councils; Davis, *One Man's Way*, 16, 19, 21, 28, 30.

138. Davis, *One Man's Way*, 96.

139. Davis, *One Man's Way*, 96–97.

140. Davis, *One Man's Way*, 77, 103–4.

141. Saperstein, "Business Relocation," 464.

142. Saperstein, "Business Relocation," 465.

143. Saperstein, "Business Relocation," 464; Goldsmith, "Urban Renewal in Detroit," 37.

144. Davis, *One Man's Way*, 99.

145. U.S. Department of Housing and Urban Development, "Major Legislation on Housing."

146. "Urban Renewal Relocation Statement," April 23, 1965, DCCR, Box 122, Folder 4.

147. Ravitz, "Urban Renewal and Relocation."

148. Saperstein, "Business Relocation," 493.

149. Saperstein, "Business Relocation," 469.

150. Sugrue, *Origins*, 41–43.

151. In her study of businesses displaced from the Elmwood Park 1 area, Saperstein reported that all local businesses stayed inside the city limits of Detroit, and all except three of those thirty businesses remained on the east side. Two-thirds moved less than three miles away from the Elmwood area. Their new locations were mostly in "socioeconomically depressed" areas similar to Elmwood Park 1. Saperstein, "Business Relocation," 447, 492.

152. Saperstein, "Business Relocation," 476.

153. Saperstein, "Business Relocation," 477.

154. Robert D. Knox, "Letter Regarding Small Business Displacement Payment," ca. 1965, DCCR, Box 122, Folder 4; Robert D. Knox, "Information Statement for Commercials Facing Displacement," ca. 1964, DCCR, Box 122, Folder 4.

155. Saperstein, "Business Relocation," 459.

156. Saperstein, "Business Relocation," 463.

157. Saperstein, "Business Relocation," 472.

158. Knox, "Letter Regarding Small Business Displacement Payment."

159. Knox, "Information Statement for Commercials Facing Displacement."

160. Saperstein, "Business Relocation," 458, 462–63.

161. City of Detroit, Detroit Housing Commission, Relocation Division, "Business and Commercial Relocation Guide," June 1963, 7, DCCR, Box 122, Folder 4.

162. Knox, "Letter Regarding Small Business Displacement Payment."

163. Saperstein, "Business Relocation," 459, 492–93.

164. Saperstein, "Business Relocation," 459.

165. Saperstein, "Business Relocation," 458–59, 492.

166. U.S. Department of Housing and Urban Development, "Major Legislation on Housing."

167. Saperstein, "Business Relocation," 459.

168. Pannill, "City Delays Purchase of Renewal Site Land."

169. Saperstein, "Business Relocation," 472–73.

170. Saperstein, "Business Relocation," 467.

171. Saperstein, "Business Relocation," 468–69.

172. Saperstein, "Business Relocation," 471.

173. Saperstein, "Business Relocation," 465–66.

174. Saperstein, "Business Relocation," 477–78.

175. Saperstein, "Business Relocation," 445.

176. Saperstein, "Business Relocation," 457.

177. Saperstein, "Business Relocation," 466.

178. Saperstein, "Business Relocation," 465–66.

179. Saperstein, "Business Relocation," 474.

180. Marsha Music, "A View of Resistance, from a Record Shop Life," in *Sonic Rebellion: Music as Resistance: Detroit 1967-2017*, ed. Jens Hoffmann (Detroit: Museum of Contemporary Art Detroit, 2018), 133–34.

181. Moon, *Untold Tales, Unsung Heroes*, 361–62; and Suzanne E. Smith, *Dancing in the Street*, 42, 101.

182. Quoted in Moon, *Untold Tales, Unsung Heroes*, 361.

183. Justine Wylie, *Detroit's Near Eastsiders: A Journey of Excellence Against the Odds, 1920's-1960's* (Detroit: Detroit Black Writers Guild for the Near Eastsiders, 2008), 29, emphasis in original.

184. Quoted in Moon, *Untold Tales, Unsung Heroes*, 74.

185. Quoted in Moon, *Untold Tales, Unsung Heroes*, 362. See also Mitchell, interview, 7–8.

Chapter 8

1. Detroit City Plan Commission, *Detroit Urban Renewal* (Detroit, Michigan, 1963), http://hdl.handle.net/2027/mdp.39015071335148.

2. Russ J. Cowans, "Medical Center Site Selection Stirs Area," *Michigan Chronicle*, December 4, 1943.

3. Cowans, Medical Center Site."

4. Albert J. Mayor, "Public Housing, Urban Renewal and Racial Segregation in Detroit," June 1962, JPC, Series II, Box 83, Folder 17.

5. "Property Owners Ready to Fight Medical Center," *Michigan Chronicle,* October 7, 1944.

6. "Property Owners Ready to Fight."

7. Cowans, "Medical Center Site."

8. For example, Black entrepreneurs and homeowners in the area bounded by Holbrook, Russell Oakland, and East Grand Boulevard established the Northend Community Association in 1955 "to try and guarantee a fair price for homes that have been condemned for razing." Business owners founded the Clay-Oakland Merchants Association in their neighborhood for the same purpose. "Exclusive Route of Expressway: A Tribune Service," *Detroit Tribune,* September 24, 1955.

9. Charles J. Wartman, "Citizen Group Announces Views on Medical Center," *Michigan Chronicle,* March 17, 1945.

10. Wartman, "Citizen Group Announces."

11. United Housing Committee on Medical Center resolution, reprinted in Wartman, "Citizen Group Announces."

12. Cowans, "Medical Center Site."

13. Clarence Anderson, "Unfinished Business," *Michigan Chronicle,* February 26, 1944.

14. Anderson, "Unfinished Business."

15. Harriet Saperstein, "Business Relocation: Owners' Views," in *Change and Renewal in an Urban Community: Five Case Studies of Detroit,* ed. Eleanor Paperno Wolf and Charles Nathan Lebeaux (New York: Praeger Publishers, 1969), 474.

16. Wallace Tyler, "Is Urban Renewal Blight or a Boon to the Negro?" *Detroit Courier,* September 15, 1962.

17. United Housing Committee on Medical Center resolution.

18. Wartman, "Citizen Group Announces."

19. Anderson, "Unfinished Business."

20. Anderson, "Unfinished Business."

21. Detroit City Plan Commission, *Detroit Urban Renewal.*

22. Booker T. Washington Trade Association, "The Position of the Booker T. Washington Trade Association Toward the Proposed Medical Center Plan and Other Renewal Public Investment Proposals," August 6, 1956, DCCR, Part 3, Box 36, Folder 2.

23. Booker T. Washington Trade Association, "The Position of the Booker T. Washington Trade Association."

24. United Housing Committee on Medical Center resolution.

25. Angela D. Dillard, *Faith in the City: Preaching Radical Social Change in Detroit* (Ann Arbor: University of Michigan Press, 2007), 262.

26. "What About a Medical Center?" *Michigan Chronicle,* October 16, 1948.

27. Booker T. Washington Trade Association, "The Position of the Booker T. Washington Trade Association."

28. Booker T. Washington Trade Association, "The Position of the Booker T. Washington Trade Association," underline in the original.

29. Booker T. Washington Trade Association, "The Position of the Booker T. Washington Trade Association."

30. Booker T. Washington Trade Association, "The Position of the Booker T. Washington Trade Association."

31. Tyler, "Is Urban Renewal Blight or a Boon to the Negro?"

32. Ernest Shell, "The Spectator" (newspaper clipping), DCCR, Part 3, Box 36, Folder 2.

33. Shell, "The Spectator."

34. Shell, "The Spectator."

35. Shell, "The Spectator."

36. Dillard, *Faith in the City*, 257–62; "Urban Renewal Means Negro Removal," *Detroit Illustrated News*, September 17, 1962; Richard B. Henry, "'GOAL' Defines Position on Urban Renewal," *Detroit Illustrated News*, March 5, 1962; Richard B. Henry, "Urban Renewal: Patrick and the Real Issues," *Detroit Illustrated News*, April 2, 1962; "'GOAL' Asks New Approach in Urban Renewal," *Detroit Illustrated News*, April 23, 1962; Albert B. Cleage Jr., "Negro Churches Can Not Be Forced out of Medical Center," *Detroit Illustrated News*, February 12, 1962; Albert B. Cleage Jr., "Blight: A City's Guilt," *Detroit Illustrated News*, February 5, 1962.

37. Robert J. Mowitz and Deil S. Wright, *Profile of a Metropolis: A Case Book* (Detroit: Wayne State University Press, 1962), 18.

38. Wendell E. Pritchett, "The 'Public Menace' of Blight: Urban Renewal and the Private Uses of Eminent Domain," *Yale Law & Policy Review* 21, no. 1 (2003): 1–2.

39. Dillard, *Faith in the City*, 261–62; Henry, "'GOAL' Defines Position on Urban Renewal"; Henry, "Urban Renewal: Patrick and the Real Issues."

40. Saperstein, "Business Relocation," 463.

41. Saperstein, "Business Relocation," 465.

42. Cited in Mowitz and Wright, *Profile of a Metropolis*, 42.

43. "Merchants Protest Delay in X-Way Construction," *Detroit Tribune*, July 1, 1961.

44. Luther Webb, "Individual Protests Heard at Council Public Hearing," *Detroit Courier*, January 23, 1960.

45. Joe T. Darden et al., *Detroit: Race and Uneven Development* (Philadelphia: Temple University Press, 1987), 173, 286n46.

46. Mildred Smith, "Letter to the Detroit Housing Commissioners from the Research Park Relocation Council," April 28, 1966, DCCR, Box 122, Folder 4.

47. Saperstein, "Business Relocation," 446.

48. Saperstein, "Business Relocation," 485.

49. Booker T. Washington Trade Association, "The Position of the Booker T. Washington Trade Association."

50. Ed Davis, *One Man's Way* (Detroit: E. Davis Associates, 1979), 71–77, 97.

51. Davis, *One Man's Way*, 103–4.

52. Davis, *One Man's Way.*

53. Booker T. Washington Trade Association, "The Position of the Booker T. Washington Trade Association."

54. Davis, *One Man's Way*, 99–100.

55. Davis, *One Man's Way.*

56. Kurt Metzger and Jason Booza, "African Americans in the United States, Michigan and Metropolitan Detroit," *Center for Urban Studies Working Paper Series*, no. 8 (February 2002): 9, http://www.cus.wayne.edu/media/1356/aawork8.pdf; Coleman Young and Lonnie Wheeler, *Hard Stuff: The Autobiography of Mayor Coleman Young* (New York: Viking, 1994), 152.

57. Dillard, *Faith in the City*, 199.

58. For more on Mel Ravitz, see Roger Biles and Mark H. Rose, *A Good Place to Do Business: The Politics of Downtown Renewal Since 1945* (Philadelphia: Temple University Press, 2022), 173–84.

59. "Council Asks: Who Is Urban Renewal For?" *Detroit News*, September 12, 1962; "Urban Renewal Means Negro Removal."

60. Minutes from "Meeting in the Common Council Chambers on October 27, Called by Rev. Hood to Discuss the Problems of Small Businessmen in the Medical Center Area," October 31, 1966, DCCR, Box 122, Folder 4.

61. Hal Cohen, "Funds Wasted? Blame U.S. Policy in Slum-Fighting Lag," *Detroit Free Press*, November 28, 1963.

62. W. Arthur Thompson and Robert Greenidge, "The Negro in Medicine in Detroit," *Journal of the National Medical Association* 55, no. 6 (November 1963): 480–81.

63. Digital Scholarship Lab, "Legislative History" in "Renewing Inequality," *American Panorama*, ed. Robert K. Nelson and Edward L. Ayers, https://dsl.richmond.edu/panorama/renewal/#view=0/0/1&viz=cartogram&text=defining&city=detroitMI&loc=12/42.3830/-83.0850.

64. "Justice for Property Owners," *Detroit News*, June 14, 1966; Berl Falbaum, "Ruling May Speed Renewal Payments," *Detroit News*, June 12, 1966.

65. "Justice for Property Owners."

66. "Court Ruling May Cost City Millions," *Detroit Free Press*, December 21, 1968.

67. Thomas J. Sugrue, *The Origins of the Urban Crisis: Race and Inequality in Postwar Detroit* (1996; Princeton: Princeton University Press, 2005), 114–18; Ralph Orr, "Building Trade Jobs Elude Negroes," *Detroit Free Press*, December 26, 1968.

68. "Demand 'Fair Share' in Rebuilding of Inner City," *Michigan Chronicle*, January 8, 1969.

69. "Demand 'Fair Share' in Rebuilding of Inner City."

70. "Diggs Proposes $2 Million Negro Business Center," *Detroit Tribune*, July 18, 1959.

71. Martin Luther King Jr. to Charles C. Diggs Jr., March 25, 1958, in *The Papers of Martin Luther King, Jr., Volume IV: Symbol of the Movement, January 1957–December 1958*, ed. Clayborne Carson (Berkeley: University of California Press, 1992), 389.

72. "Diggs Proposes $2 Million Negro Business Center."

73. "Diggs Proposes $2 Million Negro Business Center."

74. Richard W. Thomas, *Life for Us Is What We Make It: Building Black Community in Detroit, 1915–1945* (Bloomington: Indiana University Press, 1992), 265–68; Carolyn P. DuBose, *The Untold Story of Charles Diggs: The Public Figure, the Private Man* (Arlington, VA: Barton Publishing House, 1998), 4.

75. "Negro Hotelman White Dies at 55," *Detroit Free Press*, July 9, 1964.

76. "Hotel Gotham" advertisement, *Michigan Chronicle*, November 20, 1943.

77. Sunnie Wilson with John Cohassey, *Toast of the Town: The Life and Times of Sunnie Wilson* (Detroit: Wayne State University Press, 1998), 154–55.

78. "Condemnation Questioned—FBI Probes Hotel Renewal Deal," *Detroit Free Press*, August 7, 1962; "Big Raid Reveals Gotham Hotel May Be White Elephant," *New Pittsburgh Courier* (National Edition), December 1, 1962; "Bet Raid Hit Hotel—Don't Buy Gotham, City Is Warned," *Detroit Free Press*, December 19, 1962. For more on the numbers raid at the Gotham Hotel, see "112 Storm Gotham Hotel in Biggest Numbers Raid," *Detroit Free Press*, November 10, 1962; "Chicago T Man Help Wreck Gotham Hotel," *Chicago Daily Defender* (Daily Edition), November 19, 1962; "Gotham Hotel Operation Detailed," *Detroit Free Press*, October 11, 1963.

79. "Hotel Gotham: Detroit's 200 Room Hostelry Is Finest in Negro America," *Ebony*, August 1947.

80. Wilson, *Toast of the Town*, 162.

81. Harry Golden Jr., "Echoes of Music and Dice Mix as the Gotham Passes," *Detroit Free Press*, July 18, 1963.

82. Ziggy Johnson, "'Zaggin' with Ziggy," *Michigan Chronicle*, August 11, 1962; Wilson, *Toast of the Town*, 162.

83. Wilson, *Toast of the Town*, 162–63.

84. "Race War Probable." *Day Book (Chicago)*, September 11, 1912.

85. Davis, *One Man's Way*, 100–101.

86. Davis, *One Man's Way*, 101.

Epilogue

1. Suzanne E. Smith, *Dancing in the Street: Motown and the Cultural Politics of Detroit* (Cambridge, MA: Harvard University Press, 1999), 12–13.

2. Smith, *Dancing in the Street*, 25.

3. Juliet E. K. Walker, *The History of Black Business in America: Capitalism, Race, Entrepreneurship* (New York: Twayne, 1998), 301; Smith, *Dancing in the Street*, 255.

4. Smith, *Dancing in the Street*, 228, 239–40; Walker, *The History of Black Business*, 302, 319–21, 324, 326, 367.

5. Rita Griffin, "Motown's New Veep, GM Tells Firm's Future Plans," *Michigan Chronicle*, June 24, 1972, cited in Smith, *Dancing in the Street*, 239.

6. Smith, *Dancing in the Street*, 22, 181–208, 213–14, 218–20, 229.

7. Smith, *Dancing in the Street*, 193; Sidney M. Bolkosky, *Harmony & Dissonance: Voices of Jewish Identity in Detroit, 1914–1967* (Detroit: Wayne State University Press,

1991), 266, 269; Angela D. Dillard, *Faith in the City: Preaching Radical Social Change in Detroit* (Ann Arbor: University of Michigan Press, 2007), 201; Marsha Music, "A View of Resistance, from a Record Shop Life," in *Sonic Rebellion: Music as Resistance: Detroit 1967–2017*, ed. Jens Hoffmann (Detroit: Museum of Contemporary Art Detroit, 2018), 135.

8. Detroit Urban League and Philip Meyer, *The People Beyond 12th Street: A Survey of Attitudes of Detroit Negroes After the Riot of 1967* (Detroit: Detroit Urban League and the Detroit Free Press, 1967).

9. Sidney Fine, *Violence in the Model City: The Cavanagh Administration, Race Relations, and the Detroit Riot of 1967* (East Lansing: Michigan State University Press, 2007).

10. Coleman Young and Lonnie Wheeler, *Hard Stuff: The Autobiography of Mayor Coleman Young* (New York: Viking, 1994), 176.

11. Elaine Latzman Moon, *Untold Tales, Unsung Heroes: An Oral History of Detroit's African American Community, 1918–1967* (Detroit: Wayne State University Press, 1994), 386, 389. For more on Romney's views on urban renewal, see "Romney Decries Slum Program," *Detroit Free Press*, May 16, 1962; "Romney Asks Local Fund to Clear Slums," *Detroit News*, May 16, 1962; and "Detroit's Slum Problem Demands a Local Cure," *Detroit Free Press*, May 17, 1962.

12. Ed Davis, *One Man's Way* (Detroit: E. Davis Associates, 1979), 101–2.

13. Davis, *One Man's Way*, 103.

14. Quoted in Moon, *Untold Tales, Unsung Heroes*, 373.

15. Quoted in Moon, *Untold Tales, Unsung Heroes*, 383, 78. Thousands of Chinese American residents were dispersed throughout Detroit after urban renewal disintegrated their community. This included the displacement of Chinese-owned businesses located in Detroit's original Chinatown near Michigan Avenue and Third Street. "Chinatown Lost: Forlorn Area Is Buried in the Cass Corridor," *Detroit Free Press*, November 26, 1989; "Is There a Chinatown in Detroit?" *Detroit Free Press*, January 15, 1966; George Cantor, "Year of the Rabbit (4661) Arrives with a Quiet Hop," *Detroit Free Press*, January 26, 1963; Kathie Norman, "The New China Town: Quaint Shops and Exotic Eaters Are Sparking a Rebirth Along Cass," *Detroit Free Press*, November 3, 1963. For more on the Chinese American community in Detroit, see Helen Zia, *Asian American Dreams: The Emergence of an American People* (New York: Farrar, Straus and Giroux, 2000), 55–81.

16. Quoted in Moon, *Untold Tales, Unsung Heroes*, 373.

17. Davis, *One Man's Way*, 142.

18. Ed Vaughn, interview by Blackside, Inc., June 6, 1989, *Eyes on the Prize II: America at the Racial Crossroads, 1965 to 1985, Henry Hampton Collection, Washington University Film and Media Archive, http://digital.wustl.edu/cgi/t/text/text-idx?c=eop;cc=eop ;rgn=main;view=text;idno=vau5427.0309.166*; Jeanne Theoharis, *The Rebellious Life of Mrs. Rosa Parks* (Boston: Beacon Press, 2013), 191, 194; James Smethurst, *The Black Arts Movement: Literary Nationalism in the 1960s and 1970s* (Chapel Hill: University of North Carolina Press, 2005), 225.

19. Smith, *Dancing in the Street*, 197; Theoharis, *The Rebellious Life of Mrs. Rosa Parks*, 194.

20. Smith, *Dancing in the Street*, 46, 198–200; Music, "A View of Resistance," 133–34.

21. Moon, *Untold Tales, Unsung Heroes*, 362.

22. Moon, *Untold Tales, Unsung Heroes*, 362–63.

23. Moon, *Untold Tales, Unsung Heroes*, 363.

24. Moon, *Untold Tales, Unsung Heroes*, 363.

25. Moon, *Untold Tales, Unsung Heroes*, 364.

26. Quoted in Moon, *Untold Tales, Unsung Heroes*, 364.

27. Music, "A View of Resistance," 134.

28. Moon, *Untold Tales, Unsung Heroes*, 364.

29. Smith, *Dancing in the Street*, 77–78.

30. Robert Oakman Neighborhood Association, "Lest We Forget," *Detroit Illustrated News*, May 7, 1962.

31. Rev. Albert B. Cleage Jr., "Selective Patronage," *Detroit Illustrated News*, April 23, 1962. For more on Reverend Cleage and selective buying efforts, see Dillard, *Faith in the City*, 255.

32. Smith, *Dancing in the Street*, 77–78.

33. Smith, *Dancing in the Street*, 78–79. For more on Charles Diggs Jr.'s civil rights activism, see Suzanne E. Smith, *To Serve the Living: Funeral Directors and the African American Way of Death* (Cambridge, MA: Belknap Press, 2010), 120–23, 128–29, 132–33, 155; Robert E. Weems Jr. and Lewis A. Randolph, *Business in Black and White: American Presidents and Black Entrepreneurs in the Twentieth Century* (New York: New York University Press, 2009), 68–69; and Robert Singh, *The Congressional Black Caucus: Racial Politics in the U.S. Congress* (Thousand Oaks, CA: Sage Publications, 1998), 51–58.

34. In 1963 Martin Luther King Jr. participated in Detroit's "Walk to Freedom" march and delivered a speech that was a precursor to his famous "I Have a Dream" speech. Malcolm X also delivered his "Message to the Grass Roots" speech in Detroit in 1963. Smith, *Dancing in the Street*, 21–28, 54–56, 79, 85–89; Angela D. Dillard, "Religion and Radicalism: The Reverend Albert B. Cleage, Jr., and the Rise of Black Christian Nationalism in Detroit," in *Freedom North: Black Freedom Struggles Outside the South, 1940–1980*, ed. Jeanne Theoharis and Komozi Woodard (New York: Palgrave Macmillan, 2003), 166–68; Thomas J. Sugrue, *Sweet Land of Liberty: The Forgotten Struggle for Civil Rights in the North* (New York: Random House, 2008), 298–301.

35. Smith, *Dancing in the Street*, 78–79.

36. Carolyn P. DuBose, *The Untold Story of Charles Diggs: The Public Figure, the Private Man* (Arlington, VA: Barton Publishing House, 1998), 7–8.

37. For more on the history of African Americans and chain stores, see Lizabeth Cohen, *Making a New Deal: Industrial Workers in Chicago, 1919–1939* (New York: Cambridge University Press, 1990), 152–53; Tracey Deutsch, *Building a Housewife's Paradise: Gender, Politics, and American Grocery Stores in the Twentieth Century* (Chapel Hill: University of North Carolina Press, 2010), 52–53; and Traci Parker, *Department Stores and the Black Freedom Movement: Workers, Consumers, and Civil Rights from the 1930s to the 1980s* (Chapel Hill: University of North Carolina Press, 2019).

38. Moon, *Untold Tales, Unsung Heroes*, 88; Barthwell's Drug Stores, "Tenth Anniversary Bulletin, 1933–1943," 1943, DPL, Digital Collections, Resource ID: bh013369, https://digitalcollections.detroitpubliclibrary.org/islandora/object/islandora%3A224500; Snow F. Grigsby, *Ambitions That Could Not Be Fenced In* (Detroit: Research Bureau for Negroes and Minority Groups, Post War Economic Security, 1945); Jerome Hansen, "Negro Faces Rough Fight in Business," *Detroit Free Press*, June 20, 1957. In the 1950 U.S. Census Sidney Barthwell's wife, Gladys, is listed as "co-proprietor" of the drugstore chain. Seventeenth Census of the United States, 1950, Detroit, Wayne, Michigan, Enumeration District: 85-23, page 8.

39. Smith, *Dancing in the Street*, 11, 79, 86.

40. "Black, Buy Black," *Detroit Illustrated News*, September 28, 1964; Dillard, *Faith in the City*, 255.

41. Smith, *Dancing in the Street*, 92, 241. Richard H. Austin was born in Stout's Mountain, Alabama, on May 6, 1913. After migrating to Detroit in 1924, Austin became a certified public accountant, the first African American CPA in Michigan, in 1941. While Austin lost his 1969 bid for Detroit mayor, he went on to have a distinguished public service career, which spanned more than thirty years. Austin was the longest-serving secretary of state in Michigan history (1971–94). Richard H. Austin, interview by Monroe Walker, January 4, 1985, 2 audiocassettes, DPL; "Richard H. Austin Biographical Sketch" (State of Michigan), Secretary of State. http://www.michigan.gov /documents/sos/Richard_H_Austin_bio_512617_7.pdf.

42. Heather Ann Thompson, "Rethinking the Collapse of Postwar Liberalism: The Rise of Mayor Coleman Young and the Politics of Race in Detroit," in *African-American Mayors: Race, Politics, and the American City*, ed. David R. Colburn and Jeffrey S. Adler (Urbana: University of Illinois Press, 2001), 233.

43. Thompson, "Rethinking the Collapse of Postwar Liberalism," 225, 227; Smith, *Dancing in the Street*, 244–45.

44. Thompson, "Rethinking the Collapse of Postwar Liberalism," 241.

45. Thomas J. Sugrue, *The Origins of the Urban Crisis: Race and Inequality in Postwar Detroit* (1996; Princeton: Princeton University Press, 2005), 5.

46. Roger Biles and Mark H. Rose, *A Good Place to Do Business: The Politics of Downtown Renewal Since 1945* (Philadelphia: Temple University Press, 2022), 141–62; Joe T. Darden et al., *Detroit: Race and Uneven Development* (Philadelphia: Temple University Press, 1987), 150–77; Heather Ann Thompson, *Whose Detroit? Politics, Labor, and Race in a Modern American City* (Ithaca, NY: Cornell University Press, 2004), 205.

47. Sugrue, *Origins*, 268–70.

48. Howard Gillette Jr., *The Paradox of Urban Revitalization: Progress and Poverty in America's Postindustrial Era* (Philadelphia: University of Pennsylvania Press, 2022), 39.

49. Biles and Rose, *A Good Place to Do Business*, 233–56; Gillette, *The Paradox of Urban Revitalization*, 39–65.

INDEX

activism and urban renewal, 17, 219–40
Allen family (Fred and Callie), xvi, 1–2, 8–9, 50, 157
Angelou, Maya, 74–75, 277n1
Austin, Richard H., 140, 251, 324n41
automobile industry, 34–35, 45–46, 103, 153, 155, 252. *See also* Ford Motor Company
autonomy: and entrepreneurship, 10, 19–20, 41, 56, 59, 67, 205, 226–27; and illegal business, 78–80, 95. *See also* women, Black

Bagnall, Robert W., 272n76
Baldwin, Davarian, 82, 282n92
banking, 54. *See also* business (Detroit), by industry
Barthwell family (Sidney and Gladys), xi, 93, 161, 164–66, 251, 324n38
Battle, Joe Von (Joe's Records), xiv, 216, 248–49
Beck, E. M., 22
Bee Dew Laboratories. *See* Nash, Vivian
Bethel AME Church, xi, 91, 112, 122, 129, 219, 221
Biltmore Hotel, xi, 57
Binga, William (Binga Row), 51
Black Bottom, 3, 8, 14, 15, 57, 153, 169, 194, 198, 245–46, 253; ethnic diversity of, 46–47; geographic boundaries of, vii, 161; illicit activities in, 75, 77–78, 83, 95; origin of the term, 256n10; policing of, 81; urban planning and, 180–81, 183–86, 188, 197, 226
Black business district, viii, 3–4. *See also* Black Bottom; Paradise Valley
Black capitalism, 10–11, 251–52, 259n34
Black epistemologies, 304n28

Black Star Line, 57–58
Black towns, 22
Black Wall Street (Tulsa, Oklahoma), 7, 22, 30–31
Black, Nannie, 139, 144, 155
Bledsoe, Harold E., 81
blight by announcement, 13, 206–7, 236, 238
blind pig (drinking establishment), 246
Blount, Louis C., 155, 157
Booker T. Washington Grocery, xii. *See also* Gordy family
Booker T. Washington Trade Association (BTWTA), xii, xvi, 2, 91, 103, 113–15, 122, 127–51, 155–57, 163, 175, 178–79, 250; and urban renewal, 221, 226–29, 233–36
boycott, 128, 249–50. *See also* campaigns and slogans
Boykin, Ulysses W., xiii, 80–81, 83, 88–89, 110, 115, 117
Bradby, Robert, xvi, 61–62, 72, 103, 111, 221
Bristol family (Agnes and Vollington), xii, 70, 105, 134–35
business (Detroit), by industry, 63, 92, 130, 152, 166, 171, 177–78, 201; automobile sales and service, xii, 60, 135, 155, 167, 207–9, 220; banking and loans, xv, 64–65, 71–72, 92–93, 106, 133, 150, 155, 206; barber shop, xiv, 51, 105, 120, 154, 168, 191, 215; beauty culture (hair and cosmetics), xi, xiii, 66–67, 105–6, 141–42, 144, 154, 191; coal and ice, 52, 109; confectionary, 38, 76, 188, 215; construction, 41, 53, 94, 108, 123, 239; distribution, xv, 67, 172, 174–75, 205–6; drug store, xi, xvi, 58, 93, 122, 161, 166, 173, 222, 251; entertainment venue (club,

business (Detroit) (*continued*)
    theater), xiii, 52–53, 58, 149, 168–71, 188;
    flowers, 123, 173; funeral and burial, xii,
    xiii, xvi, 49–50, 58, 70, 71–72, 97, 102, 105,
    106–8, 133–35, 162, 180, 222, 232, 239–41,
    250; garments, 64, 65; grocery, xii, 60, 108,
    113, 118, 210; hospital, xv, 2, 72, 106, 152,
    175–76; hotel, xi, xiv, xvi, 57, 62, 92,
    172–74, 241; insurance, xiv, 64, 93–94, 97,
    106, 123, 134, 150, 154, 155, 222, 229, 240;
    laundry, xvi, 1–2, 8–9, 58, 157; leisure
    (pool hall, bowling), 168, 188, 233;
    manufacturing, xi, 63–64, 114, 127, 140,
    142, 144, 173–75, 205–6; movers, 47, 50,
    114; music shop, xiv, 63, 167, 191, 216,
    248–49; newspaper, xii, xiii, xv, 59, 82, 93,
    142, 154; peddling, 15, 109, 115;
    photography, 110; printing shop, 203–5;
    real estate, 51–52, 78, 94, 144, 150, 155,
    157; resorts and country clubs, 154–55,
    176–77; restaurant and bar, xiv, 58, 63, 86,
    168–69, 173, 187–88, 191; retail store
    (other), 192, 247; shoe sales and repair, xv,
    58, 76, 133, 135; tailors and cleaners, xvii,
    1, 76, 194, 206; taxicab, 47. *See also*
    business (Detroit), professionals in;
    gambling; liquor
business (Detroit), professionals in, 63, 166,
    175, 178; accountant, 140, 251, 324n38;
    architect, 3; attorney, 43, 58, 81, 89, 94, 96,
    150, 152; dentist, 41, 90; physician, xv, 39,
    41, 48, 49, 55, 68–69, 72, 106, 121, 240.
    See also professionals
business schools. *See* education

campaigns and slogans: buy Black, 11, 251;
    buycott, 128; Don't Buy Where You Can't
    Work, 128, 295n4; double-duty dollar,
    112, 128; selective-buying, 249–50
Canada, 77–78, 84–85, 155
capital, startup, 47, 49, 64, 66, 76, 167–68;
    illegal business as source of, 92–93
Chicago, 24, 34, 36, 38, 40, 64, 65, 77–78, 82,
    107, 112, 154, 156, 157, 168. *See also* race
    riots
Chicago Defender, xv, 26, 34, 36–37, 39, 173,
    194, 266n56
children. *See* youth and children
Chinese, 47, 247, 322n15

Chrysler Freeway, xiv, xvi, 180–81, 189–93,
    197, 216–17, 232, 250–51
churches, 55–56, 111–12, 148, 204, 230. *See
    also* Bethel AME Church; Second Baptist
    Church
citizenship, economic, 5, 17, 234–35
class, 15, 55–56, 112, 123, 132, 182–86, 192;
    Black elite, 56, 89; middle class, 23–24, 28,
    71, 130; working class, 120, 141, 195
Cleage, Albert B. Jr., 230, 249–51
Cohen, Lizabeth, 188–89
Cole family businesses, 49–50, 102, 106–7
communism, 103, 119–26
Community Market Corporation, 60–61
competition, white, 8–9, 56, 104, 113, 137,
    152, 154, 251, 283n110; in Jim Crow
    South, 21, 23, 26, 29; in numbers game,
    94–95
Connolly, Nathan D. B., 6
convict leasing, 21
Cooper, Brittney, 262n53
cooperativism, economic, 45, 55–62, 71–73,
    111, 114, 117, 128
cosmetology. *See* business (Detroit), by
    industry; education
culture, Southern: canning, 142; food, 63;
    guns, 81–82
Current, Gloster B., 154–55
Curtis, Austin W., xi, 173–75, 177, 205–6,
    213

Dancy, John C., xv, 28, 39–40, 53, 61–62,
    103, 110, 159, 175, 199, 270–71n49,
    275n118
Darrow, Clarence, 69–71, 305n38
Davis, Edward, xii, 135, 155, 164, 167, 181,
    186, 207–9, 234, 236–237, 243, 246–247
debt peonage, 20–21
Denby, Charles, 79, 104, 159–61, 164, 166
depression, industrial (1920–1921), 44,
    53–55, 61–62, 103, 111. *See also* Great
    Depression
Detroit Association of [Colored] Women's
    Clubs (DAWC), xii, xvi, 123–24
Detroit Contender, xii, 19, 43, 59–60, 67, 107
Detroit Housewives League (DHL), xii, xv,
    16, 103, 113–16, 122, 127–51, 155–57,
    163, 175–76, 178, 250, 294n2. *See also*
    National Housewives League

Detroit Independent, xiii, 65, 82, 93
Detroit Institute of Commerce, xiii, 145–47
Detroit Memorial Park Cemetery, xvii,
    71–72, 122
Detroit Negro Business League, 113. *See also*
    National Negro Business League (NNBL)
Detroit Tribune, xiii, 82, 105, 106, 118, 154,
    162, 191
Development of Our Own, 114, 117–18,
    291n93
DeVere, Eleanora A., xiii, 65–67
Diggs family: Charles C. Jr., 97, 239–40,
    250–51; Charles C. Sr., xiii, 58, 72, 97,
    106, 110, 117, 122, 123, 133, 239–41, 250,
    285n125; Mamie, xiii, 133–34, 250
Dillard, Angela, 113
discrimination, racial, 44–45, 56, 111, 175,
    225–231, 235, 237; in accommodations,
    57; in cemeteries, 71; in entry to business
    sectors, 21; in real estate practices, 8–9,
    50–51, 68–69, 180; in supply chain, 8–9.
    See also housing; lending
discrimination, sex, 130–31, 134–35, 141, 176
Du Bois, W. E. B., 55, 262n53, 263n2
Dudley, Herbert L., 150, 152

economic thought, Black, 14, 24, 34, 55, 57,
    74–75, 116–17, 119–21, 126
economic white supremacy, 4, 17, 20–22, 33,
    44, 68, 70, 117, 179, 181, 186–87, 252–53
education, 140, 169; beauty culture, 141,
    144, 151, 300n109; business, xiii, xiv, 16,
    61, 65, 113, 132, 138–39, 143–51;
    vocational, xvi, 145. *See also* Detroit
    Institute of Commerce; Lewis Business
    College; Slade-Gragg Academy of
    Practical Arts; Tuskegee Institute
    (Alabama)
Elliotorian Business Women's Club (EBWC),
    132, 150, 178
Ellis, Ruth, 203–5, 314n112
eminent domain, 185–86, 188, 229–31, 238,
    243
employment: Black business as creator of
    opportunities, 2, 62, 64, 67, 87, 109, 114,
    140–41, 143, 147, 150, 169, 174, 176,
    210–11, 222, 251; unemployment, 53–55,
    61, 102–3, 145, 252
Enterprise Garage, 60–61

entertainment. *See* business (Detroit), by
    industry; Paradise Valley
entrepreneurs, Black: motivations for
    entrepreneurship, 10; motivations for
    migrating, 12, 14, 16, 20, 27, 33–41; white
    support of, 50, 59, 167. *See also* ideologies
    of Black entrepreneurs; migrant
    entrepreneurship; women, Black
entrepreneurship, conception of, 15. *See also*
    migrant entrepreneurship
Exodusters, 21–22

failure, business, 102, 106–7, 110
family, 37, 41, 49, 213. *See also* migration
family business, 203–4; women's contribu-
    tions to, 2, 49, 132–37, 151, 176, 251,
    324n38
farm, 27, 41, 114, 116, 136, 142
Father Divine, 114–15
fire: arson, 28, 31–32, 206, 247–48;
    suspicious, 9
Ford Motor Company (FMC), 45, 50, 61, 70,
    79–80, 84, 95, 207, 250, 251
Forest Club. *See* Wilson, Sunnie
Franklin, Ceciline (Babe), 204–5, 314n112
fraternal organizations, xvii, 121, 123–24,
    293n116
free enterprise, 7–8, 26, 34, 119, 258n22
freedom enterprise, dreams and aspirations
    related to, 1, 4–5, 12, 20, 41, 60, 95, 140,
    169, 175
freedomenterprise.org, 262n50
freeways. *See* highway construction
Fuqua, Christina, 127, 157

Gaines, Carlton W., 150, 155, 157
gambling, 75–78, 80, 171; Associated
    Numbers Bankers, 94–95; auxiliary
    industries, 91; Black opposition to, 82–83,
    89; numbers game, 87–100, 241, 281n79;
    Policy Writers Association of Metropoli-
    tan Detroit labor strike, 90–91. *See also*
    women, Black
Garvey, Marcus, 11, 45, 56–62, 73, 117, 272n76
GI Bill, xiv, 147–48, 167
Gordy family, xii, 108–10, 135–36; Berry Jr.,
    26, 245; Berry Sr., 26–27, 33, 41, 53;
    Bertha (née Fuller), 108, 135–37. *See also*
    Motown Records

Gotham Hotel, xiv, 83, 172–74, 241–42
graft, Mayor Reading scandal, xiii, 97–100, 285n140
Gragg, Rosa Slade. *See* Slade-Gragg Academy of Practical Arts
Great Depression, 16, 102–11, 114, 125–26; Black illegal business during, 75, 87, 90, 100
Great Lakes Mutual Insurance Company, xiv, 64, 93, 134–35, 146, 150, 154–55, 222, 229, 286n141
Great Migration, 3, 11, 41; waves of, 15–16, 32, 144, 153–54, 158, 168. *See also* migration
Greenidge, Robert, 49, 72
Grooms, R. Louise. *See* Detroit Institute of Commerce
Group on Advanced Leadership (GOAL), 230–31

hair. *See* business (Detroit), by industry
Hall, Jacquelyn Dowd, 6, 257n17
Hastings Street, 3, 14, 17, 47, 153, 161, 163, 166, 168–71, 178–79, 181, 189–93, 197, 216–17
Haynes, George E., 78
health, 9. *See also* mental health
Highland Park, Michigan, 45, 203, 248
Highway Act: of 1944, 188; of 1956, 189
highway construction, 14, 184–85, 187–93, 205, 216–17, 234, 311n43. *See also* Chrysler Freeway
home-based business, 65, 203–5
Hood, Nicholas, 237
Hood, Samuel, 9
Hooker, John Lee, 170–71
Housewives League. *See* Detroit Housewives League; National Housewives League
housing: affordable, 159, 183, 194–95, 198–99; racial discrimination in, 47, 51, 187, 198, 220. *See also* restrictive covenants
Housing Act: of 1949, 194–95; of 1954, 194–95; of 1956, 209; of 1964, 209–11, 213, 238; of 1965, 211–12, 238
Howard family (William H. and Carrie Watson), 49
Hughes, Langston, 173, 241

I-75. *See* Chrysler Freeway

I-375. *See* Chrysler Freeway
ideologies of Black entrepreneurs, 10, 19, 55–56, 60, 114–18. *See also* economic thought, Black
illegal business, 15–16, 74–101, 282n92
immigrants, white, 46–47, 77, 158–59, 284n118
infrapolitics, 10
International Peace Mission. *See* Father Divine
Iota Phi Lambda (Black businesswomen's sorority), 145

Jackson, William Ellis, 107–8
Japanese, 117–18
Jewish relations with Black Detroiters, 47, 77, 94, 157–58, 161–66, 246
Jim Crow South, 7, 20–33, 158, 252

Kelley, Robin D. G., 6
King, Martin Luther Jr., 239–40, 245, 323n34
Ku Klux Klan (KKK), xv, 16, 31, 55, 67–68, 276n131

labor: industrial, 46, 53, 62, 79, 145, 153, 157, 159; temporary migrant, 36–37
Lee, Everett, 12, 260n42
lending, 106; racial discrimination in, 1, 8, 21, 49, 72, 76, 92–93, 133, 213, 239. *See also* business (Detroit), by industry; loan sharks
letters of migrants, 14, 26, 33–40
Lewis Business College (LBC), xiv, 145, 147–51, 177
Lewis, Violet T., xiv, 131, 145, 147–51, 177
liquor, 172–73; bootlegging, 76–77, 81, 84–87; legalization of, 86–87. *See also* Prohibition
loan sharks, 206, 315n128
Louis, Joe, 94, 96–97, 100, 168
lynching, 7, 20, 22–23, 26, 29–33, 68–69, 160–61, 242, 266n46, 272n1

Maben, Haywood, xiv–xv, 119–21, 291n94
Malcolm X, 117, 323n34
Malloy family (Helen and Lorenzo), xv, 128, 132–33, 135, 139
map, vii, viii, 190, 197, 202, 224; digital, 262n50
Marshall, Thurgood, 173

massacre: Atlanta, Georgia (1906), 23; Tulsa, Oklahoma (1921), 22, 30–31; Wilmington, North Carolina (1898), 27–28. *See also* race riots

mayors of Detroit: Cobo, Albert, 183–85, 309n12; Gribbs, Roman S., 251; Jeffries, Edward, 182, 309n12; Reading, Richard, 97. *See also* graft, Mayor Reading scandal

mayors, Black unofficial, 99, 156, 303n18

mental health, 106–7

Mercy Hospital, xv, 55, 175–76

Michigan Chronicle, xv, 125, 223, 225, 227

Michigan People's Finance Corporation (MPFC), xv, xvii, 65, 71, 92–93, 122, 275n118, 283n100

Mickens, Marsha (aka Marsha Music), 216–17, 248–49

migrant entrepreneurship, 11–13, 44, 63, 71, 95, 178, 202, 217, 242, 252–53

migrant identity, 11, 95, 158

migrants from: Alabama, xv, xvi, xvii, 50, 55, 81, 135, 162, 167, 173, 176, 180, 194; Florida, 39, 68; Georgia, xi, xii, xiv, xv, xvi, 27, 41, 108, 116, 119, 136–137, 142, 154, 155, 176, 215, 216, 248, 251; Grenada, British West Indies, xii; Kentucky, xii, 59, 107; Louisiana, xii, 96, 207; Mississippi, xiii, xvi, 1–2, 106, 133, 281n67; North Carolina, xvi, 28, 40, 122; South Carolina, xiii, 65; Texas, 107–8; Virginia, xii; Washington, D.C., 155; West Virginia, xi, 173

migration: chain, 27, 40; as flight from violence, 26–27, 33; kinship networks, 40, 108, 136, 147; motivations, 12, 31, 299n80; push-pull factors, 12, 20, 22, 34–35, 37–38, 260n42, 261n43; return, 54, 103–4, 107–8; sites of origin, 45, 88, 108, 116; Southern advocates for emigration, 23–24. *See also* entrepreneurs, Black; Great Migration; letters of migrants; migrants from; women, Black

Mitchell, Leroy, 93, 98, 161, 164, 166–67, 168, 173, 189

Mosley, Bill, 93

Motown Records, 26, 136, 245, 259n34

Muhammad, Elijah, 116–17, 240–41. *See also* Nation of Islam

murder, 9, 23, 29, 69, 82, 160, 194, 205. *See also* lynching

Music, Marsha. *See* Mickens, Marsha

Muslims. *See* Nation of Islam

mutual aid societies, 111–12. *See also* fraternal organizations

NAACP (National Association for the Advancement of Colored People), xvi, 2, 23, 55, 154, 159, 163, 173, 199, 225, 250, 272n76, 305n38

nadir of American race relations, 32

Nash, Vivian (Bee Dew Laboratories), xi, 142–44, 151

Nation of Islam (NOI), 103, 114–18, 250, 291n93

National Housewives League, 127, 133, 144–45, 156–57, 295n4

National Negro Business League (NNBL), xvi, 2, 24, 133, 139, 156–57, 234, 236. *See also* Detroit Negro Business League

National Recovery Administration (NRA), 105

nationalism, Black, 11, 45, 56, 58, 60, 62, 115–18. *See also* Nation of Islam; UNIA (Universal Negro Improvement Association)

"negro removal," 181, 230, 243

New Deal, 105, 110–11, 258n22. *See also* National Recovery Administration; Works Progress Administration

North Carolina Mutual Life Insurance Company, 111, 262n51

Northcross family (Daisy and David), xv, 55, 176. *See also* Mercy Hospital

Norwood, Walter (Norwood Hotel), 92, 172. *See also* Gotham Hotel

Old Detroiters, 43, 46, 102; advantages in business, 47–51, 66; conflict with Southern migrants, 51

Pakeman, Al "Geechy," 99

Paradise Valley, 3, 8, 14–15, 17, 46, 153, 158, 168–79, 245–46, 253; entertainment scene in, 169–72, 216; geographic boundaries of, vii, 161; urban planning and, 180–81, 188, 197, 219

Paradise Valley Distributing Company (PVDC), xv, 172

Parham, Bettie E., 120–21

Parkside Hospital (Dunbar Hospital), 2, 176

Patrick, William T. Jr., 237
Peck family, xii, 111–12; Fannie B. (née McCampbell), 129, 132, 137, 139, 145, 157; Fannie Peck Credit Union, 133; William H., 91, 129–30, 132, 157, 221
People's Grocery Store (Memphis), 23
policing, 53, 78, 81, 118, 158, 160, 164–65, 246–48; and numbers game, 95–100
policy. *See* gambling
political power, 55, 193, 249, 251–52; lack of formal, 20
politics, formal, 97, 122, 251–52. *See also* mayors of Detroit
population (Detroit): Black, 12, 43, 48, 62, 153, 195; demographic shifts, 44–47, 77–78, 144–45, 152–53, 167, 182–83, 219, 246
Poston brothers (Robert and Ulysses), xii, 19, 59–62, 274n98
professionals, 37, 56, 120, 129, 132, 150; entrepreneurialization of, 48–49, 175–77. *See also* business (Detroit), professionals in
Prohibition, 75, 85; end of, 86–87, 94; in Michigan, 84, 280n52. *See also* liquor
property ownership: land, 22, 24, 27, 33, 51; residential, 43, 51–52, 69–70, 72, 208, 220–22, 236, 243
property rights, 4, 70, 229–31. *See also* eminent domain
prostitution. *See* sex work

queer entrepreneurs. *See* Ellis, Ruth; Franklin, Ceciline (Babe)

race riots (race war), 23; Beaumont, Texas (1943), 163; Bluefield, West Virginia (1912), 28–30; Chicago (1919), 69; Detroit (1943), 17, 149, 152–53, 157–68, 179, 219; Detroit (1967), 166, 246; Lonoke County, Arkansas (1897–1898), 25–26; Sherman, Texas (1930), 32; Washington, DC (1919), 69. *See also* massacre; Red Summer of 1919
racial capitalism, 4, 126, 128, 165–66, 179, 181, 184, 186–87, 212, 216, 218, 241, 252–53, 268n6; archival erasure and, 14, 182, 199–200; Black quotidian analysis of, 34, 74–76, 100–101, 217; definition of, 6, 257n17; features of Northern, 44, 49, 56,
68; violence and, 6–7, 10, 13, 15–17, 20–25, 33, 41–42, 44, 67–71, 153, 158, 160–61, 242
racial prejudice among northern whites, 67–68, 304n28
Ransom, Reverdy, 23–24
Ravitz, Mel J., 186, 206, 237
Red Summer of 1919, 31
reparations, 5–6, 243
respectability politics, 82, 130–31
restrictive covenants, 68, 187, 198, 220
retirement, forced, 205, 215–16
Reuther, Walter, 183–84
Roane, Irving. *See* Gotham Hotel
Robinson, Cedric, 6
Roxborough family: Charles Jr., 96–97, 284n118; Charles Sr., 96, 284n117; John, 89, 91, 94, 96–97, 99–100, 286n141

Saperstein, Harriet, 200–202, 209, 212–13, 215, 233
scams, 52, 83
Scottsboro Boys, 126
Second Baptist Church, xvi, 61, 72–73, 111–12, 221
segregation, 8, 44, 47–48, 67–68, 149, 160, 187, 198–99, 210
self-defense, armed, 23, 31, 69–70
sex work, 77–78, 80–81, 171
Shabazz, Betty, xv
sharecropping, 20–21
Slade-Gragg Academy of Practical Arts, xvi, 124, 145, 147
small business, 11, 15
Small Business Administration (SBA), 210, 213, 237
Smith, Willis Eugene, xvi, 50, 135, 162, 180
Southern whites in Detroit, 158–59, 160–61, 304n28
Spann, Louis, 81–82
sports, 168
Straker, David Augustus, 48
Stuart, Merah S., 259n35, 262n51
Sugrue, Thomas, 184, 252
suicide, 106–7
Supreme Linen and Laundry. *See* Allen family (Fred and Callie)
Sweet, Ossian, 16, 36, 39, 41, 44, 68–71, 106, 305n38; and brother Otis, 41; and wife Gladys, 68–69, 71

Tanzy Hotel (Benjamin W. Tanzy), xvi,
54–55, 62, 271n56
Theus Photo Service (Lula J. and John J.
Theus), 110
Thomas, Alfred E. Sr., 176–77
Thomas, Richard W., 104
Thompson, Cynthia (Best Apron Shop), 64
Tolbert, Gertrude J., 138, 144
Tolnay, Stewart, 22
Toodle, Aaron Conklin, xvi–xvii, 121–23,
222; and wife Hattie, 122
trauma, 182, 216, 242, 253
Tribune Independent, xvii, 122. *See also*
Detroit Tribune
Turner, Alexander, 69–70
Tuskegee Institute (Alabama), xi, 38, 107,
108, 120, 124, 173–74
Twelve Horsemen Civic Center (IBPOEW).
See fraternal organizations
Tyson, Timothy, 124

UNIA (Universal Negro Improvement
Association), xiv, 11, 45, 55–61, 72, 103,
111, 117
urban crisis, 12, 252–53
Urban League, 14; Chicago, 33, 35–36;
Detroit, xv, 28, 36, 51, 53, 55, 61, 73, 77,
80, 92–93, 103–4, 110, 159, 175, 199, 227,
229–30, 266n56, 270n49, 275n118
urban planning, 4, 7, 17, 181–86, 217–18,
220–21, 243–44, 252–53. *See also* highway
construction; urban renewal
urban rebellions. *See* race riots
urban renewal, 12–13, 14, 195–96; and
business destruction, 153, 167–68,
199–217, 241, 314n92; and displacement,
166, 186, 191, 198–99, 201, 203, 205, 209,
214–15, 229, 246, 248; Elmwood Park
project, 185, 195–96, 200–203, 208–16,
225, 231, 233; and financial assistance,
211–14, 234; Gratiot project, 184–85,
195–200, 205, 313n83; Medical Center
project, 181, 185, 195–96, 206, 219–30,
234–37, 239–41. *See also* activism and
urban renewal

Vaughn, Edward (Vaughn's Bookstore),
247–48
vendors, Black, 2–3, 87, 123, 176
vice, 77; campaigns against, 78, 89, 95

violence: directed toward Black entrepreneurs, 9–10, 13, 16, 23, 25, 27–30, 32; at
Ford Motor Company, 79–80; intimidation and threats of, 25–27, 29, 33, 70;
political, in Jim Crow South, 28; as risk
factor for Black entrepreneurship, 7, 16,
20, 25, 33, 69, 71, 76, 81, 149, 194; white
entrepreneurs as perpetrators of, 23, 28.
See also lynching; massacre; migration;
murder; race riots; racial capitalism

Waddles, Charleszetta, 90, 171
Walker, Juliet E. K., 11, 114, 245
Walker, Madam C. J., 15, 66–67, 147
Warren, Francis H., 43
Washington, Booker T., 262n53, 263n2. *See
also* Booker T. Washington Trade
Association
Washington, Forrester B., 36, 51–52, 54, 65,
77–78, 270n49, 275n121
Watson, Edward, 49
Watson, Everett, 91, 94–95, 97–100
Wayne County Better Homes (WCBH), 2–3,
94
Wayne State University, 157, 185–86, 219,
221, 223, 227, 241, 251, 253
wealth: accumulation, 8, 89; loss of
accumulated, 5, 13, 31–33, 161, 181–82,
206, 208, 216–18, 225, 243, 253; racial
gap, 5; state-sponsored redistribution, 4,
186
Weare, Walter B., 111–12
Wells, Ida B., 23
white flight, 165–67, 182, 219, 252
white supremacy. *See* economic white
supremacy
White, John. *See* Gotham Hotel
White, Walter, 23–24, 159, 163–65, 305n38
Williams, Eric, 6
Williams, Robert F., 124–25
Wilson, Sunnie (Forest Club), xiii–xiv,
88–89, 91–92, 95, 100, 149, 160–61,
168–70, 177, 241–42
Wolcott, Victoria, 92, 130, 282n92
women, Black: autonomy, 65, 205;
employment, 275n121; entrepreneurs, 16,
64–67, 127–51, 154–55, 202, 210–11,
275n121; labor conditions, 65, 80, 141;
migration motivations, 37, 299n80; in
numbers game, 90, 281n79. *See also*

women, Black (*continued*)
  Detroit Housewives League; discrimina-
  tion, sex; Elliotorian Business Women's
  Club; Iota Phi Lambda (Black business-
  women's sorority)
Woodson, Carter G., 33
Works Progress Administration (WPA),
  110–11, 152
World War I, 35, 44, 52–53
World War II, 144–45, 153. *See also* GI Bill
Wright, A. G., 105, 222

YMCA, 2
Young, Coleman, 47, 119–20, 161, 177,
  251–52; father William C., xvii, 85, 184,
  194; on illicit activities, 75–76, 83–85, 89,
  95, 97; on urban renewal, 182–83, 193–94,
  205, 207
youth and children, 1, 23, 27, 34, 37, 41, 47,
  68, 83, 84–85, 109, 136, 140–41, 143–44,
  147–48, 163, 164, 171, 172, 174, 248–49,
  277n1. *See also* family business
YWCA, 163

ACKNOWLEDGMENTS

The intellectual journey that led to this book began while I was an under-graduate business student at Wayne State University. Joseph Baynesan, Queen Loundmon, and Mary K. Clark changed the course of my life and helped me pursue graduate study through their work with the Ronald E. McNair Postbaccalaureate Achievement Program. Danielle McGuire served as my McNair faculty supervisor and was instrumental in helping me start to think like a historian and supported me as I applied for history PhD programs. At Wayne State I also met several mentors for whom I am forever thankful, especially Alicia Nails, Elizabeth Faue, and Liette Gidlow.

This project would not have been possible without the amazing scholars who trained me to be a historian at Rutgers University-New Brunswick. I am deeply grateful to my dissertation advisor, Mia Bay, and committee members, Deborah Gray White, Jennifer Mittelstadt, and Robert E. Weems Jr. They provided guidance and encouragement at every stage of graduate school, writing the dissertation, and transforming the dissertation into a book. I also appreciate all of the professors at Rutgers who trained me including Minkah Makalani, Ann Fabian, Suzanne Lebsock, Nancy Hewitt, and Seth Koven. I am also thankful for the mentorship of Marisa Fuentes, Clement A. Price, Christina Strasburger, and Walter Rucker.

I have thought this project through with the help of many friends and colleagues. Thank you to Jesse Bayker, Jasmin Young, Dara Walker, Miya Carey, Carolina Alonso Bejarano, Marlene Gaynair, Kaisha Esty, Ashley Lawrence, Beatrice Adams, Les Arthur, Adam Wolkoff, Don Ramen, and Julia Katz. Thanks also to Alix Genter for your wonderful editing services. Participants in the Rutgers Center for Historical Analysis's 2017–2018 Black Bodies seminar directed by Maria Fuentes and Bayo Holsey helped me think through key concepts for the framing and significance of my project. Thank you especially to Brittany Cooper and Kali Gross. Presenting my research at York University's Harriet Tubman Institute produced stimulating conversation. Colleagues including Molly Ladd-Taylor, Anne Rubenstein, Andrea Davis, and Gregory Mixon engaged with the project in useful ways. At Rutgers-Camden I am grateful for my colleagues in the History Department, Africana Studies, and the Center for Urban Research and Education, particularly Lorrin Thomas and Andrew Shankman, for engaging with my work. I cannot thank Tanisha Ford, Mark Wilson, and Shennette Garrett-Scott enough for reading and engaging with the manuscript at a key stage. Their comments and conversations on the draft were invaluable. Michelle Stephens and my cohort of early career faculty fellows at the Rutgers Institute for the Study of Global Racial Justice (ISGRJ) helped me consider the relationship between Black business, Black capitalism, and racial capitalism. Writing groups with Candace Miller, Nichole Jenkins, and Latoya Teague provided community and accountability for completing revisions for the manuscript. I am extremely grateful for my Penn Press editor, Bob Lockhart, who understood my vision for this project from day one and was so attentive in seeing this project through every step of the way. The manuscript's anonymous reviewers offered crucial feedback that I am immensely thankful for. I also appreciate the American Business, Politics, and Society series editors, especially Andrew Wender Cohen, who offered insightful comments.

I have benefited from the mentorship and advice of so many people. I am grateful for RU Mafia members Melissa Cooper, Shannen Dee Williams, Vanessa Holden, Stephanie Jones-Rogers, Felicia Thomas, Arika Easley-Houser, Mekala Audain, John Adams, Leigh-Anne Francis, Amrita Meyers, and Tiffany Gill. Thank you to Deborah and Marisa for your mentorship while I was the Scarlet and Black postdoctoral associate at Rutgers. Erica Armstrong Dunbar and Jocelyn Wills have been generous with their time as formal and informal mentors. Thank you to Corrine Castro and Sangeeta Lamba of the Rutgers Faculty Diversity Collaborative. Mentorship from the "Blackademics" at Rutgers-Camden, especially Keith Green, Oscar Holmes IV, and Lisa Lewis, has been invaluable. The community support at Easton's Nook in Newark, New Jersey, helped me push out important parts of this book. Thank you to Nadine Mattis and Jackie Mattis for creating such a wonderful intellectual space, for the love and care, and for the amazing food!

This work benefited greatly from exchanges with audiences and commenters at various seminars and conferences including Harvard's Business History Seminar, the Lees Seminar at Rutgers-Camden, the Seminar on the History of American Capitalism at Johns Hopkins Institute for Applied Economics, Global Health, and the Study of Business Enterprise, the Association for the Study of African American Life and History, the Business History Conference, the American Historical Association, the Organization of American Historians, the Berkshire Conference on the History of Women, Genders, and Sexualities, and the Urban History Association. Many thanks in particular to Davarian Baldwin, Devin Fergus, Brandon Winford, Suzanne Smith, Susie Pak, Louis Galambos, Nathan Connolly, Jessica Ann Levy, Walter Friedman, Edie Sparks, Shane Hamilton, and Mary Yeager.

I appreciate the librarians and archivists who aided my research at the Burton Historical Collection (Detroit Public Library), particularly Romie Minor and Mark Bowden; LaNesha DeBardelaben, Melissa Samson, and Ashley Reynolds at the Charles H. Wright Museum Archives; and the staff at the Walter P. Reuther Library, Archives of Labor and Urban Affairs (Wayne State University). Sources from the Archives of Michigan and the Bentley Historical Library (University of Michigan) were also invaluable for the project. Thank you to Rutgers cartographer Michael Siegel for creating maps for the book.

This book would not have been possible without financial support from several institutions and organizations. I received research support from Rutgers University-Camden's Faculty of Arts and Sciences and DEI Council, the Institute for the Study of Global Racial Justice (ISGRJ) at Rutgers, and the Faculty of Liberal Arts & Professional Studies at York University (Toronto). An Albert J. Beveridge Grant from the American Historical Association aided in my research and Alfred D. Chandler Jr. travel grants from the Business History Conference allowed me to present my work and receive constructive feedback. I also am grateful for an Andrew W. Mellon Dissertation Completion Fellowship at Rutgers University-New Brunswick School of Arts and Sciences. This book has been published with the assistance of a subvention award from the Claudia Clark–Rebecca Gershenson–Megan McClintock Memorial Fund of the History Department of Rutgers-New Brunswick.

Thank you to my entire family, including my parents, Ervin Boyd Sr. and Tamra Boyd. My dad taught me to pay "special attention" to everything I do and continues to inspire my scholarly pursuits. I am grateful for the encouragement of my siblings Ervin Jr., Ondranice, Calen, and Leah, my first "editor" and partner in crime at Wayne State. I am also grateful for the kindness and generosity of Inga and Andrey Bennett, Dustin Cast, and Aunnalea Boyd.

Last but not least, Jesse, words cannot describe my appreciation for your love and support throughout this entire journey. Thank you for everything!